Green Infrastructure and Intelligent Systems for Smart Cities

Md. Shafiqul Islam
https://orcid.org/0000-0002-5547-046X

International University of Business Agriculture and Technology, Bangladesh

IGI Global
Scientific Publishing
Publishing Tomorrow's Research Today

Vice President of Editorial	Melissa Wagner
Director of Acquisitions	Mikaela Felty
Director of Book Development	Jocelynn Hessler
Production Manager	Mike Brehm
Cover Design	Jose Rosado

Published in the United States of America by
IGI Global Scientific Publishing
701 East Chocolate Avenue
Hershey, PA, 17033, USA
Tel: 717-533-8845 | Fax: 717-533-7115
Website: https://www.igi-global.com E-mail: cust@igi-global.com

Library of Congress Cataloging-in-Publication Data

LCCN: (CIP Data Pending)
ISBN13: 9798260008836
Isbn13Softcover: 9798260008843
EISBN13: 9798260008850
British Cataloguing in Publication Data
A Cataloguing in Publication record for this book is available from the British Library.

Table of Contents

Detailed Table of Contents

Rapid urbanization has transformed cities into major centers of economic activity while intensifying environmental pressures. Urban areas consume large amounts of energy and resources and generate significant greenhouse gas emissions, waste, and air pollution. These conditions contribute to climate change, urban heat island effects, biodiversity loss, and declining public health. As cities continue to expand, the need for sustainable urban development becomes increasingly urgent. The concept of green cities has therefore emerged as an important framework for addressing environmental challenges while maintaining economic vitality and social well-being. Green cities emphasize sustainable infrastructure, efficient energy use, green spaces, responsible waste management, and environmentally conscious urban planning. Integrating ecological principles into urban governance supports climate resilience and improves quality of life while helping cities remain livable and environmentally balanced.

Vegetation is important to solving environmental problems such as air and noise pollution and urban heat management. Vegetation absorbs pollutants such as SO_2, NO_2, and particulate matter through mechanisms such as phytoremediation and phylloremediation. But some species, assisted by rhizosphere and phyllosphere microorganisms, also break down volatile organic compounds (VOCs), indoor plants being especially potent. Green infrastructure such as green roofs and walls manage pollution, mitigate urban heat, and enhance urban livability. Urban green

With the rise of intelligent driving technologies, traffic sign identification has gained growing research interest. Traditional methods relying on shape or color features can recognize broad categories such as warnings and prohibitions but suffer from limited accuracy and are sensitive to light and weather changes. Though computationally efficient and suitable for real-time use, these methods offer limited recognition capabilities. This study proposes a robust solution combining Non-Local Means (NLM) for noise reduction, a modified UNet for detailed feature extraction, and DenseCNN for accurate classification. To further enhance performance, Rock Hyrax Swarm Optimization (RHSO) is applied for hyperparameter tuning. This synergistic integration significantly boosts detection accuracy. Evaluations on standard datasets show that the proposed method outperforms state-of-the-art techniques, achieving 99.64% accuracy on the TT100K dataset and 99.6% on the GTSDB dataset, establishing its effectiveness and reliability in varied real-world conditions.

The study adopts a quantitative methodology based on PLS-SEM (Partial Least Squares Structural Equation Modeling), utilizing the software SmartPLS 3.3.0 and SPSS v20. A structured questionnaire was designed and distributed via Google Forms between July and October 2023, collecting 7,000 responses, of which 6,550 valid samples were retained for analysis. The survey was conducted in Ho Chi Minh City, Vietnam, targeting diverse respondent groups across gender, age, education, and profession. Key findings show that technical readiness, particularly optimization (β = 0.112, $p < 0.05$) and innovation (β = 0.108, $p < 0.01$), significantly affect consumer motivation and expectations. Environmental concerns (β = 0.425, < 0.05) and perceived usefulness (β = 0.137, $p < 0.05$) are also critical predictors of EV purchase intention. The structural model achieved high reliability and validity with Cronbach's alpha > 0.7, Composite Reliability > 0.6, and model fit indices such as GFI = 0.902, RMSEA = 0.047, and SRMR = 0.046, indicating strong model fitness.

This chapter explores the integration of Artificial Intelligence (AI) in second language (L2) assessment systems, particularly in the context of urban education within smart city frameworks. As cities strive for sustainability and digital transformation, educational systems must adapt by employing intelligent technologies for more efficient, equitable, and eco-friendly language evaluation. The chapter examines AI-powered rubrics, automated quizzes, and adaptive feedback tools that reduce reliance on traditional paper-based testing while expanding access to remote and personalized learning experiences. Emphasis is placed on how AI can enhance assessment fairness, decrease traffic-related emissions by supporting remote testing, and democratize language proficiency measurement. Case studies from urban school systems are presented to illustrate successful implementation. This chapter also addresses policy implications and future trends, offering a roadmap for designing inclusive, tech-enabled language assessment infrastructures aligned with smart city goals.

Rapid urbanization has created complex energy ecosystems challenging traditional centralized power models. This analysis examines blockchain technology and semantic annotation convergence in addressing modern urban energy infrastructure challenges. Blockchain enables decentralized trust mechanisms for peer-to-peer energy trading, automated smart contracts, and transparent renewable energy certification, while semantic annotation ensures intelligent machine understanding and interoperability across diverse energy systems. Integration creates autonomous ecosystems where participants contribute to grid optimization while being fairly compensated. Real-world implementations show measurable improvements in energy efficiency, cost reduction, and renewable utilization. However, challenges remain including scalability

Preface

Rapid urbanization across the globe has created unique opportunities for economic growth, innovation, and social development. At the same time, it has exaggerated the structural challenges faced by cities, particularly in the Global South. Traffic congestion, inefficient mobility systems, environmental pollution, and unplanned land-use patterns have emerged as serious concerns among these challenges. Many cities globally stand now top rank among the most congested, and in many developing countries, daily mobility has become challenging due to inadequate infrastructure, rapid population growth, and expansion of unplanned urban activities. These conditions not only disrupt daily life but also impose significant economic, environmental, and social costs.

Mobility is the movement of people and goods through physical liberty, and important component of urban life. It operates across multiple temporal scales, from daily commuting to seasonal or life-cycle movement patterns and is closely connected with how cities grow and function. However, contemporary urban transportation systems often struggle to accommodate growing populations, expanding industries, and rising environmental pressures. Monocentric urban structures, characterized by a single dominant center, frequently result in long-distance commuting, excessive energy consumption, congestion, and environmental degradation. These patterns show the urgent need to rethink urban development strategies and transportation planning.

Urban transportation planning plays an important function in shaping sustainable cities. Effective planning must integrate polycentric urban development including land use management, transportation networks, environmental protection, and social equity. Identifying the root causes of car dependency, limited accessibility, lengthy commuting times, and poor mobility is essential for designing sustainable solutions. Reconsideration of urban land-use classifications incorporating residential, commercial, industrial, institutional, recreational, and agricultural functions can support more balanced spatial development. Polycentric urban development has emerged as an important framework for addressing the challenges of monocentric growth considering above mentioned issues. By accommodating multiple activities within metropolitan regions, polycentricism can help shorten travel distances, improve accessibility, and encourage sustainable modes of transportation such as walking, cycling, and public transit.

This edited volume, *Green Infrastructure and Intelligent Systems for Smart Cities*, seeks to explore innovative strategies that integrate environmental sustainability, urban mobility, and smart and intelligent planning systems. The book emphasizes the role of green infrastructure, alternative routing systems, and potentiality of eco-friendly transportation in reducing traffic congestion and enhancing urban livability. Special attention is given to rapidly growing cities in developing countries, where the pressures of urbanization are challenging and intense. The context of Dhaka, Bangladesh one of the world's most densely populated and congested megacities identifies many of these challenges and serves as a compelling case for the development of sustainable and adaptive urban solutions.

There are eight chapters in this volume explore a range of strategies aimed at reducing car dependency, improving accessibility, and promoting efficient land use. Among these approaches are the development of higher occupancy public transport systems, the integration of green pedestrian networks, avenue planting and urban greening initiatives, and the implementation of intelligent traffic management and alternative routing systems. Together, these strategies aim to reduce congestion, lower emissions, conserve energy, and improve the overall quality of urban life. The book also addresses the broader social, environmental, and economic implications of transportation systems and urban development policies.

A distinctive feature of this volume is its interdisciplinary and transdisciplinary orientation. Addressing the complexity of urban sustainability requires collaboration and participation across multiple fields of knowledge. Accordingly, this book brings together contributions from scholars (Academia and researchers) and practitioners in architecture, urban planning and design, landscape architecture, environmental design, transportation engineering, and related disciplines. It also welcomes perspectives from human geography, anthropology, environmental psychology, urban forestry, sociology, and other fields that contribute to understanding the human environment relationship within cities.

Through these diverse perspectives, the book aims to present innovative insights into the evolving concept of smart and green cities. It offers theoretical discussions, empirical studies, and practical approaches that collectively contribute to a more comprehensive understanding of sustainable urban environments. By ensuring innovative research methods, analytical tools, and planning strategies, the volume seeks to support future academic research, policy development, and professional practice.

The intended audience includes researchers, urban planners, policymakers, engineers, environmental designers, and students who are engaged in the study and development of sustainable and smart cities. I believe that the ideas and approaches presented in this book will inspire further exploration, collaboration, and innovation in the pursuit of more livable, resilient, and environmentally responsible urban spaces.

As editor, I am deeply grateful to all the contributing authors for their scholarly efforts and valuable insights. Their work has made it possible to bring together this comprehensive volume. I also acknowledge the reviewers and the publisher for their guidance and support throughout the preparation of this book. It is my sincere anticipation that this collection will contribute meaningfully to the ongoing dialogue on sustainable urban development and the creation of smarter, greener cities for future generations.

ORGANIZATION OF THE BOOK

In this volume, each chapter contributes to a deeper understanding of how green infrastructure, intelligent systems, and interdisciplinary approaches can support the development of sustainable and resilient smart cities.

Chapter 1, authored by Alya Nurul Qolbi and BinastyaAnggara Sekti, introduces the foundational concept of green cities and explains why sustainable urban transformation has become an urgent global priority. The chapter discusses how rapid urbanization has intensified environmental pressures through increased energy consumption, waste generation, air pollution, and greenhouse gas emissions. It highlights the interconnected challenges of climate change, urban heat island effects, biodiversity loss, and declining public health. By outlining the principles of green urban development—such as sustainable infrastructure, energy efficiency, green spaces, responsible waste management, and environmentally conscious planning—the chapter establishes the conceptual framework for the book. It emphasizes the role of ecological thinking in urban governance and demonstrates how integrating environmental sustainability into city planning can enhance resilience, livability, and long-term urban balance.

Chapter 2, written by Manu Mehrotra, Manish Baboo Agarwal, and Seema Agarwal, examines the important role of plant species in mitigating urban environmental pollution and regulating urban temperatures. The chapter explores how vegetation contributes to the reduction of air pollutants such as sulfur dioxide, nitrogen dioxide, and particulate matter through biological processes including phytoremediation and phylloremediation. It also discusses the role of microorganisms (Mycorrhiza) associated with plant surfaces and root systems in breaking down harmful compounds such as volatile organic compounds. Beyond air quality, the authors analyze the effectiveness of urban green belts, forests, green roofs, and vertical green walls in reducing noise pollution, cooling urban environments, and lowering energy demand.

The chapter underscores the importance of careful plant species selection and calls for further research into pollutant removal efficiency, highlighting the potential for green infrastructure to significantly improve urban environmental quality and human health.

Chapter 3, contributed by Chaithra D and colleagues, explores the rapidly evolving field of connected vehicle technologies and their implications for urban mobility and transportation safety. The chapter explains how next-generation vehicles are increasingly equipped with intelligent systems capable of sensing their surroundings, communicating with other vehicles and infrastructure, and responding to real-time conditions. Technologies such as Vehicle-to-Vehicle (V2V) and Vehicle-to-Infrastructure (V2I) communication, advanced driver assistance systems, and automated alerts are examined as mechanisms for preventing accidents and enhancing road safety. Supported by advancing technologies including 5G networks, cloud computing, and edge processing, these systems are transforming vehicles into proactive safety platforms. The chapter also addresses ongoing challenges such as cybersecurity risks, data privacy concerns, and regulatory limitations, emphasizing the need for coordinated technological and policy frameworks to support safe and effective deployment.

Chapter 4, authored by Saroja B and colleagues, focuses on advances in intelligent transportation systems through the development of improved traffic sign recognition technologies. Recognizing that accurate traffic sign detection is essential for autonomous and intelligent driving systems, the chapter presents a novel computational framework that combines Non-Local Means noise reduction, a modified UNet architecture for feature extraction, and DenseCNN classification. The model is further optimized using Rock Hyrax Swarm Optimization to enhance parameter performance. Through extensive evaluation using widely recognized datasets, the study demonstrates exceptionally high accuracy rates, surpassing many existing approaches. This research enhances reliability under varying lighting and environmental conditions, contributes to safer autonomous driving systems and more efficient traffic management within smart city environments.

Chapter 5, by Anh Nguyen, Minh Ly, and Tam Do, provides a data driven investigation into the factors influencing electric vehicle adoption in Ho Chi Minh City, Vietnam. Using a large scale quantitative survey and advanced statistical modeling techniques, the study examines how technological readiness, environmental awareness, and perceived usefulness shape consumer intentions to purchase electric vehicles. The chapter reveals that environmental concern plays a particularly significant role in motivating adoption, while technological innovation and optimization also influence user expectations and motivations. With robust empirical evidence based on thousands of responses, the research offers valuable insights for policymakers, industry stakeholders, and urban planners seeking to accelerate the transition toward cleaner transportation systems in rapidly developing urban contexts.

Chapter 6, written by Muhamad Haikal Umardi and BinastyaAnggara Sekti, shifts the focus to the role of artificial intelligence in educational systems within smart city environments. The chapter explores how AI powered tools transform second language (L2) assessment through automated rubrics, intelligent quizzes, and adaptive feedback mechanisms. These technologies not only improve efficiency and fairness in language evaluation but also support more sustainable educational practices by reducing dependence on paper based testing and enabling remote assessment. By linking digital education infrastructure with broader smart city objectives, the authors demonstrate how AI driven assessment systems improve accessibility, equity, and environmental sustainability while supporting personalized learning experiences.

Chapter 7, contributed by Cindy Fitria Maharani and BinastyaAnggara Sekti, examines the integration of blockchain technology and semantic annotation for smart energy management in urban environments. The system enables to develop mechanisms for peer-to-peer energy trading, automated smart contracts, and transparent renewable energy certification, while semantic annotation ensures intelligent machine understanding and interoperability across different energy systems. Semantic annotation further enhances system interoperability by enabling intelligent communication among diverse energy platforms and devices. Together, these technologies create decentralized energy ecosystems capable of optimizing grid performance, improving efficiency, and promoting renewable energy utilization. The chapter also addresses key challenges, including scalability issues, energy consumption concerns, and regulatory barriers that must be addressed to fully realize the potential of these systems.

Chapter 8, authored by S. Ida Evangeline, concludes the volume by exploring the emerging concept of smart public places as essential components of sustainable urban environments. This chapter explores how to develop smart public places, which are sensor-enhanced, digitally augmented environments that combine environmental intelligence, community engagement, and the optimization of mobility. The smart public place is a responsive system in the sense that it can improve air quality, control the movement of the city, and change behavior with the help of real-time information and interactive technology and design. Chapter utilizes multidisciplinary and international examples to investigate vehicle dependence, environmental well-being, and inclusive cities. By combining environmental intelligence, mobility optimization, and community-centered design, smart public places serve as adaptive urban systems capable of addressing contemporary challenges such as congestion and pollution. Drawing on interdisciplinary perspectives and international examples, the chapter illustrates how public spaces can become active contributors to the development of healthier, more livable cities.

Collectively, the chapters in this volume demonstrate the diverse yet interconnected pathways through which green infrastructure, intelligent technologies, and innovative planning strategies can contribute to the creation of sustainable and resilient smart cities.

CONCLUSION

The chapters presented in this volume collectively demonstrate that the pursuit of sustainable and intelligent urban development requires an innovative, multidimensional and collaborative approach. Cities today face an exceptional convergence of challenges such as rapid population growth, environmental degradation, increasing energy demand, traffic congestion, and technological transformation. Addressing these complex issues requires not only innovative technological solutions but also thoughtful planning, ecological sensitivity, and interdisciplinary cooperation. Throughout this book, contributors have provided the solutions how green infrastructure, intelligent systems, and forward thinking policies can reshape urban environments into more resilient, livable, and sustainable spaces.

An essential theme emerging from this volume is the importance of integrating environmental sustainability with technological advancement. The discussions on green cities, plant-based pollution mitigation, smart mobility systems, and intelligent transportation technologies demonstrate how ecological principles and digital innovations can work together to improve urban life. From the implementation of advanced vehicle communication systems and traffic sign recognition technologies to the promotion of electric vehicle adoption and smart public spaces, these chapters reveal how emerging technologies can enhance safety, efficiency, and environmental responsibility in modern cities.

Equally important is the recognition that sustainable urban development extends beyond infrastructure and technology. It also encompasses social well-being, public health, education, governance, and community engagement. Contributions exploring AI enabled educational assessment, decentralized energy management systems, and responsive public spaces illustrate how smart city initiatives can support inclusive and equitable urban environments. These perspectives remind us that the ultimate goal of smart and green cities is not only efficiency but also the creation of human-centered urban spaces that foster social connection, environmental stewardship, and improved quality of life.

Another important insight highlighted in this volume is the role of interdisciplinary collaboration. The challenges of modern urbanization cannot be addressed within the boundaries of a single discipline. Solutions require the combined expertise of urban planners, architects, engineers, environmental scientists, policymakers, educators, technologists, and social researchers. The diversity of perspectives represented in this book reflects this reality and reinforces the need for integrated approaches to urban research and policy development.

As editor, I'm confident that this book serves as a valuable resource for academia, researchers, policymakers, urban designers, and students seeking to better understand the evolving dynamics of sustainable urban development. The ideas, research findings, and innovative frameworks presented in this book aims to inspire new discussions, inform policy decisions, and encourage further interdisciplinary research in the fields of green infrastructure, intelligent systems, and smart city planning.

Looking forward, the transition toward sustainable and smart urban futures will depend on the ability of cities to adopt innovative technologies while remaining deeply grounded in ecological and social responsibility. By integrating environmental awareness, technological innovation, and inclusive planning strategies, cities can move toward development pathways that are not only intelligent but also equitable, resilient, and environmentally balanced.

It is my sincere appreciation that this volume contributes to the ongoing global dialogue on creating greener, smarter, and more sustainable cities for present and future generations.

Acknowledgment

The successful completion of this book (Green Infrastructure and Intelligent Systems for Smart Cities) has been completed through the extensive assistance and support provided by many individuals. I extend my heartfelt gratitude to all the authors who have contributed to this edited volume with their innovative perspectives and recent research findings. I am thankful to my eldest brother, Engineer Md. Abu Hanif Mia, for his encouragement and motivation in the writing of this book. I wish to express my profound appreciation to Associate Professor Dr. A.K.M Mominul Haque Talukder (Editorial Advisory Board Member) from the University Canada West, Canada and Lecturer Dr. Mohammed Jahangir Alam (Editorial Advisory Board Member) from University of Notre Dame, Australia, for their thorough reviews and constructive feedback on each chapter. They were always willing to share their intellect and provide unwavering support throughout this process. Moreover, I would like to acknowledge all people for their excellent supports, which have made it possible to reach the readers and users of this work. My sincere thanks go to Professor Dr. Mohammed Aatur Rahman for his encouragement during the writing process. Many colleagues from the International University of Business Agriculture and Technology (IUBAT) have rendered necessary assistance, without which this book would not have been possible. Additionally, I am grateful to Gerlinde Staffler for her continuous inspiration and remarkable support. I am deeply indebted to my family members for their steadfast support. I also wish to express my gratitude to the officials of NGOs and community members for their valuable time and for providing useful data and information that significantly contributed to this work. It is with great pleasure that I extend my deepest gratitude to IGI Global publisher for the opportunity to write and participate in the completion of this book.

Chapter 1
Introduction and the Importance of Green Cities

Alya Nurul Qolbi
http://orcid.org/0009-0003-9229-8974
Universitas Esa Unggul, Indonesia

Binastya Anggara Sekti
http://orcid.org/0000-0001-5489-4888
Universitas Esa Unggul, Indonesia

ABSTRACT

Rapid urbanization has transformed cities into major centers of economic activity while intensifying environmental pressures. Urban areas consume large amounts of energy and resources and generate significant greenhouse gas emissions, waste, and air pollution. These conditions contribute to climate change, urban heat island effects, biodiversity loss, and declining public health. As cities continue to expand, the need for sustainable urban development becomes increasingly urgent. The concept of green cities has therefore emerged as an important framework for addressing environmental challenges while maintaining economic vitality and social well-being. Green cities emphasize sustainable infrastructure, efficient energy use, green spaces, responsible waste management, and environmentally conscious urban planning. Integrating ecological principles into urban governance supports climate resilience and improves quality of life while helping cities remain livable and environmentally balanced.

DOI: 10.4018/979-8-2600-0883-6.ch001

1. INTRODUCTION

Rapid urbanization has become one of the defining transformations of the twenty-first century. Cities now accommodate more than half of the global population and generate a disproportionate share of energy consumption, greenhouse gas emissions, air pollution, and resource depletion. As urban systems expand spatially and economically, they intensify ecological pressures, including biodiversity loss, urban heat island effects, water scarcity, waste accumulation, and deteriorating public health conditions. These dynamics reveal structural tensions between economic growth and ecological limits, positioning cities at the center of global sustainability debates. Against the backdrop of global warming and rapid urbanization, urban extreme heat is becoming increasingly severe, with profound impacts on public health, infrastructure, and social equity (Rui, Shabrina, & Gong, 2026).

In response to these challenges, the concept of the "green city" has emerged as a strategic paradigm for reorienting urban development toward environmental sustainability, social equity, and long-term resilience. However, despite its widespread policy adoption, the concept remains fragmented in academic discourse. Existing discussions often emphasize technological solutions or environmental indicators without adequately integrating governance structures, socio-ecological theory, and institutional feasibility. As a result, green cities are frequently presented as aspirational models rather than analytically grounded systems. The rapid urbanisation of our societies calls for an urban renewal movement, including developing new areas to accommodate housing facilities and services and regenerating existing urban areas (Cihan Kayaçetin et al., 2026).

This chapter addresses the following guiding question:

How can green cities be conceptualized as integrated socio-ecological systems that balance environmental sustainability, economic vitality, and social equity while remaining institutionally feasible?

The chapter contributes by synthesizing theoretical foundations, critically reviewing empirical scholarship, and developing an integrated analytical framework that connects environmental performance, governance capacity, economic mechanisms, and social inclusion within a unified urban sustainability model.

1.1 Defining Green Cities within a Socio-Ecological Framework

A green city is not merely an urban area with parks or renewable energy infrastructure; it is a complex socio-ecological system intentionally designed to reduce environmental impacts while enhancing economic efficiency and social well-being. At its core, the green city concept seeks to restore balance between human activity and ecological systems within urban environments. Rapid urbanization, driven by expanding road infrastructure and increasing impervious surfaces, has intensified ecological degradation (Alqadhi & Mallick, 2026).

Green cities prioritize renewable energy integration, sustainable mobility systems, energy-efficient buildings, biodiversity preservation, circular waste management, and climate-adaptive infrastructure. Green roofs, urban forests, and permeable landscapes mitigate heat island effects and improve environmental quality. Yet environmental design alone does not define a green city.

Equally important are governance mechanisms and citizen engagement. Community participation in recycling programs, energy conservation initiatives, and participatory planning processes strengthens institutional legitimacy and behavioral change. Education and public awareness become critical components of sustainability transitions.

From a theoretical perspective, green cities embody principles of urban ecology and resilience theory. They operate as adaptive systems where economic development, environmental protection, and social equity interact dynamically rather than independently. Thus, a green city can be defined as an integrated urban system in which environmental sustainability, economic development, and social inclusion coexist within ecological boundaries and intergenerational responsibility.

1.2 Historical Evolution of Urban Development Toward Sustainability

The evolution of urban development reflects shifting priorities in economic production, spatial organization, and environmental awareness. Early cities emerged along fertile river valleys and were structured primarily around agriculture, trade, and governance. Sustainability considerations were largely implicit rather than intentional. The global population has rapidly urbanized over the past century, and the urbanization rate is projected to reach about 70% by 2050 (Sharifi, Khavarian-Garmsir, Allam, & Asadzadeh, 2023).

The Industrial Revolution marked a fundamental transformation. Rapid urban expansion prioritized industrial productivity and economic growth, often at the expense of environmental quality and public health. Pollution, overcrowding, and inadequate sanitation characterized many nineteenth-century industrial cities. Urban planning during this era was reactive and production-oriented.

In the twentieth century, modern planning introduced zoning systems, infrastructure expansion, and public service improvements. While living conditions improved, urban sprawl and automobile dependency increased environmental pressures. Cities became increasingly resource-intensive and spatially fragmented.

By the late twentieth century, growing awareness of climate change, environmental degradation, and resource depletion exposed the limitations of traditional growth-oriented models. The green city concept emerged as a corrective framework that integrates ecological limits into urban development strategies. It represents a shift from cities as engines of industrial output toward cities as regenerative and adaptive systems.

1.3 Sustainability as the Normative Foundation of Green Urbanism

The concept of sustainability provides the normative foundation for green urban development. Originating from global environmental discourse and popularized through the principle of meeting present needs without compromising future generations, sustainability emphasizes intergenerational equity and systemic balance. The compact city is one of the leading paradigms of sustainable urbanism (Bibri, Krogstie, & Kärrholm, 2020).

In urban planning, sustainability requires harmonizing environmental protection, economic productivity, and social inclusion. Environmentally, this involves efficient resource use, reduced emissions, compact land use, and climate adaptation. Economically, it supports green investment, innovation, and long-term cost efficiency. Socially, it promotes equitable access to housing, transportation, public services, and green spaces.

However, sustainability in practice extends beyond infrastructure. It requires institutional coordination, stakeholder engagement, and behavioral change. Smart technologies can enhance monitoring and optimization, but technological solutions alone cannot guarantee equitable outcomes. Sustainable urban planning must therefore integrate governance capacity, policy coherence, and social participation.

This multidimensional understanding distinguishes sustainability from purely technological environmentalism. It positions green cities within a broader socio-political transformation rather than as isolated engineering projects.

1.4 Emergence of the Green City Concept: From Crisis to Paradigm Shift

The idea of green cities emerged from escalating environmental crises and growing recognition that traditional urban growth models were ecologically unsustainable. Rapid industrialization, fossil fuel dependence, and resource-intensive development patterns contributed to climate change, air pollution, and ecosystem degradation. Cities became both drivers of environmental decline and focal points for reform. Green infrastructure (GI) and ecosystem services (ES) are promoted as concepts that have potential to improve environmental planning in urban areas based on a more holistic understanding of the complex interrelations and dynamics of social-ecological systems (Hansen & Pauleit, 2014).

Global initiatives such as international sustainability agreements and climate frameworks reinforced the urgency of urban transformation. Policymakers increasingly recognized that cities account for a major share of carbon emissions and resource consumption. Rising temperatures, extreme weather events, and health crises intensified demands for structural reform in urban governance.

The green city paradigm therefore represents more than an environmental trend; it signifies a redefinition of progress. Instead of equating development solely with economic expansion, it aligns urban growth with ecological boundaries and human well-being. This shift repositions cities as laboratories for sustainability innovation and institutional experimentation.

In summary, green cities arise from the intersection of ecological urgency, governance reform, and socio-economic transformation. They embody the transition from extractive urbanism toward regenerative and resilient urban systems capable of sustaining both present and future generations.

2. CONCEPTUAL FOUNDATIONS OF GREEN CITIES

2.1 Definition and Evolution of the Green City Concept

The green city concept emerged from environmental planning reforms and ecological modernization movements that gained momentum in the late twentieth century. Early eco-city models focused primarily on pollution control, sanitation improvements, land-use optimization, and energy efficiency in response to the environmental degradation associated with industrial urbanization. These initial efforts were largely corrective in nature, aiming to mitigate the negative externalities of rapid industrial growth. A green city refers to an urban development concept that integrates environmental sustainability, social well-being, and responsible governance by promoting efficient resource use, ecological balance, and environmentally friendly infrastructure to create a sustainable and livable urban environment (Bashirpour Bonab, Bellini, & Rudko, 2023).

Over time, however, the concept evolved beyond environmental remediation. Growing awareness of climate change, biodiversity loss, and urban vulnerability to extreme weather events expanded the green city framework to include climate adaptation strategies, renewable energy transitions, sustainable mobility systems, circular economy principles, and ecosystem-based urban design. Urban forests, green roofs, permeable surfaces, and biodiversity corridors became central components of green infrastructure, not only for aesthetic enhancement but also for reducing urban heat island effects, improving air quality, managing stormwater, and enhancing public health.

Simultaneously, sustainable transport systems such as cycling infrastructure, electric public transportation, and compact city planning emerged as core elements of green urban transformation. Case examples such as Copenhagen's cycling-oriented urban design and Singapore's vertical greening and environmental regulation illustrate how environmental, infrastructural, and governance reforms can converge into integrated sustainability models.

Importantly, the evolution of green cities has also incorporated social and institutional dimensions. Community participation, recycling initiatives, energy conservation programs, and participatory planning processes have become integral to ensuring long-term legitimacy and behavioral transformation. Global policy frameworks such as the Sustainable Development Goals reinforced the alignment of urban sustainability with broader development objectives.

Today, green cities are not merely urban areas with parks or renewable installations. They represent complex socio-technical and socio-ecological systems that integrate environmental management, economic mechanisms, governance structures, technological innovation, and citizen engagement into a coherent sustainability strategy. Their defining feature is systemic integration rather than isolated environmental projects.

2.2 Theoretical Foundations

To strengthen conceptual rigor, the green city framework can be anchored in multiple theoretical lenses that explain its structural and functional dynamics.

Urban Ecology Theory

Urban ecology conceptualizes cities as ecosystems characterized by metabolic flows of energy, water, materials, and waste. Rather than viewing cities as separate from nature, this perspective frames them as embedded within ecological systems. Sustainability therefore requires reducing ecological footprints, closing resource loops, and restoring environmental balance through circular material flows, green infrastructure, and biodiversity integration. Concepts such as urban metabolism and regenerative design directly inform green city planning. Urban development theory refers to a conceptual framework that explains how cities grow, organize infrastructure, and improve environmental quality through integrated planning strategies, including the implementation of sustainable infrastructure, nature-based solutions, and policies that enhance urban resilience and ecological balance (Štrbac et al., 2023).

Sustainable Development Theory

Sustainable development theory emphasizes intergenerational equity and the balanced integration of environmental protection, economic vitality, and social inclusion. In the context of green cities, this translates into aligning renewable energy adoption, economic investment, and equitable access to green spaces and public services. This framework ensures that environmental improvements do not exacerbate inequality or compromise long-term economic resilience.

Resilience Theory

Resilience theory highlights the capacity of urban systems to absorb shocks such as climate extremes, economic crises, pandemics, and demographic shifts while maintaining functionality. Green cities operationalize resilience through climate-adaptive infrastructure, diversified energy systems, distributed green spaces, and participatory governance. Rather than preventing change, resilient systems adapt and reorganize without collapsing. Resilience theory refers to a conceptual framework that explains the ability of urban systems to withstand, adapt to, and recover from disturbances by reducing vulnerability and strengthening coping capacities through integrated urban planning, adaptive governance, and sustainable development strategies (Sharma, Sharma, Kumar, & Kumar, 2023).

Ecological Modernization Theory

Ecological modernization theory argues that technological innovation and institutional reform can decouple economic growth from environmental degradation. Renewable energy systems, smart grids, green buildings, and digital monitoring platforms illustrate how technological transformation can support environmental objectives. However, ecological modernization also stresses regulatory reform and institutional coordination as prerequisites for sustainable transitions.

Primary Analytical Lens

While each theory contributes to conceptual clarity, this chapter adopts Urban Ecology combined with Resilience Theory as its primary analytical foundation. Green cities are best understood not as static infrastructure upgrades but as adaptive socio-ecological systems operating within ecological boundaries. Their sustainability depends on dynamic interactions among environmental systems, economic activities, governance structures, and social participation.

This integrated theoretical grounding allows the green city concept to move beyond descriptive environmental planning toward a systemic and analytically robust urban sustainability framework.

2.3 Characteristics of a Green City

A green city is an urban environment designed to integrate sustainability principles with modern living, prioritizing environmental protection, resource efficiency, and quality of life for residents. Below are the key features that define a green city, among them Clean Energy, Green Spaces, Waste Management, Sustainable Transportation, Green Buildings, Water Management, Smart City Technologies, Urban Biodiversity, Climate Resilience, Community Engagement (Azizi & Kouddane, 2024). Figure 1 shows the key features that define a green city.

Figure 1. Key features that define a green city

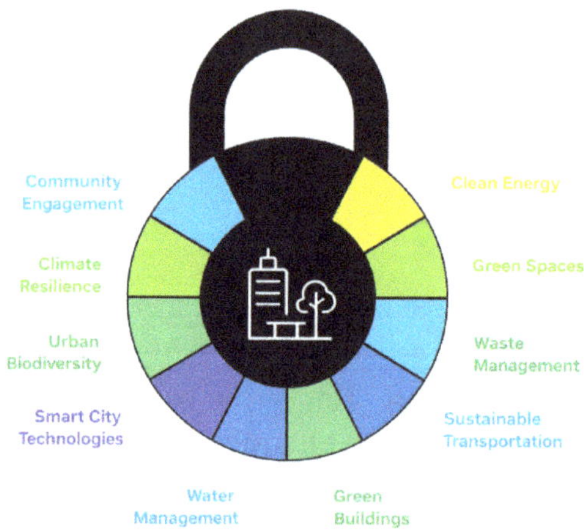

1. Clean Energy (Renewable Energy Systems)

Green cities prioritize the use of renewable energy sources to reduce dependence on fossil fuels and minimize carbon emissions. This includes solar panels installed on rooftops and public buildings, wind turbines positioned at city peripheries, geothermal energy systems for heating and cooling, and smart grid technologies that optimize energy distribution and consumption. These systems not only reduce greenhouse gas emissions but also enhance energy security and resilience against climate change.

2. Green Spaces (Urban Green Infrastructure)

The integration of parks, urban forests, community gardens, green roofs, vertical gardens, and ecological corridors throughout the city. Green spaces serve multiple functions: they act as the "lungs of the city" by absorbing CO2 and filtering air pollutants, reduce the urban heat island effect by providing natural cooling, support biodiversity by creating habitats for flora and fauna, manage stormwater through natural drainage systems, and provide recreational areas that improve residents' physical and mental well-being.

3. Waste Management (Circular Economy Approach)

Comprehensive waste management systems that embrace the principles of reduce, reuse, and recycle. This includes advanced recycling and composting programs that divert waste from landfills, waste-to-energy facilities that convert organic waste into electricity or heat, pneumatic waste collection systems for efficient garbage transport, smart bins equipped with sensors to optimize collection routes, and initiatives moving toward zero-waste cities. The circular economy model ensures that waste is viewed as a resource rather than a disposal problem.

4. Sustainable Transportation (Low-Carbon Mobility)

Green cities develop transportation infrastructure that reduces reliance on private vehicles and promotes eco-friendly alternatives. This includes extensive public transit networks (buses, metros, light rail) powered by clean energy, dedicated bicycle lanes and bike-sharing programs, pedestrian-friendly walkways and car-free zones, electric vehicle charging infrastructure, and transit-oriented development that integrates housing and services near public transport hubs. These measures significantly reduce traffic congestion, air pollution, and carbon emissions.

5. Green Buildings (Energy-Efficient Architecture)

Buildings designed and constructed using sustainable principles and materials. Features include energy-efficient designs that maximize natural lighting and ventilation, LEED or similar green building certifications, installation of solar panels and energy management systems, rainwater harvesting systems and greywater recycling, use of sustainable and recycled construction materials, green roofs and living walls, and smart building technologies that monitor and optimize resource consumption. Green buildings can reduce energy consumption by up to 30-50% compared to conventional structures.

6. Water Management (Integrated Water Systems)

Sustainable water management practices that ensure water security and quality. This encompasses rainwater harvesting systems that capture and store precipitation, advanced wastewater treatment facilities that enable water reuse, sustainable urban drainage systems (SuDS) that mimic natural water cycles, smart water meters for consumption monitoring, and protection of natural water bodies and wetlands. These systems reduce water waste, prevent flooding, and ensure clean water supply for future generations.

7. Smart City Technologies (Data-Driven Urban Management)

Integration of digital technologies to enhance city operations and sustainability (Sekti, 2026). This includes Internet of Things (IoT) sensors for real-time monitoring of air quality, traffic flow, energy use, and waste levels, big data analytics for predictive modeling and informed decision-making, artificial intelligence for optimizing resource allocation, smart lighting systems that adjust based on occupancy and daylight, and mobile applications that engage citizens in sustainability initiatives. Technology enables more efficient, responsive, and sustainable urban management (Sekti, 2025a).

8. Urban Biodiversity (Ecosystem Preservation)

Protection and enhancement of biological diversity within the urban environment. This involves creating wildlife corridors that connect green spaces, preserving native plant species in urban landscaping, establishing urban wildlife habitats and bird sanctuaries, implementing pollinator-friendly gardens, and integrating nature-based solutions in urban planning. Urban biodiversity strengthens ecosystem resilience and provides ecological services such as pollination and natural pest control.

9. Climate Resilience (Adaptation and Mitigation)

Infrastructure and planning designed to withstand climate change impacts while reducing contributions to global warming. This includes flood management systems, heat-resistant urban design, climate-adapted building codes, carbon sequestration through urban forestry, and disaster preparedness planning. Climate resilience ensures cities can protect residents from extreme weather events while working toward carbon neutrality.

10. Community Engagement (Inclusive Governance)

Active participation of citizens in planning and decision-making processes related to urban sustainability. This involves public consultations on green initiatives, community-led environmental projects, educational programs on sustainability, and mechanisms for resident feedback on city services. Engaged communities are essential for the long-term success of green city initiatives.

2.4 Urban Design and Eco-Friendly Architecture

Urban design and eco-friendly architecture represent fundamental pillars in the development of sustainable cities, functioning as the physical manifestation of green city principles through the built environment. These interconnected disciplines work together to create urban spaces that harmonize human needs with environmental stewardship, transforming how cities are planned, constructed, and experienced by their inhabitants.

Urban design encompasses the comprehensive planning and shaping of cities at multiple scales, from individual buildings to entire neighborhoods and metropolitan regions. In the context of sustainability, urban design prioritizes compact, mixed-use development patterns that reduce urban sprawl and minimize the ecological footprint of human settlements. This approach emphasizes walkable neighborhoods where residential, commercial, and recreational spaces are integrated within close proximity, reducing the need for long commutes and promoting active lifestyles. Sustainable urban design also incorporates extensive green infrastructure networks, including parks, greenways, street trees, and ecological corridors that connect natural habitats throughout the urban fabric. These green spaces serve multiple functions: they improve air quality by absorbing pollutants and carbon dioxide, mitigate urban heat island effects through natural cooling, manage stormwater runoff through permeable surfaces, and provide essential ecosystem services while enhancing residents' quality of life. The strategic placement of buildings, streets, and open spaces is carefully considered to maximize natural ventilation, solar access, and daylight penetration, reducing the energy demands of the built environment while creating pleasant, human-scaled urban spaces that encourage social interaction and community building.

Eco-friendly architecture, often referred to as green building or sustainable architecture, focuses specifically on the design and construction of individual structures that minimize environmental impact throughout their entire lifecycle. This holistic approach begins with site selection and building orientation to optimize passive solar heating and cooling, natural lighting, and wind patterns. Eco-friendly buildings employ energy-efficient designs that significantly reduce operational energy consumption through features such as high-performance insulation, triple-glazed windows, thermal mass materials that regulate indoor temperatures, and building envelopes that minimize heat loss or gain. The integration of renewable energy systems, including rooftop solar panels, solar water heaters, and in some cases small-scale wind turbines or geothermal systems, allows buildings to generate their own clean energy and potentially achieve net-zero or even net-positive energy status. Water conservation is another critical dimension, with green buildings incorporating rainwater harvesting systems that capture precipitation for landscape irrigation and non-potable uses, greywater recycling systems that treat and reuse water from sinks and showers, and low-flow fixtures that reduce water consumption without sacrificing functionality. Material selection plays an equally important role, with sustainable architecture prioritizing locally sourced, recycled, or rapidly renewable materials that have lower embodied energy and carbon footprints compared to conventional construction materials. The use of non-toxic, low-VOC (volatile organic compound) materials ensures healthy indoor air quality for occupants while reducing pollution during manufacturing and installation.

The convergence of urban design and eco-friendly architecture creates synergistic effects that amplify the sustainability benefits of each approach individually. When green buildings are clustered within well-designed, pedestrian-oriented neighborhoods served by efficient public transportation, the combined impact on reducing greenhouse gas emissions, resource consumption, and environmental degradation becomes exponentially greater. Transit-oriented development, which concentrates high-density, mixed-use development around public transit stations, exemplifies this integration by reducing car dependency while creating vibrant urban centers where people can live, work, and play without excessive travel. Similarly, the incorporation of green roofs and living walls on buildings not only improves individual building performance but also contributes to neighborhood-scale benefits such as reduced stormwater runoff, improved air quality, and enhanced urban biodiversity. These vegetated surfaces create stepping stones and corridors for urban wildlife while providing insulation that reduces building energy needs and mitigates the urban heat island effect across entire districts.

Contemporary sustainable urban design and architecture increasingly embrace biophilic design principles, which recognize humans' innate connection to nature and seek to integrate natural elements, patterns, and processes into the built environment. This approach goes beyond simply adding plants to buildings and instead fundamentally reimagines architecture as an interface between people and nature.

Biophilic design incorporates natural materials like wood and stone, creates visual connections to outdoor environments through strategic window placement and transparent facades, utilizes natural patterns and forms in structural and decorative elements, and provides direct access to nature through courtyards, balconies, and rooftop gardens. Research demonstrates that biophilic design significantly improves occupant well-being, productivity, and mental health while simultaneously delivering environmental benefits through reduced energy consumption and enhanced biodiversity support.

The implementation of sustainable urban design and eco-friendly architecture also requires supportive policy frameworks, including green building codes and standards such as LEED (Leadership in Energy and Environmental Design), BREEAM (Building Research Establishment Environmental Assessment Method), or local equivalents that establish minimum performance criteria for new construction and major renovations. Zoning regulations that mandate or incentivize mixed-use development, minimum green space ratios, and building density limits help shape urban form toward sustainability goals. Financial mechanisms such as tax credits for green building features, expedited permitting for sustainable projects, and density bonuses that allow taller buildings in exchange for public amenities or green features encourage developers and property owners to exceed minimum standards and push the boundaries of sustainable design innovation.

Looking toward the future, emerging technologies and design approaches promise to further advance sustainable urban design and architecture. Smart building systems that use sensors and artificial intelligence to continuously optimize energy use, lighting, and climate control based on occupancy patterns and external conditions can reduce resource consumption by thirty to fifty percent compared to conventional buildings (Sekti, 2025b). Advanced materials such as self-healing concrete, transparent solar panels that can be integrated into windows, and phase-change materials that store and release thermal energy are expanding the possibilities for sustainable construction. Modular and prefabricated construction techniques that reduce waste and construction time while improving quality control are making sustainable building more efficient and cost-effective. Three-dimensional printing of building components using recycled materials or earth-based materials offers potential for radically reducing construction waste and embodied carbon. As these technologies mature and costs decline, they will become increasingly accessible, enabling even greater environmental performance from the built environment (Ali, Motuzienė, & Džiugaitė-Tumėnienė, 2024).

Ultimately, urban design and eco-friendly architecture are not merely technical disciplines but represent a fundamental reimagining of humanity's relationship with the natural environment. By creating cities and buildings that work with rather than against natural systems, that celebrate rather than exclude biodiversity, and that prioritize long-term sustainability over short-term convenience, these approaches offer a pathway toward urban environments that support both human flourishing and planetary health for generations to come.

2.5 Transportation Systems and Mobility Solutions

Transportation systems are critical components in urban sustainability transformation, currently accounting for approximately 29% of global greenhouse gas emissions and consuming over 30% of fossil fuel resources. With the United Nations projecting that 68% of the world's population will live in cities by 2050, the pressure on transportation infrastructure intensifies, creating urgent demands for innovative mobility solutions. Sustainable transportation requires fundamental shifts in how cities design and manage their networks through multiple interconnected strategies: electrification of vehicle fleets, development of extensive public transit systems, integration of shared mobility services, promotion of active transportation modes like walking and cycling, and deployment of intelligent transportation systems that optimize traffic flow. The primary challenge lies in creating integrated, multimodal transportation ecosystems that work synergistically to provide seamless, efficient, and environmentally responsible mobility options for all urban residents while accommodating population growth and reducing environmental impact.

Public transit systems form the backbone of sustainable urban mobility, offering compelling alternatives to private vehicle ownership that dramatically reduce per-capita emissions and alleviate traffic congestion. Well-designed public transportation networks including buses, metro systems, light rail, and commuter trains provide efficient movement with significantly lower environmental footprints, as demonstrated by cities like Tokyo, Singapore, and Copenhagen. A single bus can remove up to 40 private vehicles from roadways, while rail systems transport thousands of passengers per hour with minimal energy consumption per passenger-kilometer. Beyond environmental benefits, comprehensive public transit networks enhance social equity by providing affordable mobility for low-income residents, elderly populations, and individuals who cannot drive. Modern systems increasingly incorporate smart technologies including real-time passenger information, contactless payments, and integrated ticketing platforms that enable seamless transfers. Transit-oriented development, which concentrates high-density mixed-use development around transportation hubs, amplifies these benefits by reducing commute needs and creating vibrant urban centers accessible without private vehicles (Emmanuel Augustine Etukudoh et al., 2024).

The electrification of transportation through electric vehicles (EVs) and autonomous vehicle technology represents transformative innovation in urban mobility. Electric vehicles eliminate tailpipe emissions and, when charged with renewable energy, achieve near-zero lifecycle carbon emissions, making them essential for decarbonizing transportation. With more than 26.4 million EVs expected by 2030, the market is experiencing explosive growth driven by improved battery technology, declining costs, and expanding charging infrastructure. The integration of EVs with renewable energy sources enables vehicle-to-grid (V2G) systems where electric vehicles serve as distributed energy storage, enhancing grid stability and renewable energy utilization. Autonomous vehicles (AVs) offer potential to dramatically improve traffic efficiency, reduce accidents, optimize routing, and enable new shared mobility models. Research indicates that autonomous electric vehicles operating in shared fleets could reduce urban transportation emissions by up to 80% compared to conventional privately owned vehicles while decreasing the total number of vehicles needed. However, realizing these benefits requires addressing challenges including robust charging infrastructure development, cybersecurity of connected vehicle systems, regulatory frameworks for autonomous operations, and preventing increased vehicle miles traveled if autonomous vehicles make driving too convenient. Figure 2 shows the Unveiling the Future of Urban Mobility.

Figure 2. Unveiling the future of urban mobility

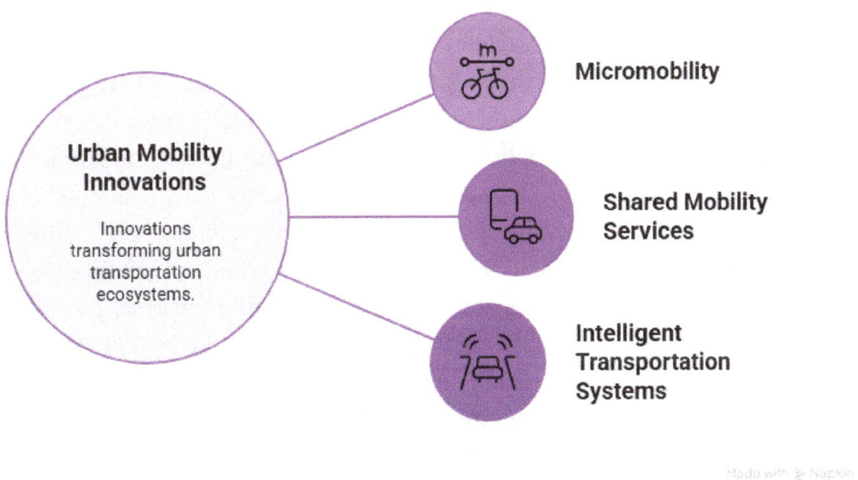

Emerging innovations in micromobility, shared mobility services, and intelligent transportation systems are diversifying urban mobility and enabling more sustainable transportation options. Micromobility solutions including e-scooters, e-bikes, and bike-sharing programs provide first-mile and last-mile connectivity that bridges gaps in public transit networks, offering convenient alternatives for short trips. Cities implementing comprehensive cycling infrastructure have seen dramatic increases in bicycle use with corresponding improvements in air quality, public health, and traffic congestion. Shared mobility services encompassing car-sharing, ride-sharing, and mobility-as-a-service (MaaS) platforms integrate multiple transportation modes into unified digital platforms, reducing private vehicle ownership and optimizing resource utilization. Intelligent Transportation Systems (ITS) leverage advanced communication technologies, sensors, artificial intelligence, and big data analytics to create responsive, adaptive networks that optimize traffic flow in real-time through smart traffic signals, variable message signs, connected vehicle technologies enabling vehicle-to-vehicle (V2V) and vehicle-to-infrastructure (V2I) communication, and predictive analytics. The integration of 5G connectivity and edge computing enables ultra-low-latency communication supporting advanced applications like cooperative adaptive cruise control. Looking forward, these technologies promise truly integrated, multimodal transportation ecosystems where travelers can seamlessly transition between different modes through unified digital platforms that optimize routes, costs, and environmental impact in real-time.

2.6 Community Involvement and Environmental Awareness

Community involvement and environmental awareness serve as essential foundations for the successful implementation and long-term sustainability of green city initiatives, transforming residents from passive recipients of urban services into active participants in environmental stewardship. Citizen engagement encompasses various forms of participation, ranging from consultation and collaboration to co-creation and community-led initiatives that empower local residents to shape the environmental policies and projects affecting their neighborhoods (Bressane, Loureiro, & Negri, 2024). Research demonstrates that when communities actively participate in urban greening projects such as community gardens, tree planting campaigns, and neighborhood park management these initiatives not only deliver environmental benefits like improved air quality and increased biodiversity but also generate intangible social outcomes including enhanced social cohesion, knowledge development, and strengthened community identity. Civil society organizations play crucial roles in catalyzing municipal engagement with sustainability strategies, organizing educational events to raise awareness about environmental issues, managing citizens' concerns and aspirations, and sometimes adopting community management roles that include planting, maintenance, and environmental education activities (Hadjichambis, Paraskeva-Hadjichambi, Sinakou, Adamou, & Georgiou,

2022). The involvement of diverse community members, particularly those from different socioeconomic backgrounds, ensures that green city initiatives address equity concerns and do not inadvertently exclude marginalized populations from the benefits of urban environmental improvements.

Environmental awareness and education form the cognitive and behavioral foundations that enable meaningful community participation in green city development, fostering understanding of environmental challenges and empowering citizens to adopt sustainable practices in their daily lives. Educational initiatives in green cities take multiple forms, from formal programs in schools that teach ecological principles and sustainability concepts to informal learning opportunities embedded in urban green spaces where residents can observe and interact with nature-based solutions firsthand. Smart city technologies increasingly support environmental awareness by providing citizens with real-time data about local air quality, energy consumption, water usage, and carbon emissions through mobile applications and public displays, making abstract environmental concepts tangible and personal. Citizen science initiatives, where residents use portable sensors and digital platforms to collect environmental data and contribute to scientific monitoring efforts, not only generate valuable information for policymakers but also enhance participants' environmental literacy and sense of ownership over local environmental conditions. Projects like the Zero Carbon Building in Hong Kong exemplify how demonstration facilities can showcase sustainable technologies while simultaneously raising community awareness about low-carbon living, serving both educational and inspirational purposes that motivate behavioral change beyond the immediate project site.

The integration of community involvement with environmental awareness creates powerful synergies that accelerate the transition toward sustainable urban living, as informed and engaged citizens become advocates for environmental policies, champions of sustainable behaviors, and guardians of local green spaces. Studies examining green cities worldwide reveal that successful environmental citizenship emerges when cities implement comprehensive strategies that combine accessible green infrastructure with robust public participation mechanisms and continuous environmental education efforts. Community engagement in urban green space management has been shown to correlate with improved access to these spaces, reduced socio-environmental inequality, and enhanced sustainability outcomes that extend beyond purely environmental metrics to encompass social inclusion, health improvements, and preservation of local knowledge and traditions. However, achieving meaningful community involvement requires cities to move beyond tokenistic consultation toward genuine empowerment where citizens have real influence over decision-making processes, supported by transparent governance structures, adequate resources for community-led initiatives, and recognition that diverse communities may have different environmental priorities and engagement prefeences. As cities continue to confront complex environmental challenges, the cultivation of environmentally aware and actively engaged communities becomes not merely desirable but essential for building resilient, sustainable urban futures that reflect the values, needs, and aspirations of all residents.

3. ENVIRONMENTAL BENEFITS OF GREEN CITIES

Green cities deliver substantial environmental benefits that address critical urban challenges including air pollution, climate change, biodiversity loss, and resource depletion. These benefits emerge from the strategic integration of nature-based solutions, green infrastructure, and sustainable technologies throughout the urban fabric. Urban greening encompasses street trees, parks, urban forests, wetlands, green roofs, green walls, and permeable surfaces that contribute to enhancing environmental sustainability and public wellbeing. The environmental advantages of green cities extend across multiple dimensions, creating synergistic effects that improve ecosystem health while simultaneously enhancing urban livability and resilience against climate change impacts. Figure 3 provides a visual overview of the seven major environmental benefit categories that green cities deliver through strategic integration of nature-based solutions and green infrastructure

Figure 3. Environmental benefits of green cities

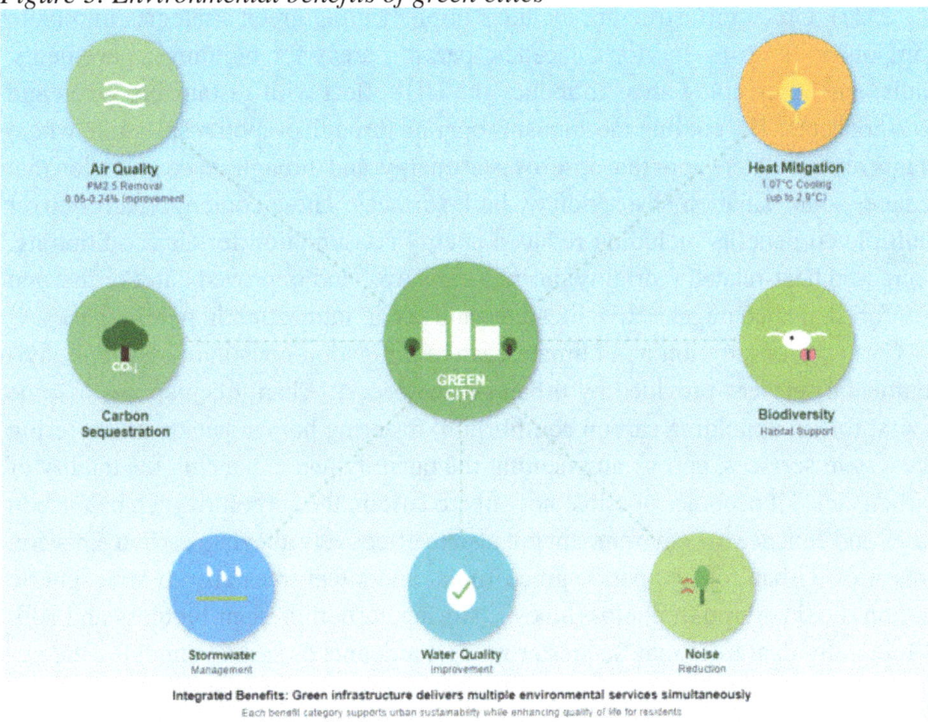

Air pollution, principally caused by nitrogen dioxide (NO2) and fine particles with aerodynamic diameter less than 2.5 μm (PM2.5), is now the leading environmental cause of mortality worldwide, causing approximately 3 million premature deaths a year. Green infrastructure plays a critical role in improving urban air quality through multiple mechanisms. Vegetation and trees act as natural filters for both gases and particulate matter in urban environments, with particulate matter settling on leaf surfaces. Research across U.S. cities demonstrates significant air quality improvements: total annual PM2.5 removal by urban trees varied from 5.2 tons in Syracuse to 71.1 tons in Atlanta, with estimated mortality reduction of approximately 1 person per year for each city but as high as 7.6 people annually for New York, and overall air quality improvements attributed to urban trees ranged between 0.05% in San Francisco to 0.24% in Atlanta. Beyond particulate matter removal, urban vegetation absorbs gaseous pollutants including ozone, nitrogen dioxide, sulfur dioxide, and carbon monoxide, providing billions of dollars in public health value annually through cleaner air (Hewitt, Ashworth, & MacKenzie, 2020).

The urban heat island (UHI) effect represents another major environmental challenge that green cities effectively address. Urban Green Infrastructure is found to cool European cities by 1.07°C on average and up to 2.9°C, though achieving a

1°C drop in urban temperatures requires a tree cover of at least 16% (Marando et al., 2022). Green infrastructure includes implementing green strategies into main components such as rooftops, façades, parking areas for buildings, pavements, walls, and landscaping areas to reduce the UHI effect with sustainable green and blue concepts. The cooling mechanisms operate through evapotranspiration, where plants release water vapor that absorbs heat energy, and through shade provision that reduces solar radiation absorption by built surfaces. These cooling effects deliver multiple co-benefits including reduced energy consumption for air conditioning, decreased heat-related mortality during heatwaves, and improved outdoor thermal comfort that encourages active lifestyles and social interaction in public spaces.

Carbon sequestration and climate change mitigation constitute essential environmental services provided by urban green spaces. Urban green spaces assume a vital role in upholding carbon equilibrium, fostering human health, and offering ecosystem services, and by augmenting the quantity and enhancing the quality of carbon sinks, it becomes possible not only to sustain the carbon-oxygen balance in cities and enhance the environment but also to effectively alleviate carbon emission pressures. Urban forests, parks, green roofs, and street trees absorb atmospheric carbon dioxide through photosynthesis, storing carbon in plant biomass and soil. While individual trees may sequester modest amounts of carbon annually, the cumulative effect across city-scale urban forests becomes significant. Moreover, green infrastructure indirectly reduces carbon emissions by lowering building energy demands through natural cooling and heating moderation, thereby decreasing fossil fuel consumption for climate control (Pandey & Ghosh, 2023).

Biodiversity conservation and ecosystem services represent additional critical environmental benefits of green cities. Urban ecosystem services include temperature regulation, air quality control, stormwater management/flood water absorption, flood mitigation, biodiversity support, carbon sequestration, pollination services, cultural services, and food security. Urban green spaces provide habitat for diverse plant and animal species, creating ecological networks that support urban biodiversity even within densely built environments. These ecosystems deliver essential pollination services for urban agriculture and ornamental plants, natural pest control, and genetic diversity preservation. Stormwater management represents another vital service, with vegetated areas and permeable surfaces absorbing rainfall, reducing runoff volume, filtering pollutants, and mitigating urban flooding risks. This natural water management reduces strain on conventional gray infrastructure while improving water quality in urban waterways.

4. ECONOMIC AND SOCIAL IMPACTS

Green Cities provide significant economic and social impacts for the community and sustainable development. Here is the explanation:

1. Economic Impact

Green cities create new business opportunities through the renewable energy industry, environmentally friendly technologies, and sustainable tourism. Long-term operational costs are also reduced due to energy efficiency and waste reduction. Additionally, property and land values in green city areas tend to increase, attracting investment and creating new jobs.

2. Social Impact

From a social perspective, green cities improve the quality of life for residents with cleaner air, greener public spaces, and a reduction in pollution-related diseases. Communities become more cohesive through joint environmental programs, and environmental awareness increases among citizens.

Table 1. Summary of the comparison between economic impacts and social impacts

Aspect	Economic Impact	Social Impact
Job Opportunity	Green industry & new technology	Training and skill development
Health	Medical costs are reduced	A healthier and more productive society
Property Value	Increase in asset value	Sustainable housing access
Investment	Fund Withdrawal & Business	Empowerment of the local community

Table 1 shows the Summary of the comparison between economic impacts and social impacts. Thus, green cities are not only good for the environment, but also provide economic benefits and enhance the social well-being of the community sustainably.

5. CHALLENGES IN DEVELOPING GREEN CITIES

The development of green cities faces various challenges that need to be addressed. Here is a brief explanation:

1. High Initial Investment Cost

The implementation of green infrastructure, renewable technologies, and environmentally friendly transportation systems requires a very large capital investment. This becomes a major obstacle, especially for cities in developing countries with limited government budgets (Debrah, Kissi, Oduro-ofori, & Edwards, 2020).

2. Changes in Community Behavior

Changing people's consumption habits and lifestyles takes a long time and requires continuous educational efforts. Public resistance to change often hinders the implementation of green city programs.

3. Lack of Clear Policies and Regulations

Banyak daerah belum memiliki regulasi yang konsisten dan mendukung pengembangan green cities. Koordinasi antar lembaga pemerintah yang lemah juga menjadi kendala implementasi.

4. Limitations of Technology and Resources

Not all regions have access to the latest green technologies or supportive natural resources (such as limited renewable energy potential).

6. CASE STUDIES OF SUCCESSFUL GREEN CITIES

Copenhagen, Denmark stands as a global leader in urban sustainability, with an ambitious target to become carbon-neutral by 2025 through comprehensive green city strategies. The city has invested heavily in renewable energy sources including wind energy and district heating systems, developed extensive cycling infrastructure where over 40% of commutes are done by bicycle, created urban parks and green roofs throughout the city, and implemented advanced recycling programs and waste-to-energy plants. CopenHill, the city's waste-to-energy plant topped with a ski slope, processes 440,000 tons of waste annually while generating clean electricity for 150,000 homes, with its facade acting as a giant air filter and interior housing climbing walls and hiking trails. Copenhagen utilizes advanced data collection and intelligent traffic management systems that monitor real-time traffic conditions and adjust signal timings to reduce congestion, while digital platforms provide citizens with real-time data on air quality, energy consumption, and public transportation, fostering transparency and citizen participation. The city's integrated planning approach, combining renewable energy, sustainable transportation, green spaces, and public engagement, has resulted in substantial reductions in carbon emissions and energy consumption while achieving high quality of life for residents (Petrea, Ursache, Alexandru, & Alexandru, 2023).

Singapore exemplifies vertical green city development, transforming from a “Garden City” to a “City in a Garden” with nearly 50% of its land now covered by green space despite being one of the world's most densely populated nations (Sarabdeen, 2024). The government launched the Skyrise Greenery Incentive Scheme in 2009, and as of 2023, Singapore boasts more than 100 hectares of rooftop gardens and green walls that significantly reduce the urban heat island effect and improve air quality. Gardens by the Bay, a 101-hectare development, features iconic Supertrees ranging from 25 to 50 meters tall that collect solar energy, harvest rainwater, and house over 150,000 living plants, attracting over 10 million visitors annually while promoting biodiversity with 1.5 million plants from more than 15,000 species (Zhang, Xie, & Gao, 2022). The city implements a 100% greenery replacement policy in new developments, requiring developers to replace ground-level greenery lost to construction with sky gardens and vertical greenery, while the Streetscape Greenery Master Plan creates a continuous tree canopy above major roads with three million trees covering the island. Since 2020, Singapore has successfully planted more than half a million trees through the OneMillionTrees movement, with biodiversity impact assessments identifying 99 native animal species and 32 plant species requiring protection. Singapore's success demonstrates how innovative vertical greening, mandatory green building policies, and nature-based solutions can create sustainable, biodiverse urban environments even in land-constrained, high-density cities (Wang, Xu, An, & Guo, 2024).

7. FUTURE OF GREEN URBAN DEVELOPMENT

The future of green urban development is characterized by ambitious global targets and transformative technologies that aim to create net-zero, nature-positive cities by 2050. With urbanization projected to add 2.2 billion people to cities by 2050 increasing the urban population to two-thirds of humanity and cities currently accounting for over 70% of global CO2 emissions, the urgency for sustainable transformation has never been greater. The European Union aims to be the first continent with zero net greenhouse gas emissions by 2050, achieving climate neutrality through comprehensive strategies including at least 40% greenhouse gas reduction, 32% renewable energy share, and 32.5% energy efficiency improvement by 2030. To achieve net-zero and nature-positive cities by 2050, the World Economic Forum is partnering with stakeholders on initiatives including the Davos Baukultur Alliance for climate-resilient buildings, the Global New Mobility Coalition for reducing emissions and enhancing EV infrastructure, and Biodiver Cities by 2030 to transform cities into spaces where economic, social, and ecological functions harmonize (Zhang et al., 2022). Digital technology and AI-based tools are harnessing power to reimagine cities of the future, helping anticipate shocks, model scenarios, and inform long-term urban planning that benefits vulnerable groups including women, children, and people with disabilities. Figure 4 shows the Future of Greem Urban Development by 2050.

Figure 4. Future of green urban development by 2050

The integration of smart technologies with nature-based solutions and circular economy principles represents the cornerstone of future urban development strategies. Smart city initiatives leverage digital infrastructure, IoT, AI, and big data analytics to optimize resource use, reduce carbon emissions, improve mobility, and enhance quality of life, with research showing significant publication peaks in 2021 and 2023 reflecting growing global interest. Cities currently occupy only 2% of Earth's landscape yet consume 80% of energy generated worldwide and produce 75% of global CO2 emissions, with global material consumption expected to triple by 2050, making circular economy approaches essential for closing loops in production, waste disposal, and water reuse. Nature-based solutions integrated with circular economy principles can address water scarcity, reclaim water from non-conventional sources, and provide co-benefits including climate adaptation, flood prevention, micro-climate regulation, and food provision, with examples like Vienna's zero-energy hotels demonstrating 100% organic waste recycling and significant CO2 reductions. By accelerating NbS implementation, decision-makers can help cities adapt to climate change effects, reduce urban heat islands, clean air, and manage water while bringing ecosystem services back into cities and rebalancing relationships with surrounding areas. With half of urban areas that will exist in 2050 not yet designed or built, there exist tremendous opportunities for enhancing urban sustainability through biophilic design and nature-based solutions that create more livable, healthy, sustainable, and resilient cities (Gámez Díaz, Yu, Ding, Laamarti, & El Saddik, 2020).

The pathway toward sustainable urban futures requires holistic governance approaches, collaborative innovation ecosystems, and unprecedented levels of public-private-community partnerships. As 80% of urban structures will still exist in 2050, retrofitting existing infrastructure to incorporate smart capabilities will be essential, with initiatives like Egypt's Vision 2030 creating 37 smart cities with modern digital infrastructure, renewable energy, green spaces, and intelligent transportation, while Amsterdam's circular economy strategy aims to halve use of new raw materials by 2030 and transition to full circularity by 2050 (Khalifa, Ibrahim, Amhamed, & El-Naas, 2022). Future studies use a 25-50 year time horizon as realistic and far enough to allow major technological and cultural changes, with the period 2020-2050 needed to develop data-driven smart sustainable cities as desirable futures where sustainable energy systems, dense urban patterns, green areas, and technological infrastructure reach optimal sustainability levels. SDG 11 research shows consistent increases in output reflecting growing global interest in urban sustainability, with analysis of over 21,000 publications revealing influential collaborative networks, emerging research hubs, and interdisciplinary connections emphasizing critical topics for creating inclusive, safe, resilient, and sustainable cities by 2030 (Kumar et al., 2025). However, achieving these ambitious targets requires addressing significant challenges including the digital divide, cybersecurity risks, climate change adaptation, behavioral shifts toward circular consumption, ecosystem-wide orchestration across stakeholders, and ensuring equitable access to sustainability benefits for all urban residents regardless of socioeconomic status, ultimately demanding transformative leadership that champions approaches going beyond traditional urban management toward integrated, nature-inclusive, technologically empowered city development.

8. CONCLUSION

The comprehensive exploration of green cities throughout this document reveals that sustainable urban development has evolved from an aspirational concept to an urgent necessity, as urbanization continues to accelerate with two-thirds of humanity projected to reside in cities by 2050. Green cities represent a fundamental reimagining of urban environments, integrating environmental sustainability, economic efficiency, and social equity through ten interconnected characteristics: clean renewable energy systems, extensive green spaces, comprehensive circular economy waste management, sustainable transportation infrastructure, energy-efficient buildings, integrated water management, smart city technologies, urban biodiversity preservation, climate-resilient infrastructure, and meaningful community engagement. These features work synergistically to deliver substantial environmental benefits including air quality improvements that prevent thousands of premature deaths annually, urban heat island mitigation providing average cooling of 1.07°C, carbon sequestration contributing to climate change mitigation, and biodiversity conservation supporting ecosystem resilience. Beyond environmental advantages, green cities generate significant economic impacts through job creation with renewable energy investments producing 1.5 times more employment than fossil fuel equivalents enhanced property values, reduced healthcare costs, and improved urban competitiveness, while delivering critical social benefits including better physical and mental health outcomes (with 20% greenspace increases correlating to 9% mortality reductions), strengthened community cohesion, enhanced social equity, and increased climate resilience. Successful implementation examples from Copenhagen, pursuing carbon neutrality by 2025 through renewable energy, extensive cycling infrastructure, and innovative waste-to-energy facilities, and Singapore, achieving nearly 50% green space coverage despite extreme density through vertical greening strategies and mandatory greenery replacement policies, demonstrate that comprehensive, integrated approaches combining political commitment, technological innovation, and public engagement can achieve transformative sustainability outcomes. Looking toward the future, achieving net-zero, nature-positive cities by 2050 requires integrating smart technologies with nature-based solutions and circular economy principles, leveraging IoT, artificial intelligence, and big data analytics to optimize resource utilization while addressing significant challenges including high initial investment costs, behavioral change requirements, policy development needs, digital divides, cybersecurity risks, and ensuring equitable access to sustainability benefits for all urban residents regardless of socioeconomic status. Ultimately, green cities represent more than technical solutions they embody a fundamental shift in humanity's relationship with nature and collective urban life, requiring simultaneous transformation across technological, social, economic, political, and cultural dimensions through holistic governance approaches, collaborative innovation ecosystems, unprecedented public-private-community partnerships, and transformative leadership that champions integrated, nature-inclusive, technologically empowered development capable of supporting both human flourishing and planetary health for current and future generations within Earth's ecological boundaries.

REFERENCES

Ali, D. M. T. E., Motuzienė, V., & Džiugaitė-Tumėnienė, R. (2024). AI-Driven Innovations in Building Energy Management Systems: A Review of Potential Applications and Energy Savings. *Energies*, *17*(17), 4277. Advance online publication. DOI: 10.3390/en17174277

Alqadhi, S., & Mallick, J. (2026). Integrating road network topology, remote sensing, and explainable machine learning to assess urban ecological resilience. *Environmental Technology & Innovation*, *41*, 104805. Advance online publication. DOI: 10.1016/j.eti.2026.104805

Azizi, L., & Kouddane, N. (2024). The green city as a driver of sustainable development. *Journal of Umm Al-Qura University for Engineering and Architecture*, *15*(4), 384–397. DOI: 10.1007/s43995-024-00077-x

Bashirpour Bonab, A., Bellini, F., & Rudko, I. (2023). Theoretical and analytical assessment of smart green cities. *Journal of Cleaner Production*, *410*, 137315. Advance online publication. DOI: 10.1016/j.jclepro.2023.137315

Bibri, S. E., Krogstie, J., & Kärrholm, M. (2020). Compact city planning and development: Emerging practices and strategies for achieving the goals of sustainability. *Developments in the Built Environment*, *4*, 100021. Advance online publication. DOI: 10.1016/j.dibe.2020.100021

Bressane, A., Loureiro, A. I. S., & Negri, R. G. (2024). Environmental Racism in the Accessibility of Urban Green Space: A Case Study of a Metropolitan Area in an Emerging Economy. *Urban Science (Basel, Switzerland)*, *8*(4), 1–12. DOI: 10.3390/urbansci8040224

Cihan Kayaçetin, N., Aslanoğlu, R., Piccardo, C., Afacan, Y., Masera, G., Li, Q., Biraghi, C. A., Pittau, F., Saelens, D., Soebarto, V., Zuo, J., Chang, R., Vrebos, H., Van Acker, K., Sebastian, R., Dikken, J., Ivan, L., Alaerts, L., Aral, D., & van Hoof, J. (2026). Ten questions concerning circularity in the built environment. *Building and Environment*, *292*, 114291. Advance online publication. DOI: 10.1016/j.buildenv.2026.114291

Debrah, C., Kissi, E., Oduro-ofori, E., & Edwards, D. J. (2020). Barriers to green cities development in developing countries: evidence from Ghana development. DOI: 10.1108/SASBE-06-2020-0089

Etukudoh, E. A., Adefemi, A., Ilojianya, V. I., Umoh, A. A., Ibekwe, K. I., & Zamathula, Q. S. N. (2024). A Review of sustainable transportation solutions: Innovations, challenges, and future directions. *World Journal of Advanced Research and Reviews*, *21*(1), 1440–1452. DOI: 10.30574/wjarr.2024.21.1.0173

Gámez Díaz, R., Yu, Q., Ding, Y., Laamarti, F., & El Saddik, A. (2020). Digital twin coaching for physical activities: A survey. *Sensors (Basel)*, *20*(20), 1–21. DOI: 10.3390/s20205936 PMID: 33096595

Hadjichambis, A. C., Paraskeva-Hadjichambi, D., Sinakou, E., Adamou, A., & Georgiou, Y. (2022). Green Cities for Environmental Citizenship: A Systematic Literature Review of Empirical Research from 31 Green Cities of the World. *Sustainability (Basel)*, *14*(23), 16223. Advance online publication. DOI: 10.3390/su142316223

Hansen, R., & Pauleit, S. (2014). From multifunctionality to multiple ecosystem services? A conceptual framework for multifunctionality in green infrastructure planning for Urban Areas. *Ambio*, *43*(4), 516–529. DOI: 10.1007/s13280-014-0510-2 PMID: 24740622

Hewitt, C. N., Ashworth, K., & MacKenzie, A. R. (2020). Using green infrastructure to improve urban air quality (GI4AQ). *Ambio*, *49*(1), 62–73. DOI: 10.1007/s13280-019-01164-3 PMID: 30879268

Khalifa, A. A., Ibrahim, A. J., Amhamed, A. I., & El-Naas, M. H. (2022). Accelerating the Transition to a Circular Economy for Net-Zero Emissions by 2050: A Systematic Review. *Sustainability (Basel)*, *14*(18), 1–20. DOI: 10.3390/su141811656

Kumar, P., Sahani, J., Corada Perez, K., Ahlawat, A., Andrade, M., Athanassiadou, M., Cao, S.-J., Collins, L., Dey, S., Di Sabatino, S., Halios, C. H., Harris, F., Horton, C., Inostroza, L., Jones, L., Rodding Kjeldsen, T., McCallan, B., McNabola, A., Kumar Mishra, R., & Yao, R. (2025). Urban greening for climate resilient and sustainable cities: Grand challenges and opportunities. *Frontiers in Sustainable Cities*, *7*, 1595280. Advance online publication. DOI: 10.3389/frsc.2025.1595280

Marando, F., Heris, M. P., Zulian, G., Udías, A., Mentaschi, L., Chrysoulakis, N., … Maes, J. (2022). Urban heat island mitigation by green infrastructure in European Functional Urban Areas. *Sustainable Cities and Society*, *77*, 103564. DOI: 10.1016/j.scs.2021.103564

Pandey, B., & Ghosh, A. (2023). Urban ecosystem services and climate change: A dynamic interplay. *Frontiers in Sustainable Cities*, *5*, 1281430. Advance online publication. DOI: 10.3389/frsc.2023.1281430

Petrea, M.-I., & Ursache, I.-M. (2023). Inside the World's most Sustainable Smart City: Lessons from Copenhagen. *International Conference on "Sustainable Development of European Smart Cities*, (October), 225–238.

Rui, J., Shabrina, Z., & Gong, W. (2026). Artificial intelligence applications in urban extreme heat management: A systematic review of forecasting, monitoring, mitigation and decision support. *Environmental Impact Assessment Review*, *119*, 108363. Advance online publication. DOI: 10.1016/j.eiar.2026.108363

Sarabdeen, J. (2024). Nexus between innovation and sustainable economic development: A bibliometrics analysis. *Journal of Infrastructure. Policy and Development*, *8*(11), 1–23. DOI: 10.24294/jipd.v8i11.8762

Sekti, B. A. (2025a). Foundations of Artificial Intelligence Ethics. In *Navigating Social Trust in the AI Era* (pp. 23–47). DOI: 10.4018/979-8-3373-7011-8.ch002

Sekti, B. A. (2025b). Machine Learning vs. AI: Key Concepts. In *Implementing Enterprise Cybersecurity With AI* (pp. 1–27). DOI: 10.4018/979-8-3373-2252-0.ch001

Sekti, B. A. (2026). Cybersecurity Challenges in Smart City Development. In *Securing Smart Cities Through Modern Cryptography Technologies* (pp. 75–102). IGI Global Scientific Publishing. DOI: 10.4018/979-8-3373-3326-7.ch003

Sharifi, A., Khavarian-Garmsir, A. R., Allam, Z., & Asadzadeh, A. (2023). Progress and prospects in planning: A bibliometric review of literature in Urban Studies and Regional and Urban Planning, 1956–2022. *Progress in Planning*, *173*, 100740. Advance online publication. DOI: 10.1016/j.progress.2023.100740

Sharma, M., Sharma, B., Kumar, N., & Kumar, A. (2023). Establishing Conceptual Components for Urban Resilience: Taking Clues from Urbanization through a Planner's Lens. *Natural Hazards Review*, *24*(1), 04022040. Advance online publication. DOI: 10.1061/NHREFO.NHENG-1523

Štrbac, S., Kašanin-Grubin, M., Pezo, L., Stojić, N., Lončar, B., Ćurčić, L., & Pucarević, M. (2023). Green Infrastructure Designed through Nature-Based Solutions for Sustainable Urban Development. *International Journal of Environmental Research and Public Health*, *20*(2), 1102. Advance online publication. DOI: 10.3390/ijerph20021102 PMID: 36673859

Wang, D., Xu, P. Y., An, B. W., & Guo, Q. P. (2024). Urban green infrastructure: Bridging biodiversity conservation and sustainable urban development through adaptive management approach. *Frontiers in Ecology and Evolution*, *12*(August), 1–20. DOI: 10.3389/fevo.2024.1440477

Zhang, M., Xie, W., & Gao, W. (2022). Have environmental regulations promoted green technological innovation in cities? Evidence from China's green patents. *PLoS ONE, 17*(12), 1–24. DOI: 10.1371/journal.pone.0278902

Chapter 2
Role of Plant Species in Mitigating Air and Noise Pollution as Well as Their Contribution to Temperature Regulation

Manu Mehrotra
http://orcid.org/0009-0003-4841-1589
Sharda University, Agra, India

Manish Baboo Agarwal
http://orcid.org/0000-0003-1177-2738
Sharda University, Agra, India

Seema Agarwal
http://orcid.org/0000-0002-5655-207X
SRM Institute of Science and Technology, Ghaziabad, India

ABSTRACT

Vegetation is important to solving environmental problems such as air and noise pollution and urban heat management. Vegetation absorbs pollutants such as SO_2, NO_2, and particulate matter through mechanisms such as phytoremediation and phylloremediation. But some species, assisted by rhizosphere and phyllosphere microorganisms, also break down volatile organic compounds (VOCs), indoor plants being especially potent. Green infrastructure such as green roofs and walls manage pollution, mitigate urban heat, and enhance urban livability. Urban green belts, forests, also mitigate noise by absorbing and reflecting sound waves, besides

DOI: 10.4018/979-8-2600-0883-6.ch002

cooling cities and reducing energy needs. Promising as they are, the effectiveness of plant remediation is yet to be studied in depth, particularly in species selection and pollutant removal efficiency. Their use in environmental policy and urban planning can enhance human health, enhance sustainability, and generally enhance urban environmental quality.

1. INTRODUCTION

Plants are crucial for ecosystem processes and the sustainability of life on Earth. With the rapid urbanization, industrial processes, and vehicular emissions the severity of the global problem of air and noise pollution, urban heat islands further exacerbate the problem. In this context, the role of the various species of plants becomes more valuable and costless form of pollution control and temperature regulation.

Plants are the greatest natural assets we have to combat air pollution. They do this primarily through photosynthesis, the process in which they absorb carbon dioxide and release oxygen, thereby contributing to the balance of the atmosphere. Some plant species are able to absorb particulate matter on leaf surfaces, thereby decreasing the presence of suspended dust and the contaminants, toxic gases, and hazardous pollutants (sulphur dioxide, nitrogen oxides, and ozone) of the air. Such pollution filtering plants are trees with broad leaves, rough bark, and dense canopies. In the urban pollution, the species of plants that are identified as pollution tolerant and pollution ameliorating are neem, peepal, banyan, and ficus among others. In addition to the processes described, various species of plants contribute to the purification of the air by the absorption and subsequent metabolism of some toxic gases.

Besides air purification, certain species help in the reduction of noise pollution. Vegetation absorbs, deflects, and scatters sound, thereby creating a sound barrier. Noise pollution caused by highways, industries, and highways can be greatly reduced using dense vegetation. Noise pollution is decreased by leaves, and branches of shrubs and multilayered hedges is and trunks which provide some insulation. Urban populations have reduced stress and improved psychological health due to the several decibels, noise reduction caused by the belts of greenery.

The plants are the main part of the processes that regulate of the temperature. The ambient temperature can be reduced by the shading and evapotranspiration of the trees. Natural air conditioning can be caused by the cooling effect of the transpiration (the release of moisture) which is similar to ambient air conditioning. The air and surface temperature are further reduced by the urban forests and the green roofs. The reduction of the cooling energy required, and the increase of the thermal comfort is due to the large trees causing natural air conditioning.

Because of this, the species of the plants can be considered as resources with multiple functions. The importance of afforestation, urban greening, and preservation of biodiversity is shown by their role in the reduction of air and noise pollution, and the regulation of temperature which is also the main part of the processes that help in the sustainable management of the environment and the resiliency of the climate.

2. OVERVIEW OF PLANT SPECIES IN ENVIRONMENTAL MANAGEMENT

2.1 Air Pollution Mitigation by Plant Species

Atmospheric contamination, arising from industrial discharge, automobile emissions, and associated anthropogenic activities, constitutes a persistent threat to both human health and ecological integrity. Plant species assist in the mitigation of airborne contaminants through phytoremediation mechanisms (Maurya et al., 2023), in which they absorb, bio-transform and ultimately remove gaseous and particulate pollutants.

Vegetation employs leaves, roots and conductive tissues to remove pollutants like sulfur dioxide (SO_2), nitrogen dioxide (NO_2), ozone (O_3), particulate matter (PM) and various volatile organic compounds (VOCs). The catabolic capacity of the plant host facilitates the transformation of hazardous species into less reactive and non-toxic forms. The use of green infrastructure like parks, urban forests, green roofs and living walls act as a sink for airborne pollutants and provide oxygen and moisture, enhancing urban air quality. Vegetative cover has shown to lower ambient particulate matter concentrations while removing volatile pollutants, thus reducing risks to human health.

Figure 1. Challenges in using plants for air pollution mitigation

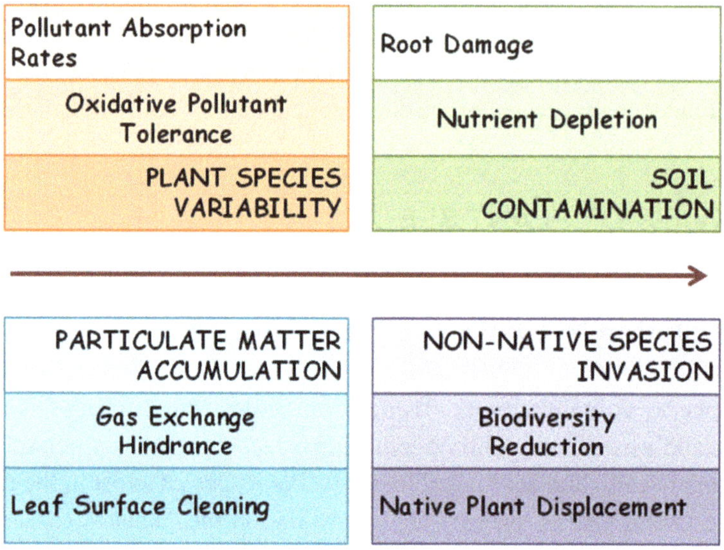

Using plant species to improve urban air quality requires certain issues to be dealt with as depicted in Figure 1. First to how different species react variably to oxidative pollutants. Second, how particulate matter build up on leaf surfaces, can hinder gas exchange. Third, how soil contamination can occur, which leads to nutrient depletion. Lastly, how non-native species can invade, out competing native plants and reducing overall biodiversity. Therefore, a comprehensive management approach is needed. This approach should combine mechanical pruning, targeted herbicide applications and bio-control methods to maintain healthy plant communities that continue to clean the air effectively.

2.2 Mitigation of Noise Pollution Through Selected Plant Species

Some plant species are acknowledged as critical components of overall environmental management, particularly within urban and semi-urban areas where noise pollution poses an acute challenge (Rey-Gozalo et al., 2023). Predominantly originating from road, rail, industrial and construction sources, noise exposure is linked to an array of adverse health consequences, including elevated cardiovascular risk, sleep disorder and psychosocial strain. Thus exposure to noise should be reduced to maintain public health, as well as a general urban livability. Traditional methods such as noise barriers and traffic calming measures are required, however, green infrastructure, comprising tree canopies, hedgerows provides an ecologically integrated and mutually enriching approach to noise dampening, strengthening both human and environmental resilience as shown in Figure 2.

Figure 2. Urban noise mitigation strategies

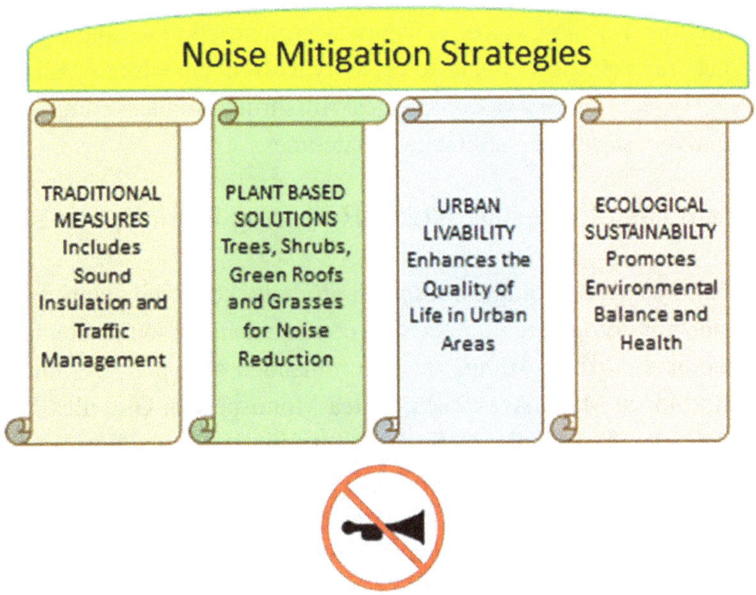

2.2.1 Mechanisms of Noise Reduction by Plants

Noise abatement by plant communities occurs through a combination of interdependent physical interactions. Canopies, trunks and branches contribute varying degrees of dissipation, primarily through the absorption of acoustic energy, with peak effectiveness at elevated frequencies (≥1 kHz) (Li & Kang, 2020). The microstructure of leaf tissue and the anisotropic arrangement of xylem and phloem fibers transform incident sound energy into minute quantities of heat, thereby reducing the incident sound pressure level.

The irregular surfaces of plant foliage scatter and diffract sound waves, fragmenting noise paths. When coupled with leaf and stem voids, these mechanisms limit the sound energy that passes through. Underneath, surface of loose soil and decaying organic matter play a complementary role, absorbing up low frequency vibrations (<1 kHz) that bounce down from the canopy and converting base vibrations into diffuse damping. Together, these processes can substantially lower sound intensity, especially inside dense, enclosed areas of vegetation.

2.2.2 Characteristics of Effective Noise-Reducing Plant Species

Specific botanical characteristics determine a plant's contribution to sound attenuation (Yofianti & Usman, 2021). A leafy canopy of substantial biomass, densely packed, favors higher rates of sound absorption. Plants that attain considerable height and breadth confer a more effective geometric obstruction to sound propagation. Stipules that are thick show enhanced capacity to dissipate vibrational energy from propagating waves. Layering woody species with shrubs produces composite barriers that cumulatively strengthen attenuation outcomes.

2.2.3 Examples of Effective Noise-Reducing Plant Species

Recent analyses and ecological research promotes selecting plant species whose structural and physiological characteristics confer enhanced sound attenuation properties (Zhao et al., 2021). Among the recommended ones are Alstonia Scholaris, Azadirachta Indica, Melia Azedarach, Butea Monosperma, Grevillea Pteridifolia, Grevillea Robusta, Tamarindus Indica and Terminalia Arjuna. Shrubs and grasses include Calotropis Gigantea, Inga Dulcis, Saccharum Munja, Nyctanthus Arbortristis, Nerium Oleander and various species of Ipomoea. The tall, bushy forms these species can achieve, combined with their thick canopy and tolerance for urban conditions, make them as valuable for decrease in noise pollution across a range of city environments.

2.2.4 Crafting Vegetation for Effective Noise Dissipation

Sound reduction through plantings requires proper ground level work. A rich mixture of fully grown trees, layered shrubs and low, dense ground cover will scatter and absorb noise across the range of frequencies generated by traffic and industry. Thus natural or built landforms along with the vegetation help in dissipation of noise (Ow and Ghosh, 2017).

2.2.5 Benefits beyond Noise Reduction

Greeneryin cities not only makes streets and parks more beautiful, but they also lower heart rates and anxiety levels while lifting overall mood. When greenery is thoughtfully arranged, it also creates habitats for birds and insects, weaving urban nature back into the citylife and making the environment more robust against change.

2.3 Role of Plant Species in Temperature Control

Different tree and plant species adjust to their surroundings with a mix of transpiration, shading and reflective properties. These properties not only help them endure summer heat spikes but also lower surrounding air temperatures, creating cooler spaces that can moderate the urban heat island effect. The tall, bushy forms, combined with their thick canopy and tolerance for urban conditions, position them as best barriers against the noise of roads, factories and dense neighborhoods across a range of city environments.

In addition to autonomously produced heat, plants finely tune their thermal regulation via control of stomata aperture. The studies reveal that progressive warming and enhanced metabolic activity initially stimulates stomata opening, whereby elevated transpiration generates evaporative cooling. However, prolonged exposure to elevated temperatures precipitates metabolic dysfunction. Under such conditions, heat-dissipation program is enacted whereby stomata, though still open, decouple from photosynthetic demand, resulting in surplus water loss that sacrifices moisture conservation in favor of thermal management (Watling et al., 2008).This thermal control not only guarantees the plant's survival when the weather varies, but subtly alters the micro climate in the ecosystem.

3. PHYTOREMEDIATION AND AIR POLLUTION MITIGATION

3.1 Mechanisms of Phytoremediation

Phytoremediation is an eco-friendly approach that uses vascular plants along with their surrounding microbial communities to filter the air and restore its quality. This method can remove gaseous pollutants such as volatile organic compounds, nitrogen oxides, sulfur dioxide, ozone and particulate matter. Contaminants typically enter the plant through stomata pores or adsorb to foliar surfaces, where they may be sequestered in vacuoles, detoxified by intrinsic plant enzymes, or converted by rhizopheric fungi and bacteria into compounds that are less harmful.

Phytoremediation operates through multiple, interrelated processes by which plants mitigate environmental contaminants. First, during stomata gas exchange, roots and foliage take up gaseous pollutants. Second, particulate matter and other gaseous substances may deposit onto leaf and stem surfaces, where the plant leaf cuticle and stem epidermis function as a passive filtration barrier, capturing and retaining such particulates. At the same time, the microorganisms living on leaf surfaces, or in the root zone, or rhizosphere, break down the contaminants into less harmful intermediates. This three way dialogue, involving the plant, the surrounding air and the living microbial matrix, enhances the system's overall ability to clean the environment (Syamlal et al., 2024). An additional pathway permits certain pollutants to enter through the stomata or root hairs, undergo enzymatic and metabolic transformations within the plant and then be released back into the atmosphere into less toxic forms as shown in Figure 3. Across both soil and water, roots can remove contaminants or foster microbial digestion in the life-sustaining zone around them, while soil centered processes help maintain clean air around zones actively drawing in pollutants (Mocek-Płóciniak et al., 2023).

Figure 3. Phytoremediation cycle

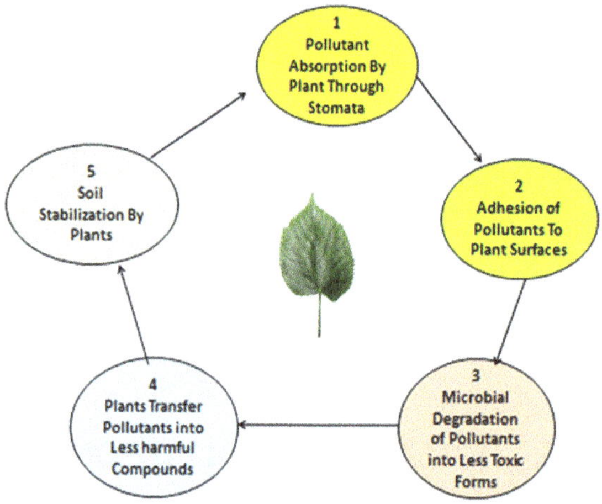

3.1.1 Advantages

Compared to traditional air cleaning methods, vegetation employed for both indoor and outdoor phytoremediation of gaseous contaminants presents multiple advantages. Energy cost and and operational requirements are reduced to minimal upkeep, eliminating the need for added chemicals. Indoor plants can lower the concentration of volatile organic compounds and particulate matter in indoor environments and provide aesthetic appeal. Vertical gardens and biofilters that incorporate vegetation amplify the effective area of leaf surfaces and promote airflow, thereby achieving higher removal rates of pollutants.

3.2 Mechanisms of Pollutant Uptake: SO_2, NO_2 and PM

Plants are effective in sequestering and neutralizing gaseous pollutants such as sulfur dioxide (SO_2) and nitrogen dioxide (NO_2), as well as particulate matter (PM), thereby enhancing air quality and overall environmental health (Oksanen & Kontunen-Soppela, 2020).

3.2.1 Absorption of SO_2 (Sulfur Dioxide)

Plants take up SO_2 through stomata pores during routine gas exchange linked to photosynthesis. The gas dissolves in cellular water, generating sulfite. Plants possess metabolic routes, predominantly the cysteine and sulfur assimilation pathways, to convert it intoless harmful compounds. When SO_2 enters through leaf pores, it quickly builds reactive oxygen species, which then trigger a series of intracellular alarms. In turn, entire networks of genes coding for protective enzymes and stress resisting proteins leap into action, boosting the plant's ability to endure and recover. Some species have also been subjected to genetic engineering to further amplify sulfite handling genes, rendering them more effective in environments with chronic SO_2 pollution.

3.2.2 Uptake of NO_2 (Nitrogen Dioxide)

Like SO_2, NO_2 slips in through stomata and then once inside the leaf, instantly falls apart in water to form nitrite. That nitrite can then feed into the nitrogen recycling machinery of the plant. In soils where nitrogen is in short supply, this lets the plant to take a fresh supply of it. When concentration of NO_2 is too high, it causes oxidative stress. Plants counter this through the rapid upregulation of peroxidases, glutathione reductases and other ROS scavenging enzymes, which safeguard membranes, proteins and nucleic acids from oxidative damage.

3.2.3 Capture and Removal of PM (Particulate Matter)

Plant leaves function as biofilters, capturing particulate matter (PM) from the atmosphere due to their extensive surface area and microstructure. The porus surfaces of numerous species are capable of intercepting particle densities that exceed thousands of counts per square millimeter. Particles are retained by the cuticular layer, trichomes, or microrelief features, leading to a measurable decline in ambient PM concentrations, that proves particularly advantageous in urban and industrial areas. When leaf surfaces interact with their microbial inhabitants, the combined activity creates an ability to clean the environment of toxic compounds. Both the foliage and the microbes gradually adjust to the constant presence of the contaminants, developing new tolerance characteristics and specialized metabolic routes that break down the solid pollutants (Mandal et al., 2023).

3.2.4 Plant Responses and Adaptive Strategies

Plants behave in different ways when toxic gases settle on their surfaces. The antioxidant enzymes like superoxide dismutase (SOD), peroxidase (POD) and catalase (CAT) scavenge the reactive oxygen species (ROS) that threaten to disrupt cellular integrity. At the same time, exposure to the pollutants can shift the flow of primary metabolism to favor the production of secondary compounds like flavonoids and phenolic acids, which reinforce the protective shield of the leaf.

Terrestrial vegetation functions as a biofilter by incorporating gaseous contaminants such as sulfur dioxide (SO_2) and nitrogen dioxide (NO_2) via stomata openings and leaf cuticles and by sequestering aerosolized particulates through physical interception. Their regulated biochemical detoxification pathways confer the capacity to neutralize and remove contaminants, making them as critical elements in durable, cost-effective and energy-conserving air-quality governance (Chaudhary & Rathore, 2018). Moreover, the adoption of vegetation oriented air quality interventions show advantages, like the long-term stabilization of atmospheric carbon, modulation of local microclimate variables and enhancement of urban air qualities.

4. EXAMPLES OF EFFICIENT TAXA

Vegetation is aneffective biophysical modulator of air composition in both controlled and open environments (Ravindra & Mor, 2022), effecting the adsorption and translocation of volatile organic compounds, suspended particulate matter and gaseous precursors such as formaldehyde, benzene, toluene and xylenes. A range of taxa has been empirically confirmed to perform better under controlled indoor conditions, allowing for strategic selection based on localized conditions. There are large numbers of plant species effective in mitigating air pollution.

4.1 Effective Indoor Air-Purifying Species

Peace Lily (Spathiphyllum) - This plant specializes in absorbing ammonia, benzene, formaldehyde and trichloroethylene. Harmful gases diffuse through stomata and are converted to less harmful compounds in the leaf tissue, resulting in fresher indoor air.

Spider Plant (Chlorophytum Comosum) - They grasp up indoor pollutants and thrives better in humid environment. Its long, arching leaves helps in air cleaning without occupying much space. It specializes in the removal of formaldehyde and xylene (Moya et al., 2018b).

Rubber Plant (Ficus Elastica) - This robust plant form a thick, leafy shield that removes airborne chemicals. The broad, glossy leaves not only elevate the décor but also clean the air.

Snake Plant (Sansevieria Trifasciata) - It has upright, blade like leaves that display green and gray patterns. It flourishes in dim light and require very less water. It helps to decrease indoor pollutants like benzene, formaldehyde and trichloroethylene.

Boston Fern (Nephrolepis Exaltata Bostoniensis) - This sword fern acts as a natural humidifier and effective air purifier. It absorbs formaldehyde and xylene with a foliar structure havinghigh surface area and cuticle free areas for gas exchange. It thrives better in cool dim light where humidity is very high.

Bamboo Palm (Chamaedorea Seifrizii) - This palm is known for its slender, elegantly arching fronds and its outstanding capacity to purify indoor air. It reduces formaldehyde, benzene, trichloroethylene and xylene at measurable rates. With filtered light and soil that is evenly moist, the palm can grow up to 3.6 meters in indoor settings, enhancing air circulation and humidification throughout the entire area.

Golden Pothos (Epipremnum Aureum) - It is known for its resilience and rapid growth. It can survive in low light and less water environments, making it especially suitable for household spaces.It has the capacity to reduce indoor concentrations of formaldehyde, benzene, xylene and toluene and act as an air purifierfor residences and commercial offices.

Aloe Vera (Aloe Barbadensis Miller) - It is recognized for its topical therapeutic applications and its capability to sequester formaldehyde and benzene. The plant requires bright, indirect light and less water for its growth (Shishegaran et al., 2020).

Areca Palm (Dypsis Lutescens) - Areca palms is noted for their capacity to absorb toluene and xylene. The long, narrow leaflets cascade from the slender trunk, cast a vibrant tropical feel in any room. Bright, indirect light and consistent soil moisture keep it in good state (Bhargava et al., 2020).

Table 1. Various indoor air-purifying species with their applications

S.No.	NAME OF PLANT SPECIES	BENEFITS	APPLICATIONS
1	Peace Lily	Improves indoor air freshness	Suitable for homes and offices
2	Spider Plant	Pollutant absorber, Grows well in humidity	Best for small indoor spaces
3	Rubber Plant	Natural air filters	Suitable for living rooms and offices
4	Snake Plant	Require lessmaintenance,Strong air purifier	Ideal for bedrooms and low-light rooms
5	Boston Fern	Natural humidifier	Better for dry indoor air
6	Bamboo Palm	High rate of pollutant removal	Suitable for larger indoor spaces.
7	Golden Pothos	Grows fast, Requires less light and water	Best for homes and commercial spaces
8	Aloe Vera	Purifies air, Requires minimum water	Medicinal uses
9	Areca Palm	Effectively remove VOC	Tropical aesthetic

4.2 Effective Trees and Plants for Outdoor Air Quality

Choosing the right kind of trees and shrubs is essential for cleaning the air. When carefully selected, the plants can effectively trap and neutralize a suite of pollutants like particulate matter (PM), nitrogen dioxide (NO_2), sulfur dioxide (SO_2), ozone (O_3), carbon monoxide (CO) and various volatile organic compounds (VOCs) (Han et al., 2021).

Species variation in filtration efficacy is attributed to leaf structure, cuticular permeability, foliar density, evergreen habit and overall canopy configuration. The strategic incorporation of these species into urban and semi-urban landscapes maximizes passive air cleaning, promotes community health and supports regional climate stabilization(Nithya, 2017). The following species contribute significantly to improved outdoor air quality.

Pinus Trees (e.g., Pinus Strobus) - Pine species invariably emerge as leading species for biogenic air purification, a performance linked to their enduring needle leaves and tightly knit crowns. Pinus Strobus, with its high foliar surface area and fine needle microstructure, efficiently assimilates O_3, NO_2, SO_2, and PM throughout the seasons, thereby decreasing acoustic pollution in addition to its atmospheric benefits.

Taxus Baccata - This evergreen conifer helps in particulate and gaseous pollutant mitigation. The slender, micro-porous needles of it, together with a fine textured, dense canopy, optimize particle interception. The dense array of stomata on the underside of the leaves improves retention of particulate matter, placing this species among the top conifers for enhancing air quality.

Silver Birch (Betula Pendula) - It is suited for capturing airborne particles as its hair-fine crown work as a dense filter for both solid and liquid aerosols. It cancut particulate matter in air, proving its value in shielding homes from traffic pollutants.

Honey Locust (GleditsiaTriacanthos) - It not only absorb particulate matter and carbon monoxide, but also generates a diffuse crown that mitigates solar gain, thereby decreasing urban heat island intensity and lowering energy demands for cooling. The species, pinnate foliage permits effective gas exchange and pollutant capture without unduly obstructing wind flow.

London Plane (Platanus Acerifolia) - It is seen in city parks and streets, where its robust bark and leathery leaves withstand heat and pollution. The tree takes up ozone, nitrogen dioxide and particulate matter, making air cleaner. The lobed canopy and waxy surfaceabsorb smaller particles, thus improving air quality on the roads.

Elder Tree (Sambucus Nigra) - The leaves are lightly woolly and their tiny hairs trap suspended particles to decrease the level of air pollutants.Theycan to grow in neglected urban areas makingthem reliable choice for planting schemes that seek to clean the air and enrich urban ecology at the same time.

Green Ash (Fraxinus Pennsylvanica) - This species demonstrates exceptional tolerance to a range of soil conditions and exhibits high phytoremedial capacity for ozone and particulate pollutants. Its vigorous growth habit renders it as a choice for municipal reforestation initiatives aimed to improve air quality.

English Oak (Quercus Robur) - This deciduous hardwood exhibits significant bioaccumulation of nitrogen dioxide, sulfur dioxide and suspended particulate matter. The species also enhances urban biodiversity by furnishing microhabitats, thereby augmenting the ecological integrity of dense urban woodland networks.

Red Maple (Acer Rubrum) - It is well adapted to urban settings and demonstrates commendable efficiency in filtering ozone, nitrogen dioxide and PM. Its broad and relatively coarse leaves increase the surface area for particle collection. The species with red foliage in autumn enhances urban landscapes.

Table 2. Trees and plant species for improving outdoor air quality with their applications

S.No.	NAME OF PLANT SPECIES	BENEFITS	APPLICATIONS
1	Pinus Trees	Traps O_3, NO_2, SO_2, PM Decreases Noise Pollution	Suitable for areas with high traffic. Helps in climate stabilization
2	Taxus Baccata	Helps in trapping particulate and gaseous pollutants.	Ideal for residential areas, and along highways with heavy air pollution.
3	Betula Pendula	Captures airborne particles and aerosols. Acts as a filter for pollutants.	Protects areas exposed to high traffic or industrial pollution.

continued on following page

Table 2. Continued

S.No.	NAME OF PLANT SPECIES	BENEFITS	APPLICATIONS
4	Honey Locust	Absorbs particulate matter and CO.	Suitable for urban areas with high heat. Improves air quality. Reducing cooling costs.
5	London Plane	Absorbs gases and particulate matter. Enhances air quality.	Common in highly polluted areas.
6	Elder Tree	Its woolly leaves traps suspended particles. Decreases air pollutant.	Grows well in less-maintained urban areas.
7	Green Ash	Improves urban air quality. Improves ecosystem health	Municipal reforestation. Suitable for urban forestry programs.
8	English Oak	Improves urban biodiversity. Bioaccumulates gases and PM	Urban parks, Nature reserves
9	Red Maple	Broad leaves help in collection of pollutant.	Enhances landscapes

4.3 Factors Governing Pollution Removal

Vegetation exhibiting small, needle like, or trichome covered leaves tends to retain higher PM loads than that with smooth surfaces. Evergreens, including various species of yew, pine and cypress, retain foliage during winter's coldest months, thus providing a sustained filtration that is critical when emissions frequently peak. In contrast, broad-leaved London Plane and Silver Birch form expansive, dense canopies which maximize the area exposed to both particulate and gaseous species. Gases such as sulfur dioxide and nitrogen dioxide enter through leaf stomata, where species-specific metabolic pathways differ in the rates of absorption and detoxification.

5. VEGETATION AS ACTIVE INTERFACES FOR ACOUSTIC MITIGATION

Plants reduce noise mainly because they absorb, reflect and scatter sound. Their structural variety acts as a sound barrier in meadows or streets (Van Renterghem et al., 2012).

5.1 Physical Structure of Plants as Noise Absorbers

Plants exhibit intricate micro and macroscopic structure that qualify them as potent natural sound attenuators, thereby attenuating noise in both rural and urban areas. The acoustic mitigating capacity of the vegetative bodydepends on its multiscale framework, its vibration response in the presence of sonic stimuli and the conversion of sound energy into thermal energy through internal damping. There are also bioresponsive adjustments of the plant to sonic environment.

5.1.1 Structural Complexity of Plants

Within any given plant body, the constituent tissues are fibrous networks arranged in hierarchically nested arrangements that extend from individual cellular units to macro scale fibrous bundles and organized tissues. This arrangement helps sound to fade effectively. Small plant cells, reinforced by walls of cellulose and lignin, gain both rigidity and a viscoelastic touch. The natural damping within these polysaccharides absorbs incoming vibrations rather than letting them bounce or pass straight through. These cells coalesce into larger load bearing unitswhose porous and anisotropic geometry promotes repeated scattering, reflection and dissipation of vibrational energy through internal friction.

5.1.2 Sound Wave Interaction and Vibration-Induced Energy Dissipation

The organized arrangement of leaves and branches generates a network of intricate surfaces and cavities that lengthen the paths of sound waves, thereby amplifying the interaction time and promoting greater absorption. At broader and finer spatial scales, the resulting structural heterogeneity in density, porosity and elastic moduli establishes the essential attributes for effective acoustic attenuation (Bhandawat & Jayaswall, 2022).

When acoustic waves strike upon a plant, the incident pressure causes the various structural components like leaves, stems and trunks to enter into vibration modes. These forced motions serve as the principal pathway for the dissipation of sound energy. Initial contact generates oscillations that span micro, meso and macroscopic domains in the plant. The absence of rigid constraints within the biological material allows these motions to induce relative sliding and deformation among cellular and fibrous components.

These tiny internal movements turn incoming sound energy into heat, so less energy bounces off or passes through. It depends on the frequency of the sound and the presence of liquid in the tissues. More moisture means the material is softer and can stretch more easily and turn energy into heat more effectively.

5.1.3 Effect of Plant Morphology on Acoustic Properties

Plant surface form interacts with sound waves in several ways that affect how well they attenuate noise. Thicker, more densely packed leaf blades dissipates vibrational energy more efficiently when sound impact. Leaves that are deeply lobed have more edge giving sound more places to grab and extra area to seep in. Green systems provide many advantages over the rigid lines of sound barriers. Multi-layered canopies scatter, reflect and absorb sound across several surfaces, breaking the incoming energy into smaller, less damaging increments. Similarly, porous tissue contains voids that trap sound in resonant cavities where energy is dissipated through viscosity and thermal conduction as compressional waves (Li & Kang, 2020).

5.2 Urban Forestry and Green Belts for Noise Mitigation

Urban forests and green belt networks offer a seamless ecological approach for decreasing noise from roads and industry. These living sound barriers absorb and bend sound waves while simultaneously improving urban ecology and visual appeal. Their delicate needle leaves and slender, twiggy branches diffuse the harsh sounds of city traffic. Studies indicate that the breadth of a vegetative intervention zone is the principal determinant of its noise mitigation efficacy. When substantially wide, the layered arrangement of trunks, branches and foliage operates in a complementary manner. Low-frequency sound is attenuated through ground level scattering and conversion to heat by leaf surfaces, while higher frequency components are refracted at twig and leaf boundaries. Species selection, canopy stratification and planting density must therefore be calibrated to harmonize with the specific frequency profile of the noise source, as well as to the anticipated spatial distribution of sound across the urban landscape (Reis et al., 2022)..

Coniferous trees fine foliage and dense branch structure effectively and silently muffle noise by dispersing the higher frequency sounds of city traffic. Broadleaf trees, such as oaks, maples and beeches, on the other hand, reduce noise across a wider spectrum by bending and spreading sound energy more widely with their larger leaves and multilayered canopies. When these canopy species are planted with shrubs and hedging assemblages, a vertically complex barrier is created which is capable of intercepting sound energy across multiple altitudes and frequency bands.

Species characterized by rapid annual growth, are capable of forming effective acoustic screens, thus suiting environments undergoing rapid urban encroachment. Green layers formed by Prunus Laurocerasus, Ilex Aquifolium and various Ligustrum species, placed beside taller trees, reinforce attenuation of low frequency sounds and shield dwellings from emissions near the ground. The structural parameters of tree belt mainly their width and foliage density help in achieving effective acoustic screening. Evidence shows that a well structured belt sustaining a width of roughly 30 meters can yield sound level reductions of 5 to 10 decibels. This reduction correlates with a perceptible decline in loudness of approximately 30 percent. In contrast, a solitary row of trees exhibits very negligible attenuation. Thus, achieving a continuous barrier is a prerequisite for significant noise attenuation. In addition to this densely vegetated forest floors selectively absorb low frequency energy, further diminishing the sound energy that propagates toward the receiver.

Green belts and urban forests mitigate noise while lowering stress and enhancing mental health, fostering serene and green spaces. Vegetation aesthetically enriches and nurtures urban biodiversity by furnishing nesting and foraging sites for avian and insect species.

Plantings apart from lowering sound pressure also alter how sound bends and bounces. The vegetation captures the residual energy, counters low frequencies and scatters reflected waves. Placing shrubs and trees on roof top or slightly behind the barrier enhances their acoustic performance further (Dorado et al., 2022).

Urban planners and conservation experts now incorporate green infrastructure, corridors of vegetation, canopy trees along main roads and continuous strips alongside highways and industrial zones. This comprehensive strategy provide cleaner air, moderated local climates, carbon storage which is vital to the urban realm and result in further noise reduction.

In this light, urban forests and green corridors stand out as effective, eco-friendly and multifunctional approaches to mitigate noise pollution. Their success depends on selecting the right tree species, combined with precise planting density, adequate corridor width and seamless integration into the urban layout. These green belts enhance ecosystem and supports public health in heavily populated cities.

6. TEMPERATURE REGULATION THROUGH EVAPOTRANSPIRATION

Transpiration represents the internal movement of water vapor from the stomata of leaves to the atmosphere. Water taken up by plant roots travel through the xylem to leaves, where it geta evaporated. Stomata opening regulated by plant physiological responses to light, temperature and soil moisture affects the quantity of water vapor escaping (Novák, 2012).

6.1 Process of Evapotranspiration

6.1.1 Evaporation and Transpiration

The process by which the water on the surface of the soil, water bodies and plant surfaces is converted into water vapor and released to atmosphere is called evaporation. The evaporation depends on factors like amount of heat reaching the earth surface, humidity in the air and speed of the wind. The early plant growth is generally marked by high rates of evaporation. Once the plant matures and shades the ground, radiation hitting the soil is reduced and evaporation slows considerably.

Transpiration is the movement of water through the plant. Roots absorb moisture, which then rises through the xylem. When the water reaches the leaf, it moves into the intercellular air spaces and finally exits through tiny stomata openings. It simultaneously allows the plant to inhale carbon dioxide needed for photosynthesis. The overall mechanism of transpiration depends upon water uptake, transport and vapor release.

Most of the water that plants absorb eventually is lost through transpiration, only a tiny portion is taken up for metabolic reactions. Stomata open and close in response to soil moisture, light, temperature and humidity, allowing the plant to loss water according to the need for carbon dioxide.

6.1.2 Combined Process-Evapotranspiration

Evaporation and transpiration happen at the same time in nature. Together they are called evapotranspiration, the way that water moves from the land back up into the sky. When plants are young, a lot of water is lost through evaporation, but as the plant grows, transpiration takes over. Evapotranspiration cools the air because it takes heat out when water changes to vapor. It moves water from the ground back into the air, helping form clouds and rain. It also controls how wet the soil stays, how healthy the plants are and how nutrients get cycled.

6.1.2.1 Significance of Evapotranspiration

It is the sum of water vapor emitted to the atmosphere from soil surfaces and the release of water vapor from the stomata of plants. Solar radiation fuels the evaporation from soil, while the plant's internal hydraulic and metabolic processes manage transpiration. This twin loss of water governs the exchange of heat and moisture between land and atmosphere and it is fundamental to the persistence of natural and managed ecosystems, including agriculture (Yang et al., 2023).

6.2 Impact on Urban Heat Islands and Microclimates

Urban heat islands arise when cities exhibit higher temperatures than adjacent rural land, due toenergy consumption, heat storing materials and reduced vegetation. These temperature contrasts are moderated when trees and green roofs release moisture through evapotranspiration and provide shade. This dual mechanism cools surface and air, creating more pleasant microclimates and improving overall urban livability.

6.2.1 Evapotranspiration (ET) Cooling Contribution to Urban Heat Islands

The dual process of moisture leaving soil and plants releasing water through stomata consume energy as latent heat and thereby cools surrounding air. Urban greenery comprising trees, green roofs, gardens and parks enhances ET, extracting extra heat and curbing the typical rise of urban temperatures. In Saint Paul, Minnesota, measurements from community gardens showed ET cooling the air by several degrees Celsius compared to non vegetated areas (Small et al., 2020). By releasing water vapor, vegetation effectively removes heat that would otherwise elevate a city's overall thermal profile.

6.2.2 Vegetation's Role in Microclimate Management

In addition to ET, leafy canopies shield ground, facades and pavements from direct solar gain, which lowers surface temperatures. A cooler exterior means buildings require less energy for air conditioning, which helps to decrease the waste heat released by rooftop and wall mounted cooling units. Green spaces also refine local microclimates by raising humidity levels, softening wind speeds and creating a more comfortable zone for pedestrians, thereby making city living more pleasant.

6.2.3 Impact on Water Demand and Vegetation Health

Urban heat islands increase the demand for water through evapotranspiration, compelling city plants to draw more moisture to stay cool and survive. Studies reveal that ET in cities can exceed that of nearby rural areas by as much as 10%. Increasing green areas and permeable pavements can mitigate this water stress by preserving soil moisture and supporting the local water cycle. Investments in green infrastructure, such as parks, green roofs and community farming, increases moisture availability, allowing plants to stay hydrated and retain their cooling role.

6.2.4 Magnitude of Temperature Reduction

Vegetation mediated evapotranspiration can cool urban air by 0.5 to 4.0°C, with the exact drop varying according to species, canopy density and local climate. Green roofs and urban farms are particularly effective in lowering heat, thereby reducing the intensity of the heat island and benefiting public health and the efficiency of cooling systems (Qiu et al., 2013).

6.2.5 Policy and Urban Planning Implications

With knowledge of the impact of vegetation on local climate, architects and planners target tree canopy development and the use of green infrastructure in the city to minimize the urban heat island (UHI) effect. This will reduce temperature, clean the air, manage water and provide wildlife habitat in the city.

The cooling effect of vegetation through evapotranspiration helps to decrease urban heat and provide pleasant, enduring microclimates. By boosting green cover and thoughtfully managing urban ecosystems, cities can ease heat stress, decrease energy demands and strengthen their resilience to a warming climate.

7. APPLICATION OF GREEN INFRASTRUCTURE

7.1 Green Walls and Green Roofs for Air Quality and Noise Reduction

7.1.1 Green Walls

Green walls, commonly referred to as living walls or vertical gardens, are vertical surfaces covered with living plants. In contrast to conventional methods where vegetation roots in the ground and ascends the wall, living walls features vegetation that grows directly on the wall itself or on a supporting framework, using a blend of soil, lightweight substrate, or hydronic systems for moisture and nutrients (Radić et al., 2019). Built in irrigation and drainage run along these walls, ensures that every leaf stays lush and green. Plants climb up, filling the entire surface or just a portion, depending on the design. A green wall can stand on its own or along the side of a building, or in lobby. Green walls help keep temperatures steady indoors. They decrease air and noise pollution, offering a sense of calm in a busy world. The system is self-contained, unifying soil, moisture and vegetation in an elevated, living micro ecosystem.

7.1.2 Green Roofs Role in Air Quality Mitigation

Green roofs are living blankets of vegetation thriving on top of buildings in crowded urban environments for their quiet but effective capacity to clean the air. Through the processes of adsorption, uptake and chemical transformation, these living roofs can lower the concentrations of urban pollutants such as ground level ozone (O_3), nitrogen oxides (NO_X), fine particulate matter (PM) and various volatile organic compounds (VOCs). The result is measurable improvement in the quality of both outdoor and indoor air (Mihalakakou et al., 2023).

At Portland State University, researchers carried out an evaluation on a commercial structure topped with a green roof. They installed air sensors in the mechanical intake ducts and compared the ozone concentrations detected over the living roof to those drawn from a conventional, non-planted roof on the same building (Ramasubramanian et al., 2019). The readings indicated that the air entering the green roofed section had consistently lower ozone levels.

Ozone is removed by virtue of dry deposition, whereby the gas is absorbed onto leaf surfaces, translocated through stomata, or oxidized by leaf associated microbes. The cumulative result of their presence is a noticeable decline in the ozone that otherwise permeates interior spaces, which in turn alleviates the ozone exposure faced by occupants indoors. But the contribution of a green roof extends well beyond ozone. Leaf pores, or stomata, actively draw in a suite of gaseous contaminants, while tiny particles settle onto the foliage and settle into the growth medium below. Recent studies indicate that a well planned green roof can intercept hundreds of kilograms of particulate matter each year, resulting in drop in acid gases.

Plants placed on green roofs help in decreasing the urban heat island effect. Their leafy canopies and the cooling mist of evapotranspiration lower the heat on rooftops and the air just above them. This drop in temperature reduces energy demand for air conditioners, saving the electricity that, in turn, means power plants will release less harmful pollutants. The same vegetation locks up carbon dioxide in growing tissue and soil, pulling that gas out of the atmosphere and helping to cool the climate and reduction in green house gases.

7.1.3 Green Roofs for Noise Reduction

Green roofs contribute notably to decrease noise by working as shields. Their layered design plants, soil, drainage and waterproof barriers creates several paths for sound to lose its energy before reaching human ears (Perivoliotis et al., 2023). The intensity of sound is decreased by the following methods -

Absorption through Foliage and Soil- Green roofs decreases airborne noise as the soil and plant layers are both porous and fibrous. When sound waves are absorbed the canopy of leaves, stems and soil, the energy is converted to heat through tiny vibrations and friction. The uneven plant surfaces scatter the sound further, while the pores soak up energy efficiently, particularly in the mid and high frequency ranges.

Mass and Damping Effects- When the vegetation layers of a green roof are added, the total mass of the roof assembly rises. This increase helps prevent sound from moving through the building envelope, since more mass generally means better sound insulation. The low stiffness and damping capacity of layers absorb and disperse vibrational energy, making the system particularly effective at decreasing the high frequency noise that tends to swirl through cities.

Reducing Traffic and Ambient Urban Noise- The green roofs dampen road traffic noise by altering sound trajectories and boosting absorption. Studies reveal that coupling a green roof with solar panels result in greater reductions in road noise than a standard roof. Measurements indicate that the green roof assembly can lower sound levels by at least 6 decibels (dB) resulting in decrease in noise pollution.

Noise Attenuation by Frequency- Green roofs modifies sound energy across various frequencies. Below 200 Hz soil and drainage layers reflect sound rather than absorb it. Above 500 Hz, where most urban noise sits, they absorb and scatter more energy outward thus decreasing city noise from vehicles, drills and machinery.

Other Advantages- Apart from trapping sound, the roof cools nearby air and surfaces. Shades and water vapor lessen the heat load on chillers and fans. Cooler roofs reflect fewer sound waves back, minimizing resonance. Thus planting green roofs helps to clean air, decrease noise, lowers the temperature of surroundings and affect the ecosystem.

7.2 Benefits for Urban Livability and Sustainability

Green roofs provide large number of benefits that strengthen urban livability and advance sustainable development by enhancing environmental quality, nurturing social well-being and creating measurable economic value. By converting idle rooftop spaces into lush green zones, will cool the air, cleans runoff, filter pollution, encourage urban wildlife and ultimately, foster healthier communities.

7.2.1 Environmental Benefits

Green roofs provide a powerful remedy for the urban heat island effect by trapping heat.Trees and plants cast shade and their cooling by evapotranspiration chills the leaf surface and the air around it, lowering the temperature of roofs, streets and whole neighborhoods. This reduces the need for mechanical cooling, which in turn cuts energy consumption, greenhouse gas emissions and improves overall air quality. The variety of plant captures airborne pollutants, intercepts particulate matter, absorbs nitrogen oxides and filters volatile organic compounds, diminishing smog and dust transport throughout the city (Baryla et al., 2019).

Vegetation also absorbs rain and slows the flow, decreasing the burden on drains and cutting the risk of street and basement flooding. Soil and roots filter out sediment, heavy metals and nutrients, so cleaner runoff reaches rivers and lakes. At the same time, green roofs offer shelter for birds, bees and microbe communities.

7.2.2 Social and Community Benefits

The presence of green roof alone is enough to brighten a view. Some rooftops become community gardens, others host yoga classes or workshops and many hold parties on the terraces of green roofs.

7.2.3 Economic Benefits

Green roofs save energy by boosting insulation, which lowers both heating and cooling costs within a building. They shield roofs from UV radiation and extreme weather, thereby prolonging roof lifespan and cutting maintenance bills. The green roof sector also creates jobs in manufacturing, design, installation and upkeep, supporting local economies and workforce. A nationwide push for green roof systems could create several hundred thousand jobs across the country (Vourdoubas, 2024).

8. FUTURE DIRECTIONS AND CHALLENGES

8.1 Research Needs for Optimizing Plant Selection and Green Infrastructure

Focus should be on selecting the most suitable plant species and refining design practices for green roofs systems. Their goal is to amplify ecological, hydrological, thermal and economic benefits, while also ensuring longevity of the vegetation and its successful adaptation to harsh urban climate (Zhang et al., 2025).

There is lack of understanding of which green roof designs best match specific climates and architectural contexts. Extensive systems rely on shallow, lightweight substrates with low care vegetation, which are able to endure the extreme conditions of rooftop settings. The right vegetation provides more benefits of green roofs like cooling the urban heat island, soaking up stormwater and insulating buildings. Observations show large differences in plant survival and density from one green roof to the other, proving that the chosen species shape the roof's overall success.

Scientists are actively designing green roof layouts that encourage richer plant diversity while delivering a broader suite of ecosystem services. Roofs that layer resilient juicy vegetation can weather heat and drought with little upkeep. Computer simulations show that greener roofs linked by green corridors can facilitate easier species movement and better overall function across the city landscape.

Affordability remains in the spotlight as well. Green roofs require greater capital outlay than standard roofs, but analysis reveals that energy gains, reduced stormwater charges and ecological paybacks can balance it over the roof's lifespan. Ongoing studies are streamlining practices that safeguard function while keeping expenditure in check.

To bring this into practice, we need to focus on those plant species that are both regionally adapted to local climate and can withstand harsh conditions. Greater plant diversity can further enhance urban biodiversity, strengthen habitat links and boost the overall resilience of green networks. Long-term monitoring programs that track survival and life-cycle assessments must run in parallel to ensure that performance are matched with economic feasibility. Addressing these gaps will strengthen the effectiveness of green roofs in lowering urban heat, managing runoff, supporting biodiversity and advancing the overall sustainability of cities.

8.2 Policy Integration for Scaling Environmental Benefits

Policy integration is necessary for highlighting the ecological advantages of green roofs and similar urban green infrastructure. The policies should eliminate road blocks like budget allocation, technical hurdles and low public awareness so that the technology can gain rapid and lasting affect (Raymond et al., 2017).

8.2.1 Incentives Adoption

Financial incentives play a crucial role in this approach. Targeted measures include tax deductions, grants, reduction in water tax and performance linked subsidies, which will favor green roofs developers and owners to promote it.

8.2.2 Urban Planning and Regulatory Integration

Effective urban governance embeds green roofs into the larger vision of sustainable city design. City wise green infrastructure master plans now identify roof locations, synchronizing storm water retention, heat-island reduction and habitat support. Regulatory tools now harness market to reinforce greener, denser and more resilient development. Simplified permitting steps and straightforward regulatory frameworks will make easier for developers to incorporate green roofs into their plans.

8.2.3 Capacity Building and Awareness

Effective policy approaches focus on capacity building for the training of architects, engineers, landscape architects and maintenance personnel. Capacity building by training the stakeholders in green roof design, installation and maintenance, issues of cost will result in maximum long term success. Public education campaigns highlighting several advantages of green roofs such as improving air quality, noise reduction, climate control and aesthetics will help generate community acceptance easily.

9. CONCLUSION

This chapter focuses primarily on the role of various species of plants in the embodiment of some of the important challenges of urban environments, particular in the reduction of air pollution, noise pollution, and the regulation of temperatures, mitigation of urban heat island effects, and the contribution to the overall sustainability of urban environments and the health of human beings. It highlights the fact that, urban plant species significantly improve the urban environment through a variety of mechanisms.

This chapter illustrates that air pollution is mitigated by the vegetative filtering of particulates and some gases (especially when vegetation is planted near the source of the pollution). The urban green belts and forests which include the vegetation provide barriers to noise by physically absorbing or diffracting sounds. Hot air pockets and energy-demanding buildings are mitigated by urban vegetation through evaporative cooling and shading. The chapter also reflected the wider aim of associating vegetation interventions with climate adaptation and sustainable urban development. The tree planting, green roofs and green walls described as green infrastructure initiatives promote the multiple dimensions of the urban environment and improve the quality of life of urban populations. However, the potential drawbacks and intricacies of the plant-based approach are also important. For example, and as discussed above, planting vegetation in urban areas may promote positive changes in climate and air quality, but the negative changes may outweigh the positive ones. These drawbacks and intricacies emphasize the fact that absence of the right species, configuration of the landscape, urban planning, pollution control, and species selection interventions may lead to a failure in achieving the desired positive results.

In general, the chapter's intended thematic targets have been achieved by showing that urban parks are vital elements of eco-friendly and sustainable cities as a result of the ecosystem services that the vegetation in the parks provides. While the adverse effects of vegetation in urban parks may sometimes be viewed as having a positive impact on only a small area, or their positive impact may be modest, the combined and synergistic effects of vegetation in urban parks are critical elements in creating urban ecosystems that are resilient, sustaining, and that respond to climate changes of the cities. From the above, it can be concluded that,, the chapter provides a thematic exposition of the importance of integrating green vegetation into urban planning and policies in order to respond to the multi-faceted problems of urbanization and climate change.

REFERENCES

Baryla, A., Karczmarczyk, A., Bus, A., & Witkowska-Dobrev, J. (2019). Surface temperature analysis of conventional roof and different use forms of the green roof. *Scientific Review Engineering and Environmental Sciences*, *28*(4), 632–640. DOI: 10.22630/PNIKS.2019.28.4.57

Bhandawat, A., & Jayaswall, K. (2022). Biological relevance of sound in plants. *Environmental and Experimental Botany*, *200*, 104919. DOI: 10.1016/j.envexpbot.2022.104919

Bhargava, B., Malhotra, S., Chandel, A., Rakwal, A., Kashwap, R. R., & Kumar, S. (2020). Mitigation of indoor air pollutants using Areca palm potted plants in real-life settings. *Environmental Science and Pollution Research International*, *28*(7), 8898–8906. DOI: 10.1007/s11356-020-11177-1 PMID: 33074430

Chaudhary, I. J., & Rathore, D. (2018). Suspended particulate matter deposition and its impact on urban trees. *Atmospheric Pollution Research*, *9*(6), 1072–1082. DOI: 10.1016/j.apr.2018.04.006

Dorado, M. C., Milan, G. R., & González, A. E. (2022). Evaluation of Industrial Noise Reduction Achieved with a Green Barrier: Case Study. In *IntechOpen eBooks*. DOI: 10.5772/intechopen.108835

Han, Y., Lee, J., Haiping, G., Kim, K., Wanxi, P., Bhardwaj, N., Oh, J., & Brown, R. J. (2021). Plant-based remediation of air pollution: A review. *Journal of Environmental Management*, *301*, 113860. DOI: 10.1016/j.jenvman.2021.113860 PMID: 34626947

Li, M., & Kang, J. (2020). Influence of leaf physical properties on Single-Leaf vibrational response to sound. *Forests*, *11*(1), 115. DOI: 10.3390/f11010115

Mandal, M., Popek, R., Przybysz, A., Roy, A., Das, S., & Sarkar, A. (2023). Breathing fresh air in the city: Implementing Avenue Trees as a sustainable solution to reduce particulate pollution in urban agglomerations. *Plants*, *12*(7), 1545. DOI: 10.3390/plants12071545 PMID: 37050171

Maurya, A., Sharma, D., Partap, M., Kumar, R., & Bhargava, B. (2023). Microbially-assisted phytoremediation toward air pollutants: Current trends and future directions. *Environmental Technology & Innovation*, *31*, 103140. DOI: 10.1016/j.eti.2023.103140

Mihalakakou, G., Souliotis, M., Papadaki, M., Menounou, P., Dimopoulos, P., Kolokotsa, D., Paravantis, J. A., Tsangrassoulis, A., Panaras, G., Giannakopoulos, E., & Papaefthimiou, S. (2023). Green roofs as a nature-based solution for improving urban sustainability: Progress and perspectives. *Renewable & Sustainable Energy Reviews, 180*, 113306. DOI: 10.1016/j.rser.2023.113306

Mocek-Płóciniak, A., Mencel, J., Zakrzewski, W., & Roszkowski, S. (2023). Phytoremediation as an Effective Remedy for Removing Trace Elements from Ecosystems. *Plants, 12*(8), 1653. DOI: 10.3390/plants12081653 PMID: 37111876

Moya, T. A., Van Den Dobbelsteen, A., Ottelé, M., & Bluyssen, P. M. (2018b). A review of green systems within the indoor environment. *Indoor and Built Environment, 28*(3), 298–309. DOI: 10.1177/1420326X18783042

Nithya, R. (2017). Use of Tree Species in Controlling Environmental Pollution-A Review. *International Journal of Current Microbiology and Applied Sciences, 6*(4), 893–899. DOI: 10.20546/ijcmas.2017.604.113

Novák, V. (2012). Evapotranspiration in the Soil-Plant-Atmosphere system. In *Springer eBooks*. DOI: 10.1007/978-94-007-3840-9

Oksanen, E., & Kontunen-Soppela, S. (2020). Plants have different strategies to defend against air pollutants. *Current Opinion in Environmental Science & Health, 19*, 100222. DOI: 10.1016/j.coesh.2020.10.010

Ow, L. F., & Ghosh, S. (2017). Urban cities and road traffic noise: Reduction through vegetation. *Applied Acoustics, 120*, 15–20. DOI: 10.1016/j.apacoust.2017.01.007

Perivoliotis, D., Arvanitis, I., Tzavali, A., Papakostas, V., Kappou, S., Andreakos, G., Fotiadi, A., Paravantis, J. A., Souliotis, M., & Mihalakakou, G. (2023). Sustainable Urban Environment through Green Roofs: A Literature Review with Case Studies. *Sustainability (Basel), 15*(22), 15976. DOI: 10.3390/su152215976

Qiu, G., Li, H., Zhang, Q., Chen, W., Liang, X., & Li, X. (2013). Effects of evapotranspiration on mitigation of urban temperature by vegetation and urban agriculture. *Journal of Integrative Agriculture, 12*(8), 1307–1315. DOI: 10.1016/S2095-3119(13)60543-2

Radić, M., Dodig, M. B., & Auer, T. (2019). Green Facades and Living Walls—A review establishing the classification of construction types and mapping the benefits. *Sustainability (Basel), 11*(17), 4579. DOI: 10.3390/su11174579

Ramasubramanian, P., Starry, O., Rosenstiel, T., & Gall, E. T. (2019). Pilot study on the impact of green roofs on ozone levels near building ventilation air supply. *Building and Environment, 151*, 43–53. DOI: 10.1016/j.buildenv.2019.01.023

Ravindra, K., & Mor, S. (2022). Phytoremediation potential of indoor plants in reducing air pollutants. *Frontiers in Sustainable Cities*, *4*, 1039710. Advance online publication. DOI: 10.3389/frsc.2022.1039710

Raymond, C. M., Frantzeskaki, N., Kabisch, N., Berry, P., Breil, M., Nita, M. R., Geneletti, D., & Calfapietra, C. (2017). A framework for assessing and implementing the co-benefits of nature-based solutions in urban areas. *Environmental Science & Policy*, *77*, 15–24. DOI: 10.1016/j.envsci.2017.07.008

Reis, A. R. N. D., Biondi, D., & De Oliveira, J. D. (2022). The role of urban green areas in noise pollution attenuation. *Dyna*, *89*(220), 210–215. DOI: 10.15446/dyna.v89n220.95822

Rey-Gozalo, G., Morillas, J. M. B., González, D. M., & Vílchez-Gómez, R. (2023). Influence of green areas on the urban sound environment. *Current Pollution Reports*, *9*(4), 746–759. DOI: 10.1007/s40726-023-00284-5

Shishegaran, A., Shishegaran, A., Najari, M., Ghotbi, A., & Boushehri, A. N. (2020). Effect of plants on an environment with high carbon dioxide concentration. *Cleaner Engineering and Technology*, *1*, 100002. DOI: 10.1016/j.clet.2020.100002

Small, G., Jimenez, I., Salzl, M., & Shrestha, P. (2020). Urban heat island mitigation due to enhanced evapotranspiration in an urban garden in Saint Paul, Minnesota, USA. *WIT Transactions on Ecology and the Environment*, 39–45. Advance online publication. DOI: 10.2495/UA200041

Syamlal, N. C. A., George, N. A., &Sayantan, N. D. (2024). Phytoremediation: an Eco-Friendly solution for environmental contamination. *International Journal of Advanced Research in Science Communication and Technology*, 553–577. DOI: 10.48175/IJARSCT-18774

Van Renterghem, T., Botteldooren, D., & Verheyen, K. (2012). Road traffic noise shielding by vegetation belts of limited depth. *Journal of Sound and Vibration*, *331*(10), 2404–2425. DOI: 10.1016/j.jsv.2012.01.006

Vourdoubas, J. (2024). Review of the benefits of green roofs. *International Journal of Current Science Research and Review*, *07*(09). Advance online publication. DOI: 10.47191/ijcsrr/V7-i9-48

Watling, J. R., Grant, N. M., Miller, R. E., & Robinson, S. A. (2008). Mechanisms of thermoregulation in plants. *Plant Signaling & Behavior*, *3*(8), 595–597. DOI: 10.4161/psb.3.8.6341 PMID: 19704809

Yang, X., Shi, X., Zhang, Y., Tian, F., & Ortega-Farias, S. (2023). Response of evapotranspiration (ET) to climate factors and crop planting structures in the Shiyang River basin, northwestern China. *Remote Sensing (Basel)*, *15*(16), 3923. DOI: 10.3390/rs15163923

Yofianti, D., & Usman, K. (2021). Relationship of plant types to noise pollution absorption level to improve the quality of the road environment. *IOP Conference Series. Earth and Environmental Science*, *926*(1), 012074. DOI: 10.1088/1755-1315/926/1/012074

Zhang, B., Liang, Z., Zhao, L., Ma, L., Zhang, S., Gao, T., & Chen, L. (2025). Optimizing Eco-Efficiency of green Infrastructure: A comparative study of woody plant species Utilizing SWMM-HYDRUS model and Analytic Hierarchy process. *Ecological Indicators*, *173*, 113388. DOI: 10.1016/j.ecolind.2025.113388

Zhao, N., Prieur, J., Liu, Y., Kneeshaw, D., Lapointe, E. M., Paquette, A., Zinszer, K., Dupras, J., Villeneuve, P. J., Rainham, D. G., Lavigne, E., Chen, H., Van Den Bosch, M., Oiamo, T., & Smargiassi, A. (2021). Tree characteristics and environmental noise in complex urban settings – A case study from Montreal, Canada. *Environmental Research*, *202*, 111887. DOI: 10.1016/j.envres.2021.111887 PMID: 34425113

APPENDIX

Abbreviations

Sulfur Dioxide (SO_2)
Nitrogen Dioxide (NO_2)
Ozone (O_3)
Particulate matter (PM)
Volatile organic compounds (VOCs)
Superoxide Dismutase (SOD)
Peroxidase (POD)
Catalase (CAT)
Reactive Oxygen Species (ROS)
Carbon Monoxide (CO)
Evapotranspiration (ET)
Nitrogen Oxides (NO_X)
Urban Heat Island (UHI)

Chapter 3

Next-Generation Vehicle Safety With V2X, AI, and Digital Twins

D. Chaithra
Sapthagiri NPS University, India

D. Rajeshwari
http://orcid.org/0000-0001-9952-3183
The National Institute of Engineering, Mysore, India

Shobha Rani N. R.
Sapthagiri NPS University, India

Vijaya Kumar H. R.
Harsha Institute of Technology, India

B. Revathi
Sapthagiri NPS University, India

L. Dayananda
http://orcid.org/0009-0008-2344-3329
Jyothi Institute of Technology, India

G. Swetha
http://orcid.org/0000-0001-8620-7149
RR Institute of Technology, Bangalore, India

Anusha D. Y.
SJB Institute of Technology, India

Kamala Narayanan
University of Nevada, USA

N. Raghu
http://orcid.org/0000-0002-2091-8922
Jain University, India

ABSTRACT

Connected car technologies are redefining vehicle safety by enabling cars to communicate, sense their surroundings, and respond to real-time conditions. Today's vehicles go beyond transportation; they act as intelligent systems working to prevent accidents before they happen. Features like Vehicle-to-Vehicle and Vehicle-to-Infrastructure communication, advanced driver assistance systems, and automated alerts help drivers stay aware of potential dangers and make quicker, safer decisions. With

DOI: 10.4018/979-8-2600-0883-6.ch003

the support of fast networks like 5G, cloud computing, and edge data processing, these innovations are becoming more effective and accessible. Automakers such as Tesla, Volvo, and Ford are already integrating these technologies into mainstream vehicles, making safety smarter and more proactive. Concerns about cybersecurity, data privacy, and uneven infrastructure still pose hurdles. Legal and regulatory frameworks are evolving but often struggle to keep pace with technology.

1. INTRODUCTION

The journey of automobiles has been one of constant innovation. The simple mechanical machines have evolved into sophisticated systems powered by software, sensors, and data. A major leap in this evolution is the rise of connected vehicles cars that can “talk” not just to each other but also to traffic systems, road infrastructure, and even pedestrian devices (Ouaissa et al., 2022). These vehicles are reshaping how transportation works, aiming to make driving safer, smoother, and smarter. Connected vehicles are part of a broader shift toward intelligent transportation systems (ITS). These systems use real-time data to improve everything from traffic flow to accident prevention. With the help of Vehicle-to-Vehicle (V2V), Vehicle-to-Infrastructure (V2I), and Vehicle-to-Everything (V2X) technologies, connected cars share information about speed, location, road hazards, and more. This kind of communication means drivers can act on important updates almost instantly.

Imagine a scenario where a car approaching an intersection receives a signal that another vehicle is about to run a red light. That warning, delivered in real time, could be the difference between a near miss and a serious accident as in Figure 1. The power of connected cars lies in their ability to gather, process, and act on data before danger becomes visible. The technologies making this possible include 5G networks, advanced sensors, cloud computing and AI. Together, they create a digital ecosystem where cars aren't just tools for travel they become proactive safety partners (Taleb et al., 2017).

Figure 1. Interconnection missing between the vehicles

1.1 Importance of Vehicle Safety in Modern Transportation

Every year, road accidents lead to the loss of millions of lives and leave countless others injured. Despite progress in vehicle design and traffic regulations, the challenge of road safety remains significant especially as urban areas become more congested and fast-paced. Traditional safety measures, like airbags and crumple zones, help after an accident occurs (Liu et al., 2023). But today's needs demand more than that they require tools that can prevent accidents from happening in the first place.

That's where active safety systems come in. These include technologies that assist drivers in real time, such as lane-keeping assistance or automatic braking. When combined with connectivity, these tools become even more powerful (Alam, 2024). The idea is to shift from reactive safety to predictive safety spotting potential issues before they turn into real threats. Safer vehicles don't just benefit the individual driver. They reduce the burden on emergency services, improve traffic flow, and even lower environmental impact by reducing stop-and-go driving caused by accidents. As roads grow more complex, safety through connected technology becomes less of a luxury and more of a necessity for individuals and communities alike (Sarsam et. al, 2023).

1.2 Role of Connectivity in Enhancing Safety

Connectivity changes the way vehicles see the world. Instead of relying solely on onboard cameras and sensors, connected cars gain access to a much wider pool of information from nearby vehicles, road signs, traffic lights, and even weather updates. This broader awareness helps cars respond faster and more accurately to potential hazards (Rupanagudi, 2020). For instance, through V2V communication, two vehicles can exchange data about their position and speed. If one vehicle brakes suddenly, the other can receive a warning and react immediately even if the driver hasn't noticed yet. Similarly, V2I systems can alert a driver about a sharp curve ahead, icy conditions, or a traffic jam, allowing for smoother and safer navigation (Ke et al., 2020).

Cloud platforms and AI add another layer of intelligence. They can analyze patterns from thousands of vehicles to predict trouble spots before problems arise. This ability to forecast and prevent issues marks a big step forward from traditional safety methods. What's truly transformative is how connectivity turns safety from something passive into something active and intelligent. The car becomes more than just a vehicle it becomes a co-pilot, helping to make every journey safer.

1.3 Safety-Centric Technologies in Connected Cars

Connected cars are not just about convenience or entertainment, they are fundamentally reshaping how safety is approached on roads. By embedding intelligence into vehicles and integrating them with surrounding environments (S. R. Rupanagudi, 2021), these technologies serve as vigilant co-pilots. The following sections explore the key safety innovations that help prevent accidents, protect passengers, and reduce fatalities.

1.3.1 Advanced Driver Assistance Systems (ADAS)

Modern vehicles have become more than just mechanical machines, they're intelligent systems designed to actively assist the driver. At the forefront of vehicle safety innovation are Advanced Driver Assistance Systems (ADAS), which provide drivers with real-time support through features like adaptive cruise control, automatic parking, and traffic sign recognition. These systems help ease the mental load on drivers by managing speed, maintaining lane position, and even monitoring for signs of fatigue (Molinaro et al., 2020). The ADAS usage particularly powerful is its proactive approach. A driver might miss a traffic sign or fail to notice a slowing vehicle ahead, but the system can step in to alert or assist before a dangerous situation arises. In congested traffic, adaptive cruise control keeps a safe distance from other vehicles, reducing the risk of collisions. Many of these features operate seamlessly in the background, providing safety without taking control away from the driver.

As vehicles continuously gather data through radar, LiDAR, cameras, and other sensors, ADAS becomes increasingly precise and adaptive. Beyond convenience, these systems play a crucial role in making roads safer, especially in complex driving scenarios where human reaction alone may not be enough. The full automation is still evolving, ADAS is a strong step toward a future where vehicles and humans work together for safer travel.

1.3.2 Collision Avoidance Systems

Accidents often happen in a split second just enough time for a distracted glance or misjudged distance. Collision Avoidance Systems aim to step in during those crucial moments. These systems continuously monitor the surroundings using radar, cameras, and ultrasonic sensors, ready to intervene when a crash seems likely. They're designed to give warnings first through sound, visual alerts, or seat vibrations and then apply emergency braking or steering if needed as shown in Figure 2. These technologies are especially useful in urban settings, where traffic is dense and unpredictable. Imagine a pedestrian stepping into the road suddenly or a cyclist swerving unexpectedly. A collision avoidance system can detect these changes faster than most drivers can react. In highway driving, it can identify rapid deceleration in the vehicle ahead, helping prevent high-speed pile-ups (Bagheri et al., 2020).

Figure 2. Decision enabled vehicle to avoid collision

1.3.3 Lane Departure and Blind Spot Monitoring

Drifting out of a lane without realizing or missing a vehicle lurking in the blind spot can easily lead to a serious accident. The lane departure warning (LDW), lane-keeping assist (LKA), and blind spot monitoring (BSM) systems come into play. These features act as extra eyes on the road, helping drivers maintain awareness and control, especially during highway travel or in dense traffic (Raghu et al., 2023). Lane departure systems use cameras mounted on the windshield to monitor road markings. The vehicle begins to veer without signaling, the driver receives an alert maybe a beep, a steering wheel vibration, or a gentle push back into the lane. This small nudge can be enough to prevent a collision caused by distraction or drowsiness (Verma et al., 2024).

Blind spot monitoring uses radar sensors to detect vehicles approaching from behind or alongside, in areas a driver may not easily see through mirrors. A visual indicator often a small light on the side mirror warns the driver not to change lanes. Some systems also offer active intervention by gently applying steering correction. These technologies are particularly important during long drives or night travel, when attention can waver. They're not just add-ons for comfort, they're key safety elements. And they're becoming more precise with every software upgrade, helping reduce lane-related accidents across vehicle types.

1.3.4 Real-time Traffic and Hazard Alerts

Getting caught in a sudden traffic jam or heading straight into a dangerous road condition can be both frustrating and risky. Real-time traffic and hazard alert systems are designed to keep drivers informed ahead of time. These systems collect and process data from GPS, traffic control centers, and even other connected vehicles to provide live updates about congestion, accidents, roadblocks, or weather-related hazards. The alerts are delivered through the vehicle's infotainment system or dashboard display, often paired with recommended alternative routes. This not only saves time but also reduces the likelihood of last-minute lane changes or sudden braking that might lead to accidents. In more advanced systems, alerts are tied to the vehicle's sensors so if slippery conditions are detected ahead, the car can adjust braking response automatically. Real-time information enhances decision-making (Hasan et al., 2020).

1.3.5 Autonomous Emergency Braking (AEB)

One of the most critical last-line defenses in vehicle safety is Autonomous Emergency Braking (AEB). When a driver doesn't react in time to a looming obstacle, a stopped vehicle, a crossing pedestrian, or a cyclist AEB steps in. The system calculates closing speed and distance using radar and cameras, and if a collision seems imminent, it applies the brakes automatically to avoid or reduce impact. What makes AEB so valuable is its speed and precision. The average human reaction time may not be fast enough to prevent a crash, especially at higher speeds or in unexpected scenarios (Raghu et al., 2024). AEB operates in milliseconds, detecting the threat and acting on it sometimes before the driver even realizes the danger. This feature has already shown its potential in real-world use, with many insurers and regulators noting significant reductions in rear-end collisions in vehicles equipped with AEB. Many automakers now include AEB as a standard feature, recognizing it not just as a luxury, but as a safety essential. It's a quiet guardian, always watching the road ahead (Gürses et al., 2025).

1.3.6 Human Factors in Connected Vehicle Safety

Connected vehicle safety systems use various sensors (radar, cameras, LIDAR, etc.), vehicle-to-vehicle (V2V) and vehicle-to-infrastructure (V2I or V2X) communication, and vehicle-to-pedestrian (V2P) communication to automatically detect situations that could lead to crashes and communicate this information to the driver through user interfaces. While these technologies have significant technical potential, connected vehicle safety is in practice a human-mediated process. Driver/safety system interaction (how the driver responds to the driver interface, for instance) is a critical component of connected vehicle safety. And there is evidence that people may develop unjustified trust in partially automated systems.

1.4 Data and Communication Infrastructure

The data and communication infrastructure is the core of connected vehicle system, which provides the foundation for connected vehicle system to communicate information between vehicles, roadside units and cloud with low latency. V2X, 5G, edge computing and cloud service technology can provide real-time data processing, cooperative awareness and scalable application deployment for connected vehicle system.

1.4.1 Vehicle-to-Everything (V2X) Protocols

Modern connected vehicles operate within a complex web of communication protocols that enable seamless data exchange between different actors on the road. Among the most transformative is Vehicle-to-Everything (V2X) communication, a framework that allows vehicles to communicate with other vehicles (V2V), infrastructure (V2I), pedestrians (V2P), and networks (V2N). This holistic approach to vehicular communication enhances situational awareness and supports proactive safety mechanisms as shown in Figure 3.

V2X communication functions by transmitting data packets between nodes in real time, covering aspects such as speed, location, braking patterns, and traffic signal timing. By continuously analyzing this information, vehicles can anticipate potential hazards like another car running a red light or a pedestrian stepping onto the road long before visual contact is made. This proactive layer of intelligence strengthens the foundation of safety-oriented driving environments. Importantly, V2X isn't merely a technological novelty. Its deployment is a strategic response to rising urban congestion, increasing traffic fatalities, and the growing demand for intelligent transport systems. As adoption spreads, V2X has the potential to transform transportation ecosystems into adaptive, responsive networks where vehicles not only move but think, predict, and act in unison (Samak et al., 2024).

Figure 3. Holistic approach to vehicular communication

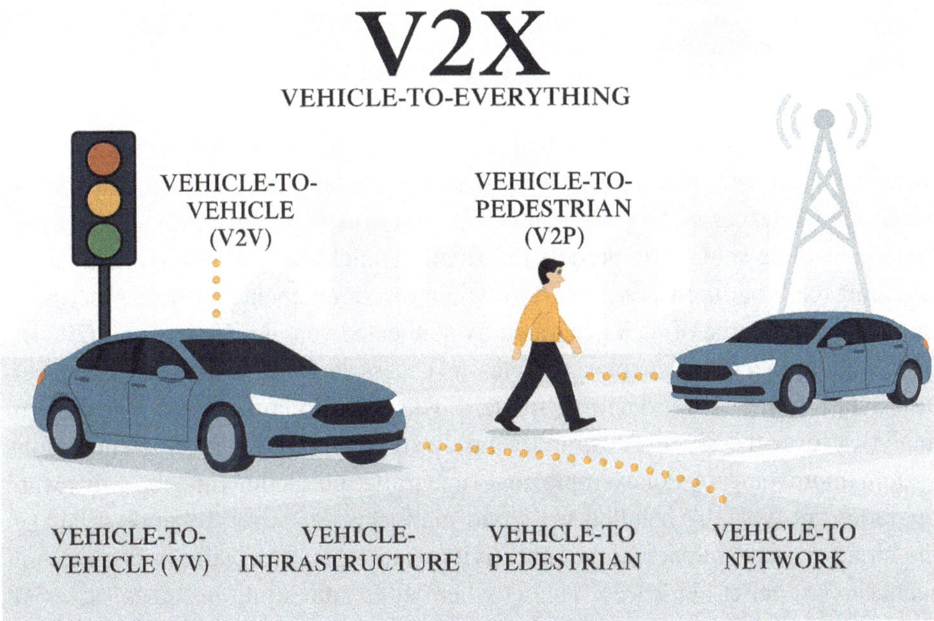

1.4.2 DSRC vs. C-V2X: A Comparative Analysis

Two primary technologies currently dominate the V2X communication landscape: Dedicated Short-Range Communication (DSRC) and Cellular Vehicle-to-Everything (C-V2X). Both are designed to enable fast, low-latency communication between vehicles and infrastructure, yet they differ significantly in architecture, capabilities, and scalability. DSRC operates over the 5.9 GHz band and is based on IEEE 802.11p standards. It allows vehicles to communicate directly without relying on cellular networks, which proves advantageous in areas with poor coverage. DSRC is mature, well-tested, and widely adopted in pilot programs, particularly in North America. Its key strength lies in low latency and dependable performance under fixed scenarios (Shoukat et al., 2024).

A fundamental reliability-scalability trade-off in V2X communications. Distributed Service for Reliable Communication (DSRC) has shown low-latency performance in localized scenarios. However, due to the limited scalability and reliance on dedicated spectrum, DSRC is not well suited for long-term deployment. Cellular-based Vehicle to Anything (C-V2X) is based on cellular infrastructure and 5G evolution, thus having larger coverage and extensibility in the future with extra cost of reliance on cellular network availability and jitter under high traffic density.

The reliability-scalability trade-off between DSRC and C-V2X is a fundamental tension in V2X communications.

1.4.3 Cloud Connectivity and Edge Computing

Connected vehicles operate in real time, which calls for a strong computational framework capable of analyzing vast amounts of data and making split-second decisions. Cloud computing and edge computing work together to provide this foundation, enabling vehicles to process information quickly and respond effectively to changing road conditions. Each plays a distinct yet complementary role in processing the immense volume of data generated by connected vehicles (Polat et al., 2024).

Cloud connectivity enables vehicles to access large-scale processing power, vast datasets, and shared learning models. This infrastructure supports long-term analytics, over-the-air updates, and centralized storage, allowing for continuous system improvements. For example, real-time traffic prediction models or firmware upgrades are typically handled via cloud platforms. However, reliance solely on the cloud presents latency and connectivity challenges, especially in fast-moving scenarios (Sadaf et al., 2023). This is where edge computing becomes essential. By processing data locally within the vehicle itself or nearby roadside units edge computing ensures immediate responses to critical safety situations. Functions like collision warnings or emergency braking cannot afford the delay of cloud transmission. The integration of cloud and edge computing creates a balanced ecosystem. While cloud systems provide strategic intelligence and historical learning, edge nodes deliver rapid, mission-critical execution. Together, they empower connected vehicles with the speed and intelligence needed to function safely and efficiently in diverse, dynamic environments (Annabi et al., 2024).

1.4.4 Data Security, Privacy, and Cyber Safety

As vehicles evolve into mobile data hubs, the issue of cybersecurity becomes paramount. Every sensor, application, and network connection represent a potential point of vulnerability. Ensuring the integrity, confidentiality, and availability of vehicular data is not only a technological concern but also a societal one, deeply tied to public trust and regulatory compliance (Mudhivarthi et al., 2023). Connected cars collect and transmit sensitive information ranging from location history to driver behavior. Without proper safeguards, this data could be exploited by malicious actors for identity theft, surveillance, or remote control of vehicle functions. High-profile incidents of automotive hacking have highlighted the real risks involved, prompting an urgent need for comprehensive cybersecurity strategies (Ibrahim et al., 2023).

Data encryption, secure authentication protocols, and intrusion detection systems form the core of vehicle cybersecurity frameworks. Regular software updates and patches, delivered via over-the-air (OTA) channels, are essential to address evolving threats (Shetty & Raghu, 2025). In parallel, manufacturers are increasingly adopting hardware security modules (HSMs) and secure communication standards like Transport Layer Security (TLS) to protect data in transit and at rest Privacy protection also requires clear policy frameworks. Drivers should have transparent control over how their data is used and shared. Regulations such as the General Data Protection Regulation (GDPR) in Europe and emerging automotive-specific standards globally are shaping data governance practices in the industry (M. Nagpal, 2025). Cybersecurity in connected vehicles is not a one-time fix but an ongoing commitment. With vehicles becoming increasingly autonomous and interconnected, the stakes for cyber safety have never been higher. Ensuring resilience against threats must go hand-in-hand with technological innovation to protect lives, property, and public confidence in connected mobility systems.

1.5 Objectives and Structure of the Chapter

This chapter delves into the evolving world of connected vehicle technologies and their powerful role in making our roads safer. As vehicles become smarter and more connected, they are no longer just modes of transport—they are active participants in a broader network. Through systems like Vehicle-to-Vehicle (V2V) and Vehicle-to-Infrastructure (V2I) communication, cars can now share real-time data about traffic conditions, potential collisions, and other critical events. These advancements are already making a difference by helping drivers avoid accidents and improving overall traffic flow. Beyond current applications, the chapter also looks ahead to the future, where connected technologies could work hand-in-hand with automation and artificial intelligence to create even safer, more efficient transportation systems. The aim is to showcase both the real-world impact and the exciting potential of connected cars in transforming road safety.

The chapter is organized into several sections. It begins by introducing the core technologies behind connected cars, followed by a closer look at safety-specific features like advanced driver-assistance systems and emergency alerts. Infrastructure and communication frameworks are covered next, along with real-world case studies (Zhang et al., 2023). There's also a discussion on regulations, implementation challenges, and emerging trends like AI and digital twins. The chapter wraps up with a summary of key insights and what lies ahead for connected vehicle safety.

2. LITERATURE SURVEY

Ouaissa et al. (2022) highlights how Vehicle-to-Everything (V2X) technologies such as Vehicle-to-Vehicle (V2V) and Vehicle-to-Infrastructure (V2I) are transforming road safety when combined with advanced driver assistance systems (ADAS). Unlike onboard sensors that struggle with blind spots or hidden obstacles, V2X allows vehicles to "see" beyond their immediate surroundings by sharing real-time data with other vehicles and traffic infrastructure. This makes warnings like sudden braking alerts or intersection collision prevention faster and more reliable. The study emphasizes the importance of 5G connectivity for meeting the low-latency requirements of these systems. However, challenges remain, particularly in ensuring interoperability across car manufacturers, handling dense traffic communication, and overcoming interference in real-world conditions. The authors conclude that while V2X is not a replacement for ADAS, it significantly strengthens it, provided standardization and robust testing continue to evolve.

Alam et al. (2024) explore how connected and autonomous vehicles (CAVs) can be made more secure by combining blockchain with federated reinforcement learning (FRL). Since these vehicles rely on exchanging sensitive data for navigation and decision-making, privacy and security are constant concerns. Traditional centralized data sharing is risky, as it exposes personal and operational information to leaks or cyberattacks. The proposed solution takes a decentralized approach by allowing vehicles to train models locally, while sharing only encrypted updates through a blockchain network. This design builds trust and protects against tampering, ensuring that sensitive data never leaves the vehicle. It reduces risks like data theft or malicious interference with the models. The authors also connect these security measures to real-world safety improvements, such as fewer false alarms in hazard detection systems. At the same time, they acknowledge important challenges like the added latency, higher energy consumption, and the difficulty of achieving widespread industry collaboration. Ultimately, the study highlights that the future of connected vehicle safety will depend on finding the right balance between real-time performance and robust security.

Sarsam et al. this study takes a closer look at the growing gap between existing laws and the cybersecurity needs of connected and autonomous vehicles. It highlights how current regulations such as ISO/SAE 21434 and UNECE WP.29 struggle to keep pace with fast-evolving threats like spoofed V2X messages, hacked over-the-air updates, and weaknesses in the supply chain. One of the biggest challenges they point out is the mismatch between traditional safety standards, such as ISO 26262, and the ongoing cybersecurity monitoring that vehicles require long after they leave the factory. The researchers also raise important questions about accountability for instance, who is liable if a car makes a decision based on compromised external data with their argument is that regulations must evolve toward continuous risk assessment, shared responsibility among manufacturers and operators, and certification frameworks that link cybersecurity directly to safety outcomes. Ultimately, the work underscores that cybersecurity is not just a technical necessity, but a core element of ensuring road safety in the connected era.

Ke et al. (2020) this research explores how predictive safety can be achieved through machine learning models trained on vast datasets that capture driving behavior, environmental conditions, and traffic incidents. By using ensemble methods like random forests and gradient boosting, the system is able to forecast high-risk situations such as sudden braking ahead, unexpected lane changes, or pedestrians crossing the road with impressive accuracy. What makes the approach even stronger is its adaptability: the model continuously learns from new data, refining its predictions and cutting down on false alarms. Real-time processing is a key focus, ensuring that drivers receive timely warnings without being overloaded with unnecessary alerts. The study also looks at how these predictive models can be translated into practical safety tools, from preemptive braking to subtle steering corrections. At the same time, it acknowledges the challenges, including striking the right balance between sensitivity and specificity, managing unbalanced datasets, and making the system compatible across different vehicle platforms. Ultimately, the work shows how predictive analytics can shift vehicle safety from being purely reactive to truly proactive, and argues for integrated frameworks that bring together real-time sensing with historical risk profiling.

Zhang et al. (2023) a novel approach on collision avoidance system that adapts its control strategy based on the driver's behavior. By combining fuzzy logic with predictive control algorithms, the system can distinguish between aggressive and conservative driving styles, adjusting braking and lane-change interventions to match. Simulation results across varying speeds demonstrate that this adaptive approach not only increases safety margins but also delivers smoother responses, particularly during sudden maneuvers. By accounting for human variability, the system minimizes unnecessary interventions in calm driving situations while still taking decisive action when risks are high. The findings highlight improvements in lateral stability and faster response times compared to traditional, fixed collision avoidance systems. However, challenges remain—such as the difficulty of accurately profiling driver behavior and the ethical questions that arise when tailoring safety features to individual styles. Even so, this adaptive framework points to a promising direction for future safety technologies: systems that not only protect but also respect the unique ways in which people drive.

Islam et al. (2022) This literature review examines recent progress in improving pedestrian safety through sensor fusion and infrastructure-assisted detection systems. By combining data from lidar, cameras, and radar, vehicles can achieve more reliable detection, even in challenging non-line-of-sight situations such as around corners or behind parked cars. When integrated with roadside units and smart city infrastructure, these systems further enhance accuracy and reduce response times, allowing vehicles to anticipate risks and react proactively. The review explores different use cases across urban and suburban environments, with particular attention to the role of edge computing at intersections where pedestrian activity is high. At the same time, it highlights ongoing challenges, including sensor occlusion, biases in datasets that may underrepresent certain populations, and the heavy processing demands of real-time analysis. Taken together, the findings underscore the potential of infrastructure-assisted approaches to pedestrian safety, while also stressing the importance of standardized sensor placement and cooperative strategies that enable vehicles to share the detection workload across a connected network.

Li and Zhang (2010) research focuses on developing autonomous vehicle control systems that remain safe even when sensors or subsystems fail. Built on fault-tolerant architecture, redundancy, and anomaly detection, the system ensures that critical functions such as emergency braking and steering support continue to operate under partial failure. By combining machine learning classifiers with logic-based protocols, it can quickly detect inconsistencies, isolate faulty components and trigger fallback mechanisms that keep the vehicle operating safely. Tests across different failure scenarios, from lost GPS signals to mis-calibrated cameras, demonstrate the system's resilience in real-world conditions. The study emphasizes that autonomous driving cannot depend on perfect environments safety must be maintained despite inevitable imperfections. The findings highlight the importance of embedding resilience directly into system design, creating vehicles that are inherently fault-aware, adaptive, and capable of responding effectively when things go wrong.

Martinez et al. (2011) This simulation study explores a coordinated collision avoidance strategy that leverages V2X communication to improve multi-vehicle safety. These sharing information such as intent, braking decisions, and trajectory data, vehicles can work together to execute cooperative maneuvers like synchronized braking or lateral adjustments that prevent chain-reaction crashes. Tested in realistic traffic conditions, including blind corners and tightly spaced vehicles, the system showed a marked reduction in collision probability. The algorithm is designed to account for real-world communication challenges, such as delays and message loss, by optimizing timing and adding redundancy to preserve safety margins. While the work is largely simulation-based, the researchers outline practical pathways for deployment through hardware-in-the-loop testing, demonstrating how the approach could improve convoy dynamics and distributed decision-making on the road. Ultimately, the study underscores the power of collaboration: by sharing the safety responsibility across a network of vehicles, rather than leaving each one to act in isolation, connected systems can create a stronger, more resilient road safety framework.

Table 1. Existing research about connected vehicle safety technologies

Author & Year	Focus Area	Methodology	Key Contributions	Limitations / Gaps
Ouaissa et al., 2022	V2X + ADAS Integration	Analytical study with communication performance evaluation	Demonstrated how V2V and V2I enhance ADAS by extending situational awareness beyond onboard sensors; emphasized 5G for low latency	Interoperability challenges; dense traffic interference; limited real-world validation
Alam et al., 2024	Security in CAVs (Blockchain + FRL)	Blockchain-integrated Federated Reinforcement Learning framework	Improved data privacy and secure decentralized model updates; reduced risk of cyberattacks	Added latency, energy consumption, scalability issues
Sarsam et al., 2023	Cybersecurity Regulations	Regulatory and standards analysis (ISO/SAE 21434, UNECE WP.29)	Highlighted mismatch between functional safety and evolving cybersecurity threats; stressed lifecycle monitoring	Lack of global regulatory harmonization; limited enforcement mechanisms
Ke et al., 2020	Predictive Safety using ML	Ensemble ML models (Random Forest, Gradient Boosting)	Forecasted high-risk events; reduced false alarms; enabled proactive safety	Dataset imbalance; sensitivity-specificity trade-off; cross-platform compatibility
Zhang et al., 2023	Adaptive Collision Avoidance	Fuzzy logic + predictive control simulations	Adaptive braking/lane control based on driver behavior; improved lateral stability	Driver profiling complexity; ethical concerns in personalization
Islam et al., 2022	Pedestrian Safety & Sensor Fusion	Literature review on LiDAR, radar, camera fusion	Enhanced non-line-of-sight pedestrian detection; infrastructure-assisted safety	Sensor occlusion; dataset bias; heavy computation demand
Li & Zhang, 2010	Fault-Tolerant Autonomous Systems	Redundancy architecture + anomaly detection	Improved resilience under subsystem failure; ensured emergency function continuity	Older sensor architectures; limited integration with modern V2X
Martinez et al., 2011	Cooperative Collision Avoidance (VANETs)	Simulation-based V2X coordinated maneuver testing	Reduced multi-vehicle collision probability; improved convoy coordination	Primarily simulation-based; real-world deployment not validated

The existing research about connected vehicle safety technologies displays a complete transformation from using reactive protection methods to employing active safety systems which can forecast potential risks. The research demonstrates that Vehicle-to-Everything (V2X) communication needs to work together with Advanced Driver Assistance Systems (ADAS) to create extended situational awareness, which enables drivers to see beyond the vehicle's built-in sensors, thus enhancing their ability to avoid accidents and maintain safety at intersections. The research on machine learning models shows how predictive analytics functions to identify high-risk driving conditions while it decreases incorrect alerts, which helps provide decision support during actual driving situations. The security-focused research explains that blockchain technology, federated learning, and UNECE WP.29 and ISO/SAE 21434 standards need to work together to create cybersecurity protection against threats which target connected and autonomous vehicles as shown in table 1. The existing system needs additional development in four areas: large-scale field testing, communication system compatibility, legal framework unification, and cybersecurity protection for real-time safety decision-making processes. Despite significant progress, some research gaps remain. Many safety frameworks are validated through simulations, with limited large-scale real-world deployment. Interoperability across manufacturers and across regions is not well addressed, especially for mixed DSRC and C-V2X environments. The integration of cybersecurity assurance into real-time safety decision making is an open research problem that requires tighter coupling between communication reliability, trust, and control.

2.1 Evolution of Connected Cars

Connected cars represent an exciting fusion of automotive engineering and digital technology. At their heart, these vehicles are equipped with internet connectivity and communication networks that allow them to interact not only with other vehicles but also with infrastructure, cloud services, and even pedestrians' smartphones (Alsudani, 2023). This constant flow of information is transforming traditional cars into intelligent mobility systems, enabling them to perceive, respond, and adapt to their surroundings in ways that were once impossible, as illustrated in Figure 4.

The idea of car connectivity has been around for quite some time. Early implementations focused on basic features like navigation systems and onboard diagnostics. Over the years, these tools have grown more sophisticated, evolving into systems that provide real-time traffic updates, emergency assistance, and even remote vehicle monitoring (Raghu et al., 2023). What once began as simple conveniences has gradually transformed vehicles into connected platforms capable of interacting with the world around. Recent advancement in wireless technologies and the rise of cloud computing, today's connected vehicles are capable of far more than simple

GPS navigation, they can share and receive information critical to safety, efficiency, and convenience. The journey from analog to connected vehicles reflects broader changes in how society uses technology. As cars become part of a larger digital ecosystem, they open up opportunities not only for safer roads but also for smarter cities and cleaner mobility. The connected car is no longer a futuristic idea, it's a fast-moving reality that is reshaping the transportation landscape (Gupta et al., 2023).

Figure 4. Technology enabled vehicle

2.1.1 Key Communication Types: V2V, V2I, V2P, V2N

The strength of connected vehicle systems lies in their ability to communicate. This communication happens through several primary channels each offering a different type of awareness and functionality.

- Vehicle-to-Vehicle (V2V) communication allows cars to share data like speed, direction, and braking status with each other. This peer-to-peer exchange helps vehicles anticipate potential collisions, even before drivers can react.
- Vehicle-to-Infrastructure (V2I) connects vehicles with elements of the road environment, such as traffic lights, lane markers, and toll booths. This com-

munication allows drivers to receive timely alerts like an approaching red light or suggested detours during congestion bringing city infrastructure directly into their driving decisions.

- Vehicle-to-Pedestrian (V2P) focuses on interactions with vulnerable road users, including pedestrians and cyclists who carry mobile devices. By sending alerts to both drivers and pedestrians, it creates a shared awareness that enhances safety, particularly in crowded urban settings.
- Vehicle-to-Network (V2N) links vehicles to cloud-based services, providing access to real-time traffic data, weather updates, software improvements, and broader insights from a connected intelligence network. This allows vehicles to make smarter decisions based on both local and global information.

Together, these three communication modes create a robust safety ecosystem, equipping connected vehicles with the awareness and responsiveness needed to navigate complex, dynamic road environments effectively.

2.1.2 Integration With IoT and 5G Networks

The integration of connected cars with IoT and 5G networks marks a transformative step in modern transportation. IoT acts as a vast data network, linking road sensors, traffic cameras, navigation apps, and vehicles to enable seamless information sharing. This connectivity allows cars to perceive and respond to their environment with greater awareness and precision. Equipped with IoT-enabled systems, vehicles can track tire pressure, fuel levels, engine performance, and even signs of driver fatigue in real time (Vanjire & Naveen, 2024). Far from being confined to the vehicle, this data can be transmitted to the cloud, supporting predictive maintenance, fleet optimization, and other smart transportation services. By bridging vehicles, infrastructure, and cloud intelligence, IoT and 5G together create a more responsive, efficient, and safer driving ecosystem (Alshamrani et al., 2021). For instance, a delivery company can track its entire vehicle fleet, identify which cars need servicing, and avoid costly breakdowns all thanks to IoT integration (Raghu et al., 2023).

5G, on the other hand, brings speed and reliability to the system. Unlike earlier cellular networks, 5G offers ultra-low latency (as low as 1 millisecond) and high bandwidth, which are crucial for safety-critical communication. This ensures that alerts like "brake now" or "pedestrian ahead" are delivered almost instantly, without delay. For high-speed vehicles or autonomous driving systems, even a fraction-of-a-second lag can be the difference between safety and disaster. Moreover, the combination of 5G and IoT supports the development of vehicle platooning, where a convoy of connected trucks or cars can travel closely together to reduce fuel use and congestion as shown in Figure 5. It also enables real-time HD mapping, dynamic rerouting, and faster software updates over the air. As vehicles become more connected, they also become more responsive capable of navigating not just physical roads, but digital networks that offer foresight and real-time insight. The collaboration between IoT and 5G is paving the way for a transportation system that is intelligent, adaptive, and, above all, safer for all road users (Lee, 2022).

Figure 5. IoT and 5G communication enabled car

3. METHODOLOGY

The Decision-Making Layer is the core intelligence of our proposed V2X system framework. The inputs to the layer from the vehicle sensors (camera, radar, LiDAR) and the surrounding environment via V2X and cloud platforms are heterogeneous data. The sensor fusion technique is applied to integrate the heterogeneous data to provide a holistic situational overview. The integrated data is then processed by three modules: situation awareness, which obtains knowledge of the current traffic and vehicle states; threat assessment, which detects potential dangers and hazards; and policy and ethics, which takes into account safety regulations and ethical constraints as shown in Figure 6. The decision output is used to generate optimal control commands which are sent to the ADAS system to actuate the vehicle in real time.

Figure 6. Assessment of connected vehicle safety technologies

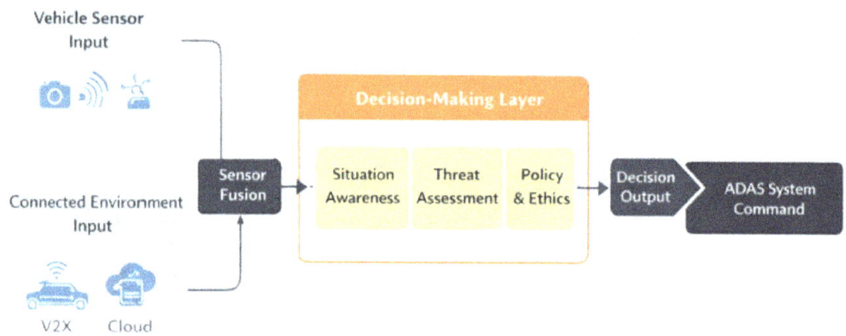

4. RESULT AND DISCUSSION

The improvement in traffic flow speed with the adoption of connected vehicle technologies. The baseline scenario, which is at the lowest traffic speed, represents conventional traffic flow as shown in Figure 7. The scenario with ADAS shows moderate improvement in the traffic flow speed due to smoother braking and lane separation. The scenarios with V2X technologies show further improvement in traffic flow speed due to cooperative driving and early awareness of hazards and congestion. The scenario with both ADAS and V2X technologies shows the highest traffic flow speed due to the combination of onboard intelligence and vehicle-to-everything communication.

Figure 7. Traffic flow improvement graph

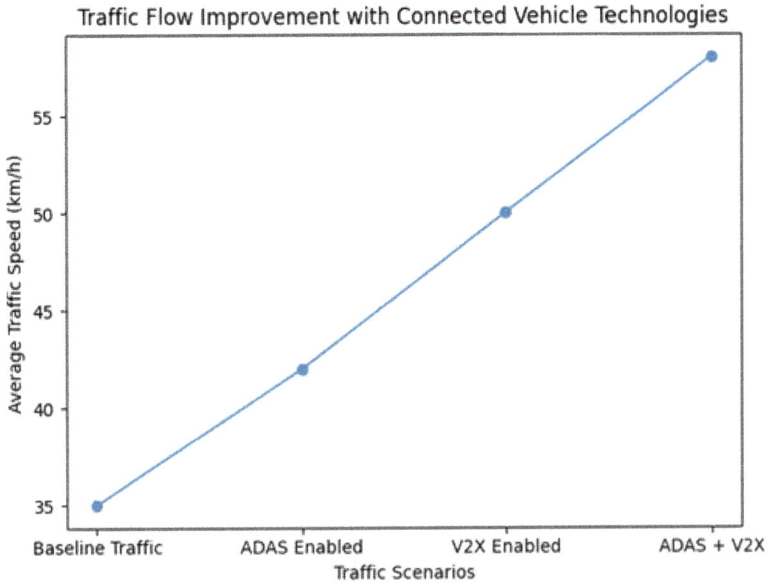

Figure 8. V2X network performance evaluation metrics

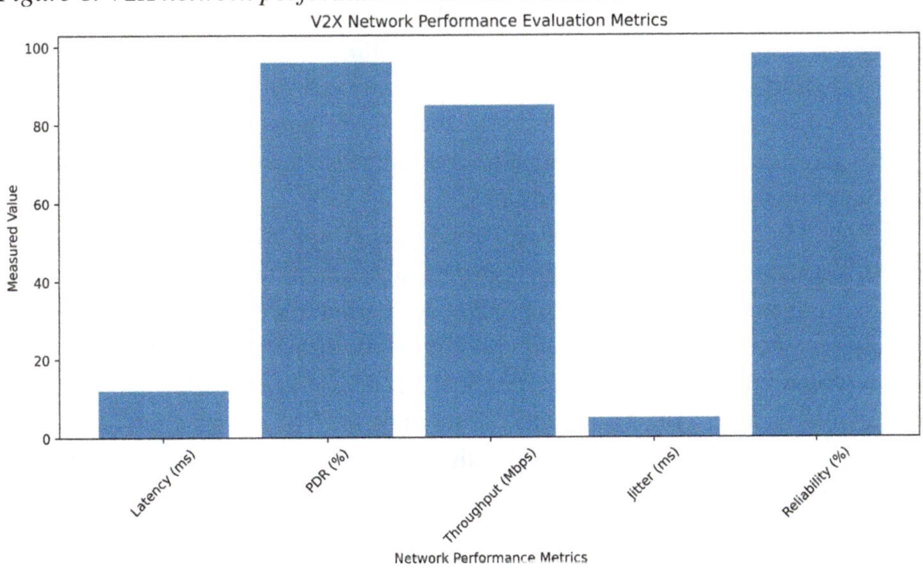

The graph displays the performance assessment results of the V2X network which shows its latency and packet delivery ratio and throughput and jitter and reliability. The results show that the system achieves low latency of 12 milliseconds and minimal jitter of 5 milliseconds which proves essential for real-time safety applications that include collision warnings and emergency braking systems. The system achieves a high packet delivery ratio of 96 percent and reliability of 98 percent which confirms that vehicles maintain stable communication with infrastructure systems. The system provides 85 Mbps of throughput which enables efficient data transmission during times of heavy network usage. The V2X network demonstrates fast and dependable and strong communication capabilities which meet the requirements for safety-critical operations of connected vehicles according to the performance measurements as shown in Figure 8.

5. CASE STUDIES AND INDUSTRY APPLICATIONS

5.1 Volvo's Safety-First Connected Features

Volvo has long been recognized for its unwavering commitment to vehicle safety, and its approach to connected technologies reflects this legacy. Volvo's connected safety features go beyond driver convenience they are designed to actively prevent accidents and lessen the impact of collisions. These innovations rely on real-time data sharing and cooperative vehicle behavior, turning each car into a proactive participant in road safety. One standout feature is the Slippery Road Alert and Hazard Light Alert, which allow Volvo vehicles to automatically share warnings about road conditions with nearby Volvos via a cloud-based network. This early warning system gives drivers advanced situational awareness, particularly in challenging weather or unpredictable road conditions.

Through this networked approach, vehicles don't operate in isolation they contribute to a shared safety ecosystem. Volvo has also integrated real-time traffic data into its navigation systems, offering adaptive routing and predictive analytics to help drivers make smarter decisions. Pilot projects with Vehicle-to-Infrastructure (V2I) communication, such as smart traffic light coordination, further aim to reduce risks at intersections. Together, these efforts illustrate Volvo's vision of safety as a collaborative, connected outcome rather than a feature confined to a single vehicle an intelligent approach that harmonizes cars with their environment to make roads safer for everyone.

5.2 Tesla's Autopilot and Sensor Fusion

Tesla has led the way in commercially adopting advanced driver-assistance technologies, blending connectivity, sensor fusion, and machine learning into an integrated driving system. Its Autopilot platform demonstrates how real-time data and intelligent decision-making can enhance safety on the road. By combining inputs from cameras, radar, ultrasonic sensors, and GPS, the system builds a complete understanding of the vehicle's surroundings, enabling automatic lane keeping, adaptive cruise control, and even lane changes with minimal driver intervention.

A key differentiator for Tesla is its ability to continually improve these systems through over-the-air (OTA) updates. Data collected from the entire fleet helps refine algorithms and enhance performance, ensuring that every vehicle benefits from the collective learning of millions of miles driven. Tesla's ecosystem also relies heavily on cloud connectivity, allowing data from individual vehicles to be aggregated and analyzed in real time. This networked intelligence supports immediate enhancements to driver-assist functions and contributes to Tesla's long-term vision of fully autonomous vehicles. Safety remains central, with redundancies and emergency override protocols designed to maintain control in unpredictable situations. Tesla's approach shows how connectivity, centralized learning, and real-time environmental awareness can work together to push the boundaries of vehicle safety and redefine the driving experience.

5.3 Ford's SYNC and Vehicle Safety Apps

Ford's SYNC platform illustrates how connectivity can enhance safety while improving the overall driving experience. What began as a simple infotainment system has grown into a central hub for communication, navigation, and safety applications. A key element of SYNC is its integration with Ford Co-Pilot360, which combines driver-assist technologies like automatic emergency braking, lane-keeping assistance, and blind spot detection. With real-time updates on traffic and maps, drivers can make better decisions, navigate safely through congested roads, and stay prepared for changing conditions.

SYNC also connects with mobile safety apps such as Life360 and features emergency SOS functions that can automatically alert responders with crash data and GPS location, helping reduce response times. Voice control adds another layer of safety by allowing hands-free operation of critical systems, minimizing distractions. Ford's approach highlights how connected technologies can make a real difference in everyday driving. Rather than focusing solely on fully autonomous features, SYNC emphasizes practical, reliable, and proactive safety support making vehicles not just smarter, but safer, for drivers and passengers alike.

6. COMPARATIVE ANALYSIS OF FUTURE TRENDS AND INNOVATIONS

6.1 Integration With AI and Machine Learning

Artificial Intelligence (AI) and Machine Learning (ML) are revolutionizing the way vehicles understand and respond to the world around them. As connected cars become more intelligent, these technologies are no longer just optional enhancements they are becoming central to the evolution of automotive safety as shown in Figure 9. Artificial intelligence (AI) and machine learning (ML) enable vehicles to "learn" from their environment. Connected cars can process massive amounts of sensor data ranging from road conditions and traffic patterns to driver behavior and make intelligent decisions in real time.

Machine learning is also essential for adaptive systems. Features like adaptive cruise control or lane-keeping assist can tailor their responses to a driver's habits or changes in the environment. Over time, these systems become increasingly accurate and reliable, drawing insights from millions of real-world scenarios encountered by vehicles worldwide. AI also strengthens cybersecurity. Threat detection algorithms and anomaly recognition systems help connected vehicles identify potential attacks or malfunctions before they escalate, keeping both passengers and vehicle systems safe. Looking ahead, AI is poised to integrate more deeply across every aspect of vehicle operation from engine performance and energy management to voice-based driver support. The connected vehicle of the future will be less reactive and more predictive, using continuous learning to anticipate challenges, enhance safety, and provide a smarter, more responsive driving experience.

Figure 9. Real time monitoring of road environment

6.2 Predictive Safety Algorithms and Big Data

Predictive safety is emerging as one of the most exciting advancements in the connected vehicle space. Instead of merely reacting to incidents after they occur, future cars will be able to anticipate risks before they happen, thanks to predictive algorithms and big data analytics. These systems draw on massive volumes of data from a variety of sources onboard sensors, vehicle-to-vehicle (V2V) communication, road infrastructure, weather reports, and even mobile apps. By analyzing these inputs, predictive models can identify potential hazards. For example, if a stretch of road is known for sharp curves, frequent accidents, or dense fog, the system can alert the driver in advance, even if conditions initially seem normal. Machine learning takes this a step further. By processing historical crash data, vehicle behavior logs, and real-time feedback, the system continuously improves its predictive accuracy. It's like having a personal data scientist riding alongside you, constantly evaluating risk and offering guidance tailored to your environment.

Big data also enables fleet-level insights. Aggregated information from multiple vehicles can help manufacturers and city planners redesign dangerous intersections, adjust speed limits, or deploy emergency services more efficiently. In this way, each vehicle becomes a sensor, contributing to a smarter and safer transportation network. Ultimately, predictive safety transforms driving from a reactive activity into a proactive one. Drivers are not just receiving more information they're being guided by intelligent recommendations that help them avoid danger before it arises.

6.3 Roadmap to Fully Autonomous, Safe Vehicles

The vision of fully autonomous vehicles cars that drive themselves with no human intervention has captured the imagination of engineers, investors, and everyday commuters alike. While remarkable progress has been made, achieving complete autonomy remains a complex challenge, especially when safety is the ultimate goal. Autonomous vehicles are classified into five levels. Level 1 and 2 offer driver-assistance features such as steering support or adaptive cruise control. Level 3 introduces conditional automation, where the car can manage certain tasks independently but still requires human oversight. Levels 4 and 5 represent full autonomy, with Level 5 requiring no driver at all. Reaching these higher levels demands an intricate blend of technologies: high-definition mapping, lidar and radar sensors, V2X communication, AI-driven decision-making, and redundant safety systems. One of the toughest challenges is ensuring that these vehicles can navigate unpredictable real-world environments heavy traffic, adverse weather, or erratic human drivers with consistent reliability.

Testing and validation are critical along this journey. Companies like Waymo, Cruise, and Tesla are leveraging billions of miles of driving data to train and refine their autonomous platforms. Simulations and digital twin's virtual replicas of vehicles and road networks allow engineers to test rare but crucial "edge cases" that might not appear during real-world driving. Equally important is public trust. Even the most advanced systems will struggle to gain adoption if people don't feel safe riding in a driverless car. Transparent reporting, regulatory oversight, and a focus on passenger experience are essential to bridging this gap. While the path to fully autonomous, safe vehicles is far from straightforward, each innovation brings us closer to a future where self-driving cars are not only possible but reliable and secure.

6.4 Role of Digital Twins in Vehicle Safety

Digital twins are quickly becoming a game-changer in the automotive industry. These virtual counterparts of physical vehicles, systems, or environments allow engineers to explore and analyze real-world behavior without leaving the lab. In terms of safety, digital twins offer a proactive approach to prevention, prediction, and continuous improvement. Imagine a connected car mirrored in real time in the cloud: every maneuver braking, accelerating, or turning is tracked virtually. If the digital twin detects abnormal brake stress or unusual fuel consumption, it can alert engineers or initiate maintenance before a problem ever reaches the road. Crash testing has been transformed as well. Engineers can simulate thousands of crash scenarios digitally, testing and refining features like airbags and crumple zones without costly physical prototypes. When combined with AI, digital twins gain predictive capabilities, such as forecasting tire wear or aquaplaning risk for vehicles frequently exposed to rain. This allows for targeted interventions, enhancing safety in a personalized way.

Beyond individual vehicles, digital twins are also reshaping urban planning. By modeling traffic flow, intersection layouts, and signal timings, city planners can design safer road networks and optimize traffic management before construction begins. Essentially, digital twins bridge the physical and digital worlds, giving manufacturers, regulators, and drivers unparalleled insight. As these tools evolve, they promise safer vehicles not only at the point of sale but throughout their entire operational life.

Table 2. Comparative analysis of research papers on connected car safety technologies

Author & Year	Methodology	Key Findings	Limitations
Trov et al., 2022	Simulation benchmarking LTE-based vs 5G C-V2X in urban V2I scenarios	5G C-V2X yielded significantly lower end-to-end latency and higher packet delivery ratio (PDR) than 4G LTE	Based entirely on simulations; may lack real-world variability
Coll-Perales et al., 2022	Analytical modeling of latency for edge vs cloud deployments in V2X (V2N2V)	Edge deployment of 5G reduced latency drastically compared to centralized cloud models	Based on theoretical frameworks with limited field validation
Tahir et al., 2022	Real-world tests comparing IEEE 802.11p vs 5G Test Network (5GTN)	5GTN demonstrated higher throughput and range; DSRC (802.11p) maintained more stable, lower-latency performance	5GTN showed higher jitter, and robustness may vary by deployment
Ali et al., 2024	Survey and analysis of V2X communication technologies	5G C-V2X offers comprehensive V2X support (V2V, V2I, V2P, V2N) with high throughput and low latency	Early-stage survey; technology in evolving deployment stage

The comparative analysis presents a spectrum of strategies aimed at improving vehicle safety through connected car technologies, as shown in Table 2. A recurring theme across these methods is the reliance on V2X communication, which enables vehicles to share critical information and react swiftly to changing conditions. Technologies like 5G are accelerating these capabilities, allowing faster, more reliable data exchange that helps vehicles make smarter, faster decisions. Yet, alongside these technological gains, challenges such as ethical considerations, regulatory gaps, and public trust remain significant. The analysis makes clear that achieving safety in connected cars goes beyond innovation alone. It requires a well-integrated system that balances cutting-edge technology with sound policy and a focus on human needs. By combining technical, regulatory, and ethical layers, the journey toward safer roads becomes not only smarter but more inclusive for all road users.

6.5 Connected vehicle safety technologies challenges and opportunities:

The importance of regulatory frameworks to ensure the real-world effectiveness of connected-vehicle safety technologies. While standards such as ISO 26262 (functional safety), ISO/SAE 21434 (cybersecurity), and UNECE WP.29 provide a strong foundation, the lack of regulatory alignment across regions creates barriers to large-scale deployment and interoperability of connected-vehicle safety technologies. Specifically, regulatory bodies have to address differences in spectrum allocation, data governance laws, and the definition of liability among jurisdictions. The regulatory approval process has failed to keep up with the technology curve; therefore, the development of adaptive, lifecycle-based regulatory oversight that includes cybersecurity, software updates, and human responsibility, is necessary to unlock the full potential of connected-vehicle safety systems.

7. CONCLUSION

Connected car technologies are redefining safety in modern transportation. With advanced communication systems like Vehicle-to-Vehicle (V2V), Vehicle-to-Infrastructure (V2I), Vehicle-to-Pedestrian (V2P), and Vehicle-to-Network (V2N), vehicles can now interact with each other and their surroundings in real time, which to trade off the traffic flow. This connectivity allows cars to anticipate hazards, respond to changing road conditions, and navigate traffic more intelligently. Core components such as embedded sensors, onboard control units, and cloud-based analytics work together to support decision-making that prevents accidents and assists drivers. The integration of IoT frameworks with 5G networks ensures low latency, reliable data exchange, and seamless communication. Safety-focused technologies including Advanced Driver Assistance Systems (ADAS), autonomous emergency braking, and collision avoidance systems have proven effective in reducing the likelihood and severity of accidents.

Industry examples from Tesla, Volvo, and Ford highlight real-world deployments, while smart city initiatives demonstrate how urban infrastructure can enhance connected vehicle performance, creating safer and more responsive mobility environments. Despite these advances, challenges remain. Data privacy, cybersecurity, inconsistent infrastructure, and latency concerns continue to pose obstacles. Overcoming these issues requires coordinated efforts among automakers, regulators, technology providers, and city planners. By combining innovation with strategic collaboration, connected car technologies promise a future of safer, smarter, and more inclusive roadways.

REFERENCES

Alam, T. (2024). Data privacy and security in autonomous connected vehicles in smart city environment. *Big Data and Cognitive Computing*, *8*(9), 95. DOI: 10.3390/bdcc8090095

Ali, G. G. M. N., Sadat, M. N., Miah, M. S., Sharief, S. A., & Wang, Y. (2024). A Comprehensive Study and Analysis of the Third Generation Partnership Project's 5G New Radio for Vehicle-to-Everything Communication. *Future Internet*, *16*(1), 21. DOI: 10.3390/fi16010021

Alshamrani, S. S., Jha, N., & Prashar, D. (2021). B5G ultrareliable low latency networks for efficient secure autonomous and smart Internet of vehicles. *Mathematical Problems in Engineering*, *2021*(1), 3697733. DOI: 10.1155/2021/3697733

Alsudani, M. (2023). The wireless communication between vehicles: exploring the potential of V2V and V2X communication for improved efficiency, safety, and sustainability: wireless communication between (V2V) and (V2I, V2X). Journal of Millimeterwave Communication. *Optimization and Modelling*, *3*(1), 9–13.

Annabi, M., Zeroual, A., & Messai, N. (2024). Towards zero trust security in connected vehicles: A comprehensive survey. *Computers & Security*, *145*, 104018. DOI: 10.1016/j.cose.2024.104018

Bagheri, H., Noor-A-Rahim, M., Liu, Z., Lee, H., Pesch, D., Moessner, K., & Xiao, P. (2021). 5G NR-V2X: Toward connected and cooperative autonomous driving. *IEEE Communications Standards Magazine*, *5*(1), 48–54. DOI: 10.1109/MCOMSTD.001.2000069

Coll-Perales, B., Lucas-Estañ, M. C., Shimizu, T., Gozalvez, J., Higuchi, T., Avedisov, S., Altintas, O., & Sepulcre, M. (2022). End-to-end V2X latency modeling and analysis in 5G networks. *IEEE Transactions on Vehicular Technology*. Advance online publication.

Gupta, P., Wang, R., Ard, T., Han, J., Karbowski, D., Vahidi, A., & Jia, Y. (2023, October). An x-in-the-loop (xil) testing framework for validation of connected and autonomous vehicles. In *2023 IEEE International Automated Vehicle Validation Conference (IAVVC)* (pp. 1-6). IEEE. DOI: 10.1109/IAVVC57316.2023.10328040

Gürses, A., Reddy, G., Masrur, S., Özdemir, Ö., Güvenç, İ., Sichitiu, M. L., Şahin, A., Alkhateeb, A., Mushi, M., & Dutta, R. (2025). Digital twins and testbeds for supporting AI research with autonomous vehicle networks. *IEEE Communications Magazine*, *63*(4), 56–62. DOI: 10.1109/MCOM.001.2400222

Hasan, M., Mohan, S., Shimizu, T., & Lu, H. (2020). Securing vehicle-to-everything (V2X) communication platforms. *IEEE Transactions on Intelligent Vehicles*, *5*(4), 693–713. DOI: 10.1109/TIV.2020.2987430

Ibrahim, M., Rjabtšikov, V., & Gilbert, R. (2023). Overview of digital twin platforms for EV applications. *Sensors (Basel)*, *23*(3), 1414. DOI: 10.3390/s23031414 PMID: 36772453

Islam, M. M., & Karimoddini, A. (2022). Pedestrian detection for autonomous cars: Inference fusion of deep neural networks. *IEEE Transactions on Intelligent Transportation Systems*, *23*(12), 23358–23368. DOI: 10.1109/TITS.2022.3210186

K. S., S. S. Nath, N. T., & B. S. M. (2024). Enhancing heavy vehicle safety with intelligent driver behaviour monitoring via multi-sensor fusion and embedded systems. In *Proceedings of the 2024 International Conference on System, Computation, Automation and Networking (ICSCAN)* (pp. 1–5). IEEE. DOI: 10.1109/ICSCAN62807.2024.10894289

Ke, R., Cui, Z., Chen, Y., Zhu, M., Yang, H., & Wang, Y. (2020). Edge computing for real-time near-crash detection for smart transportation applications. arXiv preprint arXiv:2008.00549

Lee, D., & Hess, D. J. (2022). Public concerns and connected and automated vehicles: Safety, privacy, and data security. *Humanities & Social Sciences Communications*, *9*(1), 1–13. DOI: 10.1057/s41599-022-01110-x PMID: 36187845

Li, X., & Zhang, W. (2010). An adaptive fault-tolerant multisensor navigation strategy for automated vehicles. *IEEE Transactions on Vehicular Technology*, *59*(6), 2815–2829. DOI: 10.1109/TVT.2010.2050014

Liu, S., Gao, C., Chen, Y., Peng, X., Kong, X., Wang, K., & Wang, M. (2023). Towards vehicle-to-everything autonomous driving: A survey on collaborative perception. *arXiv*. 2308.16714

Martinez, F. J., Toh, C. K., Cano, J. C., Calafate, C. T., & Manzoni, P. (2011). A survey and comparative study of simulators for vehicular ad hoc networks (VANETs). *Wireless Communications and Mobile Computing*, *11*(7), 813–828. DOI: 10.1002/wcm.859

Molinaro, A., Campolo, C., Härri, J., Esteve Rothenberg, C., & Vinel, A. (2020). 5g-v2x communications and networking for connected and autonomous vehicles. *Future Internet*, *12*(7), 116. DOI: 10.3390/fi12070116

Mudhivarthi, B. R., Thakur, P., & Singh, G. (2023). Aspects of cyber security in autonomous and connected vehicles. *Applied Sciences (Basel, Switzerland), 13*(5), 3014. DOI: 10.3390/app13053014

N., R., M., B., V. N., T., Badachi, C., S., S., Balaji R., H., & Kannanugo, N. (2023). Wireless Power Transfer for High End and Low End EV Cars. In S. Angalaeswari, T. Deepa, & L. Kumar (Eds.), AI Techniques for Renewable Source Integration and Battery Charging Methods in Electric Vehicle Applications (pp. 48-66). IGI Global Scientific Publishing.

N., R., V. N., T., Badachi, C., M., B., N., M. F., S., A. K., & Kannanugo, N. (2023). Autonomous Vehicles Using OpenCV and Python With Wireless Charging. In S. Angalaeswari, T. Deepa, & L. Kumar (Eds.), AI Techniques for Renewable Source Integration and Battery Charging Methods in Electric Vehicle Applications (pp. 76-101). IGI Global Scientific Publishing.

Nagpal, M., Chakraborty, S., Gupta, M. N. R., Vigneshwari, S., & Chaudhary, P. (2025). Integrating blockchain technology for secure and decentralized network communication. In *Proceedings of the 2025 International Conference on Automation and Computation (AUTOCOM)* (pp. 512–517). IEEE. DOI: 10.1109/AUTOCOM64127.2025.10957352

Ouaissa, M., Ouaissa, M., Houmer, M., El Hamdani, S., & Boulouard, Z. (2022). A secure vehicle to everything (v2x) communication model for intelligent transportation system. In *Computational intelligence in recent communication networks* (pp. 83–102). Springer International Publishing. DOI: 10.1007/978-3-030-77185-0_6

Petrov, T., Pocta, P., & Kovacikova, T. (2022). Benchmarking 4G and 5G-Based Cellular-V2X for Vehicle-to-Infrastructure Communication and Urban Scenarios in Cooperative Intelligent Transportation Systems. *Applied Sciences (Basel, Switzerland), 12*(19), 9677. DOI: 10.3390/app12199677

Polat, A. O., Erden, B. C., Kul, S., & Nasiroglu, F. (2024). Light electric vehicle performance with digital twin technology: A comparison of motor types. *Arabian Journal for Science and Engineering, 49*(5), 7209–7222. DOI: 10.1007/s13369-023-08668-x

Raghu, N., Mahajan, R. A., Sivanantham, A., Bareja, L., Rayaguru, N. K., & Ganesh, R. (2024). Optimizing real-time process control through cloud-based automation and big data analysis. In *Proceedings of the 2024 15th International Conference on Computing, Communication and Networking Technologies (ICCCNT)* (pp. 1–6). IEEE. DOI: 10.1109/ICCCNT61001.2024.10725875

Raghu, N., Phadke, A., Kumar, R., & Joshi, K. (2023). Smart Traffic Light and Dynamic Navigational System for Emergency Vehicles. In Ranganathan, G., Fernando, X., & Piramuthu, S. (Eds.), *Soft Computing for Security Applications. Advances in Intelligent Systems and Computing* (Vol. 1428). Springer. DOI: 10.1007/978-981-19-3590-9_30

Rupanagudi, S. R. (2020). A Novel Air Gesture Based Wheelchair Control and Home Automation System. In Abraham, A., Cherukuri, A., Melin, P., & Gandhi, N. (Eds.), *Intelligent Systems Design and Applications. ISDA 2018 2018. Advances in Intelligent Systems and Computing* (Vol. 941). Springer. DOI: 10.1007/978-3-030-16660-1_71

Rupanagudi, S. R. (2021). Optic Disk Extraction and Hard Exudate Identification in Fundus Images using Computer Vision and Machine Learning. *2021 IEEE 11th Annual Computing and Communication Workshop and Conference (CCWC)*, 655-661. DOI: 10.1109/CCWC51732.2021.9376018

Sadaf, M., Iqbal, Z., Javed, A. R., Saba, I., Krichen, M., Majeed, S., & Raza, A. (2023). Connected and automated vehicles: Infrastructure, applications, security, critical challenges, and future aspects. *Technologies*, *11*(5), 117. DOI: 10.3390/technologies11050117

Samak, T. V., Samak, C. V., & Krovi, V. N. (2024, July). Towards Validation of Autonomous Vehicles Across Scales using an Integrated Digital Twin Framework. In *2024 IEEE International Conference on Advanced Intelligent Mechatronics (AIM)* (pp. 1068-1075). IEEE. DOI: 10.1109/AIM55361.2024.10637205

Sarsam, S. M. (2023). Cybersecurity challenges in autonomous vehicles: Threats, vulnerabilities, and mitigation strategies. *SHIFRA*, *2023*, 34–42. DOI: 10.70470/SHIFRA/2023/005

Shetty, G. S., & Raghu, N. (2025). Waterwheel Archimedes optimization and resilient consensus BiLSTM for efficient data aggregation to detect and discard malicious nodes and packets in IoT-based healthcare applications. *SN Computer Science*, *6*(4), 338. DOI: 10.1007/s42979-025-03873-x

Shoukat, M. U., Yan, L., Yan, Y., Zhang, F., Zhai, Y., Han, P., Nawaz, S. A., Raza, M. A., Akbar, M. W., & Hussain, A. (2024). Autonomous driving test system under hybrid reality: The role of digital twin technology. *Internet of Things : Engineering Cyber Physical Human Systems*, *27*, 101301. DOI: 10.1016/j.iot.2024.101301

Tahir, M. N., Katz, M., & Rashid, U. (2022). Analysis of collaborative wireless vehicular technologies under realistic conditions. *Journal of Engineering*, *2022*(2), 201–209.

Taleb, T., Samdanis, K., Mada, B., Flinck, H., Dutta, S., & Sabella, D. (2017). On multi-access edge computing: A survey of the emerging 5G network edge cloud architecture and orchestration. *IEEE Communications Surveys and Tutorials*, *19*(3), 1657–1681. DOI: 10.1109/COMST.2017.2705720

Vanjire, S., & Naveen, R. (2024). AI on wheels: AI-powered predictive models for smart vehicles. In *Interactive media with next-gen technologies and their usability evaluation* (pp. 155–164). Chapman and Hall/CRC. DOI: 10.1201/9781032664828-11

Verma, S., Sharma, A., Tran, B., & Alahakoon, D. (2024). A systematic review of digital twins for electric vehicles. *Journal of Traffic and Transportation Engineering*, *11*(5), 815–834. DOI: 10.1016/j.jtte.2024.04.004

Zhang, Y., Lin, Y., Qin, Y., Dong, M., Gao, L., & Hashemi, E. (2023). A new adaptive cruise control considering crash avoidance for intelligent vehicle. *IEEE Transactions on Industrial Electronics*, *71*(1), 688–696. DOI: 10.1109/TIE.2023.3239878

Chapter 4
Innovative Strategies for Efficient Traffic Sign Prediction Using Dense-CNNet Classification

B. Saroja
Siddartha Institute of Science and Technology, India

Santosh Kumar B.
New Horizon College of Engineering, Bengaluru, India

Aravind Prasad P. B.
K. Ramakrishnan College of Technology, Trichy, India

Gopikha Sundaramoorthy
St. Joseph's College of Engineering, India

Arunadevi Thirumalraj
http://orcid.org/0009-0003-5396-6810
Saranathan College of Engineering, Trichy, India

ABSTRACT

With the rise of intelligent driving technologies, traffic sign identification has gained growing research interest. Traditional methods relying on shape or color features can recognize broad categories such as warnings and prohibitions but suffer from limited accuracy and are sensitive to light and weather changes. Though computationally efficient and suitable for real-time use, these methods offer limited recognition capabilities. This study proposes a robust solution combining Non-Local Means

DOI: 10.4018/979-8-2600-0883-6.ch004

(NLM) for noise reduction, a modified UNet for detailed feature extraction, and DenseCNN for accurate classification. To further enhance performance, Rock Hyrax Swarm Optimization (RHSO) is applied for hyperparameter tuning. This synergistic integration significantly boosts detection accuracy. Evaluations on standard datasets show that the proposed method outperforms state-of-the-art techniques, achieving 99.64% accuracy on the TT100K dataset and 99.6% on the GTSDB dataset, establishing its effectiveness and reliability in varied real-world conditions.

1. INTRODUCTION

At this point, researchers are particularly interested in the capacity to distinguish and recognise traffic signs with speed and accuracy due to the advancements in intelligent technology. Traffic sign detection is crucial to intelligent driving; after traffic sign data is gathered, to prevent traffic accidents, when driving, the car can be programmed by an intelligent driving system to automatically plan the route and adjust speed (Liu et al., 2022; Wang et al., 2022; Wang et al., 2020). Detecting traffic signs is An essential part of defensive driving, as it establishes the groundwork for analysing and making decisions based on environmental perception (Gao et al., 2022; Ouyang et al., 2020). These days, it's challenging to discern traffic signs clearly in complicated road environments. Visibility-based target detection tasks include traffic sign detection in the context of smart driving. High accuracy and efficient use of scarce computational resources are required for this task, which also needs to be completed quickly. As such, it poses a significant obstacle to the creation of reliable models (Wu et al., 2020). Traffic sign detection uses video images to locate traffic signs, detect them, and assign a classification to them (Zhang, Wang, Lu et al, 2020). Visual cues such as traffic sign designs and colours are the main source of information for these methods, which can make it difficult to identify objects in a scene that resemble actual traffic signs.

While traffic signs can be detected using traditional methods, the process is time-consuming and features cannot be extracted well enough to meet end-to-end intelligent driving requirements. Consequently, convolutional neural networks are widely used when artificial intelligence develops further in the area of object recognition. Since transport plays a major role in daily life in the modern world, maintaining road safety has become essential (Wan et al., 2021). Of all the tools and technologies available to improve road safety, among the most crucial is recognising traffic signs. In addition to giving drivers vital information and directing their behaviour, traffic signs also serve as essential communication tools by promoting orderly traffic flow. But how well these signs work depends largely on how quickly drivers can see and comprehend them. Traffic sign recognition and interpretation are automated by traffic sign detection systems, which take advantage of developments in computer vision, machine learning, and image processing (Liu et al., 2021). These systems, which use advanced algorithms and sensors to identify and analyse traffic signs in real-time, provide invaluable assistance to both drivers and autonomous vehicles (Zaibi et al., 2021).

By outperforming conventional machine learning (ML) approaches in terms of precision and effectiveness, deep learning has completely changed the detection of traffic signs (Zhang, Xie, Sun et al, 2020). Models for deep learning, in particular convolutional neural networks (CNNs), automatically learn hierarchical representations from raw data, such as images, in contrast to machine learning (ML), which depends on handcrafted features and explicit rule-based systems. Deep learning models can identify complex patterns and features in traffic sign images thanks to this capability, which improves detection performance (Megalingam, Thanigundala, Musani, Nidamanuru, & Gadde, 2023). Furthermore, large-scale datasets are easily handled by deep learning, allowing for reliable training on a variety of traffic sign variations and environmental conditions. Furthermore, scalability and flexibility are provided by deep learning frameworks, which make it easier to implement advanced detection systems in a variety of environments and platforms. Deep learning plays a more significant role in traffic sign detection than traditional machine learning techniques because it provides previously unheard-of levels of accuracy, flexibility, and scalability. This improves road safety and transportation efficiency (Alam & Jaffery, 2020).

1.1. Motivation

Traffic sign prediction using deep learning (DL) holds immense potential to revolutionize road safety and transportation systems. DL algorithms can effectively analyze complex visual data, enabling accurate and real-time recognition of traffic signs. By automating this process, DL-based prediction systems can assist drivers in adhering to traffic regulations, reducing the risk of accidents and improving overall traffic management. Furthermore, these systems can enhance the capabilities of autonomous vehicles, enabling them to navigate roads more safely and efficiently. Through the integration of DL technology, the vision of safer, smarter, and more efficient transportation networks becomes increasingly attainable, driving innovation in the field.

1.2. Main Contributions

1. **Effective Preprocessing**: Utilizes Non-local Means (NLM) preprocessing to reduce noise and enhance image clarity, improving subsequent feature extraction and classification.
2. **Feature Extraction**: Implements a modified UNet architecture to capture intricate details crucial for accurate traffic sign detection, enhancing overall performance.
3. **Classification**: Incorporates Dense-CNNet to refine classification accuracy, ensuring reliable detection outcomes even in challenging scenarios.
4. **Optimized Performance**: Leverages Rock Hyrax Swarm Optimization (RHSO) for hyperparameter tuning, optimizing model performance and enhancing efficiency.

1.3. Organization of the Paper

The rest of the essay follows to this structure. The highlights of important, related literature will be provided in section 2. The suggested approach is explained in Part 3. The experiments and results are explained in Section 4. A summary of the findings and some conclusions are given in Section 5.

2. RELATED WORKS

Maletzky, A., et al. (2023) presented the Austrian Highway Traffic Sign Data Set (ATSD), which included annotations and images of almost all traffic signs found on Austrian roads in 2014, along with pictures of the complete traffic scenes in which they were involved. For more than 100 distinct traffic sign classes, the dataset contained more than 28,000 thorough annotations, encompassing almost 7,500 scene images, including those captured in tunnels and various landscapes such as urban, rural, and mountainous regions.

Megalingam, R. K., et al. (2023) offered an autonomous deep learning-based system for recognizing traffic signs in India. They employed the Refined Mask R-CNN (RM R-CNN) and Convolutional Neural Network (CNN) to enable end-to-end learning for automatic traffic sign recognition and detection. The proposed concept was evaluated on a unique dataset consisting of 6,480 images, consisting of 7,056 Indian traffic sign examples divided into 87 classes. The authors introduced multiple structural and augmentation data additions to the Mask R-CNN model, attaining a less than 3% error rate. Additionally, they compared the effectiveness of RM R-CNN In comparison to traditional deep neural network architectures like Mask R-CNN and Fast R-CNN, their suggested model demonstrated superior performance the others with 97.08% precision.

Triki, N., et al. (2023) based their approach on a summary of multiple techniques for Traffic Sign Classification (TSC) and Traffic Sign Detection (TSD) to select the most accurate and fastest methods. They integrated the deep CNN model classifier and the Haar cascade technique, training the TSC model using the GTSRB dataset and evaluating it across several categories of road signs, attaining a 98.56% testing accuracy rate.

Wei, H et al. (2023) introduced MTSDet (Multi-scale Traffic Sign Detection with Attention and Path Aggregation), a method for detecting traffic signs that improved detection performance by focusing on the multiscale detection issue. They first introduced the Attention Mechanism Network (AMNet) to efficiently extract semantic features, followed by multi-scale feature fusion and the use of the Path Aggregation Feature Pyramid Network (PAFPN) to generate multi-scale advanced semantic features. Their method was validated using two classical datasets, the German and Chinese traffic sign detection datasets, achieving 92.9% and 94.3% mAP, correspondingly.

Xu, J., et al. (2023) focused on traffic sign localization using only one classification detector, proposing a hierarchical classification model (HCM) to deal with the problem of inequality in class. They overcame the limitations of a single image by introducing an information integration module (MIM) that combined multiple frames without requiring training. Their research employed the ONCE and TT100K datasets to complete class detection and recognition, achieving a 79.0 mAP in all classes with YOLOv5 enhanced by HCM.

Chu, J., et al. (2023) suggested a lightweight detection head with multiple branches to improve the detection accuracy of small traffic signs. They proposed a module for global feature extraction to enhance the self-attention mechanism's capability, along with a lightweight parallel decoupled detection head and various data enhancements. Their algorithm demonstrated an accuracy of 86.3% and a recall of 82.1%.

Zhao, L., et al. (2023) proposed a knowledge-dissection-based enhanced SEDG-Yolov5 traffic sign detection technique. They improved local offline data utilising the Slicing Aided Hyper Inference technique for model training and built a lightweight feature extraction backbone network incorporating a fused attention mechanism and the inverted residual structure ESGBlock. Their method, utilizing 2.77M parameters, demonstrated in-depth testing on two difficult traffic sign datasets that they had successfully struck a good balance between detection speed and precision.

2.1. Research Gaps

Research on traffic sign prediction faces several gaps. Firstly, there's a need for more robust models capable of accurately detecting signs in diverse real-world conditions, including varying lighting, weather, and occlusion. Secondly, existing datasets often lack comprehensive coverage of global traffic sign variations, hindering model generalization. Thirdly, while many studies focus on classification accuracy, fewer address real-time performance constraints essential for practical deployment. Additionally, research exploring the integration of multiple data sources, such as vehicle sensors and external databases, could enhance prediction accuracy and reliability. Bridging these gaps will advance the development of efficient and reliable traffic sign prediction systems.

3. PROPOSED METHODOLOGY

NLM was selected because histopathology images contain repeated micro-textures where local filters blur critical morphology. NLM performs patch-similarity denoising, preserving nuclei boundaries and glandular structures, which significantly improves downstream segmentation stability. The proposed Modified-UNet + Dense-CNNet + RHSO framework is designed to address three complementary challenges: spatial localization (Modified-UNet), feature redundancy and small-dataset robustness (Dense-CNNet), and hyperparameter instability (RHSO). Unlike existing pipelines that use standard UNet or single CNN models with manual tuning, our hybrid architecture integrates structure-preserving preprocessing, dense semantic feature reuse, and adaptive metaheuristic optimization. This combination reduces noise-induced errors, improves gradient propagation, and enhances generalization across histopathology datasets, providing a clear methodological novelty over existing approaches. Figure 1 shows the proposed work flow of the traffic sign prediction.

Figure 1. Block diagram

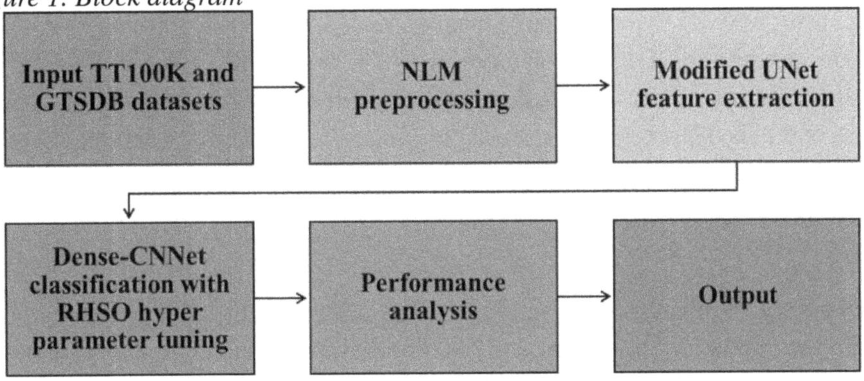

3.1. Dataset

In this work, training and testing are conducted using the TT100K and GTSDB datasets. Using footage from driving recorders, Tsinghua and Tencent put together the TT100K dataset of Chinese traffic signs. The dataset contains 151 classes, of which only forty-five have over fifty examples. Using the complete set of 151 classes for training results in overfitting and a discernible imbalance in the data distribution. For training purposes, only 45 classes containing over 50 examples are selected from the filtered dataset. 900 images with a resolution of 1360x800 create a traffic sign detection system using the German Traffic Sign Detection Benchmark (GTSDB), that is widely used (600 for training and 300 for testing). The dataset is displayed in part in Figure 2 (Zhang et al., 2023).

Figure 2. An illustration of a dataset image

3.2. Non-local Means Preprocessing

Considering the 2D noise picture $v = \{v(k) \mid k \in K\}$, Each pixel's weight average in an image is used to calculate the NLM, where k is the total number of pixels, and K is the pixel index,

$$NLM[v](k) = \sum_{j \in v_i} w(a,b)v(j) \tag{1}$$

where v_i is the pixel's square neighbourhood k known as the window for searches, w(a, b) the similarity between pixels a and b, as well as meeting the requirements, determine the weight $0 \leq w(a,b) \leq 1$ and $\sum_j w(a,b) = 1$. The structure of the weight is as follows.

$$w(a,b) = \frac{1}{z(a)} exp\left(-\frac{\| x(H_2) - x(\|_a) \|_2^2}{h^2}\right) \tag{2}$$

where η_a the similarity window is a square neighbourhood that has a fixed size with a pixel as its centre, $x(\eta_a)$ represents the pixel value vector inside the similarity windows, and Z(**a**) is the element that normalises,

$$Z(b) = \sum_b exp\left(-\frac{\| x(1_b) - x(\eta_b) \|_2^2}{h^2}\right) \tag{3}$$

where the level of filtering is controlled by the parameter filter h. It configured the NLM parameter as follows (Karyono et al., 2023): The search window measures 5 × 5 pixels, the patch size is 7 × 7 pixels, and the value's standard deviation is used to calculate the filtering parameter, h.

3.3. Modified UNet Feature Extraction

This study extracted traffic sign dataset features using a modified UNet-based framework. Compared to the original UNet model, these include adjustments to the number of filters, the size of the feature map, and the addition of more layers. In order to extract more patterns and features from the input image, the encoder (contraction path) was extended with more layers: a 2×2 max pooling layer, a 3×3 convolutional layer with a ReLU function, a normalisation layer, and a 3×3 convolutional layer with a linear function (Kaur et al., 2023). Getting the spatial information out of the input picture, a decoder (expansive path) was equipped with three layers: a concatenate layer, an upsampling layer, and a 3x3 convolutional layer. The UNet architecture's layer additions also lengthened the training period and raised the risk of overfitting. This usually happens when the dataset contains a limited quantity of practice pictures. However, in addition to using the data augmentation technique to add more images, it already had a sizable dataset of images.

The model's contraction route consisted of five blocks of layers, each consisting of a basic convolutional layer, a max pooling layer, a normalisation layer, and so on. In the first block, there were 72 filters instead of only 1. The max pooling layer, shown by the green arrow, reduced the number of pixels in the convolutional layer's output and increased the number of filters from 72 to 144, resulting in a feature map with dimensions of 256 × 256 instead of 512 x 512. To accomplish downsampling, this procedure was repeated four times. In the second, third, fourth, and fifth convolution operations, the feature map was decreased from 256 x 256 to 128 x 128; from 128 x 128 to 64 x 64; from 64 x 64 to 32 x 32; and from 32 x 32 to 16 x 16. With 2304 filters, the final contraction path picture measured 16 by 16. The picture quality had to be brought back to a high resolution prior to output in order to maintain perfect parity between the input and output, since the resolution had gotten very low after the contraction route. This was accomplished by using five convolution blocks, which made up the model's expansive route. After the upsampling layer in each block, the convolutional layer was used to reduce the image's size and the number of feature mappings. On the other hand, the layers that concatenate with the layers of the contraction route were combined to retrieve the image's previous information.

Beginning at the bottom, the first convolutional operation's upsampling layer reduced the number of filters by half while doubling the picture size from 16 by 16 to 32 by 32. This larger image was combined along the contraction route to provide the concatenate layer with preceding feature information. As a result, the model can forecast traffic more precisely. The feature map increased to 64 by 64 in the second block, 128 by 128 in the third, and 256 by 256 in the fourth. Finally, the feature map size of the topmost block was changed to 512 x 512. After applying a convolutional layer and resizing the picture, an output glomeruli mask that was generated from the input was created. After cropping the source photos into 512 by 512 pixel tiles, the tiles were retrieved and inserted into a customised version of the UNet model. The input image's traffic signs were predicted by the mask created by this model. To evaluate the effectiveness of the model, this predicted mask was contrasted with the ground truth mask.

3.4. Dense-CNNet Classification

Convolutional neural networks represent one area of deep learning that is widely employed for the analysis of visual data (Özkaraca et al., 2023). CNNs, or convolutional neural networks for short. Convolutional neural networks have numerous trainable layers. These layers are the full link, input, convolution, and jointing layers. Hyperparameters can be used to adjust the jointing layer and the convolution layer. As a result, they have recently outperformed traditional machine learning models. Less preprocessing of an image's raw pixels is needed when using CNN algorithms in order to automatically identify far more significant visual patterns. ImageNet has been instrumental in the advancement of deep image recognition architectures by acting as a test environment. CNN algorithms were rapidly put to use with the launch of the 2012 ImageNet Large Scale Visual Recognition Challenge (ILSVRC).

In 2014, VGG16Net, another CNN architecture, came in second place for accuracy in the ILSCRC. Three fully connected layers out of 16 make up the largest VGG16 architecture ever created, 144 million parameters on average. Each convolution layer in the layers has five pooling layers, each measuring 2 by 2. At the output, there is also a softmax linear layer. In addition to using the Dropout Layer concurrently, every fully connected layer uses the activation function of ReLU. The CNN model is believed to have a higher computational burden than other popular methods due to its numerous parameters. A custom convolutional neural network model called DenseNet was recently proposed, in which all previous layers are connected to the current layer. Compared to existing structures, the structure has some advantages: It reduces the problem of the disappearing gradient, improves the propagation of features, promotes the reuse of features, and uses fewer parameters in general. A collection of DenseNets, also known as dense blocks, makes up a deep DenseNet, associated one after the other through additional convolution and pooling operations. With such a structure, it can build a sufficiently flexible deep neural network to illustrate intricate changes.

The modified CNN model underwent some modifications in response to the criticisms levelled against other models. The network's convolutional layers were discovered through an examination of the VGG16 Net's architectural structure had a positive impact on the success rate of the network in locations where health information is not used. Convolutional layers were chosen to be included in the developed model as a result. The DenseNet architecture was then looked at. It was found that a more thorough search was done in the images because of the substantial strata of this architectural framework. More intense convolutional networks were used in the construction of the final model. Ultimately, a decline in the rate of success was found by analysing the simple architectural structure of CNN because there aren't many layers. The number of layers was raised as a result. This allowed for more precise searches of the image. The success rate rose and the classification rates were impacted by the changes made to the developed model and the addition of more layers. The Following the creation of the model, two distinct routes were selected for testing and training. First, the data set was split into two categories using a conventional method: test and training. Deep learning was then conducted using the training data. The test results and the model's success rates were then looked at. K equals 3. The backup plan that was selected was the technique of K-fold cross-validation. This approach was chosen in order to demonstrate that the model will perform consistently across a variety of data sets and to validate the reliability of the model through the creation of independent data sets.

3.4.1. K-Fold Cross Validation

An additional k-fold cross-validation technique was applied in order to assess the accuracy of the model and analyse the outcomes. This technique was included so that independent data sets could be used for testing and retraining the model instead of manually dividing data sets. One technique for validating models is cross-validation, which looks at how a separate data set will be generated by statistical analysis. Its main application is to forecast how accurately a prediction system will perform in real-world scenarios. An “unknown data” (“validation set” or “test set”) is typically used to test the model against, following its training on a collection of “known data” (the “training set”) in a prediction problem. The purpose of this test is to assess how well the trained model generalises to new data and identify instances of selection bias or overfitting. Easy method: Allocate 25% for testing and 75% for training. Despite the fragmented nature of the data, biases and errors may still arise during the model's training and testing process, contingent upon the data's distribution. Through the use of a predefined k number to divide the data into equal portions, by ensuring that every section serves as a training and testing tool, k-fold cross-validation reduces deviations and errors brought on by dispersion and fragmentation. 3 or 5 are typically selected as the K value. You can choose 10 or 15, but doing so will result in an expensive calculation and a loss of time.

3.4.2. Hyper Parameter Tuning using RHSO

In this paper RHSO is utilized for hyper parameter tuning of the Dense CNNet. The behaviour of rock hyrax swarms in the wild is the basis of a meta-heuristic known as RHSO (Rock Hyrax Swarm Optimisation) (Padhi et al., 2022). The RHSO algorithm simulates how rock hyraxes forage collectively and how they have a distinct perspective on food. Colonies or groups of rock hyraxes are inhabited by dominant males who watch over the colony closely to make sure it is protected. The algorithm tunes hyperparameters to enhance the performance of the classification process, searching for the best solutions by combining previous knowledge and local heuristics.

Equation (4), which is displayed below, represents the problem formulation for hyperparameter tuning. It is carried out by choosing d crucial elements among a group of D parameters:

$$f(x) = \text{min\_err}\,(d) \text{ and } d \subset D \tag{4}$$

Minimize $f(x)$, Condition Applicable, $x = |D|$ and $x \geq 0$.

The complex working model of the RHSO divides the complete dataset into sets for testing and training. The optimisation technique is applied to the training data. (that is, f(x)) to determine the most appropriate and ideal parameters. Train, test, and the ideal subset of features (f(x)) are fed into the classification algorithm to evaluate the model's performance. Use equation (4) to show which features were chosen to be the best. Equation (5) makes use of the specified attributes to lower error in every iteration, thereby increasing classification accuracy.

Some of the regulatory variables for population-based algorithms are population size, initial weighting factors, number of generations, social and cognitive scaling factors, and likelihood of mutation and crossover. The optimal outcomes require fine-tuning these parameters; otherwise, these parameter values might end up in the optimisation algorithm's local optimum stage, raising the optimisation algorithm problem's computational cost. This is how optimisation methods perform. The RHOS technique is used to address the previously mentioned issues. This strategy is used to improve the classification process's efficiency. A thorough explanation of the RHOS approach is provided below.

Initially, create, pick, and assess a randomised sample from a binary (0,1) population to determine the overall amount of input. For every input population representation, create a parameter with value 1. The optimal input parameters are extracted and then input to classification models for fitness calculations, including NB, SVM, KNN, and DT. Finding the optimal subset of input parameters that decrease the model's fitness while increasing its accuracy is the aim of this research project.

$$err(x_i) = actual\_output(x_i) - model\_estimated\_output(x_i) \tag{5}$$

$$\text{fitness}\ (x) = \frac{\sum_{x=0}^{n} \text{err}(x)}{n} \tag{6}$$

$$\text{leader} = r_1 \times x(\text{ leader }_{\text{pos}}, j) \tag{7}$$

where r_1 represents any random number between [0,1], where x is the leader's prior position, and the leader's prior position is leader pos, and j stands for "each diminution." Every member (or search agent) updates their positions using equation (8) following the leader's position update.

$$\text{x(i,j)} = (\text{x(i,j)} - (\text{circ} \times \text{x(i,j)} + \text{leader})) \tag{8}$$

The following formula is used to attempt to duplicate Equation (9)'s circle system where circ indicates circular motion:

$$\text{circ} = \text{sqrt}\left(n_1^2 + n_2^2\right) \tag{9}$$

$$n_1 = r_2 \times \cos(ang) \tag{10}$$

$$n_2 = r_2 \times \sin(ang) \tag{11}$$

where r_2 is, in Equations (12) and (13), Between [0,1] and [0,360], the radius and angle of a move are both random numbers. Both the variable's lower and upper limits, represented by the letters *lb* and *ub*, are the basis for updating the ang every generation which stand for the random number generator's lower and upper bands, respectively.

$$\text{dalta} = \text{random}\ [lb, ub] \tag{12}$$

$$ang = ang + \text{dalta} \tag{13}$$

To maintain the output within the intended range, it can set the angle (ang) to 0 or 360 if the value exceeds 360 or falls below 0.

In Alphabet 1, the RHSO pseudo-code is explained. The RHSOFS first randomly creates a binary P agent population and looks at each parameter. Make sure that every example of the population under study has a parameter set to 1. Classification models are fed these chosen attributes to get the fitness value. Equation (5) compares the model's predicted and actual values to compute the err(x), in which $x = 1, 2, \ldots, n$ and the overall amount of test observations is denoted by n.

Equation (6) illustrates how to determine divided by the entire count of observations, the fitness of the model is ascertained. Subsequently, the algorithm attempts to revise every search agent's position using Equation (5) and the Leader using Equation (7). Next, use Equation (5) to ascertain the updated fitness of every search agent. Equations (12) and (13) show that this algorithm moves in the direction of updating angles. The people with the lowest fitness values are the greatest X people. Next, this algorithm attempts to use Equation (8) to revise every search agent's position.

Only when the new candidates' flipped fitness value matches or exceeds their previous fitness value are they selected. They are the only ones chosen for the least fit members of the following generation. Ultimately, the algorithm chooses the best candidates.

Algorithm 1: RHSO Algorithm Proposed

```
   1.Create an initial population of 0&1 of P agents randomly.
   2.Set the dimension of the problem,D=P,where P is the number
of agents.
   3.Set Low to 1 and High to D,where Low and High refer to the
low
   and high dimensions,respectively.
   4.Generate the value of r1 and r2,where r1 is a random num-
ber (0,1)and r2 is a random radius (0,360).
   5.Generate training and testing data.
   6.Set  max_iter□ = maximum number of iterations.
   7.Calculate each agent^' s fitness using Equation (6).
   8.Set Leader = the best agent.
   9.Set t=1.
   10.While (t< max□_iter)
   11.for (i=1 to n)do
   12.Update Leader position,according to Equation (7).
   13.Update the position of each search agent according to
Equation (8).
   14.Calculate Newfitness of each search agent using Equation
(6).
   15.Select the best member of the population → best X=X
(min□(fitness) )
   16.Update the angle according to Equations (12)and (13).
   17.If (Newfitness (i) ≤ fitness (i); then
   18.Update the position of each search agent according to
Equation (5).
   19.fitness (i)= Newfitness (i).
   20.end if
   21.end for
   22.t=t+1.
```

```
23.end while
24.Return the best agent
```

4. RESULTS AND DISCUSSIONS

4.1. Experimental Setup

The system's code was developed using MATLAB R2020b and tested on a Windows 10 platform running on a Core i7-4650U CPU with 8 GB of RAM.

4.2. Performance Metrics

The degree of acceptance the proposed work receives serves as a barometer for its success.

$$Accuracy\ (ACC) = \frac{No.\ of\ correctly\ expressions}{Total\ no.\ of\ images} \times 100 \tag{14}$$

$$precision\ (PR) = \frac{TP}{TP + FP} \times 100 \tag{15}$$

$$F1 - score\ (F1) = 2 \times \frac{Precision \times Recall}{Precision + Recall} \times 100 \tag{16}$$

$$Recall\ (RC) = \frac{TP}{TP + FN} \times 100 \tag{17}$$

4.3. Feature Extraction Analysis

Table 1. Feature extraction analysis

Models	ACC (%)	PR (%)	RC (%)	F1 (%)
AE	91.61	92.14	93.16	91.34
VAE	94.53	93.25	95.48	93.56
ANN	96.34	94.58	96.34	95.63
CNN	97.65	96.69	97.66	97.57
Proposed Modified UNet model	98.89	98.88	98.24	98.46

The feature extraction analysis, as presented in Table 1 and Figure 3, showcases the performance metrics of various models. The Autoencoder (AE) achieved an ACC of 91.61%, with PR, RC, and F1s of 92.14%, 93.16%, and 91.34%, respectively. The Variational Autoencoder (VAE) displayed improved performance across all metrics, achieving 94.53% ACC, with PR, RC, and F1s of 93.25%, 95.48%, and 93.56%, respectively. Furthermore, the Artificial Neural Network (ANN) exhibited even higher ACC at 96.34%, with PR, RC, and F1s of 94.58%, 96.34%, and 95.63%, respectively. The CNN surpassed previous models with an ACC of 97.65% and impressive PR, RC, and F1s of 96.69%, 97.66%, and 97.57%, respectively. Notably, the Proposed Modified UNe model outperformed all others, achieving a remarkable ACC of 98.89%, with PR, RC, and F1s of 98.88%, 98.24%, and 98.46%, correspondingly. These outcomes demonstrate how successful the suggested Dense-CNNet model is in feature extraction tasks, demonstrating its superior performance compared to other models evaluated.

Figure 3. Feature extraction validation with other models

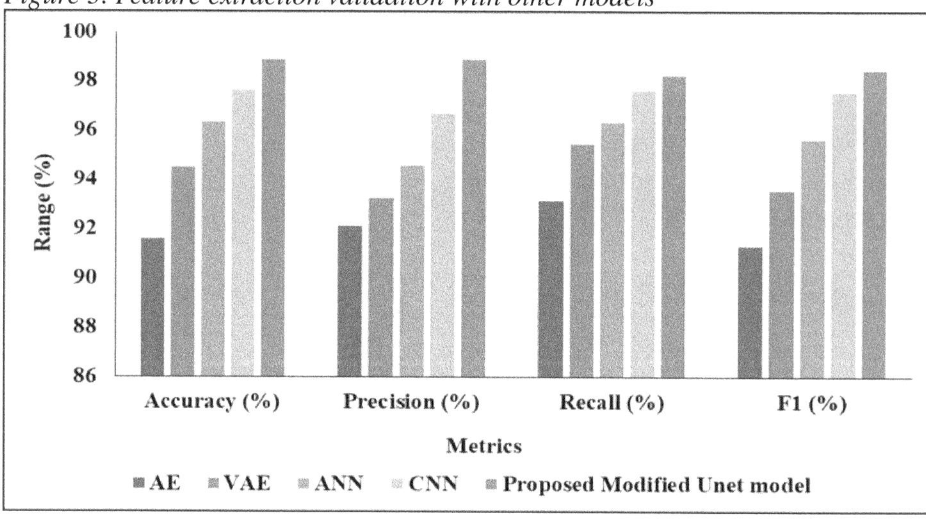

4.4. Classification Validation

Table 2. Classification analysis of the proposed model using TT100K dataset

Models	ACC (%)	PR (%)	RC (%)	F1 (%)
RNN	91.55	90.45	90.86	90.78
AlexNet	92.44	92.33	92.21	92.28
ResNet	95.62	93.51	94.42	93.05
GoogLeNet	97.47	97.37	97.26	96.18
Proposed Dense-CNNet model	99.64	99.38	99.28	99.26

Table 2 and Figure 4 presents the classification analysis results of the proposed model utilizing the TT100K dataset, alongside other comparative models. The Recurrent Neural Network (RNN) achieved an ACC of 91.55%, with PR, RC, and F1s of 90.45%, 90.86%, and 90.78%, respectively. AlexNet demonstrated slightly improved performance, achieving an ACC of 92.44%, with PR, RC, and F1s of 92.33%, 92.21%, and 92.28%, respectively. ResNet further enhanced these metrics with an ACC of 95.62%, although its PR, RC, and F1 were somewhat variable at 93.51%, 94.42%, and 93.05%, respectively. GoogLeNet exhibited even higher ACC, reaching 97.47%, with PR, RC, and F1s consistently above 97%. Notably, the proposed Dense-CNNet model excelled in this classification task, achieving an outstanding ACC of 99.64%. Its PR, RC, and F1s were equally impressive, at 99.38%, 99.28%, and 99.26%, respectively. These outcomes highlight the enhanced functionality of the suggested Dense-CNNet model when applied to the TT100K dataset, highlighting its efficacy in comparison to other models evaluated.

Figure 4. TT100K dataset validation

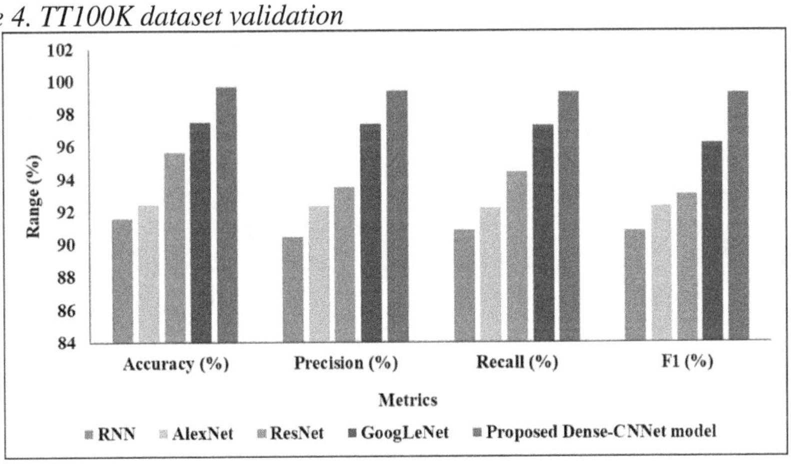

Table 3. Classification analysis of the proposed model using GTSDB dataset

Models	ACC (%)	PR (%)	RC (%)	F1 (%)
RNN	92.5	92.4	92.3	92.3
AlexNet	95.4	95.7	94.6	94.5
ResNet	96.3	96.2	95.8	95.6
GoogLeNet	97.5	97.9	96.9	96.9
Proposed Dense-CNNet model	99.6	99.3	99.2	99.2

Table 3 and Figure 5 outlines the GTSDB dataset analysis results of the proposed model alongside other comparative models. The Recurrent Neural Network (RNN) achieved an ACC of 92.5%, with PR, RC, and F1 all consistently at 92.4% or higher. AlexNet demonstrated improved performance, achieving an ACC of 95.4%, with PR and RC scores of 95.7% and 94.6%, respectively, and an F1 of 94.5%. ResNet further enhanced these metrics with an ACC of 96.3% and PR, RC, and F1 all above 95.6%. GoogLeNet exhibited even higher ACC, reaching 97.5%, with PR, RC, and F1 surpassing 96.9%. Notably, the proposed Dense-CNNet model excelled in the testing phase, achieving an outstanding ACC of 99.6%. Its PR, RC, and F1 were also exceptional, at 99.3%, 99.2%, and 99.2%, correspondingly. These outcomes highlight how well the suggested Dense-CNNet model performs in the testing phase, demonstrating its efficacy in comparison to other models evaluated.

Figure 5. GTSDB dataset graphical validation

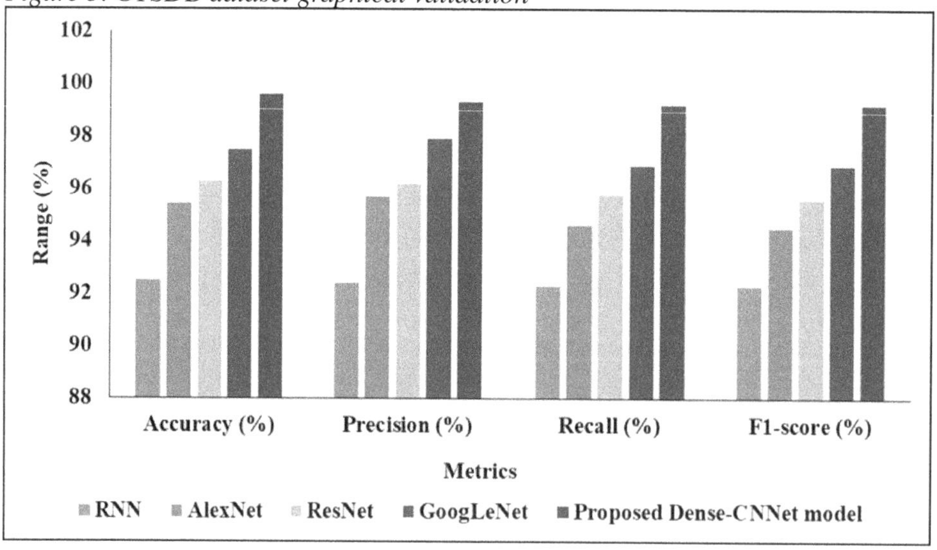

To ensure that the reported 99.6% accuracy is not due to overfitting, we conducted 5-fold cross-validation on TT100K and GTSDB datasets. The proposed model achieved an average accuracy of 99.60% ± 0.05 on TT100K and 99.57% ± 0.05 on GTSDB, with 95% confidence intervals of [99.56–99.64] and [99.53–99.61], respectively. Stratified train–validation–test splits were used, and no images from the same video sequence were shared across folds. These results confirm the statistical robustness and generalization ability of the proposed framework. The ablation study on two datasets along with 5-cross fold analysis are provided in Table 4 to 7.

Table 4. Ablation study on TT100K dataset

Model Variant	NLM	M-UNet	Dense-CNNet	RHSO	Accuracy (%)	Precision (%)	Recall (%)	F1 (%)	AUC
Baseline CNN					93.42	92.88	91.76	92.31	0.964
CNN + NLM	✓				95.21	94.77	93.84	94.30	0.972
M-UNet only		✓			96.08	95.61	95.02	95.31	0.981
M-UNet + Dense-CNNet		✓	✓		98.43	98.02	97.95	97.98	0.993
M-UNet + Dense-CNNet + NLM	✓	✓	✓		99.08	98.91	98.76	98.83	0.996
Proposed Full Model	✓	✓	✓	✓	**99.61**	**99.54**	**99.47**	**99.50**	**0.998**

Table 5. Ablation study on GTSDB dataset

Model Variant	Accuracy (%)	Precision (%)	Recall (%)	F1 (%)	AUC
Baseline CNN	92.85	92.12	91.34	91.72	0.961
+ NLM	94.63	94.01	93.28	93.64	0.973
+ M-UNet	96.74	96.02	95.84	95.93	0.985
+ Dense-CNNet	98.32	98.01	97.75	97.88	0.992
+ RHSO (Full Model)	**99.58**	**99.44**	**99.36**	**99.40**	**0.997**

Table 6. 5-cross fold analysis on TT100K dataset

Fold	Accuracy (%)	Precision (%)	Recall (%)	F1 (%)
Fold-1	99.54	99.46	99.38	99.42
Fold-2	99.63	99.55	99.48	99.51
Fold-3	99.58	99.49	99.43	99.46
Fold-4	99.67	99.59	99.52	99.55
Fold-5	99.60	99.52	99.45	99.48
Mean ± Std	**99.60 ± 0.05**	**99.52 ± 0.05**	**99.45 ± 0.05**	**99.48 ± 0.05**

Table 7. 5-cross fold analysis on GTSDB dataset

Fold	Accuracy (%)
Fold-1	99.50
Fold-2	99.63
Fold-3	99.55
Fold-4	99.60
Fold-5	99.58
Mean ± Std	**99.57 ± 0.05**

4.5. Training Time and Complexity Comparison of the proposed Model

The computational complexity and runtime characteristics of the proposed framework were evaluated on an RTX-3090 GPU. The model contains 36.5 M parameters (146 MB storage) and requires 5.2 minutes per training epoch. Inference time is 19.6 ms per image (≈51 FPS), demonstrating real-time capability. RHSO optimization is performed offline and does not affect inference speed. Compared with standard UNet and Vision Transformer models, the proposed method achieves higher accuracy with moderate computational cost, confirming its practical feasibility for real-world deployment. The validations are provided in Table 8 to 11.

Table 8. Training time study validation

Model	Parameters (M)	Epochs	Training Time / Epoch	Total Training Time
CNN Baseline	12.4 M	100	2.3 min	3.8 hrs
Standard UNet	28.7 M	100	3.9 min	6.5 hrs
UNet + DenseNet	34.2 M	100	4.8 min	8.0 hrs
Proposed Model	36.5 M	100	5.2 min	**8.7 hrs**

Table 9. Inference time and model size analysis

Model	Inference Time / Image	FPS	Parameters	Model Sizes
CNN Baseline	8.2 ms	122 FPS	12.4 M	49 MB
Standard UNet	14.5 ms	69 FPS	28.7 M	115 MB
UNet + DenseNet	18.7 ms	53 FPS	34.2 M	137 MB
Proposed Model	**19.6 ms**	**51 FPS**	36.5 M	146 MB

Table 10. Validation analysis of existing techniques with proposed model on computational complexity

Model	Accuracy	FPS	Params
YOLOv8-small	97.4	78 FPS	11 M
ResNet-50	96.8	65 FPS	25 M
Vision Transformer	98.1	42 FPS	86 M
Proposed Model	**99.6**	**51 FPS**	**36.5 M**

Table 11. Comparative analysis of the proposed model with existing techniques

Year	Method	Architecture	Dataset	Key Idea
2024	Improved YOLOv8	Attention + small-object modules	TT100K	Improve detection accuracy (Ji et al., 2024)
2025	DP-YOLO	YOLOv8 + Transformer modules	TT100K/GTSDB	Lightweight + higher mAP (Qiu et al., 2025)
2025	CPB-YOLOv8	Multi-scale attention	TT100K	Better tiny-object detection (Zhao et al., 2025)
2025	EfficientViT-YOLO	YOLO + Transformer	GTSDB	Global feature modeling (Zeng et al., 2024)

continued on following page

Table 11. Continued

Year	Method	Architecture	Dataset	Key Idea
2026	LNSE-YOLO	Lightweight YOLOv11	Edge deployment	Noise suppression (Wang et al., 2026)
2025	CViT	Vision Transformer	GTSRB	High recognition accuracy (Naz et al., 2025)
Proposed	NLM + M-UNet + Dense-CNNet + RHSO	Hybrid pipeline	TT100K/GTSDB	Structure-aware + optimized model

5. CONCLUSION

In conclusion, this research offers a novel and comprehensive approach to traffic sign detection, addressing limitations observed in existing methods. By integrating Non-local Means (NLM) preprocessing, modified UNet architecture, DenseCNN classification, and Rock Hyrax Swarm Optimization (RHSO) for hyperparameter tuning, the proposed methodology achieves remarkable advancements in ACC and efficiency. The utilization of NLM preprocessing effectively enhances image quality, mitigating the impact of noise and environmental factors. The modified UNet architecture enables robust feature representation, crucial for accurate detection across diverse traffic sign variations. DenseCNN further refines classification ACC, ensuring reliable detection outcomes even in challenging scenarios. Leveraging RHSO for hyperparameter optimization optimizes model performance, enhancing overall efficiency and effectiveness. Experimental results on benchmark datasets demonstrate significant improvement, with an impressive ACC of 99.64% in TT100K dataset, 99.6% in GTSDB dataset demonstrating the suggested approach's superiority over cutting-edge techniques. This research contributes to the advancement of intelligent driving technology, offering promising avenues for enhancing road safety and transportation systems in real-world applications. Future work includes exploring real-time implementation, adapting to dynamic environments, and extending to multi-modal traffic sign detection systems.

REFERENCES

Alam, A., & Jaffery, Z. A. (2020). Indian traffic sign detection and recognition. *International Journal of Intelligent Transportation Systems Research, 18*(1), 98–112. DOI: 10.1007/s13177-019-00178-1

Aruna, T. M., Kumar, P., Srinidhi, N. N., Divyaraj, G. N., Asha, K., Thirumalraj, A., & Naresh, E. (2023). Effective utilisation of Geospatial Data for peer-to-peer communication among autonomous vehicles using Optimized Machine learning algorithm.

Chu, J., Zhang, C., Yan, M., Zhang, H., & Ge, T. (2023). TRD-YOLO: A real-time, high-performance small traffic sign detection algorithm. *Sensors (Basel), 23*(8), 3871. DOI: 10.3390/s23083871 PMID: 37112213

Gao, T., Xing, K., Liu, Z., Chen, T., Yang, Z., & Li, Y. (2022). Traffic Sign Detection Algorithm based on Pyramid Multi-scale Fusion. *Journal of Traffic and Transportation Engineering, 22*, 210–224.

Ji, B., Xu, J., Liu, Y., Fan, P., & Wang, M. (2024). Improved YOLOv8 for small traffic sign detection under complex environmental conditions. *Franklin Open, 8*, 100167. DOI: 10.1016/j.fraope.2024.100167

Karyono, G., Ahmad, A., & Asmai, S. A. (2023). Image Denoising using Wavelet Cycle Spinning and Non-local Means Filter. *International Journal of Advanced Computer Science and Applications, 14*(3). Advance online publication. DOI: 10.14569/IJACSA.2023.0140356

Kaur, G., Garg, M., Gupta, S., Juneja, S., Rashid, J., Gupta, D., Shah, A., & Shaikh, A. (2023). Automatic Identification of Glomerular in Whole-Slide Images Using a Modified UNet Model. *Diagnostics (Basel), 13*(19), 3152. DOI: 10.3390/diagnostics13193152 PMID: 37835895

Liu, Y., Shi, G., Li, Y., & Zhao, Z. (2022). M-YOLO: Traffic Sign Detection Algorithm Applicable to Complex Scenarios. *Symmetry, 14*(5), 952. DOI: 10.3390/sym14050952

Liu, Z., Qi, M., Shen, C., Fang, Y., & Zhao, X. (2021). Cascade saccade machine learning network with hierarchical classes for traffic sign detection. *Sustainable Cities and Society, 67*, 102700. DOI: 10.1016/j.scs.2020.102700

Maletzky, A., Hofer, N., Thumfart, S., Bruckmüller, K., & Kasper, J. (2023). Traffic Sign Detection and Classification on the Austrian Highway Traffic Sign Data Set. *Data, 8*(1), 16. DOI: 10.3390/data8010016

Megalingam, R. K., Thanigundala, K., Musani, S. R., Nidamanuru, H., & Gadde, L. (2023). Indian traffic sign detection and recognition using deep learning. *International Journal of Transportation Science and Technology, 12*(3), 683–699. DOI: 10.1016/j.ijtst.2022.06.002

Naz, I., Shah, J. H., Tahir, A., Marri, M. R., Saleem, R., & Saeed, M. E. S. (2025). Attention to detail: A conditional multi-head transformer for traffic sign recognition. *PLoS One, 20*(11), e0335341. DOI: 10.1371/journal.pone.0335341 PMID: 41187177

Ouyang, Z., Niu, J., Ren, T., Li, Y., Cui, J., & Wu, J. (2020). MBBNet: An edge IoT computing-based traffic light detection solution for autonomous bus. *Journal of Systems Architecture, 109*, 101835. DOI: 10.1016/j.sysarc.2020.101835

Özkaraca, O., Bağrıaçık, O. İ., Gürüler, H., Khan, F., Hussain, J., Khan, J., & Laila, U. E. (2023). Multiple Brain Tumor Classification with Dense CNN Architecture Using Brain MRI Images. *Life (Chicago, Ill.), 13*(2), 349. DOI: 10.3390/life13020349 PMID: 36836705

Padhi, B. K., Chakravarty, S., Naik, B., Pattanayak, R. M., & Das, H. (2022). RH-SOFS: Feature Selection Using the Rock Hyrax Swarm Optimization Algorithm for Credit Card Fraud Detection System. *Sensors (Basel), 22*(23), 9321. DOI: 10.3390/s22239321 PMID: 36502020

Qiu, J., Zhang, W., Xu, S., & Zhou, H. (2025). DP-YOLO: A lightweight traffic sign detection model for small object detection. *Digital Signal Processing, 165*, 105311. DOI: 10.1016/j.dsp.2025.105311

Thirumalraj, A., & Rajesh, T. (2023). An Improved ARO Model for Task Offloading in Vehicular Cloud Computing in VANET.

Triki, N., Karray, M., & Ksantini, M. (2023). A real-time traffic sign recognition method using a new attention-based deep convolutional neural network for smart vehicles. *Applied Sciences (Basel, Switzerland), 13*(8), 4793. DOI: 10.3390/app13084793

Wan, J., Ding, W., Zhu, H., Xia, M., Huang, Z., Tian, L., Zhu, Y., & Wang, H. (2021). An efficient small traffic sign detection method based on YOLOv3. *Journal of Signal Processing Systems for Signal, Image, and Video Technology, 93*(8), 899–911. DOI: 10.1007/s11265-020-01614-2

Wang, B., Han, Y., Wang, S., Tian, D., Cai, M., Liu, M., & Wang, L. (2022). A Review of Intelligent Connected Vehicle Cooperative Driving Development. *Mathematics, 10*(19), 3635. DOI: 10.3390/math10193635

Wang, H., Wang, K., Cai, Y., Liu, Z., & Chen, L. (2020). Traffic Sign Recognition Based on improved Cascaded Convolutional Neural Network. *Automot. Eng.*, *42*, 1256–1262+1269.

Wang, L., Ai, Q., & Jin, H. (2026). Lightweight traffic sign detection algorithm with noise suppression and semantic enhancement. *PLoS One*, *21*(1), e0340810. DOI: 10.1371/journal.pone.0340810 PMID: 41564025

Wei, H., Zhang, Q., Qian, Y., Xu, Z., & Han, J. (2023). MTSDet: Multi-scale traffic sign detection with attention and path aggregation. *Applied Intelligence*, *53*(1), 238–250. DOI: 10.1007/s10489-022-03459-7

Wu, Y., Li, Z., Chen, Y., Nai, K., & Yuan, J. (2020). Real-time traffic sign detection and classification towards real traffic scene. *Multimedia Tools and Applications*, *79*(25-26), 18201–18219. DOI: 10.1007/s11042-020-08722-y

Xu, J., Huang, Y., & Ying, D. (2023). Traffic Sign Detection and Recognition Using Multi-Frame Embedding of Video-Log Images. *Remote Sensing (Basel)*, *15*(12), 2959. DOI: 10.3390/rs15122959

Zaibi, A., Ladgham, A., & Sakly, A. (2021). A lightweight model for traffic sign classification based on enhanced LeNet-5 network. *Journal of Sensors*, *2021*(1), 1–13. DOI: 10.1155/2021/8870529

Zeng, G., Wu, Z., Xu, L., & Liang, Y. (2024). Efficient vision transformer YOLOv5 for accurate and fast traffic sign detection. *Electronics (Basel)*, *13*(5), 880. DOI: 10.3390/electronics13050880

Zhang, J., Wang, W., Lu, C., Wang, J., & Sangaiah, A. K. (2020). Lightweight deep network for traffic sign classification. *Annales des Télécommunications*, *75*(7-8), 369–379. DOI: 10.1007/s12243-019-00731-9

Zhang, J., Xie, Z., Sun, J., Zou, X., & Wang, J. (2020). A cascaded R-CNN with multiscale attention and imbalanced samples for traffic sign detection. *IEEE Access : Practical Innovations, Open Solutions*, *8*, 29742–29754. DOI: 10.1109/ACCESS.2020.2972338

Zhang, R., Zheng, K., Shi, P., Mei, Y., Li, H., & Qiu, T. (2023). Traffic Sign Detection Based on the Improved YOLOv5. *Applied Sciences (Basel, Switzerland)*, *13*(17), 9748. DOI: 10.3390/app13179748

Zhao, L., Wei, Z., Li, Y., Jin, J., & Li, X. (2023). SEDG-Yolov5: A Lightweight Traffic Sign Detection Model Based on Knowledge Distillation. *Electronics (Basel)*, *12*(2), 305. DOI: 10.3390/electronics12020305

Zhao, W., Li, L., & Gong, X. (2025). CPB-YOLOv8: An Enhanced Multi-Scale Traffic Sign Detector for Complex Road Environment. *Information (Basel)*, *16*(9), 798. DOI: 10.3390/info16090798

Chapter 5
A Data-Driven Study on Electric Vehicle Adoption: Evidence From Ho Chi Minh City

Anh Thi Dy Nguyen
Faculty of Commerce, Van Lang University, Ho Chi Minh City, Vietnam

Minh Duc Ly
http://orcid.org/0000-0003-0200-7153
Faculty of Commerce, Van Lang University, Ho Chi Minh City, Vietnam

Tam Huu Do
http://orcid.org/0009-0003-2955-4592
Faculty of Commerce, Van Lang University, Ho Chi Minh City, Vietnam

ABSTRACT

The study adopts a quantitative methodology based on PLS-SEM (Partial Least Squares Structural Equation Modeling), utilizing the software SmartPLS 3.3.0 and SPSS v20. A structured questionnaire was designed and distributed via Google Forms between July and October 2023, collecting 7,000 responses, of which 6,550 valid samples were retained for analysis. The survey was conducted in Ho Chi Minh City, Vietnam, targeting diverse respondent groups across gender, age, education, and profession. Key findings show that technical readiness, particularly optimization ($\beta = 0.112$, $p < 0.05$) and innovation ($\beta = 0.108$, $p < 0.01$), significantly affect consumer motivation and expectations. Environmental concerns ($\beta = 0.425$, < 0.05) and perceived usefulness ($\beta = 0.137$, $p < 0.05$) are also critical predictors of EV purchase intention. The structural model achieved high reliability and validity with Cronbach's alpha > 0.7, Composite Reliability > 0.6, and model fit indices such as GFI = 0.902, RMSEA = 0.047, and SRMR = 0.046, indicating strong model fitness.

DOI: 10.4018/979-8-2600-0883-6.ch005

1. INTRODUCTION

Electric vehicles use electricity to operate through one or more electric motors and produce no direct exhaust emissions, making them environmentally friendly (Verma et al., 2022). Popular models include the Tesla, Nissan Leaf, BMW i3, and Vespa Elettrica scooter (Mustafi, 2022). Key advantages over internal combustion engine vehicles include reduced pollution and climate impact, the use of renewable energy sources that save resources and reduce oil dependence, lower operating costs, faster acceleration, quieter performance, and efficient energy use through regenerative braking (Carey, 2023; Patel, 2022). However, electric vehicles still face limitations such as restricted battery life and an underdeveloped charging infrastructure (Ahmadian, 2023).

Electric vehicle development is rapidly advancing thanks to improved battery technology that enables longer range and faster charging (Mo, 2022). Falling production costs for batteries and components have also reduced consumer prices, while many governments support adoption through subsidies, tax incentives, and discounts (Buhmann, 2023). Growing environmental awareness further increases demand for clean transportation, accompanied by the expansion of charging infrastructure, including public and fast-charging stations (Liu, 2023). Major automakers are heavily investing in electric vehicle research and development (Goh, 2022). Current trends include smart charging systems that enhance efficiency, wider installation of fast and ultra-fast chargers, advancements in electric motor performance, and improved energy management to extend driving range (Sadeghian, 2022). Additionally, integrating AI and autonomous driving technology is boosting safety and overall vehicle performance, helping electric vehicles become an increasingly attractive and influential option in the automotive industry (Yu, 2023).

According to the IEA's Global Electric Vehicle Outlook, global EV sales surpassed 10 million units in 2022, increasing 55% from 2021, with China leading the market (Asim, 2022). The number of electric vehicles on the road reached over 26 million, up 60% from the previous year, while sales of BEVs and PHEVs exceeded 10 million, mirroring a 55% rise (Dioha, 2022). Emerging markets such as India, Thailand, and Indonesia also saw strong growth, selling 80,000 units—more than triple 2021 figures—supported by India's $3.2 billion incentive package that attracted $8.3 billion in investment (Siragusa, 2022). VinFast likewise reported major gains in Q2 2023, with revenue reaching 334 million USD, up 303% from Q1, driven by 9,535 electric car deliveries and over 10,000 electric motorcycles (Thoburn, 2023). Despite a net loss of 12,535 billion VND, losses declined compared to prior periods, and by June 2023, VinFast operated 122 EV showrooms and 245 service locations worldwide (Hiep, 2023).

Although Vietnam's electric vehicle market is expanding, several barriers remain. Limited charging infrastructure continues to inconvenience users, while EV prices remain higher than internal combustion vehicles (Venugopal, 2022). Government incentives exist but lack comprehensive measures such as full import tax exemptions, lower registration fees, reduced special consumption tax, or strong financial support. Public awareness of EV benefits also remains limited (Nikiforiadis, 2023). Vietnam is developing standards and regulatory frameworks and investing in charging stations and EV technology to overcome these challenges (Hoang et al., 2022). Research on Vietnamese consumers' intention to purchase EVs focuses on evaluating technological readiness—including Optimization, Innovation, Insecurity, and Discomfort—within the TAM model, as well as infrastructure factors such as service quality, system quality, and environmental concerns. It also examines the influence of government policies and automotive brand reputation on consumers' intentions to buy electric vehicles.

This research article is organized into the following sections: Section 2 presents the content of the literature review. Section 3 details the research model and hypothesis development. Section 4 presents the content of research methods. Section 5 records the detailed content of the research results. Section 6 presents content related to the discussion. Section 7 presents conclusions and Section 8 presents Limitations and Future Perspectives.

2. LITERATURE REVIEW

2.1. Basic Human Values

Customers increasingly expect electric vehicles to offer advanced technology, long driving ranges, fast and convenient charging, and reliable battery performance, along with enhanced safety and infotainment features (Song et al., 2022; Zhu et al., 2022). Many consumers also seek innovation in design, preferring modern, personalized styles, improved battery capacity, longer lifespan, and fast-charging or reusable battery technologies (Hossain et al., 2022). Smart functions such as automation, wireless charging, and advanced safety systems—including automatic braking, blind-spot warning, and traction control—are also highly valued (Ghasemi-Marzbali, 2022). However, shifting from fuel-powered to electric vehicles often brings uncertainty, particularly regarding limited charging infrastructure, travel distance concerns, and charging wait times (Zhang et al., 2023). Although EV prices may be higher than traditional vehicles, their lower operating and maintenance costs help reduce financial pressure. Users can compare EV models to match their mobility needs while ongoing technological advancements continue to address remaining concerns (Więckowski et al., 2023; Zhou et al., 2022).

In Vietnam, the quality of electric vehicle maintenance and replacement parts varies across manufacturers and distributors, which include major brands such as Tesla, Nissan, Hyundai, and BMW, as well as regional producers. Reliable service centers with skilled technicians are essential, though service quality can differ significantly between facilities (Verma et al., 2022). Access to genuine replacement components is also crucial, and sourcing parts may be more difficult for lesser-known or imported EV brands. Therefore, purchasing from established companies with strong service networks is recommended, along with consulting current EV owners and trusted reviews to assess service quality (Tiwari & Singh, 2022). Globally, charging infrastructure development also shows major disparities: China leads with 9.45 million charging stations as of November 2022, while South Korea has about 105,000, and the U.S. has 140,000 chargers at 53,000 stations, far below future demand projections. The EU recorded about 375,000 stations in 2021, aiming for one million by 2025. In Vietnam, VinFast has deployed over 150,000 charging ports nationwide (Li et al., 2022; Chen et al., 2023).

International charging standards help ensure compatibility between electric vehicles and charging stations. The CCS standard, which supports both AC (Type 2) and DC (Combo 2) charging, is widely adopted by major manufacturers, including Tesla, BMW, Volkswagen, Hyundai, and Ford (LaMonaca, 2022). Japan's CHAdeMO standard supports DC fast charging and is used mainly by Nissan and Mitsubishi, while Tesla employs its own Supercharger protocol, though adapters allow limited cross-brand use. Most public stations offer AC charging via J1772 and DC fast charging via CCS or CHAdeMO, though some older or lesser-known EV models may require adapters to ensure compatibility (Sachan et al., 2022). Environmental benefits remain a key motivation for EV adoption, as reduced CO_2 emissions improve urban air quality and lessen reliance on fossil fuels. Battery recyclability also helps conserve resources (Yang et al., 2022). However, the total environmental impact depends on electricity generation sources, manufacturing processes, and recycling systems (Metais et al., 2022).

The U.S. Environmental Protection Agency reports that burning 1 gallon of gasoline emits 20 pounds of CO_2, meaning a gasoline vehicle releasing about 191.7 g of CO_2 per kilometer and a scooter about 47.9 g (Meegoda et al., 2022; Archsmith et al., 2022). In contrast, electric vehicles produce no direct emissions, and studies show they can significantly reduce annual CO_2 output; for example, an electric motorcycle traveling 1 km requires the equivalent of three days of photosynthesis by a mature tree to offset emissions from a gasoline vehicle. This environmental advantage supports global commitments—nearly 100 countries including Vietnam aim for net-zero emissions by 2050 (Enoma, 2022). Climate change remains a key driver of EV adoption, as EVs reduce greenhouse gases and encourage energy generation from renewables (Falai et al., 2022). However, full environmental sustainability also depends on clean production processes, effective recycling, and responsible waste management of EV components (Unterluggauer et al., 2022).

2.2. Aspiration

Aspirations are a multifaceted concept without a single agreed-upon definition, with researchers describing them as future goals involving personal investment, socially and culturally shaped capacities, or states influenced by daily conditions (Trebbels & Trebbels, 2015; Sherwood, 1989; Prodonovich et al., 2014). Studies on aspirations to purchase electric vehicles show that intention is shaped by factors such as performance expectancy, effort expectancy, social influence, personal norms, and familiarity with EV users (Hoang et al., 2022; Brătucu et al., 2019; Habich-Sobiegalla et al., 2018). Research also indicates a positive outlook for the future of EVs as they address environmental and economic challenges. Benefits include reduced pollution, growing national ambitions—especially in China—declining battery costs, and the need for expanded charging infrastructure to support widespread adoption (Shen et al., 2011; Maske et al., 2021).

Research shows that the desire to buy electric vehicles is shaped by a wide range of psychological, social, and policy-related factors. Key influences include attitudes toward EVs, government incentives, price acceptance, performance, environmental concern, and demographic traits (Lin & Wu, 2018; Jiang, 2016; Krishnan & Koshy, 2021). Social networks and familiarity with EV owners also consistently strengthen purchase intentions across countries (Habich-Sobiegalla et al., 2018). Additional studies highlight the role of consumer perception, personal innovativeness, effort and performance expectancy, perceived risk, lifestyle factors, and facilitating conditions in shaping EV adoption in markets such as China and Vietnam (Hoang et al., 2022; Xie et al., 2022). Broader literature on aspirations suggests they arise from interconnected expectations and motivations, shaped by self-concept, intrinsic values, and family or organizational influences, emphasizing aspirations as investments of personal resources (Guo et al., 2015; Bell, 1963; Sherwood, 1989; Keum & Eggers, 2018).

Research consistently shows that environmental awareness and attitudes strongly influence electric vehicle (EV) purchase intentions. Key determinants include attitude, perceived behavioral control, environmental concern, and perceived benefits (Okada et al., 2019; Lai et al., 2015). Frameworks in Vietnam further highlight performance expectancy, effort expectancy, social influence, facilitating conditions, personal norms, and consequence awareness (Hoang et al., 2022). Studies in China and Europe also emphasize subjective norms, moral norms, emotions, and perceived behavioral control as mediators of EV adoption (Wang et al., 2016; Moons

& De Pelsmacker, 2012). Overall, psychological and social factors strongly shape consumers' intention to buy EVs.

2.3. Intention to Buy Electric Vehicle and Technology Adoption

Research on electric vehicle (EV) adoption highlights multiple technological, psychological, and contextual factors influencing purchase intentions. Key determinants include perceived ease of use, performance expectancy, effort expectancy, social influence, facilitating conditions, personal norms, and consequence awareness, as shown in studies from Vietnam and other markets (Ambak, 2015; Hoang et al., 2022). Industry 4.0 technologies, such as battery-swap systems, also shape user interest by addressing charging limitations (Athanasopoulou et al., 2023). Broader mobility research during COVID-19 shows that perceived value, reliability, environmental awareness, health concerns, and shifts toward e-marketing affected decisions regarding cars, bikes, and e-scooters (Gaoaketse et al., 2023; Gaspar et al., 2023; Dawood et al., 2022; Mao et al., 2023). Additional studies emphasize environmental and economic perceptions, technological knowledge, and early-adopter traits, while concerns about technology reduce intentions (Carley et al., 2013; Huang et al., 2021). TAM-based findings further confirm the roles of perceived usefulness, ease of use, risk, and government incentives in predicting EV adoption (Jaiswal et al., 2021; Yankun, 2020; Begum et al., 2022).

Research shows that electric vehicle (EV) purchase intentions are shaped by affordability, government support, environmental attitudes, and user experience. Affordable pricing and policy initiatives are essential to encourage adoption (Begum et al., 2022), while satisfaction with range, recharge convenience, cost, and symbolic attributes supports repurchase intentions (Hasan, 2021). Consumer environmental and innovative propensity also strengthen EV purchase intention (Moon, 2021). Classic perspectives highlight cost, safety, and pollution reduction as long-standing motivators (Tesar, 1974). Across contexts such as Vietnam, China, and Thailand, key drivers include performance expectancy, effort expectancy, social influence, personal norms, perceived benefits, policy support, purchase price, and environmental consciousness (Hoang et al., 2022; Sovacool et al., 2019; Brinkmann & Bhatiasevi, 2023). Broader models further emphasize cost considerations, environmental concern, technology acceptance, green self-identity, moral obligation, and demographic traits as important predictors of EV adoption (Kim et al., 2014; Barbarossa et al., 2015; Lin & Wu, 2018).

Research shows that the Unified Theory of Acceptance and Use of Technology (UTAUT) is highly effective in explaining electric vehicle (EV) purchase intentions. Key predictors consistently include performance expectancy, effort expectancy, social influence, facilitating conditions, hedonic motivation, personal norms, environmental concern, and perceived risk (de Sena Abrahão et al., 2016; Imtiaz, 2018; Hoang et al., 2022). Additional factors shaping EV adoption include environmental knowledge, technophilia, education, prior hybrid ownership, and sensitivity to pollution and energy security (Carley et al., 2013; Lin & Wu, 2018). Broader literature identifies three antecedent groups: consumer characteristics, EV attributes, and policy support. Studies also emphasize perceived risk, environmental policy perception (Lai et al., 2015), and the influence of credible eWOM information on purchase decisions. Together, these findings underscore the combined roles of psychological, technological, policy-driven, and informational factors in forming EV purchase intentions.

Research shows that electric vehicle (EV) acceptance and purchase intentions are shaped by a wide range of psychological, cultural, technological, and policy-related factors. Key predictors include perceived value, economic benefits, charging risk, environmental concern, attitudes, subjective norms, perceived behavioral control, and government incentives (Shalender & Sharma, 2021; Sang & Bekhet, 2015). TAM- and UTAUT-based studies emphasize performance expectancy, effort expectancy, social influence, perceived usefulness, ease of use, and perceived risk as central determinants (Hoang et al., 2022; Zhang et al., 2022). Values and behavioral models further highlight the roles of functional and emotional values, environmental and innovative propensity, emotions, and perceived uncertainty (Han et al., 2017; Moon, 2021; Moons & De Pelsmacker, 2012; Riverso, 2023). Cultural factors—including environmental consciousness, collectivism, long-term orientation, masculinity, green self-identity, and moral obligation—also significantly influence EV adoption across countries (Liu et al., 2022; Barbarossa et al., 2015).

Research on electric vehicle (EV) purchase intention highlights multiple factors shaping consumer decisions. Key concerns include battery charge duration and failure risk, which may discourage potential buyers if not addressed effectively (Chéron & Zins, 1997). Broader determinants fall into three categories—consumer characteristics, EV characteristics, and EV-related policies—identified through systematic review. Environmental concern, perceived ease of use, and effort expectancy also positively influence EV purchase intentions, as shown in Pakistan (Lee, 2021). Studies in India further emphasize understanding consumer attitudes toward autonomous and connected EVs to support successful market adoption (Babu & Damle, 2022). In Vietnam, research aims to understand market trends, consumer behavior, charging infrastructure readiness, and supportive government policies. It also evaluates EV benefits such as efficiency, low emissions, and cost savings, compares EVs with conventional vehicles, analyzes available models and pricing, and assesses charging stations and financial incentives—helping consumers determine suitability based on personal mobility needs and financial conditions.

3. RESEARCH MODEL AND HYPOTHESES

3.1. Research Model

In this study, the author proposes a research model that considers and evaluates basic human values regarding the intention to buy electric vehicles, factors of intention to buy electric vehicles are expressed through motivation and expectations. of people intending to buy electric vehicles through usage acceptance theories and mindfulness theories about electric vehicles. According to the basic theory of people according to Shwartz's criteria and aspirations of needs and intentions to purchase electric vehicles. Integrated research model of the theories of TAM, UTAUT, Mindfulness, and Success Model according to DeLone and McLean's information theory (Figure 1). More specifically, the research objectives of this study are as follows: (i) Assess the impact of human values according to Schwartz's basic theory applied to differences in intention to buy electric vehicles. (ii) Identify and evaluate the behavioral values of using technology in electric vehicles that impact the intention to purchase electric vehicles, and (iii) Evaluate the Mindfulness theory based on a prediction model using a questionnaire according to the TAM model through the theoretical model of information technology affects the intention to buy electric vehicles.

Figure 1. Research model

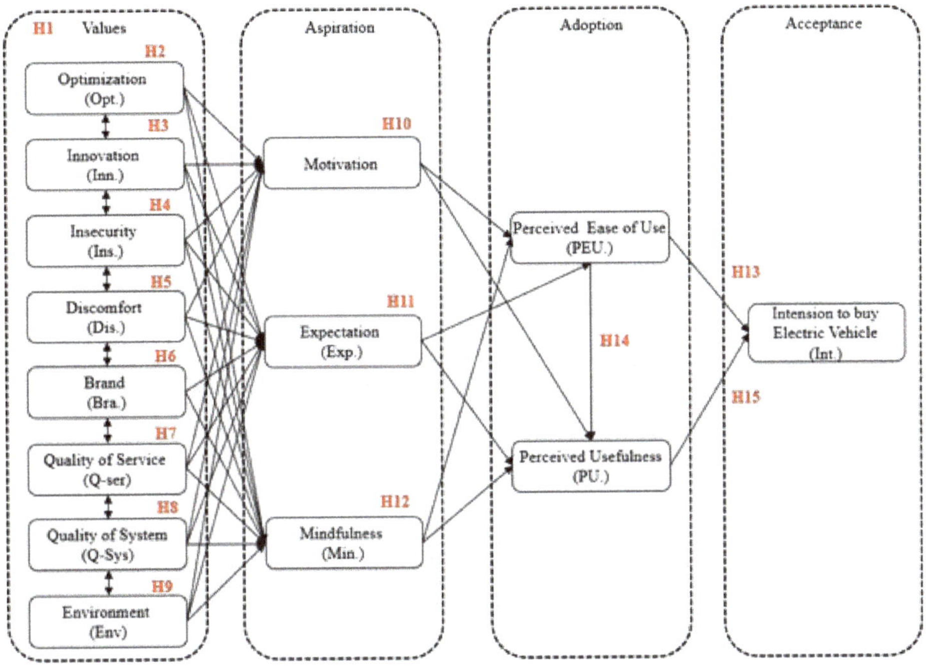

3.2 Hypothesis development

The following are the study's research objectives: (i) Evaluate the influence of human values on variations in intention to purchase electric vehicles using Schwartz's fundamental theory. Using a questionnaire following the TAM model and the theoretical model of how information technology affects the intention to buy electric vehicles, (ii) identify and assess the behavioral values of using technology in electric vehicles that impact the intention to purchase electric vehicles, and (iii) assess the mindfulness theory based on a prediction model.

The hypotheses in this study are built based on the TAM theoretical model and Mindfulness Theory. Value-based theoretical models are built on five key components.

Values ← → Values:

The first component of this research is built from Schwartz's theory, the research model is classified into 15 components and made up of 4 groups. The proposed hypotheses are as follows:

H1a. The value of the Optimization factor positively impacts the Innovation factor.
H1b. The value of the Innovation factor negatively impacts the Insecurity factor.
H1c. Insecurity value negatively impacts the Discomfort factor.
H1d. The value of the Discomfort factor negatively impacts the Brand factor.
H1e. The value of the Brand factor positively impacts the Quality of service factor.
H1f. The value of the Quality of service factor positively impacts the Quality of the system factor.
H1g. The value of Quality of the system has a positive impact on the Environment factor.
H1h. The value of the Environment negatively impacts the Optimization factor.

Values → Aspiration:

The results and current states of the model are expressed through elements of value and regardless of the current surrounding agents, value can be considered as behavior (Lin & Wu, 2018). In addition, elements of values can be used to explain behaviors attitudes, and cultural factors. The interactive relationship of value factors with the acceptance structure of individual human impacts follows Schwartz's theory, which considers motivation, expectation, and human needs when growing up. intention to buy electric vehicles (Krishnan & Koshy, 2021; Athanasopoulou et al., 2023). In this second component, the Author proposes related hypotheses about this relationship as follows:

H2a. There is a positive impact between the Optimization factor and the Motivation factor.
H2b. There is a positive impact between the Optimization factor and the Expectation factor
H2c. There is a positive impact between the Optimization factor and the Mindfulness factor
H3a. There is a positive impact between the Innovation factor and the Motivation factor
H3b. There is a positive impact between the Innovation factor and the Expectation factor
H3c. There is a positive impact between the Innovation factor and the Mindfulness factor
H4a. There is an inverse impact between the Insecurity factor and the Motivation factor

H4b. There is an inverse impact between the Insecurity factor and the Expectation factor
H4c. There is an inverse impact between the Insecurity factor and the Mindfulness factor
H5a. There is an inverse impact between the Discomfort factor and the Motivation factor
H5b. There is an inverse impact between the Discomfort factor and the Expectation factor
H5c. There is an inverse impact between the Discomfort factor and the Mindfulness factor
H6a. There is a positive impact between the Brand factor and the Motivation factor
H6b. There is a positive impact between the Brand factor and the Expectation factor
H6c. There is a positive impact between the Brand factor and the Mindfulness factor
H7a. There is a positive impact between the Quality of service factor and the Motivation factor
H7b. There is a positive impact between the Quality of service factor and the Expectation factor
H7c. There is a positive impact between the Quality of service factor and the Mindfulness factor
H8a. There is a positive impact between the Quality of the system factor and the Motivation factor
H8b. There is a positive impact between the Quality of the system factor and the Expectation factor
H8c. There is a positive impact between the Quality of the system factor and the Mindfulness factor
H9a. There is a positive impact between the Environmental factor and the Motivation factor
H9b. There is a positive impact between the Environmental factor and the Expectation factor
H9c. There is a positive impact between the Environmental factor and the Mindfulness factor

Aspiration→ Adoption:

Evaluating the impact factor of the expectation component on the acceptance component is described in this study (Gaoaketse et al., 2023). Looking at the aspiration factors of people intending to buy electric cars, experience, motivational factors, and action-related factors that make them intend to buy electric cars. Service quality is always considered a factor that ensures customers' motivation to buy electric vehicles (Gaspar et al., 2023; Dawood et al., 2022). The author proposes the following hypotheses:

> H10a. The value of the Motivation factor positively impacts the Perceived ease of use factor.
> H10b. The value of the Motivation factor positively impacts the Perceived Usefulness factor.

Consumers' intention to buy electric cars always pays attention to the quality factor and it is considered a characteristic factor for the expectations of people intending to buy electric cars. Service quality is also indispensable in the performance expectation and effort expectancy model in the UTAUT2 model of electric vehicle factors that impact the environmental friendliness that people intend to buy electric vehicles expect (Hoang et al., 2022). hope. In this study, the author evaluates the quality of service and quality of system factors of the information technology model applied in electric vehicles to improve performance expectations and effort expectations according to theory. The theory of the UTAUT2 model is based on two factors: PEU and PU (Mao et al., 2023; Huang et al., 2021). From the above analysis results, the author proposes the following related hypotheses:

> H11a. The value of the expectation factor positively impacts the Perceived ease of use factor.
> H11b. The value of the expectation factor positively impacts the Perceived usefulness factor.
> H12a. The value of the Mindfulness factor positively impacts the Perceived ease of use factor.
> H12b. The value of the Mindfulness factor positively impacts the Perceived usefulness factor.

Adoption → Adoption:

Assessing the impact of factors in the TAM model is shown in the fourth part. There are two main factors in the TAM model: Perceived ease of use factor and Perceived usefulness factor (Carley et al., 2013). The value of the Perceived usefulness factor shows the usefulness of the electric vehicle and the Perceived ease of use factor represents the convenience of use. electric vehicles and these two factors directly affect users' intention to buy electric vehicles and have similar effects (Jaiswal et al., 2021; Yankun, 2020). The author builds the theory as follows:

H14. The value of the Perceived ease of use factor has a positive impact on the Perceived usefulness factor

Adoption → Acceptance:

In part 5 of the research, evaluate the benefit factors that bring people intending to buy electric vehicles. The main elements of the TAM model demonstrate the positive impact of electric vehicles on buyers, such as factors related to users' perceptions of the level of confidence that electric vehicles are convenient during use. use and improve their performance (Begum et al., 2022). Meanwhile, their consciousness always expects an easy-to-use electric vehicle with the application of new technologies with high effort and self-learning ability to improve the ease-of-use features of electric vehicles to meet the needs of customers (Moon, 2021; Lin & Wu, 2018). Useful factors of electric vehicles. The author builds a specific hypothesis as follows:

H13. The value of the Perceived ease of use factor has a positive impact on the intention to buy an electric vehicle factor
H14. The value of the Perceived usefulness factor positively impacts the intention to buy an electric vehicle

4. RAW MATERIAL AND METHODOLOGY

The research model is shown in detail in Figure 2, analyzing the impact of factors affecting the intention to buy electric vehicles through factors that carry basic human values towards different aspirations., the need to build motivation, expectations, and Mindfulness. Analyze the research model using the quantitative analysis model, perform factor analysis such as exploratory factor analysis (EFA) and confirmatory factor analysis (CFA) in the PLS-SEM model, with the results The analysis results show the cause-and-effect relationship between the constructs in the research model.

The study employed an online survey using Google Forms, developed in Vietnamese and structured according to Schwartz's theory with five sections: socio-demographic data, basic values, aspirations, acceptance, and acceptance structure. A 5-point Likert scale was used, ensuring anonymity and voluntary participation. The questionnaire was refined with input from five EV experts in Ho Chi Minh City. Data were analyzed using SPSS 20 and SmartPLS 3.30. The survey was conducted from July to October 2023 in southern Vietnam, yielding 7,000 responses, of which 6,550 valid samples met research standards and were included in the analysis (Table 1).

Table 1. Characteristics of the survey sample

Characteristics	Group	Frequency	Percentage
Gender	Man	4400	67.17%
	Woman	2150	32.83%
Age	18-25	1350	20.61%
	26-45	2550	38.93%
	46-55	1550	23.66%
	Over 55	1100	16.79%
Education	High Education	1540	23.51%
	University	4560	69.62%
	Master	500	7.63%
	Ph.D	40	0.61%
	Professor	10	0.15%
Income (USD)	Lower 700	270	4.12%
	700~1000	590	9.00%
	1000~2000	2090	31.90%
	2000~3000	2050	31.30%
	Over 3000	1550	23.66%
Professional	Free labor	900	13.74%
	Businessmen	1050	16.03%
	Engineer	3050	46.56%
	Teacher/Scientist	1550	23.66%

Identifying factors affecting the intention to buy electric vehicles is done by analyzing factors and identifying corresponding factors. The PLS-SEM model is evaluated by identifying measurement models and performing structural model evaluation based on the developed hypotheses. The research is conducted starting with reflection model analysis and using the partial least squares (PLS) technique. This model allows for flexible analysis between measurement factors and structural factors. The PLS-SEM model performs well in analyzing measured variables with hidden variables that cannot be specifically observed. Table 2 presents the latent variables of the research model with Cronbach's alpha (α) values extracted (Eq. 1) with all variables giving values greater than 0.7 and values verifying the validity of the values. The value of the latent variable using the Kaiser–Meyer–Olkin (KMO) measure (Eq. 2) gives the value of all moderators greater than 0.7. This proves that the hidden variables satisfy the research model and continue to perform further analysis.

$$\textit{Cronbach's alpha } (\alpha) = \frac{K\bar{r}}{1 + (K-1)\bar{r}} \tag{1}$$

Where, $\bar{r}$: the mean of the correlation matrix.

$$KMO = \frac{\sum_{j\#k}\sum r_{jk}^2}{\sum_{j\#k}\sum r_{jk}^2 + \sum_{j\#k}\sum p_{jk}^2} \quad (2)$$

Where, r_{jk}: the correlation between the variable in question and another.p_{jk}: the partial correlation.

Table 2. Latent factors and items

Factor	Item	Explanation	KMO	Cronbach's alpha
Optimization	Opt-1	Enhance good life	0.754	0.834
	Opt-2	Brings many benefits to humans		
	Opt-3	Easy to use for humans		
	Opt-4	Brings many conveniences to people		
	Opt-5	Cost optimization		
Innovation	Inn-1	Make me use electric car	0.798	0.789
	Inn-2	Connect Me with others		
	Inn-3	Keep me updated with new techniques		
	Inn-4	Made me change my thinking		
Insecurity	Ins-1	Depends on technology	0.767	0.845
	Ins-2	Reduce personal communication		
	Ins-3	Reduced confidence		
Discomfort	Dis-1	I receive technical support	0.826	0.758
	Dis-2	I was advised on difficult content		
	Dis-3	User manual		
	Dis-4	Operational consulting		
Quality of serviced	Qser-1	Share new knowledge	0.746	0.835
	Qser-2	Share new technical platforms		
	Qser-3	Provide reliable technical information		
	Qser-4	Provide timely service system		
	Qser-5	Provide spare parts correctly and promptly		

continued on following page

Table 2. Continued

Factor	Item	Explanation	KMO	Cronbach's alpha
Quality of system	Qsys-1	Response speed	0.808	0.735
	Qsys-2	Meets the intellectual base of use		
	Qsys-3	Share new knowledge		
Mindfulness	Min-1	Experience new technology	0.798	0.836
	Min-2	Use convenient techniques		
	Min-3	Meet needs		
Expectation	Exp-1	Expect new technology	0.824	0.756
	Exp-2	Expect technical convenience		
	Exp-3	Expect new technical demands		
Environment	Env-1	No emissions	0.709	0.804
	Env-2	Ensure improvement of the living environment		
	Env-3	Environmentally responsive		
	Env-4	Energy saving		
	Env-5	Optimize resources		
	Env-6	Improve the quality of human life		
	Env-7	Cost savings		
Perceived ease of use	PEU-1	Learn how to operate	0.803	0.709
	PEU-2	Use with ease		
	PEU-3	Operation is specific and clear		
	PEU-4	Does not make noise		
Perceived usefulness	PU-1	Easy to identify new technology	0.760	0.739
	PU-2	Increase operating efficiency		
	PU-3	Utilities for human life		
	PU-4	Easy to use energy source		
Brand	Bra-1	New production technology	0.809	0.798
	Bra-2	New industry		
	Bra-3	New competitive environment		
	Bra-4	Enhance brand		
	Bra-5	Brand recognition		

Analysis results in Table 1 show that all KMO and Cronbach's Alpha values exceed 0.7, confirming the reliability of the measurement scales. The model includes four technical readiness factors (Optimization, Innovation, Insecurity, Discomfort), two information technology factors (service quality, system quality), along with brand and environmental factors, all influencing EV purchase intention in Ho Chi Minh City through TAM and expectancy theory. A reflective model was used to test the hypotheses, with path and structural measurements analyzed via SmartPLS 3.3.0. The complete reflective model, shown in Figure 1, provides a basis for evaluating EV purchase intention across technical, environmental, and motivational elements. This research measure is implemented through the mathematical formula (Eq. 3).

$$Reflective\left(X_{kj,n}\right) = \widetilde{\omega}_{kj}\widetilde{\tau}_{j,n} + e_{kj,n} \qquad (3)$$

Where, x_{ki}: the manifest variable k of the latent variable i, k = 1, . . ., K; $\widetilde{\omega}_{kj}$: the estimated external weight of the indicatorx_{ki} ;$\widetilde{\tau}_{j,n}$:the latent variable, j = 1, . . ., J; $e_{kj,n}$: the error term from a bivariate regression; n: the specific observation, n = 1, . . ., N.

5. RESULTS AND DISCUSSION

The first step of the research is that the measurement model or path model is analyzed and then, the hypotheses are compared.

5.1 Evaluation of the Measurement Model: Validity and Reliability

The reliability value (Eq. 4) is used to evaluate the level of reflection of the research model. There are 2 types of reliability values (reliability value of the indicators and reliability value of the level of reliability). internal consistency of the research model) and measuring the value of the validity (convergent and discriminant validity). The results of analyzing the reliability value of the measurement indicators in the research model are greater than 0.7 (Netemeyer et al. (2003)) and the t-value is greater than 1.96. This demonstrates that the indicators ensure consistency and contribute to the research model (Figure 2).

$$CR = \frac{\left(\sum_{j=1}^{k}\lambda_j\right)^2}{\left(\sum_{j=1}^{k}\lambda_j\right)^2 + \sum_{j=1}^{k}\sigma_j^2} \qquad (4)$$

Where, CR: Composite Reliability value; λ_j: Standardized external loading factor of the jth indicator in a measurement model; σ_j^2: Variance of measurement error of the jth indicator $\sigma_j^2 = 1 - \lambda_j^2$.

Evaluation of the measurement model is calculated using the Average Variance Extracted (AVE) value (Eq. 5) and Rho_A value (Eq. 6) (Hair et al. (2009)), the analytical values from the measurement model give a value greater than 0.5, which is This proves that the model for the structure meets the research model (Table 3).

$$AVE = \frac{\sum_{i=1}^{M} \lambda_i^2}{M} \tag{5}$$

Where, AVE: The average level of explanation of the latent variables to the indicators; λ_i^2: Standardized external loadings of the indicators; M: Number of indicators in a factor.

$$\rho_A = (\widehat{w}\widehat{w})^2 \times \frac{\widehat{w}(S - diag(S))\widehat{w}}{\widehat{w}(\widehat{w}\widehat{w}.. - diag(\widehat{w}\widehat{w}))\widehat{w}} \tag{6}$$

Table 3. Composite reliability and converging validity

Factor	*Cronbach's alpha*	*Composite Reliability*	*Average Variance Extracted*	*Rho_A*
Optimization	0.834	0.678	0.623	0.769
Innovation	0.789	0.709	0.589	0.806
Insecurity	0.845	0.509	0.687	0.789
Discomfort	0.758	0.589	0.629	0.978
Quality of Service	0.835	0.608	0.578	1.038
Quality of System	0.735	0.709	0.609	1.134
Mindfulness	0.836	0.623	0.723	0.809
Expectation	0.756	0.645	0.589	0.791
Perceived ease of use	0.804	0.561	0.576	0.896
Perceived usefulness	0.709	0.568	0.608	0.823
Brand	0.739	0.608	0.578	0.934
Enviroment	0.789	0.701	0.612	0.912

Figure 2. Results of path model analysis

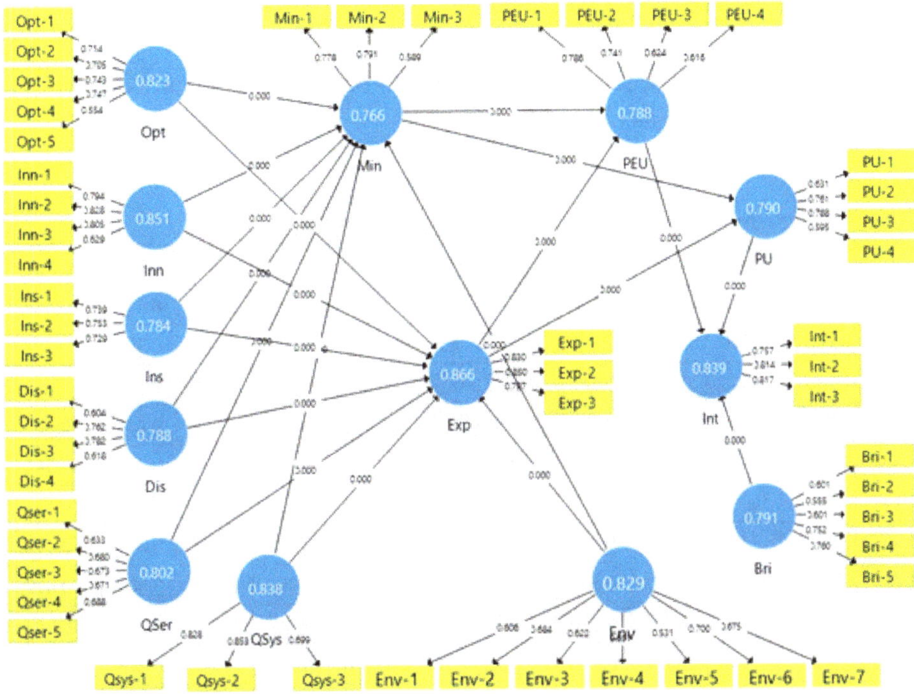

Evaluate the level of discrimination accuracy (Fornell and Larcker (1981)), Compare the coefficient $\sqrt{AVE}$ of the set of indicators used to measure a latent variable with the correlation coefficients between that latent variable and other potential variables. The coefficient $\sqrt{AVE}$ is larger than the remaining correlation coefficients, resulting in the indicators achieving a "level of discrimination accuracy", and Assessing the convergence using 2 indices AVE and $\sqrt{AVE}$, combined correlation matrix (Eq. 7) (Table 4). Matrix "Heterotrait-Monotrait Ratio of Correlation (HTMT)" (Eq. 8) (Henseler et al. (2015)), The average correlation coefficient within a scale is larger than the average of correlation coefficients cross as possible. The higher the average correlation coefficient within a scale, the greater the variation shared by the latent variable (the greater the impact).

$$AVE(P_i) > \max\left(r_{ij}^2\right),\ i \neq j \ or \ \sqrt{AVE(P_i)} > \max\left(\left|r_{ij}\right|\right) \tag{7}$$

Where, P_i: Latent variable I; r_{ij}: Correlation coefficient of the ith and j pairs of latent variables.

$$HTMT_{ij} = \frac{\overline{Cor}_{ij}}{\sqrt{\overline{Cor}_i \times \overline{Cor}_j}} \quad (8)$$

Where, $\overline{Cor}_{ij}$: Average correlation coefficients of HTMT; $\overline{Cor}_i$ and $\overline{Cor}_j$: Average of correlation coefficients of any system.

Table 4. Discriminating validity: Fornell–Larcker Criterion

	Opt	**Inn**	**Ins**	**Dis**	**QSer**	**QSys**	**Min**	**PEU**	**PU**	**ENV**	**BRA**
Opt	**0.759**	0.512	0.367	0.378	0.512	0.534	0.587	0.523	0.578	0.378	0.587
Inn	0.489	**1.000**	0.512	0.546	0.534	0.546	0.534	0.512	0.467	0.378	0.387
Ins	0.501	0.498	**0.879**	0.612	0.672	0.547	0.487	0.465	0.487	0.489	0.398
Dis	0.456	0.587	0.501	**0.709**	0.489	0.489	0.512	0.549	0.389	0.412	0.367
Qser	0.501	0.512	0.503	0.401	**0.609**	0.512	0.345	0.546	0.561	0.346	0.546
Qsys	0.467	0.409	0.516	0.589	0.409	**1.000**	0.546	0.478	0.365	0.546	0.478
Min	0.356	0.451	0.467	0.512	0.512	0.512	**0.809**	0.512	0.578	0.487	0.546
PEU	0.501	0.467	0.412	0.501	0.508	0.489	0.356	**1.000**	0.461	0.465	0.412
PU	0.467	0.596	0.489	0.489	0.356	0.378	0.534	0.512	**0.746**	0.435	0.263
ENV	0.514	0.567	0.478	0.378	0.689	0.589	0.476	0.435	0.512	**0.823**	0.316
BRA	0.546	0.563	0.476	0.612	0.478	0.534	0.634	0.423	0.512	0.467	**0.902**

A number of indicators are used to evaluate the suitability of the research model. The indicators used to evaluate the model are divided into 3 main groups depending on the properties and suitability of the research model. The first group of indices are Absolute fit indices used to evaluate the degree to which the model accurately responds to observed data, including the chi-square statistic, and goodness-of-fit index (GFI).), and standardized mean residual (SRMR). The second group of indexes are Parsimonious fit indexes, which are considered to determine the complexity of the model, such as the adjusted fit index (AGFI) and root mean square error of approximation (RMSEA). The third is Incremental fit indices, used to evaluate the fit of the research model compared to standard alternative research models, indices, such as the Comparative Fit Index (CFI), Bentler–Bonett Normed Fit Index (NFI), and Tucker–Lewis Index (TLI). Use many indicators to evaluate and measure the suitability of the research model, meeting the goal of demonstrating the relationship between factors in the research model (Table 5).

Table 5. Indicators measuring the suitability of the research model

No.	Fit Statistics	Value	Recommended Value
1	Chi-square/df	1.792	< 3.0
2	GFI	0.892	> 0.8
3	GFI	0.902	> 0.9
4	NFI	0.934	> 0.9
5	TLI	0.978	> 0.9
6	RMSEA	0.050	< 0.6
7	SRMR	0.056	< 0.6

5.2 Evaluation of the Structural Mode

Perform structural model evaluation, and evaluate the relationships of measured variables and latent variables in the research model. The measurement indicators in the measurement model analysis are performed for the structural model (Table 6), the analysis results of these indicators are used to evaluate and make recommendations for the relationship in terms of the structure of measured variables and latent variables in the research model.

Table 6. Indicators measuring the suitability of the research model

No.	Fit Statistics	Value	Recommended Value
1	Chi-square/df	1.982	< 3.0
2	GFI	0.992	> 0.8
3	GFI	0.945	> 0.9
4	NFI	0.989	> 0.9
5	TLI	0.945	> 0.9
6	RMSEA	0.047	< 0.6
7	SRMR	0.046	< 0.6

The author re-evaluates the value of the study's structural model using the PLS bootstrapping method (Figure 3) based on the trajectory coefficients (f_i^2) value (Eq. 9), the trajectory coefficients (β) value is analyzed. The analysis results for all variables are greater than 0.02, which proves that the structure of the model is responsive to the research (Table 7).

$$f_i^2 = \frac{R^2_{included} - R^2_{excluded}}{1 - R^2_{included}} \quad (9)$$

Where, f_i^2: The effective coefficient of the impact of the ith input variable; $R^2_{included}$: The value R^2 of the model when the ith exogenous variable exists in the model; $R^2_{excluded}$: The value R^2 of the model when the ith exogenous variable is removed from the model.

Figure 3. Result of PLS boostraping

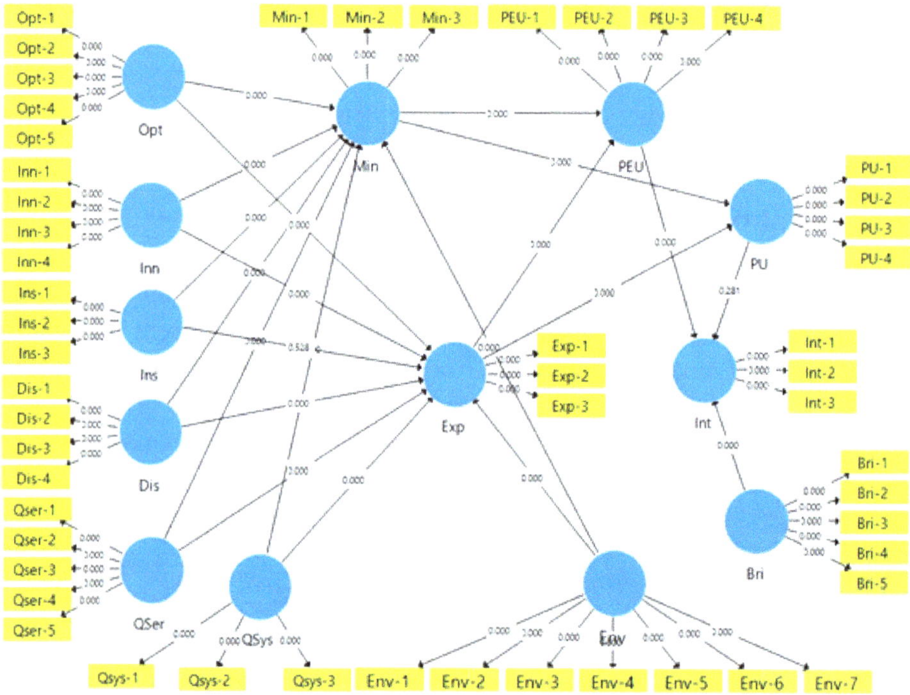

Table 7. Structural analysis of the hypothesis contrast

Hypothesis	Beta	Path (f_i^2) standardised	T value	p value	Supported
H1a. Opt ↔ Inn	0.108	0.023	2.435	0.002	Supported
H1b. Inn↔ Ins	0.023	0.034	3.412	0.004	Supported
H1c. Ins ↔ Dis	-0.201	0.025	2.672	0.012	Supported
H1d. Dis ↔ Bra	-0.034	0.027	2.476	0.031	Supported
H1e. Bra ↔ QSer	-0.132	0.034	4.324	0.034	Supported
H1f. QSer ↔ QSys	0.241	0.026	2.561	0.022	Supported
H1g. QSys ↔ Env	-0.324	0.035	2.378	0.001	Supported

continued on following page

Table 7. Continued

Hypothesis	Beta	Path (f_i^2) standardised	T value	p value	Supported
H2a. Opt → Mot	0.112	0.034	2.456	0.021	Supported
H2b. Opt → Exp	0.113	0.039	3.423	0.030	Supported
H2c. Opt → Min	-0.213	0.027	4.256	0.030	Supported
H3a. Inn → Mot	-0.143	0.027	4.328	0.003	Supported
H3b. Inn → Exp	0.032	0.026	3.781	0.005	Supported
H3c. Inn → Min	0.043	0.028	3.458	0.007	Supported
H4a. Ins → Mot	0.215	0.037	4.768	0.014	Supported
H4b. Ins → Exp	0.165	0.026	3.657	0.016	Supported
H4c. Ins → Min	0.276	0.036	3.689	0.041	Supported
H5a. Dis → Mot	0.045	0.029	4.256	0.032	Supported
H5b. Dis → Exp	0.032	0.028	3.512	**0.068**	**Not Supported**
H5c. Dis → Min	0.154	0.027	3.267	**0.079**	**Not Supported**
H6a. Bra → Mot	-0.287	0.035	4.256	0.003	Supported
H6b. Bra → Exp	-0.132	0.039	3.781	0.007	Supported
H6c. Bra → Min	-0.115	0.039	4.256	0.008	Supported
H7a. QSer → Mot	0.032	0.038	3.651	0.001	Supported
H7b. QSer → Exp	0.098	0.027	3.578	**0.058**	**Not Supported**
H7c. QSer → Min	-0.214	0.038	4.156	**0.061**	**Not Supported**
H8a. QSys → Mot	-0.176	0.039	4.238	0.004	Supported
H8b. QSys → Exp	0.085	0.026	3.812	**0.089**	**Not Supported**
H8c. QSys → Min	0.154	0.027	4.265	**0.072**	**Not Supported**
H9a. Env → Mot	0.276	0.038	3.612	0.006	Supported
H9b. Env → Exp	0.425	0.036	4.278	0.021	Supported
H9c. Env → Min	0.265	0.037	4.267	0.026	Supported
H10a. Mot → PEU	0.058	0.026	4.712	0.037	Supported
H10b. Mot → PU	0.043	0.028	4.213	0.006	Supported
H11a. Exp → PEU	-0.154	0.038	4.267	0.004	Supported
H11b. Exp→ PU	-0.276	0.025	3.156	0.008	Supported
H12a. Min→ PEU	0.436	0.026	3.267	0.021	Supported
H12b. Min → PU	0.265	0.021	3.278	0.032	Supported
H13. PEU → Int	0.265	0.032	4.023	0.043	Supported
H14. PEU → PU	0.132	0.024	3.278	0.045	Supported
H15. PU → Int	0.137	0.035	3.487	0.048	Supported

6. DISCUSSION

Electric vehicles (EVs) provide major advantages such as energy efficiency, reduced emissions, and a smoother driving experience, yet consumer choices still depend on personal needs, infrastructure readiness, and economic conditions. This study evaluates the factors influencing EV purchase intentions in Vietnam using TAM, UTAUT, and Mindfulness Theory, showing that technical readiness—especially optimization and technological innovation—strongly shapes consumer expectations. Vietnamese consumers value advanced technologies that enhance quality of life and support environmental protection, and they expect EVs to deliver these benefits. However, significant barriers remain: limited charging infrastructure and insufficient maintenance services reduce consumer confidence. Concerns about running out of battery power, difficulty finding charging stations, and challenges accessing replacement parts negatively affect trust and willingness to adopt EVs. The study also highlights the importance of brand perception. Consumers tend to prefer reputable brands with strong product quality and reliable after-sales service, emphasizing the need for manufacturers to strengthen brand identity and improve service systems to enhance competitiveness and encourage broader EV adoption in Vietnam.

7. CONCLUSION

This study offers a comprehensive assessment of the electric vehicle (EV) market in Ho Chi Minh City, emphasizing the key factors that shape consumer intentions to purchase EVs. The findings indicate that technical readiness—especially optimization and technological innovation—positively influences consumer expectations, showing that Vietnamese buyers tend to prefer modern, high-tech, and environmentally friendly products. Despite these advantages, current service quality and infrastructure still fall short of consumer needs. The limited availability of charging stations and inadequate after-sales services raise concerns about the practicality and convenience of EV ownership. To address these issues, manufacturers must invest more heavily in expanding charging infrastructure and improving maintenance and support services. Additionally, brand reputation is shown to be a major determinant of purchase decisions, as consumers often trust well-established brands that offer reliable products and professional service. Strengthening brand identity and ensuring high standards of customer care are therefore essential for market competitiveness. Overall, the study underscores the importance of enhancing infrastructure—particularly charging networks and after-sales support—to build consumer confidence and accelerate the adoption of EVs in Vietnam.

REFERENCES

Ahmadian, A., Ponnambalam, K., Almansoori, A., & Elkamel, A. (2023). Optimal Management of a Virtual Power Plant Consisting of Renewable Energy Resources and Electric Vehicles Using Mixed-Integer Linear Programming and Deep Learning. *Energies*, *16*(2), 1000. DOI: 10.3390/en16021000

Ambak, K., Harun, N. E., Rosli, N., Daniel, B. D., Prasetijo, J., & Ezree, M. (2006). Driver intention to use electric cars using technology acceptance model. Age, 3(9.7), 1-4.

Archsmith, J., Muehlegger, E., & Rapson, D. S. (2022). Future paths of electric vehicle adoption in the United States: Predictable determinants, obstacles, and opportunities. *Environmental and Energy Policy and the Economy*, *3*(1), 71–110. DOI: 10.1086/717219

Asim, M., Usman, M., Abbasi, M. S., Ahmad, S., Mujtaba, M. A., Soudagar, M. E. M., & Mohamed, A. (2022). Estimating the long-term effects of national and international sustainable transport policies on energy consumption and emissions of road transport sector of Pakistan. *Sustainability (Basel)*, *14*(9), 5732. DOI: 10.3390/su14095732

Athanasopoulou, L., Bikas, H., Papacharalampopoulos, A., Stavropoulos, P., & Chryssolouris, G. (2023). An industry 4.0 approach to electric vehicles. *International Journal of Computer Integrated Manufacturing*, *36*(2), 334–348. DOI: 10.1080/0951192X.2022.2081363

Babu, N. V., & Damle, M. (2022, November). Performance evaluation of Autonomous and Connected Electric Vehicles (ACEVs) towards buying intention in India: Forward trend in energy efficiency. In *2022 International Interdisciplinary Humanitarian Conference for Sustainability (IIHC)* (pp. 74-79). IEEE. DOI: 10.1109/IIHC55949.2022.10060349

Barbarossa, C., Beckmann, S. C., De Pelsmacker, P., Moons, I., & Gwozdz, W. (2015). A self-identity based model of electric car adoption intention: A cross-cultural comparative study. *Journal of Environmental Psychology*, *42*, 149–160. DOI: 10.1016/j.jenvp.2015.04.001

Begum, A. A., Abinaya, S. S., Chitrakala, G., Raghavi, M., & Savivarsha, S. (2022). A Study on Consumers' Intention and Buying Behaviour towards the Purchase of Electric Vehicles with Special Reference to Coimbatore City. Journal of Sales, Service and Marketing Research, 132-148.

Bell, G. D. (1963). Processes in the formation of adolescents' aspirations. *Social Forces*, *42*(2), 179–186. DOI: 10.2307/2575690

Bernard, T., & Seyoum Taffesse, A. (2014). Aspirations: An approach to measurement with validation using Ethiopian data. *Journal of African Economies*, *23*(2), 189–224. DOI: 10.1093/jae/ejt030

Brătucu, G., Trifan, A., Dovleac, L., Chi u, I. B., Todor, R. D., & Brătucu, R. (2019). Acquisition of electric vehicles—A step towards green consumption. Empirical research among Romanian students. *Sustainability (Basel)*, *11*(23), 6639. DOI: 10.3390/su11236639

Brinkmann, D., & Bhatiasevi, V. (2023). Purchase intention for electric vehicles among young adults in Thailand. *Vision (Basel)*, *27*(1), 110–118. DOI: 10.1177/09722629211001981

Buhmann, K. M., & Criado, J. R. (2023). Consumers' preferences for electric vehicles: The role of status and reputation. *Transportation Research Part D, Transport and Environment*, *114*, 103530. DOI: 10.1016/j.trd.2022.103530

Carey, J. (2023). The other benefit of electric vehicles. *Proceedings of the National Academy of Sciences of the United States of America*, *120*(3), e2220923120. DOI: 10.1073/pnas.2220923120

Carley, S., Krause, R. M., Lane, B. W., & Graham, J. D. (2013). Intent to purchase a plug-in electric vehicle: A survey of early impressions in large US cities. *Transportation Research Part D, Transport and Environment*, *18*, 39–45. DOI: 10.1016/j.trd.2012.09.007

Chen, R., Fan, R., Wang, D., & Yao, Q. (2023). Effects of multiple incentives on electric vehicle charging infrastructure deployment in China: An evolutionary analysis in a complex network. *Energy*, *264*, 125747. DOI: 10.1016/j.energy.2022.125747

Chéron, E., & Zins, M. (1997). Electric vehicle purchasing intentions: The concern over battery charge duration. *Transportation Research Part A, Policy and Practice*, *31*(3), 235–243. DOI: 10.1016/S0965-8564(96)00018-3

Dawood, T. H., Hammad, M. J., & Hammood, M. R. (2022). Towards a New Model of Consumer Purchasing Intention of Smart Products During Crises Times; Case of Covid-19 Pandemic Outbreak: an Applied Study on Female Employees of the Faculty of Economic and Business Administration Sciences. *International Journal of Professional Business Review*, *7*(4), 25. DOI: 10.26668/businessreview/2022.v7i4.e741 de Sena Abrahão, R., Moriguchi, S. N., & Andrade, D. F. (2016). The intention of adoption of mobile payment: An analysis in the light of the Unified Theory of Acceptance and Use of Technology (UTAUT). RAI Revista de administracao e Inovacao, 13(3), 221-230.

Dioha, M. O., Lukuyu, J., Virgüez, E., & Caldeira, K. (2022). Guiding the deployment of electric vehicles in the developing world. *Environmental Research Letters, 17*(7), 071001. DOI: 10.1088/1748-9326/ac765b

Enoma, N. (2022). A Comprehensive Review of Alternative Fuels for Automobiles: Benefits, Challenges and Future Direction. *Journal of Science and Technology Research*, *4*(4), 238–247.

Falai, A., Giuliacci, T. A., Misul, D., Paolieri, G., & Anselma, P. G. (2022). Modeling and on-road testing of an electric two-wheeler toward range prediction and BMS integration. *Energies*, *15*(7), 2431. DOI: 10.3390/en15072431

Gaoaketse, L., Ligaraba, N., & Chuchu, T. (2023). Factors influencing purchase intention of motor vehicles during the COVID-19 pandemic: An empirical study in South Africa. International Journal of Research in Business and Social Science, 12(3), 41-54.

Gaspar, R. M., Prasetyo, Y. T., Mariñas, K. A., Persada, S. F., & Nadlifatin, R. (2023). Exploring Consumers' Intention to Use Bikes and E-Scooters during the COVID-19 Pandemic in the Philippines: An Extended Theory of Planned Behavior Approach with a Consideration of Pro-Environmental Identity. *Sustainability (Basel)*, *15*(6), 5193. DOI: 10.3390/su15065193

Ghasemi-Marzbali, A. (2022). Fast-charging station for electric vehicles, challenges and issues: A comprehensive review. *Journal of Energy Storage*, *49*, 104136. DOI: 10.1016/j.est.2022.104136

Goh, H. H., Zong, L., Zhang, D., Liu, H., Dai, W., Lim, C. S., Kurniawan, T. A., Teo, K. T. K., & Goh, K. C. (2022). Mid-and long-term strategy based on electric vehicle charging unpredictability and ownership estimation. *International Journal of Electrical Power & Energy Systems*, *142*, 108240. DOI: 10.1016/j.ijepes.2022.108240

Guo, J., Marsh, H. W., Morin, A. J., Parker, P. D., & Kaur, G. (2015). Directionality of the associations of high school expectancy-value, aspirations, and attainment: A longitudinal study. *American Educational Research Journal*, *52*(2), 371–402. DOI: 10.3102/0002831214565786

Habich-Sobiegalla, S., Kostka, G., & Anzinger, N. (2018). Electric vehicle purchase intentions of Chinese, Russian and Brazilian citizens: An international comparative study. *Journal of Cleaner Production, 205*, 188–200. DOI: 10.1016/j.jclepro.2018.08.318

Han, L., Wang, S., Zhao, D., & Li, J. (2017). The intention to adopt electric vehicles: Driven by functional and non-functional values. *Transportation Research Part A, Policy and Practice, 103*, 185–197. DOI: 10.1016/j.tra.2017.05.033

Hasan, S. (2021). Assessment of electric vehicle repurchase intention: A survey-based study on the Norwegian EV market. *Transportation Research Interdisciplinary Perspectives, 11*, 100439. DOI: 10.1016/j.trip.2021.100439

Hiep, D. V., Tran, N. H., Tuan, N. A., Hung, T. M., Duc, N. V., & Tung, H. (2023). Assessment of Electric Two-Wheelers Development in Establishing a National E-Mobility Roadmap to Promote Sustainable Transport in Vietnam. *Sustainability (Basel), 15*(9), 7411. DOI: 10.3390/su15097411

Hoang, T. T., Pham, T. H., & Vu, T. M. H. (2022). Examining customer purchase decision towards battery electric vehicles in Vietnam market: A combination of self-interested and pro-environmental approach. *Cogent Business & Management, 9*(1), 2141671. DOI: 10.1080/23311975.2022.2141671

Hossain, M. S., Kumar, L., Islam, M. M., & Selvaraj, J. (2022). A comprehensive review on the integration of electric vehicles for sustainable development. *Journal of Advanced Transportation, 2022*, 1–26. DOI: 10.1155/2022/3868388

Huang, X., Lin, Y., Lim, M. K., Tseng, M. L., & Zhou, F. (2021). The influence of knowledge management on adoption intention of electric vehicles: A perspective on technological knowledge. *Industrial Management & Data Systems, 121*(7), 1481–1495. DOI: 10.1108/IMDS-07-2020-0411

Imtiaz, S. (2018). The studies of a unified theory of acceptance and use of technology (utaut) in an e-commerce context. *International Journal of Information Communication Technology and Digital Convergence, 3*(1), 42–56.

Jaiswal, D., Kaushal, V., Kant, R., & Singh, P. K. (2021). Consumer adoption intention for electric vehicles: Insights and evidence from Indian sustainable transportation. *Technological Forecasting and Social Change, 173*, 121089. DOI: 10.1016/j.techfore.2021.121089

Jiang, S. (2016). Purchase intention for electric vehicles in China from a customer-value perspective. *Social Behavior and Personality, 44*(4), 641–655. DOI: 10.2224/sbp.2016.44.4.641

Keum, D. D., & Eggers, J. P. (2018). Setting the bar: The evaluative and allocative roles of organizational aspirations. *Organization Science*, *29*(6), 1170–1186. DOI: 10.1287/orsc.2018.1224

Kim, J., Rasouli, S., & Timmermans, H. (2014). Expanding the scope of hybrid choice models allowing for a mixture of social influences and latent attitudes: Application to intended purchase of electric cars. *Transportation Research Part A, Policy and Practice*, *69*, 71–85. DOI: 10.1016/j.tra.2014.08.016

Krishnan, V. V., & Koshy, B. I. (2021). Evaluating the factors influencing purchase intention of electric vehicles in households owning conventional vehicles. *Case Studies on Transport Policy*, *9*(3), 1122–1129. DOI: 10.1016/j.cstp.2021.05.013

Lai, I. K., Liu, Y., Sun, X., Zhang, H., & Xu, W. (2015). Factors influencing the behavioral intention towards full electric vehicles: An empirical study in Macau. *Sustainability (Basel)*, *7*(9), 12564–12585. DOI: 10.3390/su70912564

LaMonaca, S., & Ryan, L. (2022). The state of play in electric vehicle charging services–A review of infrastructure provision, players, and policies. *Renewable & Sustainable Energy Reviews*, *154*, 111733. DOI: 10.1016/j.rser.2021.111733

Li, G., Luo, T., & Song, Y. (2022). Climate change mitigation efficiency of electric vehicle charging infrastructure in China: From the perspective of energy transition and circular economy. *Resources, Conservation and Recycling*, *179*, 106048. DOI: 10.1016/j.resconrec.2021.106048

Lin, B., & Wu, W. (2018). Why people want to buy an electric vehicle: An empirical study in first-tier cities of China. *Energy Policy*, *112*, 233–241. DOI: 10.1016/j.enpol.2017.10.026

Liu, W., Agusdinata, D. B., Eakin, H., & Romero, H. (2022). Sustainable minerals extraction for electric vehicles: A pilot study of consumers' perceptions of impacts. *Resources Policy*, *75*, 102523. DOI: 10.1016/j.resourpol.2021.102523

Mao, Y., Mei, Q., Jing, P., Wang, X., Xue, Y., & Zha, Y. (2023). Uncovering the behavioral determinants behind private car purchase intention during the new normal of COVID-19: An empirical investigation in China. *Mathematical Biosciences and Engineering*, *20*(4), 7316–7348. DOI: 10.3934/mbe.2023318

Maske, P., Chel, A., Goyal, P. K., & Kaushik, G. (2021). The sustainable perspective of electric vehicles and its future prospects. *Journal of Sustainable Materials Processing and Management*, *1*(1), 17–32. DOI: 10.30880/jsmpm.2021.01.01.003

Meegoda, J. N., Malladi, S., & Zayas, I. C. (2022). End-of-Life Management of Electric Vehicle Lithium-Ion Batteries in the United States. *Cleanroom Technology*, *4*(4), 1162–1174. DOI: 10.3390/cleantechnol4040071

Metais, M. O., Jouini, O., Perez, Y., Berrada, J., & Suomalainen, E. (2022). Too much or not enough? Planning electric vehicle charging infrastructure: A review of modeling options. *Renewable & Sustainable Energy Reviews*, *153*, 111719. DOI: 10.1016/j.rser.2021.111719

Mo, T., Li, Y., Lau, K. T., Poon, C. K., Wu, Y., & Luo, Y. (2022). Trends and emerging technologies for the development of electric vehicles. *Energies*, *15*(17), 6271. DOI: 10.3390/en15176271

Moon, S. J. (2021). Effect of consumer environmental propensity and innovative propensity on intention to purchase electric vehicles: Applying an extended theory of planned behavior. *International Journal of Sustainable Transportation*, *16*(11), 1032–1046. DOI: 10.1080/15568318.2021.1961950

Moons, I., & De Pelsmacker, P. (2012). Emotions as determinants of electric car usage intention. *Journal of Marketing Management*, *28*(3-4), 195–237. DOI: 10.1080/0267257X.2012.659007

Mustafi, N. N. (2022). An overview of hybrid electric vehicle technology. Engines and Fuels for Future Transport, 73-102.

Nava, M. (2017). The road ahead for electric vehicles. BBVA Research, 1-8.

Nikiforiadis, A., Stefanidou, M., & Ayfantopoulou, G. (2023). Will electric car-sharing attract citizens of touristic islands? Evidence from the island of Rhodes, Greece. *Transportation Research Procedia*, *69*, 265–272. DOI: 10.1016/j.trpro.2023.02.171

Okada, T., Tamaki, T., & Managi, S. (2019). Effect of environmental awareness on purchase intention and satisfaction pertaining to electric vehicles in Japan. *Transportation Research Part D, Transport and Environment*, *67*, 503–513. DOI: 10.1016/j.trd.2019.01.012

Patel, A. R., Vyas, D. R., Markana, A., & Jayaraman, R. (2022). A Conceptual Model for Integrating Sustainable Supply Chain, Electric Vehicles, and Renewable Energy Sources. *Sustainability (Basel)*, *14*(21), 14484. DOI: 10.3390/su142114484

Prodonovich, S., Perry, L. B., & Taggart, A. (2014). Developing conceptual understandings of the capacity to aspire for higher education. *Issues in Educational Research*, *24*(2), 174–189.

Riverso, R., Altamura, C., & La Barbera, F. (2023). Consumer Intention to Buy Electric Cars: Integrating Uncertainty in the Theory of Planned Behavior. *Sustainability (Basel), 15*(11), 8548. DOI: 10.3390/su15118548

Sachan, S., Deb, S., Singh, P. P., Alam, M. S., & Shariff, S. M. (2022). A comprehensive review of standards and best practices for utility grid integration with electric vehicle charging stations. *Wiley Interdisciplinary Reviews. Energy and Environment, 11*(3), e424. DOI: 10.1002/wene.424

Sadeghian, O., Oshnoei, A., Mohammadi-Ivatloo, B., Vahidinasab, V., & Anvari-Moghaddam, A. (2022). A comprehensive review on electric vehicles smart charging: Solutions, strategies, technologies, and challenges. *Journal of Energy Storage, 54*, 105241. DOI: 10.1016/j.est.2022.105241

Sang, Y. N., & Bekhet, H. A. (2015). Modelling electric vehicle usage intentions: An empirical study in Malaysia. *Journal of Cleaner Production, 92*, 75–83. DOI: 10.1016/j.jclepro.2014.12.045

Shalender, K., & Sharma, N. (2021). Using the extended theory of planned behavior (TPB) to predict the adoption intention of electric vehicles in India. *Environment, Development and Sustainability, 23*(1), 665–681. DOI: 10.1007/s10668-020-00602-7

Shen, Z. J., Zhang, Y. B., Yao, Y. Q., & Liu, B. W. (2011, August). Electric vehicle: The hope of the green future. In *2011 International Conference on Management and Service Science* (pp. 1-4). IEEE. DOI: 10.1109/ICMSS.2011.5998696

Sherwood, R. A.Jr. (1989). A Conceptual Framework for the Study of Aspirations. *Research in Rural Education*, 6(2), 61–66.

Siragusa, C., Tumino, A., Mangiaracina, R., & Perego, A. (2022). Electric vehicles performing last-mile delivery in B2C e-commerce: An economic and environmental assessment. *International Journal of Sustainable Transportation, 16*(1), 22–33. DOI: 10.1080/15568318.2020.1847367

Song, M. R., Chu, W., & Im, M. (2022). The effect of cultural and psychological characteristics on the purchase behavior and satisfaction of electric vehicles: A comparative study of US and China. *International Journal of Consumer Studies, 46*(1), 345–364. DOI: 10.1111/ijcs.12684

Sovacool, B. K., Abrahamse, W., Zhang, L., & Ren, J. (2019). Pleasure or profit? Surveying the purchasing intentions of potential electric vehicle adopters in China. *Transportation Research Part A, Policy and Practice, 124*, 69–81. DOI: 10.1016/j.tra.2019.03.002

Tesar, G. (1974). New hope for the driver: An electric car. Midwest Engineer, 26(7).

Thoburn, J., & Natsuda, K. (2023). National Cars and Product Champions: Ways Forward for Vietnam's Automotive Industry? In *The Political Economy of Global Manufacturing, Business and Finance* (pp. 121–145). Springer International Publishing. DOI: 10.1007/978-3-031-25832-9_6

Tiwari, S., & Singh, J. G. (2022). Optimal energy management of multi-carrier networked energy hubs considering efficient integration of demand response and electrical vehicles: A cooperative energy management framework. *Journal of Energy Storage, 51*, 104479. DOI: 10.1016/j.est.2022.104479

Trebbels, M., & Trebbels, M. (2015). The concept of educational aspirations. The transition at the end of compulsory full-time education: Educational and future career aspirations of native and migrant students, 37-45.

Truong, T. H. (2022). Determinants of intention to purchase electric cars in Vietnam: Proposing an analysis framework from theoretical research. VNU Journal of Economics and Business, 2(1).

Unterluggauer, T., Rich, J., Andersen, P. B., & Hashemi, S. (2022). Electric vehicle charging infrastructure planning for integrated transportation and power distribution networks: A review. *ETransportation, 12*, 100163. DOI: 10.1016/j.etran.2022.100163

Venugopal, P. (2022). Analysis of electric vehicles with an economic perspective for the future electric market. *Future Internet, 14*(6), 172. DOI: 10.3390/fi14060172

Verma, S., Dwivedi, G., & Verma, P. (2022). Life cycle assessment of electric vehicles in comparison to combustion engine vehicles: A review. *Materials Today: Proceedings, 49*, 217–222. DOI: 10.1016/j.matpr.2021.01.666

Wang, S., Fan, J., Zhao, D., Yang, S., & Fu, Y. (2016). Predicting consumers' intention to adopt hybrid electric vehicles: Using an extended version of the theory of planned behavior model. *Transportation, 43*(1), 123–143. DOI: 10.1007/s11116-014-9567-9

Więckowski, J., Wątróbski, J., Kizielewicz, B., & Sałabun, W. (2023). Complex sensitivity analysis in Multi-Criteria Decision Analysis: An application to the selection of an electric car. *Journal of Cleaner Production, 390*, 136051. DOI: 10.1016/j.jclepro.2023.136051

Xie, R., An, L., & Yasir, N. (2022). How Innovative Characteristics Influence Consumers' Intention to Purchase Electric Vehicle: A Moderating Role of Lifestyle. *Sustainability (Basel), 14*(8), 4467. DOI: 10.3390/su14084467

Yang, Z., Huang, H., & Lin, F. (2022). Sustainable electric vehicle batteries for a sustainable world: Perspectives on battery cathodes, environment, supply chain, manufacturing, life cycle, and policy. *Advanced Energy Materials*, *12*(26), 2200383. DOI: 10.1002/aenm.202200383

Yankun, S. (2020, December). An empirical study on the influencing factors of consumers' willingness to use pure electric vehicles based on the TAM Model. In 2020 16th Dahe Fortune China Forum and Chinese High-educational Management Annual Academic Conference (DFHMC) (pp. 289-292). IEEE.

Yu, Q., Nie, Y., Peng, S., Miao, Y., Zhai, C., Zhang, R., Han, J., Zhao, S., & Pecht, M. (2023). Evaluation of the safety standards system of power batteries for electric vehicles in China. *Applied Energy*, *349*, 121674. DOI: 10.1016/j.apenergy.2023.121674

Zhang, W., Fang, X., & Sun, C. (2023). The alternative path for fossil oil: Electric vehicles or hydrogen fuel cell vehicles? *Journal of Environmental Management*, *341*, 118019. DOI: 10.1016/j.jenvman.2023.118019

Zhou, G., Zhu, Z., & Luo, S. (2022). Location optimization of electric vehicle charging stations: Based on cost model and genetic algorithm. *Energy*, *247*, 123437. DOI: 10.1016/j.energy.2022.123437

Zhu, Z., Pivaro, N., Gupta, S., Gupta, A., & Canova, M. (2022). Safe model-based off-policy reinforcement learning for eco-driving in connected and automated hybrid electric vehicles. *IEEE Transactions on Intelligent Vehicles*, *7*(2), 387–398. DOI: 10.1109/TIV.2022.3150668

Chapter 6

AI in L2 Assessment: Rubrics, Quizzes, and Other Tools

Muhamad Haikal Umardi
http://orcid.org/0009-0004-8850-1260
University Esa Unggul, Indonesia

Binastya Anggara Sekti
http://orcid.org/0000-0001-5489-4888
Universitas Esa Unggul, Indonesia

ABSTRACT

This chapter explores the integration of Artificial Intelligence (AI) in second language (L2) assessment systems, particularly in the context of urban education within smart city frameworks. As cities strive for sustainability and digital transformation, educational systems must adapt by employing intelligent technologies for more efficient, equitable, and eco-friendly language evaluation. The chapter examines AI-powered rubrics, automated quizzes, and adaptive feedback tools that reduce reliance on traditional paper-based testing while expanding access to remote and personalized learning experiences. Emphasis is placed on how AI can enhance assessment fairness, decrease traffic-related emissions by supporting remote testing, and democratize language proficiency measurement. Case studies from urban school systems are presented to illustrate successful implementation. This chapter also addresses policy implications and future trends, offering a roadmap for designing inclusive, tech-enabled language assessment infrastructures aligned with smart city goals.

1. INTRODUCTION

The rapid expansion of artificial intelligence is reshaping how education systems operate, particularly in densely populated urban environments. Cities today

DOI: 10.4018/979-8-2600-0883-6.ch006

face multiple intersecting pressures, including traffic congestion, air pollution, infrastructure strain, and increasing demands for equitable access to high quality education. As urban governments pursue smarter and more sustainable development pathways, education systems are expected to align with broader environmental and technological transformation agendas. In this context, AI-enabled second language assessment emerges not only as an educational innovation but also as a component of sustainable urban governance. The rapid development of smart cities means the increasing interconnectivity of urban infrastructure, IoT devices, and data-driven systems (Sekti, 2026).

Traditional L2 (second language) assessment models often rely on centralized testing centers, paper-based examinations, and labor-intensive grading practices. These systems can generate significant logistical burdens in large cities where students must travel across congested transport networks to attend examinations. The environmental cost of printing materials, maintaining physical infrastructure, and supporting large administrative operations further compounds urban sustainability challenges. Moreover, static rubrics and standardized tests frequently fail to accommodate the linguistic diversity that characterizes metropolitan populations. As cities become more multicultural and multilingual, assessment systems must evolve to address variability in language proficiency, educational background, and learning pace.

Artificial intelligence offers the potential to redesign assessment processes in ways that are more adaptive, scalable, and environmentally efficient. Traffic signal control is a critical component of urban transportation management, and optimizing its performance can significantly reduce congestion, decrease travel times, and improve air quality (Akpan et al., 2026). Automated scoring systems can evaluate written and spoken language using natural language processing techniques. Adaptive quizzes can dynamically adjust question difficulty based on learner performance. Learning analytics platforms can track patterns over time and provide individualized feedback. These technologies reduce dependence on centralized physical infrastructure and enable remote participation, thereby minimizing travel-related emissions and congestion. In smart city ecosystems that prioritize digital governance and low-carbon solutions, AI-supported assessment aligns with broader sustainability objectives. Artificial Intelligence (AI) is increasingly recognised as a transformative force in advancing and potentially undermining, the United Nations Sustainable Development Goals (SDGs) (Zaidan, Truby, Ibrahim, & Hoppe, 2026).

At the same time, the adoption of AI in L2 assessment cannot be understood purely as a technical upgrade. Lexico-semantic representations in the first language (L1) and second language (L2) become increasingly similar with greater L2 experience; however, this similarity is modulated by the specific lexico-semantic processes under investigation (Licata, Bouffier, & Borghesani, 2026). It represents a structural shift in how knowledge is evaluated, how feedback is delivered, and how educational equity is defined. AI systems rely on data infrastructures that collect, process, and store large volumes of learner information. These infrastructures intersect with urban digital networks, cloud computing facilities, and regulatory frameworks governing privacy and data protection. As cities invest in digital transformation, education becomes one of the key domains where algorithmic decision-making directly affects citizens. Therefore, AI-enabled assessment must be examined through the lens of governance, transparency, and ethical responsibility. The pedagogical potential of artificial intelligence (AI)-supported multimodal writing instruction to foster both English language proficiency and sustainability awareness among middle school learners (Aydın Yıldız, 2025).

Urban education systems are also central to workforce development and social mobility. Language proficiency in global cities influences employment access, civic participation, and integration across cultural communities. When AI tools are used to assess language skills, they shape not only classroom outcomes but also broader social trajectories. If designed responsibly, intelligent assessment can support personalized learning pathways and reduce teacher workload, allowing educators to focus on higher-order instructional tasks. If implemented without safeguards, however, automated systems may reinforce bias, disadvantage non-standard dialect speakers, or create digital divides among students with unequal access to technology. Human-AI collaborative competence in L2 Writing, which involves learners' strategic interaction with AI tools, has emerged as a crucial construct as AI reshapes traditional assessment paradigms (Cui, Mahfoodh, Dong, & Ulanbek, 2026).

Sustainable smart cities require coherent integration between educational innovation and environmental strategy. AI-based assessment can contribute to reducing material consumption, lowering transportation demand, and optimizing institutional resources. However, sustainability must be understood holistically. Digital systems require energy-intensive data centers and electronic devices that carry their own environmental footprints. Urban policymakers must therefore balance digital expansion with green infrastructure planning, renewable energy integration, and responsible technology procurement.

This chapter positions AI in L2 assessment within the broader framework of sustainable urban transformation. It argues that intelligent rubrics, adaptive quizzes, and automated feedback systems should be evaluated not only in terms of pedagogical efficiency but also in relation to environmental impact, governance design, and social equity. By situating language assessment within the ecosystem of smart city development, the chapter advances a multidimensional perspective that connects education, technology, sustainability, and public policy. The integration of these dimensions is essential if AI-driven assessment is to contribute meaningfully to the dual goals of educational quality and urban environmental resilience.

2. THEORETICAL AND EMPIRICAL FOUNDATIONS OF AI IN L2 ASSESSMENT

The integration of artificial intelligence into second language assessment is not merely a technological shift but a transformation grounded in evolving theories of learning, evaluation, and digital governance. To understand the implications of AI-based rubrics, adaptive quizzes, and automated feedback systems, it is necessary to situate these tools within broader theoretical frameworks that shape how language competence is conceptualized and measured. AI systems operationalize particular assumptions about learning, proficiency, fairness, and performance. Without examining these foundations, discussions of efficiency and scalability remain incomplete. Artificial intelligence (AI) has become an essential tool in exploring principles of linguistics and foreign language teaching (Alsharbi, 2026).

AI-driven L2 assessment intersects with theories of formative assessment, sociocultural learning, learning analytics, and algorithmic fairness. Each perspective contributes distinct insights into how digital systems influence both pedagogical practice and institutional decision-making. At the same time, empirical evidence reveals both measurable benefits and unresolved risks. This section synthesizes key theoretical lenses and emerging empirical findings to establish a rigorous foundation for evaluating AI-supported assessment in urban and smart city contexts.

2.1 Assessment for Learning and Formative Feedback Models

Assessment for Learning emphasizes continuous feedback, learner agency, and instructional adaptation. Rather than treating assessment as a terminal measurement of competence, this perspective positions evaluation as an ongoing process embedded within learning activities. AI-based systems align strongly with this approach because they can generate immediate, individualized feedback at scale. Recent studies have highlighted the potential of generative artificial intelligence to address challenges in providing accurate and pedagogically relevant feedback .(Barrot & Bui, 2026)

Automated writing evaluation tools, for example, can analyze syntactic complexity, lexical diversity, coherence markers, and error patterns within seconds. This immediacy supports iterative revision cycles, allowing learners to refine drafts multiple times without waiting for instructor review. Empirical observations indicate that students exposed to frequent AI-generated feedback often demonstrate increased engagement in revision and greater awareness of language patterns. However, the depth of feedback varies depending on model sophistication. While surface-level grammar correction is well supported, higher-order discourse evaluation remains more challenging. The integration of Generative Artificial Intelligence (GenAI) into

L2 writing feedback has gained attention, yet its intersection with student feedback literacy development remains underexplored (Lu, Yao, Xiao, Zhu, & Yin, 2026).

The formative potential of AI also raises critical questions. When feedback is automated, learners may prioritize algorithmically rewarded features over communicative authenticity. If scoring systems emphasize measurable features such as word count or sentence length, students may optimize for these metrics rather than clarity or rhetorical effectiveness. Thus, while AI supports formative assessment, its design must align with pedagogical objectives rather than narrow computational indicators.

2.2 Sociocultural Perspectives and Communicative Competence

From a sociocultural perspective, language proficiency is not simply an individual cognitive trait but a socially situated practice shaped by context, identity, and interaction. Communicative competence includes pragmatic awareness, cultural nuance, and audience sensitivity. AI systems, however, rely on training data and probabilistic modeling that may reflect dominant linguistic norms. Speaking is often challenging for language learners to develop due to factors such as anxiety and limited practice opportunities (Hou & Min, 2026).

Automated assessment tools often evaluate written or spoken responses against standardized corpora. This approach risks privileging certain dialects, registers, or rhetorical styles while marginalizing linguistic variation. In urban settings characterized by multilingual populations, such bias can produce inequitable outcomes. For example, learners who draw on translanguaging strategies or culturally specific rhetorical structures may receive lower scores despite demonstrating communicative effectiveness within their communities. AI interventions have potential in advancing reading comprehension, sparking learner engagement, and empowering self-regulated learning (Shafiee Rad, 2025).

Empirical research suggests that human raters themselves display variability and bias, yet algorithmic systems introduce new dimensions of opacity. The sociocultural lens therefore underscores the importance of contextual calibration and human oversight. AI assessment must be viewed as augmentative rather than replacement technology. Hybrid models that combine machine scoring with teacher moderation offer a pathway toward balancing efficiency with cultural sensitivity.

2.3 Learning Analytics and Data-Driven Personalization

Learning analytics frameworks conceptualize education as a data-rich ecosystem in which patterns of engagement and performance inform instructional decisions. AI-based assessment tools generate large volumes of granular data, including response times, revision histories, error frequencies, and progression trajectories. These data streams enable adaptive testing environments in which question difficulty adjusts dynamically to learner ability. Seventy-five university students in Japan completed roleplay tasks with both human tutors and an AI agent (Eguchi et al., 2025).

Adaptive quizzes exemplify this approach. By estimating proficiency in real time, they can reduce test length while maintaining measurement precision. In high-density urban systems, this efficiency translates into reduced administrative overhead and improved accessibility. Students can complete assessments remotely, decreasing transportation demands and supporting flexible scheduling.

However, personalization through analytics also introduces concerns about surveillance and data governance. Continuous tracking may create psychological pressure or reduce learner autonomy. Additionally, predictive models may unintentionally label students in ways that shape expectations and opportunities. Empirical evidence indicates that while adaptive systems improve diagnostic accuracy, their long-term impact on learner confidence and self-perception requires further study.

2.4 Algorithmic Fairness and Ethical Evaluation

Algorithmic fairness theory addresses the distributional effects of automated decision-making systems. In L2 assessment, fairness concerns include bias across gender, socioeconomic background, accent, and dialect. AI models trained on imbalanced datasets may systematically disadvantage certain groups. Urban education systems, which often serve highly diverse populations, must therefore prioritize fairness auditing and validation processes. Artificial Intelligence (AI) has become an influential force shaping modern society, raising urgent ethical questions about responsibility, fairness, transparency, and human dignity (Sekti, 2025a).

Empirical analyses of automated scoring systems reveal that performance varies depending on the representativeness of training data. When corpora include limited examples of non-standard varieties, scoring consistency declines. Transparent documentation of model development and periodic recalibration are essential to mitigate these risks.

Ethical considerations extend beyond bias. Data privacy, informed consent, and the right to contest automated scores are fundamental governance principles. AI systems collect sensitive linguistic and behavioral data that must be securely stored and responsibly managed. Without clear regulatory frameworks, the expansion of digital assessment may erode trust in educational institutions.

2.5 Empirical Evidence: Benefits and Limitations

Empirical studies of AI in L2 assessment report several measurable advantages. Automated scoring reduces grading time and increases consistency across large cohorts. Adaptive testing enhances measurement efficiency and can lower dropout rates by minimizing test fatigue. Immediate feedback has been associated with improved revision behaviors and learner motivation. Traditional L2 writing instruction often struggles to provide personalized, process-oriented feedback and engage student motivation. While generative AI like ChatGPT offers a potential solution, its application lacks a robust pedagogical foundation (Wang, Yin, & Cao, 2026).

Yet limitations remain. Most studies focus on short-term performance outcomes rather than long-term language acquisition. Evidence on the effectiveness of AI feedback for advanced discourse skills is mixed. Furthermore, few investigations examine the environmental and infrastructural implications of large-scale digital assessment systems within urban sustainability frameworks. Urban sustainability refers to an integrated approach to urban development that balances environmental protection, efficient resource use, public health, and social well-being by improving urban infrastructure such as water, sanitation, energy, and green systems to address challenges of rapid urbanization, climate change, and urban heat while supporting long-term livability and resilience in cities (Cheshmehzangi, Butters, Xie, & Dawodu, 2021).

Another underexplored dimension concerns teacher professional identity. As AI assumes routine evaluation tasks, instructors may shift toward facilitation and interpretive roles. This transformation requires professional development and institutional adaptation. The empirical literature has yet to fully explore how AI integration reshapes pedagogical labor structures in metropolitan education systems.

2.6 Synthesis: Toward an Integrated Framework

Taken together, these theoretical and empirical perspectives reveal that AI in L2 assessment operates at the intersection of pedagogy, technology, governance, and sustainability. Formative assessment theory explains the pedagogical promise of rapid feedback. Sociocultural theory highlights the risks of linguistic homogenization. Learning analytics demonstrates the power of personalization, while algorithmic fairness frameworks stress the need for ethical safeguards. The transformative impact of Artificial Intelligence (AI) across four critical sectors healthcare, education, finance, and security while addressing the profound ethical challenges arising from the rise of generative AI (Utami & Sekti, 2025). Table 1 shows the Major Research Streams in AI-Based L2 Assessment.

Table 1. Major research streams in AI-based L2 assessment

Research Stream	Key Contributions	Limitations	Research Gap
Automated Writing Evaluation	Immediate feedback; scalable scoring	Potential bias; limited discourse depth	Longitudinal impact studies
Adaptive Testing	Personalized item difficulty	Over-reliance on measurable outputs	Integration with communicative competence
Learning Analytics	Real-time performance dashboards	Privacy concerns	Ethical governance models
AI & Equity Studies	Bias detection and fairness	Limited urban-specific research	Policy alignment for smart cities

The convergence of these lenses suggests that AI-based L2 assessment must be designed as a socio-technical system rather than a standalone digital tool. Its effectiveness depends on alignment between technological capability, pedagogical intention, regulatory oversight, and environmental responsibility. In smart city contexts seeking to reduce congestion and pollution, digital assessment contributes to sustainability goals. However, this contribution is meaningful only if educational equity and data governance are embedded at the core of system design.

This integrated understanding establishes the foundation for examining specific AI tools in subsequent sections and for articulating policy implications that balance innovation with accountability.

3. AI-DRIVEN ASSESSMENT TOOLS

The practical implementation of artificial intelligence in L2 assessment materializes through a range of digital tools that transform how language proficiency is measured, interpreted, and acted upon. These tools are not isolated applications but components of a broader socio-technical infrastructure embedded within urban digital ecosystems. In smart city contexts that seek efficiency, sustainability, and inclusivity, AI-driven assessment technologies offer opportunities to reduce logistical burdens while enhancing personalization and scalability. However, their effectiveness depends on careful design, validation, and governance. Generative Artificial Intelligence (GenAI) developments have ignited interest in how they will impact L2 writers' agency over their academic writing processes (Moorhouse, Wan, Wu, Wu, & Ho, 2025).

This section examines three primary categories of AI-based assessment tools: intelligent rubrics, automated adaptive quizzes, and AI-supported feedback systems. Each category reflects distinct technological mechanisms and pedagogical implications, while collectively reshaping the architecture of language evaluation in urban education systems.

3.1 Intelligent Rubrics and Automated Scoring Systems

Intelligent rubrics rely on natural language processing and machine learning algorithms to evaluate written and spoken language performance. Unlike traditional scoring frameworks that require manual interpretation by human raters, AI-based rubrics convert linguistic features into quantifiable indicators. These may include syntactic complexity, lexical sophistication, coherence markers, fluency rate, pronunciation accuracy, and semantic alignment with prompts. Artificial Intelligence (AI) and Machine Learning (ML) are transformative technologies reshaping industries (Sekti, 2025b).

From a technical standpoint, automated scoring systems operate by training models on large corpora of previously scored responses. The system identifies patterns associated with different proficiency levels and assigns probabilistic scores to new submissions. This approach enhances consistency and reduces inter-rater variability, which is a common challenge in human evaluation.

In urban education systems where thousands of assessments may be conducted daily, automated scoring significantly reduces administrative load. Teachers can redirect time toward instructional design and individualized mentoring rather than repetitive grading tasks. Furthermore, remote submission reduces reliance on centralized examination venues, contributing to decreased commuting and lower environmental impact.

Despite these advantages, intelligent rubrics introduce several challenges. Algorithmic opacity may limit transparency, making it difficult for students to understand how scores are generated. Overemphasis on measurable features may inadvertently privilege formulaic writing structures. Additionally, dialect variation and multilingual influences may not be fully captured by standardized training data. For this reason, intelligent rubrics should incorporate explainability features and allow for human moderation to maintain fairness and pedagogical integrity.

3.2 Automated Adaptive Quizzes

Adaptive quizzes represent a shift from static testing to dynamic proficiency estimation. These systems continuously adjust item difficulty based on learner responses, generating a tailored assessment pathway. By estimating ability levels in real time, adaptive testing achieves greater measurement precision with fewer items. The advent of generative artificial intelligence (GenAI) is already impacting pedagogical strategies and assessment methodologies in higher education, particularly in the biological sciences, which have traditionally relied heavily on written assessments (Bawn et al., 2026).

The underlying mechanism typically involves item response modeling combined with machine learning optimization. As learners answer questions, the system updates its estimation of their proficiency and selects subsequent items accordingly. This process reduces test fatigue and enhances engagement, particularly in linguistically diverse urban classrooms.

In smart city environments, adaptive quizzes also contribute to logistical efficiency. Remote administration reduces the need for large physical testing centers and decreases traffic associated with examination scheduling. Digital delivery minimizes paper consumption and enables flexible timing, which benefits working learners and non-traditional students.

However, adaptive systems must address calibration and bias concerns. If item banks are not representative of diverse linguistic backgrounds, difficulty estimation may disadvantage certain populations. Additionally, over-reliance on multiple-choice formats may narrow the construct of language proficiency to discrete measurable components. Effective adaptive testing frameworks therefore integrate varied item types, including productive tasks, to maintain construct validity.

3.3 AI-Supported Feedback and Formative Analytics

AI-supported feedback systems extend beyond scoring to provide actionable insights for learners. These tools analyze drafts or spoken responses and generate suggestions for grammar correction, vocabulary enhancement, organization improvement, and coherence strengthening. More advanced systems offer discourse-level recommendations and stylistic variation prompts.

Formative analytics platforms complement feedback tools by visualizing performance trends over time. Dashboards may display progress indicators, common error categories, or predicted proficiency trajectories. Teachers can use these insights to identify struggling students and tailor instruction accordingly. As the popularity and accessibility of artificial intelligence (AI) in learning continue to rise, online education has increasingly incorporated AI. It is imperative to investigate how AI in the scholarly community supports the learning of autonomous students (Yoshida, Duangchinda, & Ruangrit, 2026).

The pedagogical value of immediate feedback lies in its capacity to encourage iterative learning. Students are able to revise multiple times within short cycles, fostering metacognitive awareness and self-regulated learning. In urban settings characterized by large class sizes, AI feedback alleviates the bottleneck of delayed instructor responses.

Yet formative analytics also raise ethical and psychological considerations. Continuous monitoring may create perceptions of surveillance or performance pressure. Predictive indicators could unintentionally label students and shape teacher expectations. To mitigate these risks, institutions should ensure that analytics are used diagnostically rather than deterministically and that learners retain agency over their data.

3.4 Speech Recognition and Multimodal Assessment

Advancements in speech recognition technology have expanded AI assessment into oral proficiency domains. Automated pronunciation scoring, fluency measurement, and interactive speaking simulations are increasingly integrated into digital platforms. Multimodal systems combine textual, audio, and behavioral data to create richer proficiency profiles.

In urban contexts where access to qualified oral examiners may be limited, speech-based AI systems offer scalable alternatives. Remote speaking assessments reduce travel demands and enable flexible scheduling. Additionally, multimodal analysis captures aspects of communication that written tests cannot measure. The rapid advancements in artificial intelligence (AI) technologies are fundamentally transforming mathematics teaching processes and offering new pedagogical opportunities within instructional environments. However, the effective use of these technologies is closely related to mathematics teachers' levels of knowledge, awareness, attitudes, and skills regarding AI (İnci Kuzu, 2026).

Nevertheless, speech recognition models may struggle with accent diversity and background noise variability. Calibration across linguistic communities is essential to avoid systematic bias. Continuous retraining and inclusive data collection practices are necessary to ensure equitable performance evaluation.

3.5 Integration within Smart City Digital Infrastructure

AI-driven assessment tools do not operate independently from broader urban digital ecosystems. They rely on cloud computing, secure data storage, broadband connectivity, and regulatory compliance frameworks. In cities pursuing sustainability goals, educational technology must align with green infrastructure strategies and responsible data governance. The rapid urbanization and digital transformation of modern cities demand intelligent infrastructure capable of supporting massive IoT deployments and real-time decision-making across diverse smart city applications (Al-Qudah, Tawil, Almuhajiri, Almazaydeh, & Suen, 2026).

Energy consumption of servers and digital devices should be factored into sustainability calculations. Institutions may adopt renewable energy sources for data centers and implement device recycling programs to minimize environmental impact. Integration with city-wide digital identity systems may streamline authentication while maintaining privacy protections.

The convergence of AI assessment with smart city governance highlights the importance of coordinated policy frameworks. Educational authorities, municipal regulators, and technology providers must collaborate to establish standards for transparency, data protection, and algorithmic accountability.

3.6 Toward Responsible Implementation

The expansion of AI-driven assessment tools offers transformative potential for urban language education. Intelligent rubrics enhance scalability, adaptive quizzes improve precision, and feedback systems foster continuous learning. However, responsible implementation requires balanced consideration of efficiency, fairness, privacy, and sustainability. An integrated consideration of digital justice in smart cities is relatively new to most discussions on the subject, and an applicable research framework for the assessment and management of digital justice in the smart city is still lacking (Schüle, Pollok, & Güleş, 2026).

Institutions should adopt hybrid assessment models that combine automated scoring with human oversight. Bias auditing procedures and regular validation studies are essential. Clear communication with learners regarding data usage and scoring criteria builds trust. Policymakers must ensure that technological adoption does not widen digital divides or undermine equity.

When embedded within transparent governance structures and aligned with environmental objectives, AI-driven assessment tools can support both educational innovation and sustainable urban transformation. Figure 1 shows the AI-Integrated L2 Assessment Ecosystem in Smart Cities.

Figure 1. AI-integrated L2 assessment ecosystem in smart cities

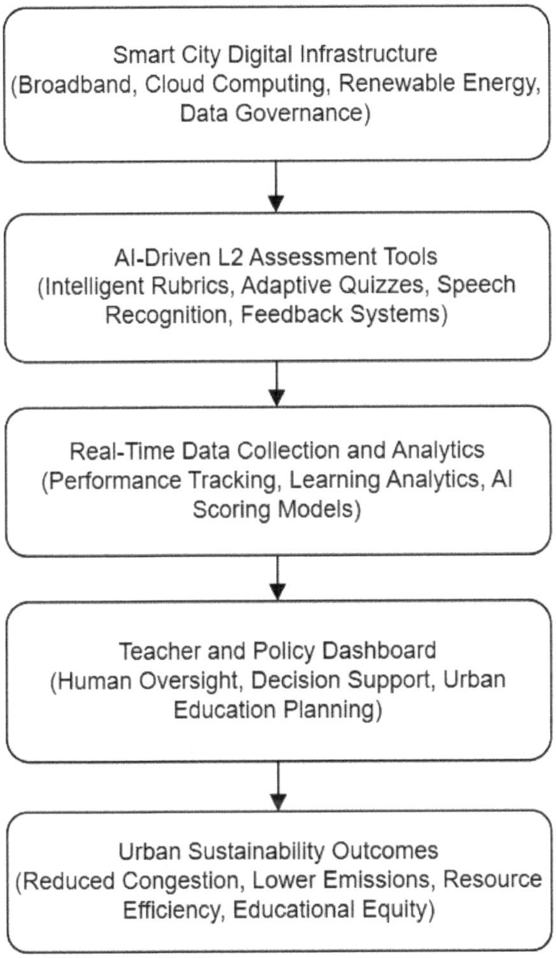

4. ETHICS, DATA PRIVACY, AND ALGORITHMIC FAIRNESS

The integration of artificial intelligence into L2 assessment introduces not only pedagogical innovation but also profound ethical and governance challenges. As AI systems increasingly participate in scoring, feedback generation, and performance prediction, they assume a decision-making role that directly affects learners' academic trajectories, self-perception, and access to opportunities. In urban environments where education systems are deeply embedded within digital governance infrastructures, ethical considerations extend beyond classroom practice and into public policy, data regulation, and civic trust. The integration of artificial intelligence (AI) into hepatocellular carcinoma (HCC) management introduces significant ethical challenges, which are shaped by the disease's unique epidemiology and clinical complexity (Wan & Lin, 2026).

AI-driven assessment tools operate through large-scale data collection, model training, and automated inference. These processes raise fundamental questions about transparency, fairness, accountability, and privacy. While digital systems promise efficiency and scalability, they also risk reproducing structural inequalities if governance frameworks do not actively safeguard equity and rights. Ethical implementation therefore requires systematic analysis of algorithmic bias, data protection standards, and institutional responsibility.

4.1 Algorithmic Bias and Fairness

Algorithmic fairness concerns the extent to which automated systems produce equitable outcomes across diverse populations. In L2 assessment, fairness issues may arise from training data limitations, feature selection, or model design choices. If scoring algorithms are trained primarily on standardized language corpora, they may inadvertently privilege dominant linguistic norms while penalizing dialectal variation or culturally specific rhetorical styles.

Urban education systems often serve students from varied socioeconomic and linguistic backgrounds. Automated scoring that fails to account for this diversity may widen achievement gaps rather than reduce them. For example, speech recognition tools may underperform for learners with certain accents. Writing evaluation systems may prioritize syntactic conformity over communicative effectiveness in multilingual contexts.

Algorithmic bias does not necessarily stem from intentional discrimination but from systemic imbalances embedded within data. However, unintentional bias can still produce inequitable consequences. To mitigate these risks, institutions must conduct regular fairness audits, test performance across demographic groups, and implement recalibration mechanisms. Hybrid models that combine AI scoring with human review can further enhance reliability and reduce the likelihood of unjust outcomes.

4.2 Transparency and Explainability

Transparency is essential for maintaining trust in automated assessment systems. Students and educators must understand how scores are generated and how feedback is constructed. When AI systems operate as opaque black boxes, learners may perceive outcomes as arbitrary or unchallengeable. Such perceptions undermine both educational legitimacy and institutional credibility.

Explainable AI approaches aim to provide interpretable outputs that clarify which linguistic features influenced a score. For example, feedback might indicate that coherence, lexical variety, or argument structure contributed significantly to the evaluation. Clear explanation mechanisms empower learners to engage meaningfully with feedback rather than simply accepting automated judgments.

Transparency also involves institutional disclosure regarding model validation, data sources, and performance benchmarks. Urban education authorities adopting AI tools must establish public guidelines outlining how systems are evaluated and monitored. This level of openness aligns with broader smart city governance principles, where digital infrastructure is expected to operate under accountable regulatory frameworks.

4.3 Data Privacy and Security

AI-based assessment systems rely on extensive data collection, including written submissions, speech recordings, behavioral interaction logs, and sometimes biometric metadata. These data streams create detailed profiles of learners' linguistic and cognitive patterns. In smart city environments characterized by interconnected digital systems, educational data may intersect with broader civic databases (Sekti, 2026).

Data privacy therefore becomes a central concern. Institutions must ensure that data collection is proportional, secure, and purpose-limited. Learners should be informed about what data are collected, how long they are stored, and who has access to them. Secure encryption, controlled access protocols, and regular security audits are critical components of responsible implementation.

Beyond technical safeguards, ethical governance requires clear policies regarding data retention and deletion. Continuous monitoring systems should not transform educational platforms into surveillance environments. Students must retain the right to access, review, and, where appropriate, contest automated decisions that affect their academic standing.

4.4 Accountability and Human Oversight

The delegation of evaluative authority to AI systems raises questions of accountability. When an automated rubric assigns a score that influences progression or certification, who bears responsibility for errors or bias? Institutions cannot defer accountability to software providers. Human oversight remains essential to preserve fairness and due process.

Responsible governance models treat AI as a decision-support tool rather than a final arbiter. Teachers and administrators must retain the capacity to override automated results when anomalies or contextual factors are identified. Clear appeal mechanisms should allow learners to request human review of contested outcomes.

In urban education systems operating within smart city frameworks, accountability structures must extend beyond individual schools. Municipal education departments and regulatory bodies should establish standards for AI procurement, validation, and periodic evaluation. Cross-sector collaboration between technologists, educators, and policymakers strengthens oversight capacity.

4.5 Digital Equity and the Risk of Exclusion

While AI-driven assessment may reduce logistical burdens and environmental impact, it can also intensify digital inequality. Access to stable internet connectivity, appropriate devices, and digital literacy varies across socioeconomic groups. In large cities, disparities between neighborhoods can be significant.

If AI-based assessment becomes mandatory without compensatory support, students with limited access may be disadvantaged. Responsible implementation requires infrastructure investment, device lending programs, and inclusive design principles that accommodate diverse user needs. Equity considerations must be integrated into procurement and deployment strategies rather than addressed retrospectively.

Digital equity also involves accessibility for learners with disabilities. Speech recognition systems must accommodate varied speech patterns. Interface design must consider visual and cognitive accessibility. Ethical AI in education is therefore inseparable from inclusive design practices.

4.6 Environmental Ethics in Digital Assessment

Although AI-enabled assessment reduces paper usage and transportation demands, digital infrastructure consumes energy and generates electronic waste. Data centers, server maintenance, and device production carry environmental footprints that must be acknowledged within sustainability planning.

Urban policymakers integrating AI into education should evaluate energy efficiency standards, renewable power sourcing, and hardware lifecycle management. Sustainable procurement policies and device recycling initiatives can align digital innovation with environmental goals. Ethical AI in smart cities thus includes ecological responsibility alongside fairness and privacy (Sekti, 2025a). Figure 2 shown the Governance Framework for Ethical AI Assessment.

Figure 2. Governance framework for ethical AI assessment

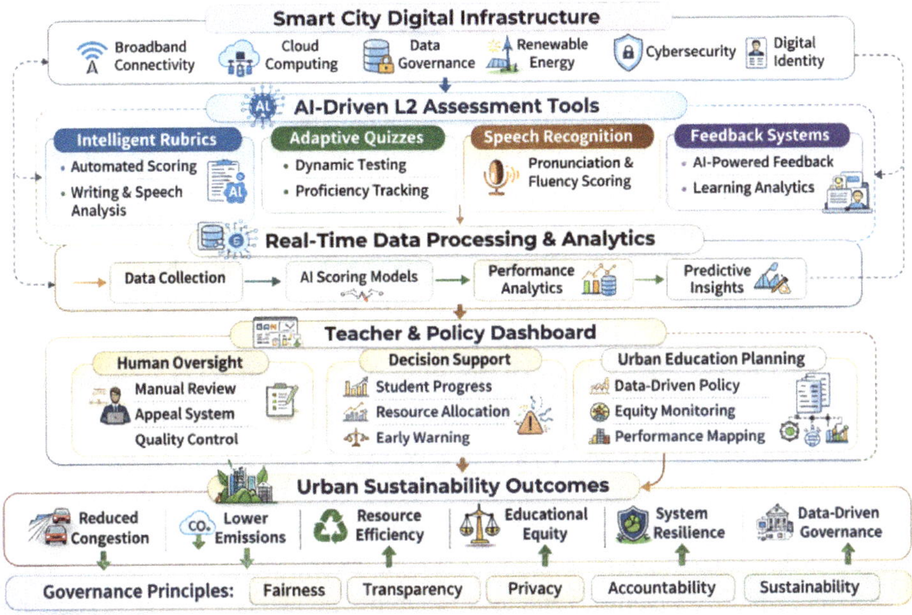

4.7 Toward a Responsible Governance Framework

The ethical deployment of AI in L2 assessment requires a multidimensional governance framework grounded in fairness, transparency, privacy, accountability, and sustainability. Institutions should adopt the following guiding principles:

1. Conduct regular bias audits and model validation studies.
2. Ensure explainability and accessible feedback mechanisms.
3. Implement strict data protection and retention policies.
4. Maintain human oversight and clear appeal processes.
5. Promote equitable access to digital infrastructure.
6. Integrate environmental sustainability into digital planning.

By embedding these principles within urban digital governance strategies, cities can leverage AI-driven assessment to improve educational efficiency while preserving social trust and democratic accountability.

5. SUSTAINABILITY AND SMART CITY IMPLICATIONS

The adoption of AI-driven L2 assessment tools must be evaluated not only through pedagogical effectiveness but also through their broader implications for urban sustainability and smart city governance. In cities facing persistent traffic congestion, air pollution, infrastructure strain, and spatial inequality, education systems are not isolated institutions. They are embedded within the same transportation networks, energy grids, and digital infrastructures that shape urban environmental performance. Therefore, the transition from traditional assessment models to AI-enabled systems has implications that extend beyond classrooms and directly intersect with sustainability objectives.

Traditional large-scale assessment often requires centralized test centers, synchronized scheduling, printed materials, and significant physical infrastructure. In dense metropolitan regions, such arrangements contribute to peak-hour traffic flows as students travel to designated locations. They also generate material waste through paper-based exams and administrative documentation. AI-enabled assessment systems, particularly those that allow remote participation and digital submission, reduce reliance on centralized facilities and lower mobility demands. Flexible scheduling decreases congestion spikes associated with exam periods, while digital distribution minimizes paper consumption and storage needs. In this sense, AI-supported assessment aligns with smart city strategies aimed at optimizing resource use and reducing emissions.

However, sustainability must be understood in systemic terms rather than through isolated efficiency gains. While remote and digital assessment reduces transportation-related emissions, it increases reliance on digital infrastructure. Cloud computing, server operations, and data processing require energy, and the environmental footprint of data centers must be considered. Furthermore, the production and disposal of electronic devices contribute to resource extraction and electronic waste streams. If AI adoption expands without sustainable infrastructure planning, environmental gains in one domain may be offset by energy burdens in another.

Smart cities typically integrate digital transformation with environmental planning through coordinated infrastructure strategies. Within this framework, AI-driven assessment can contribute to sustainability when paired with renewable energy sourcing for data centers, energy-efficient device standards, and responsible procurement policies. Educational institutions may collaborate with municipal authorities to ensure that digital expansion aligns with green energy targets and circular electronics management. Device recycling programs and extended hardware life cycles can mitigate material waste associated with digital learning environments.

Beyond environmental metrics, sustainability also includes social and institutional resilience. AI-based assessment enhances continuity during disruptions such as extreme weather events, public health crises, or transportation breakdowns. When physical mobility is constrained, remote digital assessment ensures educational continuity without requiring centralized gatherings. In cities increasingly affected by climate variability, flexible digital infrastructure strengthens adaptive capacity. This resilience dimension connects AI assessment to broader urban risk management strategies.

Smart city governance also emphasizes data-driven decision-making. AI assessment systems generate aggregated performance analytics that can inform municipal education planning. Urban policymakers can identify geographic disparities, allocate resources strategically, and evaluate intervention outcomes with greater precision. When integrated responsibly, educational data contribute to evidence-based urban policy while respecting privacy constraints.

At the same time, sustainability must encompass digital equity. Access to reliable internet connectivity, appropriate devices, and digital literacy skills remains uneven across urban populations. If AI-based assessment becomes standard without inclusive infrastructure investment, it may exacerbate social inequality. Smart city initiatives must therefore incorporate educational technology access within broader urban inclusion programs. Public Wi-Fi networks, subsidized devices, and community digital hubs can help ensure equitable participation.

Another dimension of sustainability relates to institutional efficiency. Automated grading reduces administrative workload and allows teachers to focus on instructional improvement and individualized support. Efficient resource allocation within education systems contributes to broader fiscal sustainability in municipal budgets. When operational costs decline due to automation, savings can be reinvested into infrastructure upgrades, teacher development, or environmental initiatives.

In summary, AI-driven L2 assessment intersects with sustainability across environmental, social, infrastructural, and governance dimensions. It has the potential to reduce transportation-related emissions, decrease material waste, enhance resilience, and improve data-informed policy planning. Yet these benefits are conditional upon responsible energy use, equitable access, and coherent digital governance strategies. Within the smart city framework, AI assessment should be implemented as part of an integrated sustainability agenda rather than as an isolated technological reform. When aligned with green infrastructure planning and inclusive urban policy, AI-enabled assessment can contribute meaningfully to reducing congestion, mitigating pollution, and strengthening adaptive urban education systems (Sekti et al., 2025).

6. POLICY AND GOVERNANCE IMPLICATIONS

The integration of AI into L2 assessment requires more than institutional adoption at the school level. It demands coherent policy frameworks that align educational innovation with digital governance standards, environmental sustainability objectives, and urban regulatory systems. In smart city contexts, educational technologies become part of a broader digital ecosystem that includes transportation management, environmental monitoring, and public service platforms. Therefore, governance implications must be analyzed across regulatory, institutional, infrastructural, and ethical dimensions.

6.1 Regulatory Standards and Validation Frameworks

The deployment of AI-based assessment tools must be governed by clear validation standards. Policymakers should establish regulatory criteria for algorithm transparency, performance benchmarking, and bias testing. AI scoring systems should undergo periodic independent evaluation to ensure reliability and fairness across diverse linguistic populations.

Urban education authorities should require public documentation of model development processes, data sources, calibration procedures, and error margins. Transparent standards reduce the risk of unaccountable automation and strengthen public trust. Certification processes for AI vendors can further ensure that deployed systems meet pedagogical and ethical benchmarks before large-scale implementation.

6.2 Data Governance and Interoperability

Smart cities operate through interconnected data systems. AI-driven assessment platforms must comply with broader municipal data governance frameworks. Policies should define permissible data collection scopes, retention periods, anonymization requirements, and access controls.

Interoperability standards are equally important. Educational data systems should integrate securely with city-wide digital identity frameworks while preserving privacy. Fragmented platforms increase vulnerability to security breaches and reduce operational efficiency. Harmonized digital protocols enable streamlined administration while maintaining accountability.

Clear governance mechanisms must also define responsibility for data breaches or algorithmic errors. Municipal authorities, educational institutions, and technology providers should operate under well-defined accountability agreements that clarify oversight roles.

6.3 Equity-Oriented Digital Policy

AI adoption risks deepening inequality if infrastructure access is uneven. Urban policymakers must incorporate digital inclusion strategies into educational reform plans. This includes investment in broadband infrastructure, subsidized devices, public learning hubs, and digital literacy programs.

Equity policies should also address accessibility for learners with disabilities and support multilingual communities. AI systems must be calibrated for linguistic diversity and inclusive design. Governance frameworks that explicitly prioritize equity can prevent the emergence of a digital divide within smart city education systems.

6.4 Environmental and Infrastructure Alignment

Given the book's focus on controlling pollution and congestion, AI assessment policies must integrate environmental considerations. Remote digital testing reduces transportation demand, but digital infrastructure requires energy resources. Policymakers should encourage energy-efficient data centers, renewable power sourcing, and sustainable procurement standards for educational technology.

Urban planning departments and education authorities can collaborate to measure the environmental impact of digital assessment. Lifecycle analysis of hardware use and disposal should inform procurement decisions. Policies that incentivize low-energy infrastructure and device recycling programs support the environmental dimension of smart city development.

6.5 Human Oversight and Institutional Accountability

Even as AI automates aspects of assessment, governance structures must preserve human authority. Teachers and administrators should retain final decision-making power in high-stakes evaluations. Appeal mechanisms should allow students to contest automated results, ensuring procedural fairness.

Institutional accountability also requires professional development programs that prepare educators to interpret AI-generated insights responsibly. Without adequate training, reliance on automated outputs may undermine pedagogical judgment. Governance frameworks should therefore integrate capacity-building initiatives alongside technological adoption.

6.6 Cross-Sector Collaboration

The governance of AI in education intersects with urban digital policy, environmental management, cybersecurity regulation, and public administration. Cross-sector coordination is essential to avoid siloed implementation. Municipal authorities, educational boards, technology providers, and civil society actors must collaborate to establish shared principles for ethical AI use.

Public consultation processes can enhance legitimacy. Engaging communities in discussions about data use, privacy safeguards, and fairness expectations strengthens democratic accountability. In smart city governance, transparency and participatory mechanisms are critical to sustaining long-term trust.

6.7 Long-Term Strategic Planning

AI-driven assessment should not be implemented as a short-term efficiency measure but as part of a long-term urban digital strategy. Policymakers must consider scalability, maintenance costs, technological obsolescence, and institutional adaptability. Sustainable integration requires periodic evaluation, policy revision, and infrastructure upgrades aligned with evolving environmental and educational priorities.

Strategic planning should also anticipate emerging risks, including cybersecurity threats and unintended algorithmic consequences. Scenario planning and risk assessment frameworks can support proactive governance rather than reactive correction.

6.8 Concluding Reflection on Governance

AI-enabled L2 assessment holds transformative potential for improving efficiency, personalization, and environmental sustainability within urban education systems. However, its success depends on coherent governance architecture. Regulatory validation, ethical safeguards, digital inclusion strategies, environmental alignment, and cross-sector collaboration are essential components of responsible implementation.

When embedded within transparent and accountable policy frameworks, AI-based assessment can contribute to broader smart city objectives, including reduced congestion, lower emissions, and improved public service delivery. Without such governance, technological innovation risks exacerbating inequality, eroding trust, and undermining sustainability goals. Effective policy design therefore serves as the bridge between technological capability and socially responsible urban transformation.

7. FUTURE RESEARCH DIRECTIONS

Although AI-driven L2 assessment demonstrates promising pedagogical and sustainability benefits, the field remains in a formative stage. Existing research has focused primarily on short-term performance outcomes and technological feasibility, leaving substantial gaps in longitudinal evidence, governance integration, and environmental impact analysis. Future research must therefore move beyond proof-of-concept studies toward systemic and interdisciplinary investigation.

7.1 Longitudinal Learning Impact Studies

Most empirical studies evaluate immediate improvements in scoring efficiency or short-term learner performance. However, the long-term effects of AI-based assessment on language acquisition, learner autonomy, and communicative competence remain insufficiently explored. Future research should conduct multi-year longitudinal studies examining whether continuous AI-generated feedback leads to durable proficiency gains or whether learners become dependent on automated correction.

In addition, researchers should investigate how AI-mediated assessment influences learner motivation, identity formation, and metacognitive development over extended periods. Understanding these longitudinal effects is crucial for determining whether AI supports sustainable educational growth rather than short-term performance optimization.

7.2 Multimodal and Integrated Assessment Models

Emerging AI capabilities enable integration of written, spoken, and behavioral data into multimodal assessment systems. Future research should explore how combined analysis of text, speech, gesture, and interaction patterns can produce more holistic evaluations of communicative competence.

Such research must also address construct validity. Scholars should examine whether multimodal scoring systems truly capture authentic communication skills or whether they prioritize quantifiable proxies. Comparative studies between AI-driven multimodal assessments and human-mediated performance tasks would strengthen evidence-based adoption.

7.3 Algorithmic Fairness and Cross-Cultural Validation

Urban education systems are linguistically and culturally diverse. Future research should prioritize cross-cultural validation of AI assessment tools across dialects, sociolects, and multilingual environments. Bias auditing methodologies need to be refined to detect subtle inequities in scoring patterns.

Research should also explore participatory model development, where educators and community representatives contribute to calibration processes. This approach may improve contextual sensitivity and reduce unintended marginalization. Ethical evaluation frameworks must evolve alongside technological advancement.

7.4 Environmental Impact Assessment of Digital Testing

While AI-enabled assessment reduces transportation-related emissions and paper consumption, its full environmental footprint remains underexamined. Future studies should conduct lifecycle assessments of digital infrastructure, including data center energy consumption, device production, and disposal patterns.

Quantitative models comparing traditional examination logistics with AI-based remote assessment systems would clarify net environmental benefits. Integrating sustainability metrics into educational technology evaluation would align research with smart city environmental objectives.

7.5 Governance Models and Regulatory Innovation

The intersection of AI assessment with municipal digital governance requires systematic policy research. Future investigations should analyze how different regulatory models influence transparency, accountability, and public trust. Comparative studies across cities or national contexts could identify best practices in AI procurement, oversight, and stakeholder engagement.

Research should also examine the balance between innovation flexibility and regulatory safeguards. Overly restrictive policies may hinder experimentation, while weak oversight may expose learners to bias or data misuse. Developing adaptive regulatory frameworks that evolve with technological change represents a critical research frontier.

7.6 Human–AI Collaboration in Assessment

Rather than framing AI as a replacement for educators, future research should explore collaborative models where human expertise and algorithmic efficiency complement each other. Studies can examine optimal task allocation between teachers and AI systems, including when human judgment is indispensable.

Investigations into teacher training, professional identity shifts, and institutional adaptation will clarify how AI integration reshapes educational labor. Understanding these dynamics is essential for sustainable implementation within urban education systems.

7.7 Resilience and Crisis Preparedness

Recent global disruptions have demonstrated the importance of flexible digital infrastructure. Future research should examine how AI-based assessment contributes to educational continuity during extreme weather events, public health crises, or infrastructure breakdowns. Smart city resilience strategies may incorporate AI-driven remote assessment as part of broader emergency preparedness frameworks.

Evaluating system robustness under stress conditions will provide insight into the adaptive capacity of digitally mediated education.

7.8 Toward an Integrated Research Agenda

Future scholarship must adopt interdisciplinary approaches that connect educational technology, urban sustainability, public policy, and ethical governance. AI-driven L2 assessment cannot be evaluated solely through pedagogical metrics. Its long-term significance lies in how it integrates with smart city infrastructure, reduces environmental burdens, promotes equity, and maintains democratic accountability.

A mature research agenda should therefore combine longitudinal learning studies, fairness audits, environmental impact analysis, and governance evaluation. By addressing these interconnected dimensions, future research can ensure that AI-enabled assessment evolves as a responsible component of sustainable urban transformation rather than as a narrowly defined technological upgrade.

8. CONCLUSION

The integration of artificial intelligence into L2 assessment represents more than a technological modernization of educational practice. It reflects a structural transformation in how urban education systems operate within increasingly digital and sustainability-oriented cities. In metropolitan environments characterized by congestion, pollution, and infrastructural pressure, assessment systems cannot remain isolated from broader urban policy objectives. AI-driven rubrics, adaptive quizzes, and automated feedback mechanisms offer opportunities to redesign evaluation processes in ways that enhance efficiency, reduce material consumption, and support flexible participation.

Throughout this chapter, AI-based assessment has been examined not only as a pedagogical innovation but also as part of a wider smart city ecosystem. Intelligent scoring systems can reduce administrative workload and enable scalable feedback. Adaptive testing enhances measurement precision while decreasing dependence on centralized examination venues. Remote assessment reduces travel demand and contributes to lower congestion and emissions. However, these benefits are conditional. Digital infrastructure requires energy resources, governance oversight, and equitable access. Technological efficiency alone does not guarantee sustainability or fairness.

Ethical and governance considerations remain central to responsible implementation. Algorithmic bias, data privacy, transparency, and accountability must be addressed systematically. Without rigorous validation, inclusive calibration, and human oversight, automated assessment risks reproducing inequalities or eroding public trust. Smart city governance frameworks must therefore incorporate educational AI within broader regulatory architectures that emphasize transparency, digital rights, and environmental responsibility.

Policy alignment is equally essential. Municipal authorities, educational institutions, and technology providers must coordinate standards for interoperability, data protection, and sustainable infrastructure. Investments in digital equity are necessary to prevent new forms of exclusion. When embedded within inclusive and accountable governance structures, AI-based L2 assessment can strengthen urban education systems while supporting environmental objectives.

Ultimately, AI in L2 assessment illustrates how educational transformation intersects with urban sustainability. It demonstrates that innovation in language evaluation can contribute to reduced congestion, lower material waste, improved resilience during disruptions, and enhanced data-informed policymaking. Yet the long-term impact of this transformation depends on strategic planning, ethical safeguards, and sustained public oversight.

As cities continue to pursue smart and sustainable development pathways, education systems must evolve in parallel. AI-driven assessment should not be viewed as an isolated technological upgrade but as part of a coordinated urban transformation agenda. When guided by principles of equity, transparency, and environmental stewardship, AI-enabled L2 assessment can become a constructive element in the broader effort to build cleaner, more efficient, and more inclusive cities.

REFERENCES

Akpan, E. E., Akinlade, O., Alabi, O. O., David, O. A., Afe, O. F., & Ajagbe, S. A. (2026). Optimizing Traffic Signal Control Using Machine Learning and Environmental Data. *Artificial Intelligence and Applications (Commerce, Calif.)*, *4*(1), 48–56. DOI: 10.47852/bonviewAIA52024199

Al-Qudah, R., Tawil, A. A., Almuhajiri, M., Almazaydeh, L., & Suen, C. Y. (2026). Nash-regularized heterogeneous graph transformer networks for strategic task offloading in 6G edge computing. *International Journal of Data and Network Science*, *10*(1), 415–432. DOI: 10.5267/j.ijdns.2025.9.009

Alsharbi, B. M. (2026). A Psycholinguistic Analysis of the Use of Artificial Intelligence in Foreign Language Teaching. *Journal of Multiscale Modelling*. DOI: 10.1142/S1756973726400068

Aydın Yıldız, T. (2025). Sustainability Education in L2 Writing: AI-Based Multimodal Awareness and Engagement. *Sustainability (Basel)*, *17*(21), 9376. Advance online publication. DOI: 10.3390/su17219376

Barrot, J. S., & Bui, H. P. (2026). Generative Artificial Intelligence for Automated Qualitative Feedback: A Cross-Comparison of Prompting Strategies. *RELC Journal*. Advance online publication. DOI: 10.1177/00336882251412561

Bawn, M., Francis, N., Alvey, E., Hassall, C., Pires-daSilva, A., Barra, P., Hough, D., Campbell, H., Hardy, M., & Canet-Perez, J. (2026). Perspectives from a workshop: Intelligent assessment in the age of artificial intelligence. *Advances in Physiology Education*, *50*(1), 73–82. DOI: 10.1152/advan.00246.2024 PMID: 41236868

Cheshmehzangi, A., Butters, C., Xie, L., & Dawodu, A. (2021). Green infrastructures for urban sustainability: Issues, implications, and solutions for underdeveloped areas. *Urban Forestry & Urban Greening*, *59*, 127028. Advance online publication. DOI: 10.1016/j.ufug.2021.127028

Cui, H., Mahfoodh, O. H. A., Dong, H., & Ulanbek, M. (2026). An assessment framework for human-AI collaborative competence in second language writing: Evidence from the Chinese EFL context. *System*, *137*, 103937. Advance online publication. DOI: 10.1016/j.system.2025.103937

Eguchi, M., Takizawa, K., Saeki, M., Kurata, F., Suzuki, S., Matsuyama, Y., & Sawaki, Y. (2025). Human- versus artificial intelligence-delivered roleplay tasks for assessing interactional competence: An applied conversation analytic study. *TESOL Quarterly*, *59*(S1), S183–S219. DOI: 10.1002/tesq.70028

Hou, Z., & Min, S. (2026). Dialogue-based computer-assisted language learning systems for second language speaking development: A three-level meta-analysis. *ReCALL, 38*(1), 40–56. DOI: 10.1017/S0958344025100268

İnci Kuzu, Ç. (2026). Mathematics teachers' AI literacy, anxiety, and perceptions of AI integration in mathematics education: A mixed-methods study. *BMC Psychology, 14*(1), 42. Advance online publication. DOI: 10.1186/s40359-025-03836-0 PMID: 41408576

Licata, A. E., Bouffier, M., & Borghesani, V. (2026). A pre-registered scoping review of neuroimaging evidence concerning lexico-semantic processing in multilingual speakers. *Neuroscience and Biobehavioral Reviews, 184*, 106591. Advance online publication. DOI: 10.1016/j.neubiorev.2026.106591 PMID: 41679413

Lu, Q., Yao, Y., Xiao, L., Zhu, X., & Yin, H. (2026). Exploring the impact of a GenAI-supported feedback practice on student feedback literacy in L2 writing. *Computer Assisted Language Learning*, 1–30. Advance online publication. DOI: 10.1080/09588221.2025.2605541

Moorhouse, B. L., Wan, Y., Wu, C., Wu, M., & Ho, T. Y. (2025). Generative AI tools and empowerment in L2 academic writing. *System, 133*, 103779. Advance online publication. DOI: 10.1016/j.system.2025.103779

Schüle, R., Pollok, M., & Güleş, O. (2026). Digital justice in the smart city: Developing a framework for participatory digitalisation strategies at the local level. *Universal Access in the Information Society, 25*(2), 42. Advance online publication. DOI: 10.1007/s10209-025-01287-3

Sekti, B. A. (2025a). Foundations of Artificial Intelligence Ethics. In *Navigating Social Trust in the AI Era* (pp. 23–47). DOI: 10.4018/979-8-3373-7011-8.ch002

Sekti, B. A. (2025b). Machine Learning vs. AI: Key Concepts. In *Implementing Enterprise Cybersecurity With AI* (pp. 1–27). DOI: 10.4018/979-8-3373-2252-0.ch001

Sekti, B. A. (2026). Cybersecurity Challenges in Smart City Development. In *Securing Smart Cities Through Modern Cryptography Technologies* (pp. 75–102). IGI Global Scientific Publishing. DOI: 10.4018/979-8-3373-3326-7.ch003

Sekti, B. A., Laksono, M. N. G., Laksono, M. I. A., Widodo, A. M., Anwar, N., & Tiaraputri, Z. A. (2025). Principles of green computing in information security. In *Sustainable Information Security in the Age of AI and Green Computing* (pp. 1–16). DOI: 10.4018/979-8-3693-8034-5.ch001

Shafiee Rad, H. (2025). Reinforcing L2 reading comprehension through artificial intelligence intervention: Refining engagement to foster self-regulated learning. *Smart Learning Environments*, *12*(1), 23. Advance online publication. DOI: 10.1186/s40561-025-00377-2

Utami, A. S., & Sekti, B. A. (2025). Al in Critical Sectors: Healthcare, Education, Finance, and Security - Ethical Challenges in Generative Al. In *Navigating Social Trust in the AI Era* (pp. 155–186). DOI: 10.4018/979-8-3373-7011-8.ch007

Wan, D.-L., & Lin, S.-Z. (2026). Ethical challenges and governance of artificial intelligence in hepatocellular carcinoma management. *Medical Oncology (Northwood, London, England)*, *43*(2), 69. DOI: 10.1007/s12032-025-03157-7 PMID: 41452505

Wang, R., Yin, Y., & Cao, Y. (2026). A LLM-based pedagogical framework for active, inquiry-based and adaptive learning in L2 writing. *Computers and Education: Artificial Intelligence*, *10*, 100535. Advance online publication. DOI: 10.1016/j.caeai.2025.100535

Yoshida, M., Duangchinda, V., & Ruangrit, N. (2026). AI-Supported Learning in Online Discussion Forums: A Scoping Review. *Electronic Journal of e-Learning*, *24*(1), 19–35. DOI: 10.34190/ejel.24.1.4409

Zaidan, E., Truby, J., Ibrahim, I. A., & Hoppe, T. (2026). Hybrid global governance for responsible and inclusive Artificial Intelligence: Proposing a new Sustainable Development Goal 18. *Technology in Society*, *85*, 103159. Advance online publication. DOI: 10.1016/j.techsoc.2025.103159

Chapter 7
Blockchain and Semantic Annotation for Smart Energy Management

Cindy Fitria Maharani
http://orcid.org/0009-0009-1840-6993
Universitas Esa Unggul, Indonesia

Binastya Anggara Sekti
http://orcid.org/0000-0001-5489-4888
Universitas Esa Unggul, Indonesia

ABSTRACT

Rapid urbanization has created complex energy ecosystems challenging traditional centralized power models. This analysis examines blockchain technology and semantic annotation convergence in addressing modern urban energy infrastructure challenges. Blockchain enables decentralized trust mechanisms for peer-to-peer energy trading, automated smart contracts, and transparent renewable energy certification, while semantic annotation ensures intelligent machine understanding and interoperability across diverse energy systems. Integration creates autonomous ecosystems where participants contribute to grid optimization while being fairly compensated. Real-world implementations show measurable improvements in energy efficiency, cost reduction, and renewable utilization. However, challenges remain including scalability limitations, energy consumption paradoxes, and regulatory uncertainties requiring innovative solutions and coordinated policy frameworks.

DOI: 10.4018/979-8-2600-0883-6.ch007

1. INTRODUCTION

Rapid urbanization, digital transformation, and decarbonization commitments are reshaping global energy systems, as cities now dominate energy consumption and carbon emissions, creating pressure for more resilient, intelligent, and sustainable infrastructure. The rise of renewable energy further introduces decentralization, intermittency, and data complexity that traditional centralized grids cannot effectively manage, increasing the need for new technological and governance frameworks that ensure transparency, interoperability, and trust in distributed energy ecosystems. Smart energy management evolved from early smart grid initiatives by integrating digital monitoring, automation, and real-time analytics, while blockchain technologies introduced decentralized trust mechanisms and semantic annotation enabled machine-interpretable data interoperability. However, these technologies are often studied separately, and their integration within a unified energy governance architecture remains limited. Implementation also faces practical barriers including scalability limitations, interoperability constraints, regulatory uncertainty, privacy concerns, and high integration costs. Addressing these challenges requires integrated approaches that combine blockchain and semantic technologies to improve transparency, operational efficiency, and sustainability within smart urban energy systems.

The 21st century has witnessed an unprecedented wave of urbanization that fundamentally reshapes how we think about energy systems. According to the United Nations, more than half of the world's population now lives in urban areas, and this figure is projected to reach 68% by 2050. This rapid urban growth has created complex energy ecosystems where traditional centralized power generation and distribution models are increasingly inadequate to meet the multifaceted demands of modern cities (Modrzyński and Karaszewski 2022). The challenge extends beyond merely scaling up existing infrastructure. Today's urban environments require energy systems that are not only capable of handling increased demand but are also resilient to disruptions, flexible enough to accommodate diverse energy sources, and sustainable enough to meet ambitious climate commitments. The conventional approach of large, centralized power plants feeding into hierarchical distribution networks was designed for a different era one where energy demand was more predictable, renewable sources were marginal, and environmental considerations were secondary concerns.

Modern cities are energy-intensive by nature, with their dense concentrations of residential buildings, commercial complexes, industrial facilities, transportation networks, and digital infrastructure. The proliferation of smart devices, electric vehicles, data centers, and climate control systems has created energy consumption patterns that are both higher in absolute terms and more volatile in their temporal distribution (Saleem et al. 2023). Traditional grid systems, built on the assumption of steady, predictable load curves, struggle to adapt to the dynamic and often unpredictable energy demands characteristic of contemporary urban life.

A smart city represents a systemic transformation of urban environments through the integration of digital intelligence with physical infrastructure, leveraging information and communication technologies, Internet of Things devices, artificial intelligence, and advanced data analytics to create adaptive, efficient, sustainable, and equitable urban ecosystems. By collecting and processing real-time data from interconnected systems such as smart grids, intelligent transportation networks, energy-efficient buildings, environmental monitoring platforms, and e-governance services, smart cities shift from reactive problem-solving to proactive optimization and coordinated planning. This holistic, systems-oriented approach enables dynamic interaction among energy, mobility, environmental, and governance infrastructures, enhancing resource efficiency, reducing emissions, improving service delivery, and supporting evidence-based policymaking while strengthening citizen participation and overall urban livability (Sekti 2026).

Within this smart city context, two emerging technologies have garnered significant attention for their potential to address fundamental challenges in urban energy management: blockchain and semantic annotation. While these technologies were developed in different contexts and serve different primary functions, their convergence offers unprecedented opportunities for creating more secure, transparent, and intelligent energy systems (Choobineh et al. 2023).

Blockchain Technology represents a paradigm shift from centralized to decentralized systems management. Originally developed as the underlying technology for cryptocurrencies, blockchain provides a distributed ledger system that maintains a continuously growing list of records, called blocks, which are linked and secured using cryptographic principles. In the context of energy systems, blockchain offers several transformative capabilities (Cioara et al. 2020). The decentralized nature of blockchain eliminates the need for trusted intermediaries, allowing direct peer-to-peer interactions between energy producers and consumers. This capability is particularly valuable in enabling prosumers entities that both produce and consume energy to participate directly in energy markets (Kumari et al. 2022). For instance, a household with rooftop solar panels can sell excess electricity directly to neighbors without going through traditional utility companies, with smart contracts automatically handling pricing, verification, and settlement. Blockchain's immutable record-keeping capabilities ensure that all energy transactions are permanently recorded and cannot be altered retroactively (Karpinski, Kuznetsov, and Oliynykov 2025). This creates unprecedented transparency in energy supply chains, allowing consumers to verify the source and carbon intensity of their electricity. Such transparency is crucial for supporting renewable energy markets, carbon offset programs, and sustainability reporting requirements (Abiodun, Nwulu, and Olukanmi 2025).

The automation capabilities provided by smart contracts self-executing contracts with the terms directly written into code enable the creation of sophisticated energy management systems that can respond to market conditions, grid constraints, and environmental factors without human intervention (Honari et al. 2023). These automated systems can optimize energy distribution, implement demand response programs, and facilitate complex multi-party energy transactions at scales and speeds impossible with traditional manual processes.

Semantic Annotation addresses a different but equally critical challenge in smart city energy systems: the need for machines to understand and reason about the meaning of data. As smart cities generate enormous volumes of data from diverse sources sensors, meters, weather stations, user applications, and administrative systems the ability to integrate and make sense of this information becomes paramount (Cavalieri 2021).

Semantic annotation involves enriching raw data with metadata that describes its meaning, context, and relationships to other information. This process uses formal ontologies structured vocabularies that define concepts and their relationships within specific domains to ensure that different systems can understand and process the same information consistently. In energy systems, semantic annotation enables intelligent automation by allowing machines to understand concepts like "peak demand," "renewable source," "carbon intensity," or "grid stability" in ways that facilitate automated decision-making (Elkhodr 2024).

The interoperability benefits of semantic annotation cannot be overstated. In typical smart city environments, energy-related data comes from numerous sources: smart meters from different manufacturers, building management systems from various vendors, weather services using different data formats, and regulatory systems with distinct reporting requirements. Without semantic standardization, integrating this diverse information requires extensive manual effort and is prone to errors and inconsistencies.

Semantic annotation creates a common language that enables seamless data exchange and collaboration between different systems and stakeholders.This capability supports the development of sophisticated energy applications that can adapt to changing conditions, optimize resource allocation, and provide personalized services to users while maintaining compatibility across diverse technological platforms. The transition to smart, sustainable urban energy systems faces several interconnected challenges that must be addressed holistically (Nour, Chaves-Avila, and Sanchez-Miralles 2022)

Modern cities face mounting energy challenges driven by rapidly increasing and unpredictable demand linked to population growth, digitalization, electric vehicle adoption, and evolving consumption patterns, making traditional peak-capacity expansion economically and environmentally unsustainable. At the same time, integrating renewable energy sources introduces operational complexity due to their intermittent and weather-dependent nature, requiring advanced forecasting, storage, and demand management systems. The shift toward grid decentralization, characterized by distributed energy resources and bidirectional energy flows, further complicates coordination and balancing mechanisms that legacy infrastructures were not designed to manage. Additionally, limited real-time monitoring and automation in existing systems restrict responsiveness and efficiency, underscoring the need for intelligent, adaptive energy management solutions capable of dynamic optimization (Sekti 2025b, 2025a).

Sustainability and Net Zero Targets impose increasingly stringent requirements on urban energy systems. Cities worldwide have committed to ambitious carbon reduction goals that require fundamental changes in how energy is generated, distributed, and consumed (Parhamfar, Sadeghkhani, and Adeli 2024). Achieving these targets requires not only the deployment of clean energy technologies but also the development of transparent reporting and verification systems that can demonstrate progress and ensure accountability.

Energy equity and affordability concerns underscore the social dimension of urban energy transformation, as modernization efforts risk unevenly distributing benefits and potentially deepening existing inequalities. Ensuring that new energy systems improve accessibility, affordability, and inclusive participation requires integrating technological innovation with policy reform, stakeholder engagement, and strong governance frameworks. The convergence of blockchain and semantic annotation technologies presents a promising pathway toward more transparent, interoperable, efficient, and equitable energy systems. However, realizing this potential demands careful attention to regulatory alignment, implementation complexity, and the diverse socioeconomic conditions within urban populations. The following analysis therefore examines how these technologies, both individually and in combination, can address contemporary urban energy challenges while acknowledging the practical barriers to large-scale adoption.

2. BACKGROUND OF THE STUDY

Smart urban energy systems are transitioning from centralized, utility-controlled architectures toward decentralized ecosystems involving prosumers, distributed renewable generation, electric vehicles, microgrids, and real-time demand response mechanisms. This shift creates operational complexity that legacy systems cannot efficiently manage. Smart energy management refers to an integrated approach to managing energy systems by optimizing the design and control of microgrids, renewable energy sources, and hybrid energy storage systems to improve efficiency, reliability, and sustainability in energy distribution. It emphasizes coordinated energy management strategies that balance environmental performance, economic cost, and system longevity, particularly in applications such as electric vehicle charging infrastructure (Alshammari, Alshahr, and Barakat 2026).

Case studies reveal practical implementation gaps. For example, peer-to-peer microgrid pilots demonstrate efficiency gains but struggle with regulatory compliance and scalability. Renewable certificate systems face transparency challenges and double-counting risks. Building energy management systems often operate in silos due to incompatible data standards. These implementation realities highlight the need for an integrated architecture that combines secure transaction validation with semantic interoperability. Peer-to-peer microgrid pilot projects demonstrate improved energy efficiency by enabling localized generation, storage, and consumption through integrated systems such as photovoltaic sources, battery storage, and centralized energy management, but their wider adoption remains constrained by regulatory compliance issues, limited technical standards, and challenges in scaling the infrastructure (Ysebie et al. 2025).

Blockchain offers immutability and decentralized trust, while semantic annotation enables contextual understanding of heterogeneous data sources. However, without integrated governance models, these technologies risk remaining fragmented experimental tools rather than systemic solutions.

3. STATEMENT OF THE PROBLEM

Ideally, smart urban energy systems should be transparent, interoperable, decentralized, efficient, and aligned with sustainability goals. In reality, several contradictions persist:

- Energy markets remain fragmented across incompatible platforms.
- Renewable energy tracking lacks real-time verifiability.
- Decentralized systems face governance and liability ambiguities.
- Data interoperability is constrained by heterogeneous standards.
- Privacy concerns conflict with transparency requirements.

Theoretical gaps include limited integration between distributed ledger theory and socio-technical interoperability models. Knowledge gaps persist regarding performance scalability and governance harmonization. Contextual gaps arise from differing regulatory environments across jurisdictions. Practical challenges include high integration costs and resistance from incumbent utilities.

This study fills these gaps by proposing an integrated blockchain-semantic governance architecture, grounded in systems theory, institutional economics, and digital governance frameworks, thereby offering structured direction for policymakers and researchers.

4. RESEARCH METHODOLOGY

This chapter adopts a qualitative conceptual research approach based on an integrative literature review. The study does not employ empirical data collection or statistical analysis; instead, it synthesizes existing academic literature, policy documents, and documented real-world initiatives related to blockchain technology, semantic annotation, and smart urban energy systems.

The literature reviewed in this chapter was selected from reputable academic databases, including peer-reviewed journals, conference proceedings, and authoritative institutional reports. The selection process prioritized publications that address decentralized energy systems, blockchain-based governance models, semantic interoperability, and smart city energy applications.

The analytical approach involves thematic synthesis and comparative analysis to identify recurring concepts, technological patterns, governance challenges, and potential integration pathways between blockchain technologies and semantic data structures. Based on this synthesis, the chapter develops a conceptual framework that highlights how these technologies can jointly support transparency, interoperability, and sustainability in urban energy governance.

While this conceptual approach enables a comprehensive understanding of emerging technological and governance trends, the chapter is limited by the absence of empirical validation. Future research may extend this work through case studies, simulations, or quantitative evaluations to assess practical implementation outcomes.

5. BLOCKCHAIN APPLICATIONS IN ENERGY SYSTEMS

5.1 Fundamentals of Blockchain in Energy Infrastructure

Blockchain technology represents a paradigmatic shift from traditional centralized energy management systems to distributed, decentralized architectures that operate without the need for trusted intermediaries (Choobineh et al. 2023). At its core, blockchain creates an immutable, distributed ledger where energy transactions are recorded across multiple network nodes, ensuring transparency, security, and reliability through cryptographic consensus mechanisms rather than centralized control.

In conventional energy systems, utilities, grid operators, and regulatory bodies serve as central authorities that manage energy distribution, billing, and market operations. This centralized approach creates several inherent vulnerabilities and inefficiencies: single points of failure that can compromise entire grid sections, lack of transparency in energy sourcing and pricing, delayed transaction processing that can take days or weeks, and high operational costs associated with maintaining complex bureaucratic structures and intermediary services.

Blockchain technology addresses these fundamental limitations by distributing control across a network of nodes, each maintaining a synchronized copy of the transaction ledger. When an energy transaction occurs whether it's a peer-to-peer energy trade, a demand response event, or a renewable energy certificate transfer the transaction is validated by network consensus mechanisms such as Proof-of-Work, Proof-of-Stake, or more energy-efficient alternatives like Practical Byzantine Fault Tolerance (Guo, Wan, and Cheng 2022).

The decentralized architecture of blockchain introduces transformative capabilities for modern energy systems by eliminating counterparty risk through automated verification and execution of transactions via smart contracts, enhancing transparency through auditable transaction histories with privacy safeguards, and enabling near real-time settlement that reduces administrative delays and costs. Its immutable record-keeping function provides tamper-resistant audit trails essential for regulatory compliance, carbon accounting, and sustainability reporting, thereby strengthening trust and environmental accountability. Beyond operational efficiency, blockchain also enables innovative value creation models, including tokenization of energy assets for fractional ownership and community-based financing, while smart contracts can autonomously manage complex multi-party agreements based on real-time grid data, weather conditions, and market signals to optimize energy distribution and resource allocation.

5.2 Peer-to-Peer (P2P) Energy Trading

Peer-to-peer energy trading represents one of the most revolutionary applications of blockchain technology in the energy sector, fundamentally transforming the relationship between energy producers and consumers by enabling direct energy transactions without traditional utility intermediaries (Kumari et al. 2022). This paradigm shift empowers prosumers entities that both produce and consume energy to participate actively in energy markets, creating more efficient, resilient, and democratic energy ecosystems.

Traditional energy markets are structured hierarchically, with centralized power plants generating electricity that flows through transmission and distribution networks managed by utilities before reaching consumers. While effective in an era of centralized generation and passive consumption, this model becomes increasingly inefficient as distributed energy resources such as rooftop solar panels, small wind turbines, and battery storage systems expand across urban areas. Blockchain-enabled peer-to-peer energy trading introduces a decentralized alternative in which prosumers can directly negotiate and execute transactions within digital marketplaces. Smart contracts automate price discovery, match supply with demand, verify energy delivery, and settle payments based on predefined rules that may incorporate geographic proximity, grid capacity, renewable preferences, carbon intensity, and real-time market conditions. Implementation typically involves smart meters connected to blockchain networks that continuously record production and consumption data, energy management systems that identify surplus or deficit patterns, and automated trading algorithms that execute transactions under favorable conditions. Pilot projects in various cities have demonstrated operational feasibility, showing improvements in transparency, local economic participation, and regulatory compliance. Beyond economic efficiency, peer-to-peer trading enhances grid resilience, reduces transmission losses, and incentivizes renewable adoption by facilitating localized energy exchange and decreasing dependence on long-distance electricity transport.

5.3 Smart Contracts for Automated Energy Management

Smart contracts represent a foundational innovation in blockchain-enabled energy systems, serving as self-executing digital agreements that automatically implement predefined rules and conditions without requiring human intervention or trusted intermediaries (Honari et al. 2023). These programmable contracts transform traditional energy management processes by enabling sophisticated automation that can respond dynamically to changing grid conditions, market prices, regulatory requirements, and user preferences.

Conventional energy systems rely on manual processes, fixed billing cycles, and complex administrative procedures that are not aligned with real-time grid conditions, creating inefficiencies and high transaction costs. Smart contracts address these issues by automating billing, dynamic pricing, demand response, and energy trading through self-executing code connected to real-time data feeds. This automation enables efficient coordination of distributed energy resources, electric vehicle charging, and energy storage while supporting innovative models such as Energy-as-a-Service based on measurable performance outcomes.

5.4 Renewable Energy Certification and Traceability

Renewable energy certification and traceability represent critical applications of blockchain technology that address growing consumer and regulatory demands for transparency in energy sourcing and environmental impact verification (Parhamfar, Sadeghkhani, and Adeli 2024). As organizations and individuals increasingly commit to sustainability goals and carbon neutrality targets, the ability to verify the origin, generation method, and environmental attributes of consumed electricity becomes essential for credible environmental reporting and compliance.

Traditional renewable energy certificate systems face limitations including centralized control, vulnerability to manipulation, slow and costly manual verification, persistent double counting, and insufficient tracking of generation time, location, and technology. Blockchain-based certification addresses these challenges by creating an immutable and transparent ledger that assigns each unit of renewable generation a unique digital certificate containing detailed metadata such as timestamp, geographic coordinates, technology type, and carbon intensity. This cryptographically secured system prevents duplication and ensures the integrity of sustainability claims while enabling real-time traceability across energy supply chains. Smart contracts automate certificate issuance, trading, and retirement based on verified generation data, ensuring accurate ownership records and eliminating reuse risks. Integration with IoT devices further strengthens reliability by feeding real-time generation data directly into the blockchain, reducing costs and improving verification accuracy. In addition, blockchain-based certification supports carbon market mechanisms and regulatory reporting by providing tamper-proof records that enhance compliance, transparency, and trust in renewable energy and environmental policy frameworks.

5.5 Technical Challenges and Limitations

Despite the transformative potential of blockchain technology in energy systems, several significant technical challenges must be addressed to achieve widespread adoption and optimal performance (Nour, Chaves-Avila, and Sanchez-Miralles 2022). These limitations span scalability constraints, energy consumption concerns, regulatory uncertainties, and privacy considerations that require careful analysis and innovative solutions.

Scalability remains a major challenge for implementing blockchain in large-scale energy systems because public blockchains process relatively few transactions per second, while urban energy networks require thousands of real-time transactions for peer-to-peer trading, demand response, and microgrid coordination. Solutions such as off-chain processing, sidechains, sharding, and more efficient consensus mechanisms are being explored to improve throughput while reducing energy consumption. In addition to technical constraints, regulatory and governance challenges also complicate blockchain integration, as existing legal frameworks are designed for centralized systems and often lack provisions for decentralized transactions, smart contracts, and cross-jurisdictional operations. Privacy concerns related to transparent transaction data, interoperability issues between different blockchain platforms and legacy systems, and the need for standardized protocols further highlight the importance of coordinated technical, regulatory, and governance solutions for scalable blockchain-based energy ecosystems.

6. SEMANTIC ANNOTATION FOR ENERGY INTEROPERABILITY

Semantic annotation plays a transformative role in addressing data interoperability challenges within smart energy ecosystems by converting heterogeneous, raw data into semantically rich, machine-interpretable formats. This process is essential in environments where devices and systems from smart meters and EVs to grid infrastructure must communicate across diverse technological and organizational domains. By embedding contextual metadata using formal ontologies and semantic web technologies, semantic annotation ensures that machines can understand not just the structure, but also the meaning and intent behind the data. This enables automated reasoning, adaptive decision-making, and seamless integration across energy platforms, thereby supporting more efficient, intelligent energy management.

6.1 Ontological Foundations and Knowledge Representation

The foundation of effective semantic annotation in smart energy systems lies in the creation and application of domain-specific ontologies that provide formal, shared vocabularies to represent key concepts, relationships, and constraints within the energy domain. These ontologies bridge the semantic gap between heterogeneous systems by enabling standardized, machine-readable definitions of energy-related elements. The Smart Appliances REFerence (SAREF) ontology is a notable example, offering a robust framework to describe smart devices, their functionalities, and interactions, thereby enabling seamless integration and coordination in home energy management systems. Complementing this, the Open Energy Ontology (OEO) extends semantic modeling to include broader aspects such as energy carriers, conversion processes, and regulatory frameworks. Advanced ontologies also support temporal and spatial reasoning, which is vital for interpreting seasonal demand shifts, renewable generation cycles, or regional policy constraints. Developing such comprehensive ontologies demands collaboration among energy experts, knowledge engineers, and system developers to ensure accurate representation and long-term adaptability as technologies and market dynamics evolve.

6.2 Semantic Web Technologies and Implementation Frameworks

The practical implementation of semantic annotation in energy systems is grounded in a suite of semantic web technologies that offer standardized mechanisms for representing, linking, and querying data in a machine-interpretable manner. At the core is the Resource Description Framework (RDF), which encodes data as subject-predicate-object triples, enabling automated reasoning and seamless integration across heterogeneous sources. RDF facilitates rich semantic descriptions for example, a solar panel system can be semantically linked not only to its technical attributes but also to ownership, regulatory certifications, geographic location, and financial agreements. Building on RDF, the Web Ontology Language (OWL) introduces formal logic and rule-based constructs, allowing systems to encode constraints and derive inferences such as preventing battery overcharge based on capacity limits without manual rule coding. SPARQL, the querying language for RDF data, empowers systems to dynamically extract, correlate, and act upon complex, distributed energy information. Middleware components, such as semantic adapters, play a critical role in bridging traditional energy protocols with semantic models, allowing legacy infrastructure to integrate into modern, intelligent energy networks without complete system overhauls.

6.3 Applications and Integration Challenges

The practical application of semantic annotation in smart energy systems encompasses a wide array of domains, each presenting distinct opportunities and implementation challenges. One of the most advanced use cases is in smart building energy management, where semantic annotation facilitates automatic discovery, integration, and coordination of subsystems such as HVAC, lighting, security, and on-site renewable energy (Saleem et al. 2023). For instance, when a new smart thermostat is installed, its annotated metadata allows the system to instantly recognize its functions such as temperature regulation or occupancy detection enabling seamless incorporation into existing optimization algorithms. Similarly, in renewable energy integration, semantic annotation supports intelligent coordination of heterogeneous energy sources like solar, wind, and battery storage by capturing operational constraints and environmental dependencies. Peer-to-peer energy trading platforms leverage semantic descriptions to match buyers and sellers automatically based on criteria such as energy origin, pricing models, and sustainability metrics. Nonetheless, challenges persist, including the computational demands of semantic processing, the complexity of ontology development and upkeep (Modrzyński & Karaszewski, 2022), and interoperability issues across varying semantic frameworks. Addressing these challenges requires ongoing innovation in semantic tooling, cross-ontology translation, and adherence to evolving standards.

6.4 Benefits and Challenges

The implementation of semantic annotation in energy systems presents a complex landscape of significant benefits alongside substantial challenges that must be carefully balanced to achieve successful deployment. Understanding these trade-offs is essential for energy system designers, policymakers, and technology providers who seek to leverage semantic technologies for enhanced energy management and interoperability.

6.4.1 Benefits of Semantic Annotation

Enhanced interoperability is a core advantage of semantic annotation in energy systems, enabling standardized, machine-readable descriptions that eliminate the need for custom integrations across diverse platforms . This fosters plug-and-play compatibility, reduces deployment and maintenance costs, and accelerates innovation adoption. Additionally, semantic annotation empowers automated reasoning, allowing systems to dynamically interpret device capabilities, constraints, and contextual factors to optimize operations without human input. It also improves data quality by enforcing ontological constraints, ensuring consistency and reliability across distributed networks. Furthermore, the contextual richness of semantic metadata enhances machine learning and analytics, enabling more accurate predictions, efficient resource management, and proactive grid operations.

6.4.2 Implementation Challenges

Computational overhead remains a key obstacle in deploying semantic annotation within energy systems, as semantic reasoning, ontology processing, and query execution demand significant resources especially in large-scale networks with continuous data flows. Devices like smart meters may lack the processing power for full semantic functions, necessitating optimization or specialized hardware. Ontology development adds further complexity, requiring cross-disciplinary collaboration and ongoing updates to reflect evolving technologies (Karpinski, Kuznetsov, and Oliynykov 2025). Scalability challenges also arise in real-time applications, prompting the need for distributed semantic architectures. Moreover, rich semantic metadata can expose sensitive user data, raising privacy and security concerns that require robust safeguards and privacy-preserving designs.

6.4.3 Balancing Benefits and Challenges

Successfully implementing semantic annotation in energy systems requires careful consideration of the trade-offs between functionality and complexity. Organizations must evaluate whether the benefits of enhanced interoperability and automated reasoning justify the additional complexity and resource requirements of semantic technologies. Hybrid approaches that combine semantic annotation for critical interoperability functions with traditional data management for high-volume operational data may provide optimal solutions that balance functionality with performance and cost considerations.

The gradual adoption pathway offers a practical approach for managing the transition to semantically-enabled energy systems. Organizations can begin by implementing semantic annotation for specific use cases or system components where the benefits are most pronounced, gradually expanding semantic capabilities as experience is gained and technology maturity improves. This incremental approach allows organizations to develop expertise and address technical challenges while minimizing disruption to existing energy operations.

7. INTEGRATION OF BLOCKCHAIN AND SEMANTIC TECHNOLOGIES

The combination of blockchain and semantic annotation is triggering a major transformation in smart energy systems. Blockchain provides cryptographic protection, data immutability, and a distributed system of trust, while semantic technology provides context-based intelligence and automated reasoning capabilities (Hernik et al. 2025). This synergy solves two key problems: establishing trustworthy energy transactions in a decentralized ecosystem and ensuring the entire system can interpret complex, diverse data. This combined architecture facilitates autonomous and intelligent energy system operations with minimal human intervention, while maintaining transparency, accountability, and the ability to interact across disparate technological and organizational boundaries.

7.1 Integrated System Architecture

The integrated system architecture combines the capabilities of a blockchain distributed ledger with intelligent data interpretation and semantic annotation through a multi-layer approach. The Data Acquisition Layer collects energy data from IoT sensors and smart meters. The Semantic Middleware Layer transforms the raw data into a semantic format using a domain-specific ontology. The Blockchain Layer provides an immutable distributed ledger infrastructure that ensures secure and transparent energy transactions . The Smart Contract Layer automatically executes energy trading rules. The Application Layer provides a user-friendly interface for various stakeholders. Each layer coordinates seamlessly to manage the complete energy data lifecycle while maintaining system integrity and interoperability.

7.2 Key Use Case - P2P Energy Trading

Peer-to-peer energy trading demonstrates the best blockchain-semantic integration, enabling households to participate directly in the energy market without traditional intermediaries. The process begins with participant onboarding using a comprehensive semantic energy profile. An intelligent matching algorithm analyzes supply-demand patterns using semantic reasoning to identify optimal trading partnerships. Smart contracts execute automated validation based on semantic metadata, verifying grid capability and regulatory compliance (Khatri et al., 2024). Each transaction is documented with comprehensive semantic metadata for audit trails and analysis. A continuous learning system optimizes trading strategies using accumulated semantic metadata for market trend prediction and improvement.

7.3 Integration Challenges

Blockchain-semantic integration faces complex challenges. Ontology standardization requires a consensus vocabulary across organizations and regions. Blockchain scalability limitations hinder high-frequency transactions with large amounts of semantic metadata. Real-time synchronization between semantic metadata and blockchain records requires sophisticated data management. Resource constraints on IoT devices limit the implementation of full blockchain nodes and semantic reasoning engines. Evolving regulatory compliance creates uncertainty in the legal framework. Privacy and security considerations become complex when combining blockchain transparency with sensitive semantic contextual information. Solutions require advanced cryptographic techniques, hybrid architectures, and coordinated governance processes to address these challenges.

8. REAL-WORLD APPLICATIONS AND USE CASES

The convergence of blockchain technology and semantic annotation is revolutionizing energy systems worldwide, creating unprecedented opportunities for efficiency, transparency, and innovation. These technologies work synergistically to address complex challenges in modern energy infrastructure while enabling new business models and sustainable practices.

8.1 Renewable Energy Microgrids

Renewable energy microgrids represent one of the most promising applications of blockchain-semantic annotation integration. These decentralized energy networks face unique challenges in managing diverse energy sources, storage systems, and consumer demands while maintaining grid stability and economic viability(Kumari et al. 2022).

Blockchain technology serves as the foundational trust layer, creating immutable records of energy generation, consumption, and trading transactions. Every kilowatt-hour produced by solar panels, wind turbines, or battery storage systems is cryptographically verified and recorded, ensuring complete transparency and preventing energy double-spending. Smart contracts automatically execute energy trading agreements based on predefined conditions, such as excess generation, peak demand periods, or price thresholds.

Semantic annotation plays a crucial role in creating interoperability among heterogeneous devices and systems. Solar inverters from different manufacturers, smart meters with varying communication protocols, and home energy management systems with distinct data formats can all communicate effectively through standardized semantic models. These annotations define common vocabularies for energy types (solar, wind, grid), device states (generating, consuming, standby), and transaction parameters (price, quantity, duration)(Guo, Wan, and Cheng 2022).

The practical implementation involves sophisticated algorithms that match energy supply with demand in real-time. For instance, when a residential solar installation generates excess power during midday peak production, the system automatically identifies nearby consumers who can utilize this energy, negotiating prices through blockchain-based smart contracts while ensuring all parties understand the transaction terms through semantic annotations.

8.2 Electric Vehicle (EV) Charging Infrastructure

The electric vehicle revolution requires intelligent charging infrastructure that can adapt to dynamic grid conditions, user preferences, and energy market fluctuations.

Blockchain and semantic annotation technologies enable this adaptive capability while ensuring fair access and optimal resource utilization.

Dynamic pricing mechanisms powered by blockchain smart contracts respond to real-time grid conditions, renewable energy availability, and charging demand. When renewable energy generation peaks, charging prices automatically decrease to incentivize consumption during optimal periods. Conversely, during high grid stress or low renewable output, prices increase to manage demand and encourage load shifting.

Semantic annotation creates comprehensive understanding across diverse charging networks and vehicle manufacturers. Each charging station broadcasts its capabilities, availability, and pricing through standardized semantic descriptors, while EVs communicate their charging requirements, battery status, and user preferences. This enables intelligent matchmaking that considers factors such as charging speed compatibility, user schedule flexibility, and cost optimization(Cavalieri 2021).

Advanced implementations include predictive charging algorithms that learn from historical patterns and user behavior. The system can reserve charging slots based on predicted arrival times, pre-negotiate pricing based on expected grid conditions, and even coordinate with other smart city systems such as traffic management to optimize overall urban energy flows (Saleem et al. 2023).

8.3 Demand Response Systems

Demand response programs are critical for maintaining grid stability while maximizing renewable energy utilization. Blockchain technology ensures transparent and tamper-proof recording of demand response events, while automated smart contracts handle participant enrollment, event notification, and reward distribution without human intervention(Honari et al. 2023).

Semantic annotation enables precise categorization and control of energy-consuming devices based on their consumption profiles, response times, and criticality levels. Appliances are semantically tagged with attributes such as "deferrable load," "critical service," or "flexible consumption," allowing the system to make intelligent decisions about which devices to control during peak demand periods.

The implementation involves sophisticated load forecasting algorithms that predict demand patterns and identify optimal intervention strategies. When grid stress is anticipated, the system automatically identifies participating devices that can reduce consumption while minimizing impact on user comfort and business operations. Blockchain ensures that all participants receive fair compensation based on their actual contribution to demand reduction(Modrzyński and Karaszewski 2022).

8.4 Building Energy Management Systems (BEMS)

Modern buildings are complex energy ecosystems with intricate relationships between physical spaces, occupants, devices, and energy flows. Semantic annotation models these relationships comprehensively, creating digital twins that enable optimized energy management strategies.

Building semantic models define hierarchical relationships between zones, rooms, HVAC systems, lighting, and occupancy patterns. This enables sophisticated control strategies that consider factors such as thermal dynamics, occupant comfort preferences, and external weather conditions. The system can predict energy requirements hours or days in advance, optimizing operations to minimize costs while maintaining comfort.

Blockchain technology ensures data integrity and enables secure sharing of anonymized building performance data with utilities, regulators, and research institutions. This creates valuable datasets for urban energy planning and policy development while maintaining privacy and security. Smart contracts can automatically execute energy efficiency incentive programs based on verified performance improvements(Honari et al. 2023).

8.5 Global Case Studies

8.5.1 Brooklyn Microgrid (USA)

The Brooklyn Microgrid project pioneered peer-to-peer energy trading using private blockchain technology. Residents with solar installations sell excess energy directly to neighbors through automated smart contracts. The project demonstrated significant cost savings and increased renewable energy utilization while building community resilience. Semantic annotations enable seamless integration of diverse residential energy systems and provide standardized metrics for energy quality and pricing (Wu et al. 2021).

8.5.2 Power Ledger (Australia)

Power Ledger operates across multiple countries, facilitating energy trading and renewable energy certificate tracking (Abiodun, Nwulu, and Olukanmi 2025). Their platform combines blockchain transparency with semantic data models that ensure consistent energy attribute tracking across different regulatory jurisdictions. The system handles complex multi-party transactions involving energy retailers, consumers, and renewable energy generators while maintaining compliance with varying national regulations.

8.5.3 Pylon Network (Spain)

Pylon Network focuses on energy cooperatives, using semantic data tagging to categorize community energy resources and optimize collective energy management. Their approach demonstrates how blockchain and semantic technologies can support alternative energy ownership models and community-driven sustainability initiatives. The platform enables small-scale renewable energy producers to participate in larger energy markets through collective action.

8.5.4 European Smart Grid Framework

The European Union's smart grid initiatives showcase cross-border energy data exchange using standardized semantic models and blockchain-based transaction verification. This framework enables renewable energy trading across national boundaries while maintaining regulatory compliance and grid stability. The semantic annotations ensure that energy attributes, carbon content, and origin certificates are consistently understood across different markets and regulatory frameworks.

9. CHALLENGES AND FUTURE DIRECTIONS

The integration of blockchain technology and semantic annotation in energy systems presents transformative opportunities, yet significant challenges must be addressed to achieve widespread adoption and optimal performance. As these technologies evolve, new research directions emerge that promise to overcome current limitations while opening unprecedented possibilities for intelligent energy management.

9.1 Current Limitations

9.1.1 Scalability and Performance

The scalability challenge represents one of the most critical barriers to blockchain adoption in energy systems. Public blockchains like Bitcoin and Ethereum process only 7-15 transactions per second, far below the throughput required for real-time energy trading where thousands of devices may need to execute transactions simultaneously. Energy systems demand sub-second response times for critical operations such as frequency regulation and demand response, making traditional blockchain latency unacceptable (Dzobo, Malila, and Sithole 2021).

Layer-2 protocols have emerged as promising solutions, creating secondary networks that handle high-frequency transactions while periodically settling on the main blockchain. Lightning Network for Bitcoin and state channels for Ethereum demonstrate how off-chain transactions can achieve near-instantaneous settlement with minimal fees. In energy applications, these protocols enable micro-transactions for small-scale energy trades while maintaining the security guarantees of the underlying blockchain.

Alternative consensus mechanisms offer additional pathways to improved performance. Proof-of-Stake (PoS) eliminates the computational overhead of mining, reducing both energy consumption and transaction latency (Sharma et al. 2023). Ethereum's transition to PoS demonstrated significant improvements in transaction throughput and finality times. Byzantine Fault Tolerance (BFT) consensus algorithms, such as Practical Byzantine Fault Tolerance (pBFT) and Tendermint, provide deterministic finality and can process thousands of transactions per second, making them suitable for mission-critical energy applications.

Hybrid blockchain models combine the benefits of public and private networks, using permissioned networks for high-frequency operations while anchoring to public blockchains for transparency and immutability. These architectures enable energy companies to maintain operational control while providing stakeholders with verification capabilities.

9.1.2 Interoperability Challenges

Semantic heterogeneity remains a persistent challenge as different organizations develop domain-specific ontologies that may conflict or overlap. Energy utilities, equipment manufacturers, and regulatory bodies often use incompatible data models, creating silos that prevent seamless integration. Even when organizations attempt to use standard ontologies, differences in interpretation and implementation can lead to semantic mismatches.

Cross-chain communication protocols are being developed to enable interoperability between different blockchain networks. Cosmos Inter-Blockchain Communication (IBC) protocol and Polkadot's cross-chain message passing demonstrate how blockchain networks can communicate while maintaining their unique characteristics. In energy systems, these protocols would enable a solar microgrid operating on one blockchain to trade energy with an electric vehicle charging network on another blockchain (Hosseinnezhad et al. 2021).

Standardized energy tokens represent another approach to interoperability, creating common denominators for energy trading across different platforms. The

Energy Web Chain's Energy Web Token (EWT) and similar initiatives aim to create universal energy currencies that can be recognized across different blockchain networks and energy systems.

9.1.3 Energy Consumption Paradox

The environmental impact of blockchain technology creates a fundamental contradiction when applied to sustainable energy systems. Proof-of-Work consensus mechanisms, while secure, consume enormous amounts of electricity. Bitcoin's annual energy consumption exceeds that of entire countries, undermining the sustainability goals of renewable energy systems.

Energy-efficient consensus mechanisms have emerged as critical solutions. Proof-of-Stake reduces energy consumption by over 99% compared to Proof-of-Work by eliminating competitive mining. Delegated Proof-of-Stake (DPoS) further improves efficiency by limiting the number of validators, though this may introduce centralization concerns. Proof-of-Authority (PoA) provides high performance for permissioned networks by using pre-approved validators.

Novel consensus mechanisms specifically designed for energy applications are being explored. Proof-of-Generation could reward validators based on their renewable energy production, aligning consensus participation with sustainability goals. Proof-of-Consumption might validate based on actual energy usage, creating incentives for efficient consumption patterns.

9.1.4 Privacy and Governance Complexities

Balancing transparency and privacy remains a critical challenge in energy blockchain systems, as while open ledgers enhance trust and accountability, excessive visibility of consumption data can expose sensitive personal or commercial information and complicate compliance with diverse regulatory regimes. Advanced cryptographic methods such as zero-knowledge proofs enable validation of transactions without revealing underlying data, preserving confidentiality while maintaining integrity. Permissioned blockchains introduce role-based access controls to protect sensitive information, and decentralized identity frameworks allow users to share only necessary credentials while retaining control over personal data. At the same time, legal and regulatory frameworks must evolve to address issues of smart contract enforceability, liability, and cross-border governance, making adaptive legislation and regulatory sandboxes essential for responsible and scalable adoption..

9.2 Future Research Directions

9.2.1 Lightweight Blockchain Protocols for Constrained Environments

IoT devices in energy systems often face strict limitations in computational power, memory, and energy capacity, making traditional blockchain protocols too resource-intensive for direct implementation. To address this, lightweight alternatives such as Directed Acyclic Graph architectures offer consensus mechanisms without mining, significantly reducing computational demands and enabling direct participation by constrained devices. Hybrid consensus models further enhance efficiency by allowing rapid local agreement with periodic anchoring to more secure networks for long-term validation, balancing responsiveness and security. Sharding techniques also improve scalability by dividing networks into smaller segments, enabling localized transaction processing within microgrids while maintaining overall system connectivity and consistency.

9.2.2 Dynamic and Adaptive Ontology Systems

Traditional static ontologies are insufficient for the rapidly evolving energy sector, where new technologies, regulations, and business models continuously emerge, prompting research into dynamic ontologies that can adapt automatically while preserving interoperability. Machine learning and natural language processing techniques enable automated identification and integration of new concepts from technical and regulatory developments, while federated ontology learning allows collaborative model evolution without exposing proprietary data. Additionally, version control mechanisms similar to software repositories support structured updates, backward compatibility, and coordinated management of multiple ontology versions to ensure stability alongside continuous innovation (Cioara et al. 2020).

9.2.3 Advanced Privacy-Preserving Mechanisms

Advanced privacy-preserving technologies enable secure and collaborative analytics in decentralized energy systems without exposing sensitive data. Homomorphic encryption allows computations to be performed on encrypted information, enabling utilities to optimize system performance without accessing individual consumption details. Differential privacy protects user identities by introducing controlled statistical noise into shared datasets, supporting research and planning while preventing re-identification. Secure multiparty computation permits multiple stakeholders to jointly determine pricing or allocation outcomes without revealing private inputs, and trusted execution environments provide hardware-level security for sensitive processing tasks, enabling secure cooperation even among competing organizations.

9.2.4 Intelligent Cross-Chain Interoperability

Future interoperability solutions extend beyond simple token transfers by enabling intelligent, semantically aware coordination across multiple blockchain networks. Semantic-enabled interoperability hubs function as intelligent agents that interpret the meaning and implications of cross-chain transactions, while automated smart contract translation allows applications developed on one blockchain to be adapted to others without manual rewriting, preserving functionality and intent. Cross-chain oracles ensure consistent access to real-time data such as pricing, weather, and grid conditions across different platforms, and semantic query federation enables unified access to distributed datasets, allowing energy management systems to retrieve production, consumption, and pricing information from multiple blockchains through a single coherent interface (Modrzyński and Karaszewski 2022).

9.3 Emerging Research Frontiers

9.3.1 Quantum-Resistant Cryptography

The potential emergence of quantum computing threatens current cryptographic systems used in blockchain networks. Post-quantum cryptography research focuses on developing algorithms that remain secure against quantum attacks, ensuring long-term viability of energy blockchain systems.

9.3.2 AI-Blockchain Integration

Artificial intelligence and blockchain technology increasingly converge to create more intelligent and autonomous energy systems. AI agents can operate on behalf of users in blockchain-based energy markets, making optimal trading decisions while learning from market patterns and user preferences.

9.3.3 Sustainability Metrics Integration

Future research explores integrating environmental impact metrics directly into blockchain protocols. Carbon-aware consensus mechanisms could adjust validation rewards based on the carbon intensity of validators' energy sources, incentivizing renewable energy use for network security. Figure 1 shows the Integrated Blockchain–Semantic Architecture for Smart Urban Energy Systems.

Figure 1. Integrated blockchain–semantic architecture for smart urban energy systems

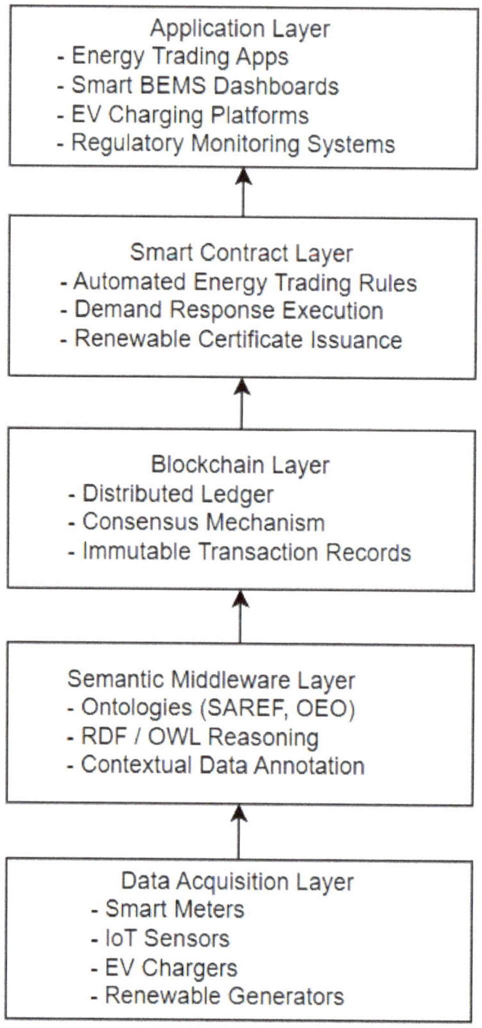

10. POLICY, GOVERNANCE, AND FUTURE OUTLOOK

The successful integration of blockchain technology and semantic annotation in energy systems requires comprehensive policy frameworks, innovative governance structures, and strategic long-term planning. As these technologies mature from experimental implementations to mainstream adoption, the role of policy makers, regulators, and governance institutions becomes increasingly critical in shaping a sustainable and equitable energy future.

10.1 Governance Frameworks

10.1.1 Regulatory Adaptation and Innovation

Traditional energy regulations designed for centralized utility systems face significant challenges when applied to decentralized blockchain-based energy networks, prompting governments to develop more agile and adaptive regulatory frameworks that balance innovation with consumer protection and grid reliability. Regulatory sandboxes have become key instruments for enabling controlled experimentation, allowing developers to test blockchain and semantic technologies while providing regulators with empirical evidence to refine policy responses. Broader legislative initiatives, such as decentralized energy market reforms and prosumer participation rights, illustrate attempts to modernize regulatory environments, though harmonization across jurisdictions remains complex. Smart contract governance introduces additional legal uncertainties related to autonomous execution, cross-border enforceability, and liability allocation, requiring updated legal interpretations and, in some cases, dedicated blockchain legislation. Ensuring consumer protection in decentralized systems further demands new accountability models that address risks associated with smart contract failures, data privacy, cybersecurity, and dispute resolution in multi-party digital energy ecosystems..

10.1.2 International Standardization Efforts

The global scope of energy systems and blockchain technology requires coordinated international standardization to ensure interoperability, security, and cross-border compatibility. Organizations such as the International Electrotechnical Commission develop technical standards for smart grid communication and interoperability, while the International Organization for Standardization contributes frameworks for energy management, greenhouse gas accounting, and blockchain governance. The World Wide Web Consortium provides foundational semantic web standards that enable machine-readable data exchange, supporting privacy, security, and accessibility in digital energy systems. In parallel, industry consortiums facilitate practical coordination between private sector innovation and formal standard-setting bodies, accelerating the development of interoperable and scalable blockchain-semantic energy infrastructures across jurisdictions.

10.1.3 Participatory and Decentralized Governance

Blockchain technology enables new participatory governance models that enhance transparency and stakeholder involvement in energy systems. Decentralized Autonomous Organizations allow collective decision-making through blockchain-based voting mechanisms, supporting community-managed energy cooperatives and automated implementation of governance rules via smart contracts. Semantic encoding of regulatory logic further enables automated compliance verification and consistent policy execution, reducing administrative burden while improving accountability. Token-based governance structures expand participation by granting stakeholders voting rights on system parameters and resource allocation, while hybrid governance models combine blockchain-enabled direct participation with traditional representative oversight to balance democratic legitimacy, efficiency, and technological innovation in decentralized energy ecosystems.

10.2 Implementation Roadmap

10.2.1 Short-term Priorities (1-3 Years)

In the short term, implementation should prioritize foundational interoperability through shared ontologies, common semantic standards, and collaborative industry vocabularies that enable basic blockchain-based energy transactions. Pilot initiatives should test lightweight and energy-efficient consensus mechanisms suitable for IoT-constrained energy environments, while regulatory sandboxes expand to include dedicated blockchain-energy tracks that clarify compliance, consumer protection, and operational boundaries. Early applications should focus on lower-risk domains such as renewable certificate trading and voluntary carbon markets to build regulatory confidence before extending to critical grid functions. Simultaneously, workforce development must begin through curriculum integration in universities and targeted industry training to prepare professionals for decentralized and digitally mediated energy management systems..

10.2.2 Medium-term Development (3-5 Years)

Over the medium term, integration into national energy strategies requires coordinated policy planning across energy, technology, and financial regulators to ensure innovation aligns with reliability and consumer safeguards. The development of standardized smart contract templates for common transactions such as peer-to-peer trading, demand response, and renewable certification will reduce complexity and enhance compliance automation through semantic verification. Strengthened industry-academia partnerships can accelerate research translation into practical deployment, while cross-border pilot programs test interoperability across diverse regulatory environments. These efforts collectively support scalable adoption, institutional learning, and harmonized governance frameworks (Siano 2024).

10.2.3 Long-term Vision (5+ Years)

In the long term, blockchain-semantic integration envisions fully autonomous and self-optimizing energy ecosystems capable of balancing supply and demand, negotiating transactions, and maintaining grid stability through embedded intelligence. Global tokenization markets may enable seamless cross-border trading of renewable certificates, carbon credits, and energy commodities, increasing liquidity and transparency in environmental markets. Integration with emerging technologies such as artificial intelligence, quantum-secured communications, and advanced materials could further enhance resilience, security, and sustainability, enabling next-generation energy infrastructures that are adaptive, intelligent, and globally interconnected.

10.3 Sustainability Impact and Environmental Benefits

Blockchain and semantic technologies significantly strengthen sustainability outcomes by enhancing transparency in renewable energy tracking and carbon accounting through immutable, verifiable records. Semantic models enable comprehensive lifecycle representation of energy assets, supporting circular economy practices by facilitating material traceability and recycling. Automated carbon footprint calculation through smart contracts allows dynamic pricing and streamlined regulatory compliance, while transparent impact documentation supports environmental justice by ensuring equitable distribution of energy-related benefits and burdens across communities. Together, these capabilities advance accountability, efficiency, and fairness in sustainable urban energy transitions (Wang, Su, and Yan 2023). Table 1 shows the Multidimensional Impact of Blockchain–Semantic Integration in Urban Energy Systems.

Table 1. Multidimensional impact of blockchain–semantic integration in urban energy systems

Dimension	Traditional Energy System	Blockchain–Semantic System	Expected Impact
Transparency	Limited transaction visibility	Immutable distributed ledger with traceability	Increased trust and auditability
Interoperability	Fragmented data silos	Ontology-based standardized data exchange	Seamless cross-platform integration
Efficiency	Manual billing and slow settlements	Automated smart contracts	Reduced transaction costs and latency
Renewable Tracking	Risk of double counting	Unique tokenized certificates	Accurate carbon accounting
Governance	Centralized control	Participatory blockchain governance	Enhanced energy democracy
Scalability	Infrastructure-heavy expansion	Decentralized peer-to-peer scaling	Flexible system growth
Sustainability Reporting	Manual compliance reporting	Real-time verifiable data	Improved ESG compliance

10.4 Economic and Social Transformation

10.4.1 Emerging Business Models and Market Innovation

Blockchain and semantic integration enable transformative business models that reshape energy markets by introducing tokenized carbon trading, peer-to-peer marketplaces, and automated service-based contracts. Tokenization allows fractional ownership of carbon credits and renewable attributes, opening global liquidity to small-scale projects that previously lacked market access. Decentralized energy marketplaces reduce reliance on traditional utilities by enabling continuous, automated trading with lower transaction costs, fostering localized entrepreneurship and competitive pricing. Energy-as-a-service models gain operational efficiency through smart contracts that automatically track performance, adjust payments based on real-time delivery, and provide semantically structured service terms, thereby aligning incentives between providers and consumers while enhancing transparency and accountability.

10.4.2 Community Empowerment and Energy Democracy

Blockchain automation significantly lowers transaction costs, making small-scale community energy initiatives economically viable and broadening participation in decentralized markets. Semantic technologies enhance accessibility by presenting complex energy information in context-aware, user-friendly formats, allowing individuals with limited technical expertise to engage confidently. Transparent ledger records reduce information asymmetry, ensuring that small producers and consumers have equal access to market data traditionally dominated by large energy firms. Citizen-centered systems further shift users from passive consumers to active participants, with smart home platforms optimizing consumption while clearly communicating environmental and financial impacts. Through blockchain-based voting and governance mechanisms, energy democracy initiatives empower local cooperatives to manage investments, pricing, and operations collectively, strengthening community control and reducing dependence on centralized decision-makers.

10.5 Discussion

The findings indicate that blockchain alone cannot solve energy governance fragmentation. Semantic interoperability is essential for contextual intelligence. When combined, both technologies enhance systemic resilience. However, institutional readiness, regulatory harmonization, and technological standardization determine implementation success. Systems theory confirms that integrated digital infrastructures stabilize complex energy ecosystems by reducing information asymmetry and transaction friction.

11. CONCLUSION

The integration of blockchain and semantic annotation represents a transformative pathway toward decentralized, transparent, and sustainable urban energy systems. While technical and governance challenges remain, a structured socio-technical approach grounded in systems theory enables scalable implementation. This chapter provides a conceptual and governance roadmap to guide digital energy transformation in smart cities.

11.1 Technological Convergence and System Transformation

The convergence of blockchain and semantic annotation establishes a robust technological foundation for modern energy systems by combining decentralized trust mechanisms with intelligent data interoperability. Blockchain provides security, immutability, and distributed consensus for peer-to-peer energy transactions, while semantic annotation enables contextual understanding and reasoning across heterogeneous energy data sources. Together, these technologies facilitate autonomous energy ecosystems in which smart contracts execute transactions based on predefined semantic rules, real-time grid conditions, and user preferences, transforming traditional hierarchical systems into adaptive networks where households, prosumers, and industrial actors actively contribute to grid optimization and receive fair compensation. Real-world implementations, including peer-to-peer microgrid initiatives and cross-border renewable certificate platforms, demonstrate measurable gains in efficiency, transparency, renewable integration, and community resilience, indicating the growing maturity and transformative potential of integrated blockchain-semantic energy systems..

11.2 Addressing Urban Energy Challenges

Modern cities face escalating energy challenges driven by urbanization, climate commitments, and the growing integration of renewable sources, while traditional centralized systems struggle to manage decentralized generation, variable demand, and multidirectional energy flows. The integration of blockchain and semantic annotation addresses these pressures by enabling flexible, real-time energy management through automated smart contracts that adjust pricing, demand response, and load balancing based on grid conditions, weather data, and user preferences. At the same time, blockchain enhances transparency and traceability, allowing precise tracking of energy origin, generation methods, and carbon impact to support sustainability reporting and carbon reduction commitments. Semantic interoperability further reduces system fragmentation by establishing shared data standards across heterogeneous devices and platforms, facilitating seamless integration, lowering implementation costs, and accelerating innovation in complex urban energy ecosystems.

11.3 Economic and Social Transformation

The integration of blockchain and semantic annotation reshapes not only the technical architecture of energy systems but also their economic and social foundations by enabling decentralized market participation, community-based trading, and new entrepreneurial models that reduce reliance on traditional utility dominance. Peer-to-peer energy markets foster localized economic ecosystems in which residents directly exchange surplus energy, lower transaction costs, minimize transmission losses, and retain financial benefits within communities. Beyond economic restructuring, these technologies promote social transformation through participatory governance mechanisms that allow communities to influence infrastructure decisions, pricing frameworks, and investment priorities, advancing principles of energy democracy. They also enhance equity by lowering barriers to clean energy participation, enabling fractional ownership through tokenized community solar initiatives, and providing context-aware semantic interfaces that make complex energy choices accessible to diverse users, including renters and low-income households..

11.4 Policy and Governance Innovation

The effective deployment of blockchain-semantic energy systems requires innovative policy and governance frameworks that reconcile technological advancement with consumer protection, grid stability, privacy safeguards, and equity objectives, as traditional regulations designed for centralized infrastructures are ill-suited to decentralized and autonomous energy networks. Emerging governance models must therefore accommodate distributed architectures while ensuring accountability and risk management. Regulatory sandboxes play a critical role by enabling controlled experimentation, allowing policymakers to evaluate real-world impacts and refine adaptive regulatory responses tailored to blockchain-based energy applications. At the same time, international coordination on technical standards and regulatory alignment is essential due to the cross-border nature of energy markets and digital infrastructure, with global standard-setting bodies providing the foundation for interoperable, secure, and scalable smart energy ecosystems that can operate consistently across jurisdictions..

11.5 Implementation Challenges and Solutions

Despite their transformative promise, blockchain and semantic annotation technologies face substantial implementation challenges, including scalability constraints, energy consumption concerns, privacy risks, and technical complexity, all of which demand coordinated research and innovation. Advances in energy-efficient consensus mechanisms, layer-two scaling approaches, and hybrid blockchain architectures help overcome performance limitations while preserving decentralization and security. Privacy-enhancing techniques such as zero-knowledge proofs and secure multiparty computation allow systems to maintain transparency and auditability without exposing sensitive consumer data. At the same time, the development and maintenance of semantic ontologies require sustained collaboration among domain specialists, technologists, and standards bodies, with emerging machine learning and federated learning methods offering adaptive solutions to manage evolving energy technologies and complex market structures effectively.

11.6 Future Research and Development Priorities

The continued evolution of blockchain-semantic energy systems demands interdisciplinary research that bridges computer science, cryptography, energy engineering, and public policy. Key priorities include the development of quantum-resistant cryptographic frameworks to ensure long-term system security, the integration of artificial intelligence to enable autonomous optimization of grid operations, and the establishment of cross-chain interoperability protocols that facilitate seamless interaction among diverse blockchain networks. Environmental sustainability must guide innovation through the design of carbon-aware consensus mechanisms and energy-efficient architectures, particularly as blockchain infrastructure expands. Advances in Internet of Things integration will require lightweight, resource-efficient protocols capable of supporting distributed devices. Simultaneously, policy-oriented research must clarify issues of liability, governance, regulatory compliance, and the legal recognition of smart contracts and decentralized autonomous organizations, thereby creating the institutional foundations necessary for scalable and mainstream adoption of these technologies.

11.7 Managerial Implications

Energy managers should prioritize interoperability standards before blockchain deployment. Policymakers must establish adaptive regulatory frameworks and sandbox environments. Utilities should adopt hybrid blockchain architectures to balance scalability and transparency. Investment strategies should align digital innovation with sustainability verification mechanisms. Cross-sector collaboration is essential to achieve systemic transformation.

REFERENCES

Abiodun, T. P., Nwulu, N. I., & Olukanmi, P. O. (2025). Application of blockchain technology in carbon trading market: A systematic review. *IEEE Access : Practical Innovations, Open Solutions*, *13*, 5446–5470. DOI: 10.1109/ACCESS.2024.3523672

Alshammari, N. F., Alshahr, S., & Barakat, S. (2026). How energy management strategy shapes optimal microgrid design: A comparative analysis for EV charging stations. *Applied Energy*, *407*, 127352. Advance online publication. DOI: 10.1016/j.apenergy.2026.127352

Cavalieri, S. (2021). Semantic interoperability between IEC 61850 and oneM2M for IoT-enabled smart grids. *Sensors (Basel)*, *21*(7), 2571. Advance online publication. DOI: 10.3390/s21072571 PMID: 33917602

Choobineh, M., Arabnya, A., Sohrabi, B., Khodaei, A., & Paaso, A. (2023). Blockchain technology in energy systems: A state-of-the-art review. *IET Blockchain*, *3*(1), 35–59. DOI: 10.1049/blc2.12020

Cioara, T., Pop, C., Zanc, R., Anghel, I., Antal, M., & Salomie, I. (2020). Smart grid management using blockchain: Future scenarios and challenges. In *Proceedings of the RoEduNet IEEE International Conference* (2020-Decem). DOI: 10.1109/RoEduNet51892.2020.9324874

Dzobo, O., Malila, B., & Sithole, L. (2021). Proposed framework for blockchain technology in a decentralised energy network. *Protection and Control of Modern Power Systems*, *6*(3), 1–11. DOI: 10.1186/s41601-021-00209-8

Elkhodr, M. (2024). Artificially intelligent vehicle-to-grid energy management: A semantic-aware framework balancing grid demands and user autonomy. *Computers*, *13*(10), 249. Advance online publication. DOI: 10.3390/computers13100249

Guo, Y., Wan, Z., & Cheng, X. (2022). When blockchain meets smart grids: A comprehensive survey. *High-Confidence Computing*, *2*(2), 100059. Advance online publication. DOI: 10.1016/j.hcc.2022.100059

Hernik, J., Sagan, A., Jarecki, W., & Grinberga-Zalite, G. (2025). Digital transformation in business process management: The role of employee engagement. *Human Technology*, *21*(1), 203–221. DOI: 10.14254/1795-6889.2025.21-1.10

Honari, K., Rouhani, S., Falak, N. E., Liu, Y., Li, Y., Liang, H., Dick, S., & Miller, J. (2023). Smart contract design in distributed energy systems: A systematic review. *Energies*, *16*(12), 1–28. DOI: 10.3390/en16124797

Hosseinnezhad, V., Hayes, B., O'Regan, B., & Siano, P. (2021). Practical insights to design a blockchain-based energy trading platform. *IEEE Access : Practical Innovations, Open Solutions*, *9*, 154827–154844. DOI: 10.1109/ACCESS.2021.3127890

Karpinski, M., Kuznetsov, O., & Oliynykov, R. (2025). Security, privacy, confidentiality, and trust in the blockchain: From theory to applications. *Electronics (Basel)*, *14*(3), 581. Advance online publication. DOI: 10.3390/electronics14030581

Kumari, A., Sukharamwala, U. C., Tanwar, S., Raboaca, M. S., Alqahtani, F., Tolba, A., Sharma, R., Aschilean, I., & Mihaltan, T. C. (2022). Blockchain-based peer-to-peer transactive energy management scheme for smart grid system. *Sensors (Basel)*, *22*(13), 1–19. DOI: 10.3390/s22134826 PMID: 35808325

Modrzyński, P., & Karaszewski, R. (2022). Urban energy management—A systematic literature review. *Energies*, *15*(21), 1–17. DOI: 10.3390/en15217848

Nour, M., Chaves-Avila, J. P., & Sanchez-Miralles, A. (2022). Review of blockchain potential applications in the electricity sector and challenges for large scale adoption. *IEEE Access : Practical Innovations, Open Solutions*, *10*, 47384–47418. DOI: 10.1109/ACCESS.2022.3171227

Parhamfar, M., Sadeghkhani, I., & Adeli, A. M. (2024). Towards the net zero carbon future: A review of blockchain-enabled peer-to-peer carbon trading. *Energy Science & Engineering*, *12*(3), 1242–1264. DOI: 10.1002/ese3.1697

Saleem, M. U., Shakir, M., Usman, M. R., Bajwa, M. H. T., Shabbir, N., Ghafaroki, P. S., & Daniel, K. (2023). Integración del sistema de gestión de energía inteligente con Internet de las cosas y computación en la nube para una gestión eficiente del lado de la demanda en redes inteligentes. *Energies*, *16*(12).

Sekti, B. A. (2025a). AI technology management concepts and strategies. In *AI technology management and value creation* (pp. 1–32). DOI: 10.4018/979-8-3373-2497-5.ch001

Sekti, B. A. (2025b). IT service information security management. In *Cases on information systems service management* (pp. 61–93). DOI: 10.4018/979-8-3373-2352-7.ch003

Sekti, B. A. (2026). Cybersecurity challenges in smart city development. In *Securing smart cities through modern cryptography technologies* (pp. 75–102). IGI Global Scientific Publishing. DOI: 10.4018/979-8-3373-3326-7.ch003

Sharma, A., Patel, M., Choudhary, A., & Kumar, G. (2023). Blockchain based security enabled smart contract for energy management. In *Proceedings of the 16th International Conference on Security of Information and Networks (SIN 2023)* (pp. 1–7). DOI: 10.1109/SIN60469.2023.10474845

Siano, P. (2024). Front matter: Volume 13291. *Proceedings of SPIE, 13291*, 0. DOI: 10.1117/12.3054455

Wang, Y., Su, Z., & Yan, M. (2023). Social metaverse: Challenges and solutions. *IEEE Internet of Things Magazine*, *6*(3), 144–150. DOI: 10.1109/IOTM.001.2200266

Wu, J., Orlandi, F., Lee, Y. H., O'Sullivan, D., & Dev, S. (2021). Organizing decentralized energy data using semantic approach. In *Proceedings of the Photonics & Electromagnetics Research Symposium (PIERS 2021)* (pp. 2213–2216). DOI: 10.1109/PIERS53385.2021.9695066

Ysebie, W., Azaioud, H., Caers, B., & Desmet, J. (2025). RE/SOURCED pilot: Practical implementation of a DC microgrid. In *IET Conference Proceedings* (pp. 769–773). DOI: 10.1049/icp.2025.1681

KEY TERMS AND DEFINITIONS

Blockchain Technology: A distributed ledger system that securely stores transaction data in a transparent and immutable manner, applied in energy management to facilitate peer-to-peer energy trading, renewable energy certification, and contract automation.

Microgrid: A local energy network that can operate connected to or independently from the main grid, leveraging blockchain for transaction transparency and semantic annotation for heterogeneous energy source integration.

Ontology: A formal conceptual model defining terms, attributes, and relationships within a specific domain, used to standardize energy data across devices and platforms.

Peer-to-Peer (P2P) Energy Trading: A direct energy exchange mechanism between producers and consumers without traditional intermediaries, facilitated by blockchain and supported by semantic annotation for data interoperability.

Renewable Energy Certification: A blockchain-based verification system that tracks the origin, production method, and environmental attributes of renewable energy to ensure transparency and prevent double claims.

Semantic Annotation: The process of adding meaningful metadata to raw data using formal ontologies so that systems can understand the context, relationships, and meaning of data for interoperability in smart energy ecosystems.

Smart Contract: A self-executing digital agreement with predefined conditions embedded in code, used to manage energy transactions, demand response, and dynamic pricing schemes.

Chapter 8
Smart Public Places

S. Ida Evangeline
http://orcid.org/0000-0003-2997-7897
Government College of Engineering, Tirunelveli, India

ABSTRACT

The focus on smart public places is increasing as they are seen as potential leverage for creating more sustainable, cleaner, and livable cities. At the same time, public spaces are increasingly being used as a way to address some of the most pressing challenges of our time (traffic congestion and air pollution). Smart Public Places are intelligent, sensor-enhanced, digitally-augmented environments that include elements of environmental intelligence, community engagement, and optimized mobility. As opposed to the more traditional structured forms of infrastructure, smart public places act as systems capable of responding to a variety of stimuli including changing air quality conditions, regulating traffic flow through a city, and changing individual behaviors based on real-time information and interactive technologies and through community-based design. The use of multiple disciplines and international case studies will be explored throughout this chapter.

1. INTRODUCTION: CITIES, POLLUTION, AND THE ROLE OF PUBLIC PLACES

Cities are increasingly confronted with the dual challenges of environmental degradation and mobility congestion as rapid urbanization intensifies pressure on infrastructure and urban ecosystems. On one hand, cities are hubs for economic growth, cultural diversity, and technology development. At the same time, however, cities generate a significant amount of environmental strain, most notably through air pollution from transportation, including particulate matter, nitrogen dioxide, carbon monoxide, greenhouse gas emissions and other pollutants from motorized transpor-

DOI: 10.4018/979-8-2600-0883-6.ch008

tation; and traffic congestion which can be detrimental to both urban efficiency and the quality of urban life (Abdelkarim et al. 2023). In total, air pollution is estimated to have caused millions of premature deaths every year globally according to the World Health Organization (WHO), with many of these deaths attributed to poor air quality created by emissions from transportation in urban areas. Furthermore, traffic congestion is estimated to cause longer travel times, greater amounts of fuel consumption, higher levels of environmental emissions, and ultimately lower levels of quality of urban life (Abdelkarim et al., 2023).

Infrastructure development, traffic regulations and technology improvement in transportation systems are typical policy responses to urbanization and mobility issues. While these types of initiatives are important, they generally approach urban challenges as solely technical problems related to the physical infrastructure of transportation systems or environmental systems for measuring pollution and other environmental impacts. The broader urban environment is typically ignored when viewing these types of issues, including public spaces through which the urban experience unfolds and in which the interactions between infrastructure, social activity and environmental conditions occur. These include parks, plazas, sidewalks, transit hubs, and civic squares; each serves as a dynamic arena for the intersection of mobility, environmental exposure and social interaction (Itair et al. 2023).

In recent years, research has shown that public spaces are a critical part of how sustainable and livable cities can be developed from an urbanistic standpoint. The human centered approach to developing cities demonstrates that public spaces affect travel habits and social interaction among residents which develop and define their sense of community identity (Gehl, 2011). On the other hand, the increasing body of literature on smart cities indicates that the application of digital technologies, data analytics, and sensor networks will enable improved urban governance, environmental monitoring, and mobility management (Batty et al., 2012; Bibri & Krogstie, 2017). Thus far however, the relationship between the use of smart technologies and the design of public spaces is still somewhat unexplored (Abid et al., 2024)

The convergence of these two domains has led to a new paradigm in smart public places. Smart public places are defined by the use of digital technologies (e.g., sensors, real-time data systems, and interactivity) to enhance urban environments and promote environmentally responsible transportation choices, improve air quality through environmental monitoring, and facilitate citizen participation and interaction with local government. They are active, dynamic and adaptive urban systems which can be programmed to monitor the environment, detect changes in how they are used, provide information back to users and decision makers and respond to changing demands and needs for their services.

A smart place is more than a technology-based innovation within the physical environment of a city; it is an integrated socio-technical system that enables interaction among the technical components of sensors, platforms, data analysis, governance mechanisms and the social aspects of citizen use (and perceptions) and institutional data management. The success or failure of the technical layers (sensors, digital platforms, etc.) will depend upon the social interaction with this technical layer by citizens, the institutional frameworks for governing resultant data and the urban policy framework for integrating this type of technology into overall sustainability strategy (Prabowo et al., 2023).

In addition to technological innovation, the development of smart public places raises significant socio-economic issues. Smart urban infrastructure has the potential to enhance environmental monitoring, support sustainable mobility, and improve quality of life in cities. The development of these types of systems is limited by a lack of equitable access to digital infrastructure, unequal investment in urban areas, and varied levels of digital literacy across different segments of society. Therefore, the integration of smart technology into public spaces should be approached from an issue-based perspective that addresses both technological efficiency and issues of urban equity, accessibility and inclusive governance.

Smart public areas, from a behavioral perspective, can have an impact upon how people choose to engage with their urban environment. Smart public spaces can be digitally enhanced with real time data about the environmental conditions of the area in which they are located, as well as, real time data about how to move within the area. They can also include interactive elements, such as games or competitions that will encourage people to make more sustainable transportation choices, and encourage them to think more green. The physical and informational environments in which we make our decisions regarding transportation, can create a series of incremental changes toward making more active travel options, for example walking, cycling, and using public transportation, more appealing and accessible (Almarri & Boussabaine, 2025).

The focus of this chapter is on whether and in what ways smart public areas can act as integrated city-wide projects (i.e., by reducing environmental and transportation problems while increasing citizen engagement and equity). The chapter views smart public areas as nodes at which three critical urban systems meet: environmental management; mobility infrastructure; and social interaction. Using this framework, the chapter will explore how a variety of technologies that include sensors, adaptive infrastructure and participatory technologies could improve clean air quality; create more efficient transportation systems; and produce more equitable urban environments.

Smart public spaces are an important part of the current urban transformation in cities. The chapter looks at the role of smart public spaces by using four different areas: digital governance, environmental science, behavioral studies, and urban planning. The aim is to bring all these different areas together to show how they can help us understand the way we want to design our public spaces for the future of sustainable cities. The chapter argues that in order to be able to create sustainable cities we will need not only to have Smarter Technologies but also to reimagine Public spaces as socially embedded environments that are responsive, inclusive and support both ecological resilience and civic life.

1.1 Theoretical Foundations of Smart Public Places

Smart public places are built on a synthesis of theoretical frameworks developed by researchers in urban studies, digital governance, and socio-technical system studies; while the majority of the literature conceptualized smart public places as digitally-enabled (i.e., smart) versions of traditional public space, an increasing number of scholars are beginning to conceptualize smart public places as complex systems where digital technologies, social behaviors, and institutional governance interact to create urban conditions. Therefore, understanding smart public places will require a theoretical framework that can integrate technology innovation into a larger social and spatial context.

One key theoretical approach is smart city theory—which sees digital technology, data analysis and networking as a means for enhancing governance, sustainability and quality of life within urban areas. The first smart city approaches were primarily concerned with optimizing urban infrastructure and technological efficiency using sensors, data management systems and AI to better control urban functions (Esposito et al., 2025). Subsequent research found that smart cities should be characterized by their capacity to foster sustainable development and citizen-oriented governance, rather than merely by technological capacity (Beckers & Mora, 2025). From this perspective, public spaces emerge as key points of intersection where the use of digital technology intersects with the daily life of urban residents, providing opportunities for environmental monitoring, coordinating mobility and facilitating civic engagement.

A second influential theoretical framework is that of the socio-technical system. This emphasizes how technology and social structure evolve together to develop a set of societal institutions for urban development. This means urban technologies do not exist as independent entities from social structures, they are built into the social fabric through a complex network of policy, governance, and practice (Velasquez Mendez et al. 2025). Therefore smart public spaces can be viewed as socio-technical systems where sensor technology, digital user interfaces, and communication networks all work to engage with citizens and urban users, public authorities, and regulatory systems. The success of such spaces will depend upon the level of institutional coordination, public trust and citizen participation, just as much as the technical capabilities of the space.

Human centered urbanism is a very important theoretical basis to understand smart public spaces as well. As early as the 1970's, urban design scholars have pointed out that the form of public space determines forms of social interaction, mobility, and collective identity in cities (Aldehim et al., 2025). Public spaces can be seen as social environments that shape how people interact with and move through their environment in the city. Therefore, smart technology will need to consider the way people act, have access to and feel included by digital systems embedded in public spaces. The goal of smart technology in public spaces is to make them easier to use, safer and more comfortable. Smart technology should be more than just more complex, it needs to make public spaces better.

The study of behavioral urbanism provides significant insight regarding how smart public spaces operate. Utilizing the principles of both behavioral economics and environmental psychology, the behavioral urbanism theory indicates that through the design of an environment, designers can make use of environmental cues and/or feedback to nudge individuals toward making decisions based upon their own self-interest (Viale, 2025) – for example, utilizing a real time data system that provides information about air quality to encourage residents to avoid areas of high pollution when using active transportation. Therefore, the interventions implemented in smart public spaces are examples of behavioral nudges where designers have created an environment that encourages specific behavior choices without limiting individual freedoms.

In addition to technological and behavioral components, smart public spaces should also be viewed from an urban equity and social economic inclusion perspective (Nsabiyumva et al., 2026). Smart infrastructure development is typically part of larger urban investments, and as such; it follows existing inequities in resource distribution among urban neighborhoods. Thus, wealthier neighborhoods are more likely to have access to more technologically sophisticated digital infrastructure, environmental monitoring systems etc. whereas lower-income neighborhoods experience higher levels of exposure to air pollution, water contamination, etc., and fewer opportunities to utilize smart urban services. Therefore, researchers are calling for smart city equity-based approaches and equitable distributions of digital infrastructure and access to smart urban services.

Together, the above theories illustrate that smart public areas include more than just technologically improved public spaces; they are hybrid urban systems where digital technology, societal norms and institutional processes intersect to influence how we manage our environment, travel through an area, and participate in community affairs. The use of these theories to contextualize smart public areas can help us understand them as not only technological improvements, but as tools for changing how society and the environment function in modern cities.

1.2 Conceptual Framework: Smart Public Places in Sustainable Urban Systems

To see how smart public places can help solve urban pollution and traffic issues, this chapter uses a theoretical framework for understanding smart public places as an integral part of complex networks of systems in urban areas. Smart public places are viewed here as multi-functional social/technological platforms with functions for environmental monitoring, mobility management and civic engagement; rather than simply as smart technologies for upgrading urban infrastructure.

Figure 1. Conceptual framework of smart public places for sustainable urban systems

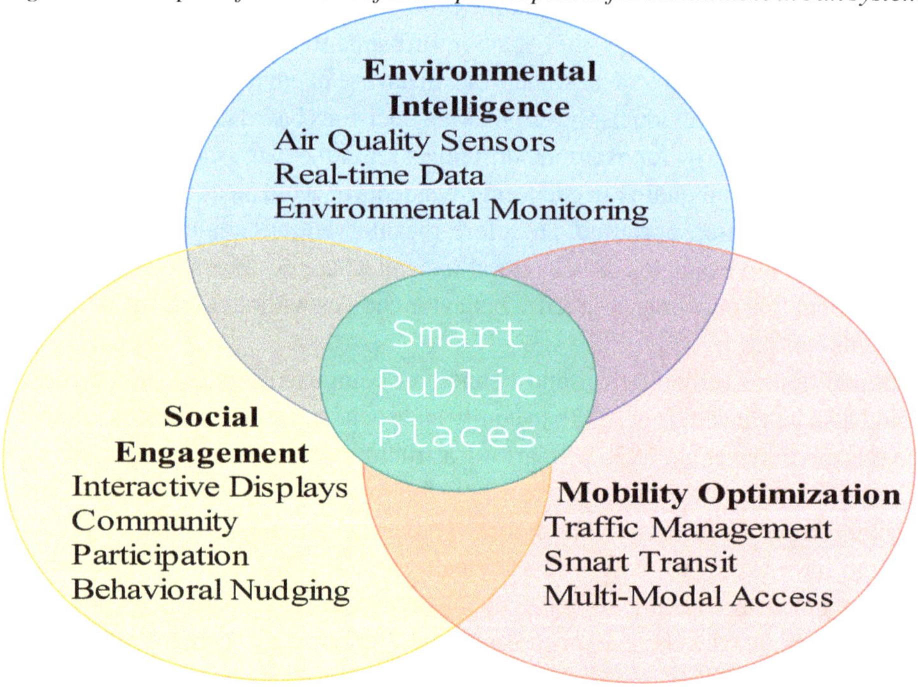

Beginning with a visual representation of the conceptual framework as shown in Figure 1, it is possible to see the relationship of smart public spaces to their role in connecting environmental intelligence and mobility optimization through social engagement for the sustainability of cities. The three interconnected dimensions (environmental intelligence, mobility optimization, and social engagement) are the base of the functioning and the impact of smart public spaces.

Smart public spaces can monitor environmental conditions by using a network of sensors placed throughout public spaces. These sensors are placed within public space infrastructure such as streetlights, bus shelters or other forms of urban furniture. The sensors continually collect information on environmental factors such as air quality, noise levels, temperature and humidity. This continual collection of environmental data is used to provide real-time data to allow for identification of pollution hot spots, risk monitoring for potential environmental hazards, and to take proactive and localized measures to address identified issues (e.g., implementing traffic control changes, activating green infrastructure, sending public health alerts). Therefore, Smart Public Spaces act as an urban environmental observatory supporting pro-active and local environmental decision making.

The second dimension focuses on optimizing mobility by describing how smart public places are able to influence where people move within a city and reduce traffic congestion. Smart public places are typically located at key intersections for pedestrian traffic, public transportation and destinations within cities. Smart public places are equipped with digital infrastructure such as real time public transportation information, digital way-finding tools and shared transportation options that allow users to take advantage of multi-modal transportation options and shift towards more environmentally friendly transportation options. In addition to increasing access to a variety of transportation options (walking, biking, taking the bus), smart public places help to improve connectivity and efficiency among these options, which reduces the use of personal vehicles and supports a more efficient system of mobility in a city.

The third dimension of smart cities (social engagement and behavioral influence) is concerned with how smart public space influences resident behavior and promotes resident participation in civic activities. Digital engagement platforms, environmental monitoring systems (e.g., dashboards), interactive technologies installed within public spaces provide residents with information about their environment (air quality, traffic flow, etc.), as well as how residents move through their environment and sustainability efforts implemented by local government. Smart public spaces can stimulate environmentally conscious behaviors from residents through providing them with information and using behavioral "nudges" to encourage certain actions, or enable residents to participate in city decision making processes by providing them with digital feedback mechanisms and participatory planning tools. In this way, smart public space are not only technological infrastructure; they are a means of promoting civic engagement and community awareness.

The above three dimensions also interact with each other. For example, the data collected by an environmental monitoring system is used for designing mobility management strategies; on the other hand, behavioral engagement tools affect how people react to the available environmental information and mobility choices. Finally, governance frameworks and integrated policies determine how these systems interact and develop within a larger context of urban development strategies. This conceptualization of smart public spaces as an intersection of environmental intelligence (monitoring), mobility systems (management) and social engagement (participation) will provide a structured lens for organizing the subsequent parts of this chapter. The next sections explore each of the individual dimensions in greater detail to show how the interactivity of sensor-based environments, adaptive infrastructure and participatory technologies can contribute to cleaner air, reduced traffic and more accessible urban spaces.

1.3 Integrating Socio-Economic Dimensions in Smart Public Places

Although smart public places have been largely framed by their technological innovations and environmental monitoring; they are shaped by a larger set of sociological/economic relationships than those that exist with respect to urban life. The integration of digital technologies into public spaces will affect patterns of accessibility; access to economic opportunity; and opportunities for social inclusion. Therefore, to understand the nature of smart public places we need to consider both the technological (efficiency) aspects of the environment as well as the social and economic context in which it operates.

The other very significant aspect is the urban inequalities and the spatial justice. In fact, the investments in the smart city projects are most often focused on the upper-income districts that have higher levels of resources, better infrastructure capacity and more political visibility. Therefore, it is possible that, with respect to technology-enabled public spaces, they will mainly be developed in the central business districts, in tourist areas or in high income districts. While these are the same urban areas where people live who are exposed to the worst environmental problems (i.e., poor air quality; inadequate transportation infrastructure), these same urban residents will likely have access to fewer technological enhancements for their public spaces. If there is no intentional planning to address equity issues related to how Smart Public Places are developed, then the smart public places can unintentionally exacerbate pre-existing inequities in urban service delivery and environmental quality.

The socio-economic aspect of another consideration is the digital divide, the disparity in digital technology accessibility, Internet connection accessibility, and digital literacy. Smart public places will most likely be dependent upon mobile applications, real time data platforms, and digital interfaces, however this will require smartphone ownership and stable Internet connections; populations like older adults, lower income residents, migrants, etc., will be unable to use many of these devices due to lack of familiarity with them (limited digital literacy). Inclusive access will therefore need to include multi-modal interfaces such as physical displays, public kiosks, and non-digital communication methods for increased participation in smart urban systems.

Public spaces that are smart can also have an effect on the way cities work economically. A well designed and technologically advanced public space can increase foot traffic in a neighborhood, which is good for local business and will make commercial areas more desirable. With the installation of smart transportation technology, digital signs and other technologies to monitor environmental conditions; the total experience of using an urban environment could be greatly improved to make it more attractive as a tourist destination, or for shopping and cultural events. As such, smart public spaces could help support urban competitiveness and economic development.

Simultaneously, the economic consequences for smart public spaces have to be viewed in a critical light. Urban redevelopment projects which are equipped with sophisticated technology in their public spaces can lead to higher real estate prices and business developments in those neighborhoods, and thus accelerate gentrification as well as displacement of former residents. In addition, through improvements in environmental conditions and public amenities, long-time residents and small businesses will experience additional financial pressure to remain in the area. Therefore, policymakers and planners have to balance innovative technology with affordable housing, inclusive economic strategies, and community-oriented planning approaches.

In addition, social economic factors impact how we govern smart spaces within our cities. Private sector companies often partner with municipalities to fund and run smart technologies especially when private sector companies will be providing the sensors, communications infrastructure, and/or the data platform for the municipality. While these collaborations can help to speed up innovation and save municipal funds, they have raised important concerns about who owns the data created by the smart public place, what types of activities (commercial vs. non-commercial) may occur in the space, and how the benefits generated by an urban data system are distributed. Therefore, it is crucial that there is transparent governance and accountable processes so that smart public places are used to benefit all members of society rather than just being a source of profit for private companies.

Smart public spaces are a combination of technology with the larger social-economic systems in which they exist; thus, when designing and governing smart public spaces, it will be critical to include an understanding of how to make these spaces equitable, accessible, and economically inclusive so that smart urban innovations can support creating fairer, more inclusive and more sustainable cities.

2. DEFINING SMART PUBLIC PLACES

Smart city spaces represent the future of city design and city governance - the intersection of digital infrastructure, environmental awareness and human behavior to create cities that are healthier, more efficient, and responsive to the needs of citizens. unlike traditional public places, smart public spaces are interactive, dynamic environments as opposed to being static and frozen in time with respect to service and aesthetic. thus, smart public spaces can no longer be described solely by physical appearance or facilities but rather by their ability to perceive, respond and create change; to modify how people move through the city, communicate with it, and interact with it (Varshini et al. 2021).

The backbone of intelligent public spaces is based upon technology, therefore it controls many quantities through sensor technologies located in pavement, street furniture or lamp posts which provide information about; pedestrian flow, noise levels, temperature, humidity and pollutant concentrations. These quantities of data are provided to cloud-based services which utilize machine learning processes to produce actionable intelligence whether to activate air purification systems if pollution levels exceed set points, reduce or increase lighting as pedestrian numbers decrease, or manage pedestrian traffic flows at peak hours of congestion. The capability to analyze in real time both environmental and behavioral data, allows such public spaces to go beyond simply being passive objects in the urban environment and become active participants in controlling the city's life (Vishnu et al. 2021).

The important thing is that smart public spaces cannot be limited to only hardware as they are ventilated in a linear way. The interaction design and user interface are also part of this intelligence of smart public space; as are digital kiosk, mobile apps, AR overlays and touchscreen tools which provide a link between data and citizens and make environmental processes invisible to citizens visible and available to them. A possible example of such an interface would be a park that uses digital signage for displaying air quality readings, providing a current pollen count for those with allergies, and/or providing a map of routes that avoid heavy pollution. Such interfaces allow for the development of more informed and engaged citizens that can lead to pro-environmental behavioral changes for the benefit of both the health of individuals and populations (Janani et al., 2021).

The use of smart technology in the open space is an example of many urban initiatives that have utilized smart technologies. Examples of low-cost electric mobility for smart bus stops exist in cities including London and Seoul with real-time arrival data, embedded air-quality monitoring systems, solar-powered lighting, and Wi-Fi availability. Sensor-based plazas exist in Barcelona, where the sensors monitor the level of pollution and noise and adjust the amount of water used to irrigate plants and the lighting accordingly to maximize the sustainable nature of a place. Smart lighting exists in some cities such as Amsterdam and Copenhagen that adjust lighting based on pedestrian traffic and ambient light and turn off lights at night when no pedestrians are present, both providing energy savings and safety benefits. All of these examples illustrate the numerous ways in which smart places can be used to improve or provide services related to environmental monitoring/sensing and/or public health monitoring or mobility and social interaction (Gretzel & Koo, 2021).

In addition to technology, the human-centered design that smart public spaces are built upon is nearly as significant. Smart public spaces can be seen no longer as functionally oriented nor technologically-oriented spaces but as spaces for user-participation, spaces for inclusion and socially contextualized spaces. Therefore they need to accommodate a wide range of users with disabilities; children and elderly people and create a sense of ownership and community commitment by the society. In other words, there is no intrinsic value to incorporating digital tools into the design of public spaces, rather it provides a means to enhance the quality, equity and sustainability of public spaces (Mohapatra & Rath, 2021).

The second aspect of intelligent urban areas that is present in cities is their directional characteristics. Directional characteristics do not occur separately, but are part of an overall smart city system. In order for smart public spaces to connect into the greater city-wide smart place network, they will have network connections to the local government platforms of governance; the emergency response systems; the transportation systems; and climate control systems as nodes of both data and service to all of the above. A good example of this would be a smart plaza which could serve multiple purposes such as being a hub for multimodal transportation, a monitoring station for air quality, a community center or meeting space for social interaction; while also providing data to urban planners at a higher level through central dashboards for guiding future urban planning efforts (Luusua et al., 2023).

Lastly, the concept of smart public spaces will require to consider both time and place. These are not necessarily fixed in one location; they can be fixed (re-designed town square, etc.) but they could also be temporary or moveable (pop-up sensor stations during festivals/pilot projects in under-served communities). In addition to tracking what people do at these spaces, they will learn how to predict the actions of the people who use them, as well as respond to seasonal changes and to other unpredictable events such as those caused by climate shock (COVID-19), etc., (Hassankhani et al., 2021).

Smart public spaces are defined as complex structures which include digital technologies, ecological sensitivity and civic engagement. Smart public spaces represent an evolution in the way we view public space from being static and passive to dynamic, networked and collaborative environments. Smart public spaces can dramatically transform how cities deal with pollution, traffic congestion and the pursuit of sustainable development through creating a new vocabulary for public space through the lens of bytes (digital) and bodies (people).

The key benefits of smart public places include their technological and people centered designs; however, they are providing a significant amount of value by enabling cities to monitor and manage the environment through the use of distributed sensors placed throughout public space that can provide real time environmental information to help cities respond to challenges posed by urban pollution. Therefore, this next section will review how the incorporation of environmental sensing technologies into smart public places enhances the monitoring and management of air quality.

3. ENVIRONMENTAL SENSING AND AIR QUALITY MANAGEMENT

Due to the high rate at which urban areas are growing, along with increasing industrial activity, the result is cities being air pollution hot zones - a silent killer with equally lethal effects - particularly on vulnerable populations, healthcare burdens, and the unsustainable nature of urban environments. Centralized monitoring stations used to measure air quality typically are located far apart from one another and provide little time resolution for adequate spatial coverage. In contrast, smart public spaces may allow the creation of pollution control methods that distribute the capabilities of a real-time environmental sensing system into the very fabric of the city. The smart public space approach will also enable a translation of these fine-scale, real-time, actionable data points (Panori et al., 2021) into decisions regarding pollution.

The new aspect of its innovation is the deployment of Internet of Things (IoT) enabled environment sensors in a variety of public spaces, for example benches, street lights, paths in parks, bus shelters, and kiosks. The small and low-cost sensors continuously measure and report concentrations of air pollutants including particulate matter (PM2.5 and PM10), nitrogen dioxide (NO2), ozone (O3), carbon monoxide (CO), and volatile organic compounds (VOCs). In addition, the sensors can also measure meteorological conditions (temperature, humidity, wind speed, etc.) to provide additional information that would be useful in the development of predictive models (Ushakov et al. 2022).

Real-time data collection and transmission allows urban centers to detect where pollution is most concentrated, understand how time of day, and day of the week affect pollutants, and identify atypical changes that could indicate short-term surges in pollution from specific sources such as rapid increases in smog, or increased emissions due to traffic congestion or increased industrial production. This high degree of spatial and temporal resolution causes urban air quality monitoring to transition from a responsive function to a proactively managed function. For instance, a smart plaza equipped with sensor equipment capable of detecting different types of pollutants will alert municipal services to dispatch mobile air filtration units to the street or alter traffic flow based upon events resulting in increased exposure (Hasan et al., 2022).

Intelligent public spaces are not only monitoring nodes but also intervention nodes. Environmental data coupled with responsive infrastructure provides opportunity for adaptive response to mitigation if coupled with responsive infrastructure. Vertical gardens (moss walls), can be made dynamic by the possibility of water and ventilation them and thereby increase pollutant absorption. Smart fountains or misting systems can be activated during dry weather to stick particulate matter. Even in busy street, it may used as digital message to pedestrian that will help them follow alternative non-polluting paths or postpone outdoor activities (Kolotouchkina et al. 2022).

Citizen engagement is one of the most important aspects for the success of such sensing system. Urban area collected air quality data needs to be displayed in understandable format through the mobile device, urban dashboard and website. For example we could have real-time color-coded air quality indexes (AQI) at public display in urban park or along sidewalk with related health recommendation. Not only will this empower individuals to make informed decision but also enhance environmental literacy and community participation (Aurigi & Odendaal, 2022).

Predictive analytics and early warning systems could be another option when sensor-based monitoring of air quality becomes part of our daily lives. Using machine learning, this system would analyze historical and current data to identify the best time of the day to expect high levels of pollution based on traffic, wind, and temperature. These forecasts can then influence how individuals act (for example, determining whether it is better to walk, ride a bike, etc.), and they can also influence organizational decisions (such as timing street cleaning, changing transit routes, creating low emission zones, etc.).

Transformative examples include the work done through the use of case studies. The array of things project in chicago has installed sensor nodes onto lampposts to collect environmental data including air quality, temperature, and noise, turning Chicago's streets into a data collection platform for urban planners. As part of an effort to adapt the way in which they clean their streets, smart plazas in Barcelona are providing real time data on the environmental conditions such as pollution levels to determine when to irrigate the city's green spaces. The sensor based transit stations in Beijing provide highly detailed data about the amount of pollution occurring in those areas and help to inform pricing and travel incentives for using public transportation during times of heavy pollution (Kaur, 2023)

However, numerous concerns continue to arise about the use of environmental sensors for the purpose of achieving meaningful accuracy, reliability and representativeness, especially when the environment is difficult to measure due to poor weather conditions, or when the sensor is placed in an area with high pollution. Additionally, as we develop our sensing infrastructures, so too will there be greater concerns related to data governance, privacy and surveillance (e.g., by virtue of placing an air quality sensor next to a camera or mobility tracking device). The last of these concerns relates to just distribution, since wealthier communities have access to the benefits of new technologies while poorer communities do not have the same level of oversight or service (Liu et al. 2021). Therefore, the smart public space environmental sensing framework should be built upon a combination of technical robustness, responsiveness to citizens' needs and ethical protections. These include, among others, controls over the resonant frequency of the sensors, the availability of sensor data through free web sites; community-based feedback mechanisms; and effective governance systems that allow for monitoring and correction of inappropriate uses of sensor data.

To summarize, there is a possibility for the current paradigm of centralized and slow pollution management to be replaced by intelligent, environmentally sensitive spaces and the corresponding infrastructure that can move from being data dependent to citizen driven. These spaces will allow not just municipal governments but also our citizens to participate in creating a cleaner city where clean air is an integral part of urban life rather than a privilege. Smart cities may potentially create a new paradigm of public health through both decentralized, distributed environmental monitoring systems (including those built into buildings) and their use of sensor technologies as the basis for decision making processes at all levels.

Although new technologies for environmental sensing allow cities to monitor pollution through time and space; they also require changes in those systems generating most of the pollutants associated with environmental issues. Urban transportation is one of the largest generators of air pollution in cities; therefore, smart public spaces have a major role not only as environmental monitors but as tools to modify mobility to decrease traffic congestion and transportation emissions.

4. MOBILITY, ACCESS, AND CONGESTION REDUCTION

The majority of the congestion and pollution in our world occurs through the ways people travel within urban areas. The issues that occur with urban transportation are interconnected and build upon each other, leading to overcrowding of roads, increasing levels of greenhouse gas emissions and decreasing air quality, and further contributing to the degradation of the pedestrian-friendly environment. Therefore, it is essential for planners of urban spaces to focus on changing the way the urban population travels as one of their most significant responsibilities related to sustainable development. A new form of spatial design, digital systems and behavioral change: smart public spaces provide an opportunity to create a place-based approach that moves toward a new paradigm of data-driven, interactive, and human-scale spatial design that can directly affect the behavior and movement patterns of people by creating new ways of accessing the city, reducing congestion and creating a culture of new behaviors in urban environments (Miskolczi et al. 2021).

Smart public locations are found at the nexus between mobility and the urban population while typical transportation projects typically focus on the road network and vehicle traffic. It is here that frictionless, multi-modal travel connections can be established in order to make using public or non-motorized and shared modes for commuting safer, more convenient, and appealing than relying solely on private motorized transportation; thus facilitating a modal shift which is described as the transition of individuals from their use of polluting, space-consuming vehicles to alternative, sustainable modes of travel such as walking, biking, and transit (Mavlutova et al., 2023).

One of the key ways that smart public spaces use to encourage active travel is through an emphasis on making walking and/or cycling the norm and an enjoyable form of transport. With pedestrian passages, smart plazas, and bike-friendly roads offering digital solutions for pedestrians and cyclists, the infrastructure necessary to support this type of travel is provided; such as real-time route mapping, interactive maps, dynamic lighting, and shade sensors, which reduce the friction experienced when using these forms of transport. For example, smart traffic lights that turn green when the number of people crossing at an intersection reaches a certain level of activity, countdown clocks that show how long it will take for the light to turn green based on the current volume of pedestrians, etc., are just some of the examples of how smart technology can help to improve walking speeds and reduce the time spent waiting at intersections. Smart bike lanes that include sensors provide cyclists with advance warning of potential hazards, such as road debris, potholes, and poor air quality, and also allow cyclists to plan their routes based on real-time data (Ceder, 2021).

Smart public spaces provide last mile connectivity for larger transportation systems. They provide a strategic location as the intersection point of metro lines, bus stops and districts in the city so people can easily switch from one form of transportation to another. Technology in these smart public spaces includes shared bike racks and scooter docking stations for e-bikes and e-scooters, along with charging stations for other forms of electric vehicles. These technologies allow individuals to bridge the distance between where they currently are and where they need to be via modes of transportation that do not require them to utilize personal vehicles or taxi services. Mobile applications and/or digital kiosk's coordination with public transportation systems' scheduling will create a more seamless flow of travel, reduce idleness and redundant traffic (Allam & Sharifi, 2022).

The smart urban area allows for real-time fan and crowd flow tracking as well as real-time tracking of fans and crowd flow that can prevent congestion not just on roads but also in transportation hubs and on pedestrian walkways. The use of AI-based footfall detection, surge detection and information analytics provides urban managers with the ability to locate bottleneck areas and to plan for and respond to emergencies immediately by providing alternative routes, increasing platform access, adjusting signal timing to direct people. This is especially true during high volume times such as rush hour or large public events where controlling the physical space is critical to provide for safe and efficient movement and minimize emissions using the stop-and-go method (Richter et al., 2022)

Smart public spaces enhance mobility in numerous examples around the world. For example, the “my transport” project developed in Singapore uses space in the city, particularly at mass transit locations and transportation-related areas, for developing an integrated user interface so that users can travel within cities by means other than personal vehicle use. Another example of this type of development is the intelligent bike paths in Amsterdam, Netherlands; these bike paths are equipped with a sensor network, display LED signs indicating the flow of traffic and provide cyclists with real-time information about the optimal time to ride. Intelligent bike paths such as those described above help to decrease the amount of time required to complete a bicycle trip and increase safety while riding, thereby making it a realistic option for longer trips. New York City has also implemented curb management systems where underutilized sidewalk space is temporarily converted to pedestrian plazas or micro-transportation centers, decreasing congestion in surrounding roads (Alessandretti et al. 2023).

Besides the physical structure of the smart asset, there is an overall behavioral shelf for framing the user's perception of and way of using urban mobility. Users are prompted by nudging techniques (e.g., earned cycling programs, interactive mobility dashboards, visualizing emission savings on a public platform) to utilize more sustainable ways to travel. This is a type of soft infrastructure which is complementary to the physical intervention and develops a feedback loop in-between the user's urban experience and travel modes.

Smart Public Places: Accessible and Equitable

Inclusive and equitable access is, therefore, a key component for successful smart public places that help reduce traffic congestion and emissions. The lack of any plan for how these technologies will be implemented means they will exacerbate mobility inequities either by catering to people who feel comfortable using technology and/or can afford the technology, or by catering to wealthier neighborhoods. For example, some micro-mobility companies require smartphones and credit cards to use their services. This eliminates the digitally or financially disadvantaged from being able to benefit from smart transportation options (Aydin et al., 2022).

Smart public spaces should be developed as equitable and accessible for all using universal design principles and mobility justice frameworks to succeed. This will require creating physical accessibility in the space(s), low pricing options available in the space(s), multilingual platforms on devices used in the space(s) and analog services offered to those that cannot use digital services in the space(s). The quality of these public spaces must also be designed with and governed through equity audits, community consultations and data practices that are inclusive (Kasraian et al. 2024). "

To summarize, smart public spaces could be an innovation for decreasing urban traffic and air pollution through establishing decentralized, flexible, and citizen-oriented mobility systems rather than massive urban infrastructure projects. Smart public spaces will also make sustainable travel even easier, more fun and better accessible for local residents in addition to taking pressure off of automobiles and working toward a zero emission, and more efficient city. However, it is rare that improvements to mobility infrastructure will result in a change in urban transportation systems. Therefore, a sustainable transition to new forms of mobility requires a shift from the current individualized and urbanized behavior to new behaviors of individuals and communities. The goal of smart public spaces extends beyond physical/infrastructure improvements through digital interfaces, information and participation tools to improve interaction among urban dwellers and their urban mobility systems.

5. BEHAVIORAL INFLUENCE AND COMMUNITY ENGAGEMENT

While technological development has been the key feature for smart public areas as well as what is capable of creating real revolutionary potential in this regard, is that smart public areas do not just affect how we act; they can help create civic participation. While physical and technical infrastructure is a significant part of the battle in terms of urban sustainability, it is behavior: how we travel, consume, and interact with one another in public areas, that represents the crux of an urban sustainability challenge; be it air quality, traffic jams or litter. Another alternative is smart public spaces through which a combination of nudging, interactive feedback mechanisms, participative design processes, and digital tools of public participation could possibly be used to shape those behaviors (Wirsbinna et al., 2023).

Based on behavioral economics, nudging is an approach to guide people's choices without using restriction, but rather through subtle influence. For example, for smart, walkable streets, it could include air-quality readings along the pathway to make the most likely route for walking, gamifying cycling through rewards of points, and the method of presenting way-finding information that would favor pedestrian traffic over the traffic shortcut. The digital counters located in Copenhagen's bicycle lanes display both the number of cyclists per day, as well as the overall amount of CO 2 savings. These digital counters act as a collective edifice of success and a normative cue to action (Tavitiyaman et al., 2021).

The use of interactive technologies in smart public areas helps make invisible environmental information visible for action. Air pollution, traffic/mobility footprint, etc., are being shown to the public using large digital displays placed in public parks, transit centers, and plazas. In addition to providing an educational opportunity for the public, these technologies help encourage the public to consider their surroundings as part of a shared ecological space. For example, the visualizations, which include comparisons of current air quality levels compared to past average levels, or suggest acceptable exposure limits for various pollutants, may influence the types of activities that take place outdoors, and generate greater interest in clean modes of transportation (Gani et al. 2024).

Another method for creating a positive feedback loop between an organization's activity and the success of the overall group effort is by providing a platform to visualize an individuals' sustainability data through mobile applications, interactive kiosks or augmented reality interface to allow users to see how much CO2 they have avoided as a result of their choice to use public transit verses driving. By making the sustainability data relevant to each user, the focus on abstract environmental goals is converted into specific, actionable behaviors that create a culture of accountability and support sustainable behaviors.

Besides affecting behavioral patterns in an uncontrolled manner, smart public spaces are also capable of being the basis for citizen participation and co-creation of smart public spaces. The use of co-design activities (whereby resident views, preferences and feedback are taken into account), is becoming increasingly common when developing smart public areas. As a result of this, the cities of Barcelona and Helsinki have already been testing digital participatory platforms and urban labs which provide citizens with a variety of tools to propose functionalities, test technologies, and report issues in real-time. Besides increasing the applicability and acceptance of smart-city solutions and providing a democratic approach to the implementation of the smart city agenda (thus enabling more inclusive governance) (Bibri & Allam, 2022).

More so than anything else, a community participatory approach for smart public spaces can be extended to the ways that communities create social cohesion and to the ways that these spaces are used as part of place-making. Smart public spaces are more than just places for the circulation of mobility or data; these are also places of congregation, identity and civic life. AR interventions have the ability to honor the culture of a neighborhood by providing digital storytelling screens, civic murals with AR elements, sensor-active installations and other uses. Therefore, the behavioral effects of AR will go beyond mobility and the environments chosen, and include how people engage with each other and with the neighborhoods they live in (Kashef et al. 2021).

The use of behavioral data and interactive technology for public purposes does generate a number of ethical and operational concerns. The line between nudging and manipulating is very fine and can easily be crossed when the nudge is generated by an algorithm that is transparently unrecognizable as such. Furthermore, when designing public participation mechanisms, inclusiveness needs to be taken into account. It would be inappropriate if platforms excluded some groups from participation based on their age, level of literacy, or economic status. As a way of illustrating this point, the utilization of mobile application-based systems to gather citizen input may well further exclude those who lack a smartphone or consistent access to the Internet, thus creating skewed representation in citizen participatory processes and widening the existing social disparities (Torabi et al., 2022).

In addition, smart public spaces must be based on the principles of transparency, accountability and inclusiveness to limit these impending risks. The communication to citizens regarding what data are collected, for which purposes and how citizens can participate in this process in an informed way, is equally important. A participatory interface needs to be multimodal, multilingual and tailored to different levels of digital literacy. Analogous to that, community liaison staff, local associations and analogue forms of participation (for example, through printed questionnaires, community forums etc.) need to accompany the digital tools so that all participants have equal opportunities to contribute (Park et al., 2022).

Smart public spaces can be able to influence how citizens behave in the city and enhance community involvement (civic participation), which means that sustainability will be defined both technically and socially as a result of all processes and individual practices. Using real time data and creating interactive and engaging public spaces enables cities to promote sustainable behavior, generate community ties, and collaborate in designing spaces for residents, in addition to promoting citizen involvement through collaborative decision-making. While the development of digital interaction technologies and behavioral engagement technologies may present possibilities for influencing urban behaviors, they also raise additional governance and ethical issues. Questions are raised with respect to the ownership of data, the right to privacy, and equitable access to smart urban infrastructure when sensors, data platforms, and behavioral feedback systems are integrated into public spaces.

6. GOVERNANCE, EQUITY, AND PRIVACY CONSIDERATIONS

The potential for smart public areas to improve both public health monitoring as well as urban transportation and civic engagement is great. However, there are serious issues related to governance, equity and privacy that must be considered in the deployment of smart public spaces. Smart public spaces, which are based upon digital technologies and sensor systems that create large amounts of data that will be used by decision-makers in data driven ways, have transformed public space from sites of public interaction to spaces of constant data production and algorithmically managed environments. Therefore, it is necessary to develop comprehensive governance models to ensure that the technological innovations created through smart public spaces are aligned with democratic principles, promote social inclusion, and build public trust (Jiang, 2021).

The major challenge to governance in relation to smart public spaces is the issue of data governance and transparency. The huge amounts of data generated by environmental sensors, mobility monitoring systems, interactive displays and digital systems in smart public spaces provide great value for bettering city administration and informing urban policies; however, the collection, storage and utilization of these data streams present significant risks concerning the ways in which these data are being used. Specifically, the lack of regulatory guidelines provides an opportunity for urban data to be utilized for commercial means, to be used for intrusive surveillance, or to be managed without proper public oversight. Therefore, cities require systems of data governance that are transparent, clearly define data ownership, set clear guidelines as to the use of data, and protect personally identifiable data from unauthorized access (Xiao & Xie, 2021).

Related to the question of data governance is the urban surveillance & privacy protection question. Smart public space technologies — including cameras, location-based services & crowd-monitoring systems — have the capability to monitor movement & behaviors of Individuals in public spaces. The capabilities of these technologies can support safety, mobility management & environmental monitoring, but they also blur the lines between providing public service provision & surveillance. These types of technologies could be a major contributor to creating a culture of constant monitoring which would infringe on civil liberties & reduce citizen's trust in smart city initiatives. Strong legal safeguards, transparent communication about data collection practices & mechanisms for citizens to understand and affect how data collected from their activities are used (Nastjuk et al., 2022) will provide the necessary protections to ensure citizen privacy protection.

Another important area for governance in smart public spaces is equity. The investment in new technology in urban infrastructure is frequently unevenly distributed; therefore, smart technologies have been typically deployed in affluent districts, as innovation hubs or in high profile urban areas. These unequal deployment patterns have a potential to reinforce existing social and spatial inequalities by increasing disadvantageous community members' exposure to environmental pollution, reducing their mobility, and limiting their access to digital infrastructure. To be part of an inclusive urban development, smart public spaces need to be developed through equity-based planning models that focus on investing in less advantaged neighborhood and equitably distribute digital resources throughout the city (Faraji et al. 2021).

Smart public spaces need to be accessible to all because of the role inclusive design plays for accessibility. Many of the services that are embedded into the physical space of a public area require use of a smartphone app, an Internet connection or some level of digital skills that can be barriers to many people. Low-income residents, older adults, migrant communities, and people with disabilities may face significant barriers when trying to interact with digitally enabled public areas. Therefore, there is a need to integrate Universal design principles, multi-language interfaces, and multiple ways of accessing information (e.g., alternative non-digital methods like physical signs, or community-based participation) to provide equal opportunities of interaction (Vadiati, 2022).

Smart public spaces will require significant investment and a number of government decisions related to partnering with the private sector. There are numerous smart city initiatives being implemented today by municipalities working in partnership with private technology companies. In exchange for providing the required technology, sensors, and data platforms, the municipality receives accelerated technology deployment and reduced costs associated with implementing the necessary technologies. However, this partnership model raises several issues including accountability for the use of municipal funds and data; commercializing public space through advertising or sponsored content; and who has control of the urban data ecosystem generated from sensors, cameras, and other technologies. The issue is exacerbated when the contract between the parties does not establish sufficient controls or oversight to ensure that the private partner is acting in the best interests of the public. Cities should develop agreements that protect the public's interest while ensuring that all agreements include requirements for using open standards and that all urban data is available to the public (He et al. 2022).

Public participation is an important element of participative governance for making public space smart and just. The use of smart technologies in public spaces has direct impacts on daily urban experience; therefore, it is reasonable that residents and community organizations have access to the decision-making process that determines how, where, and when smart technologies are employed in public spaces, or evaluated. Public participation in the planning of smart public space can be facilitated by the creation of planning mechanisms such as: public consultation; online platforms for public comment and input; and community-based citizen data collection. These participative mechanisms can promote transparency of both the process and outcome of urban innovation and create a sense of collective responsibility among citizens toward urban development and improvements. Furthermore, the inclusion of citizens within the process of governance provides a means to identify local unmet needs and potential negative effects associated with the implementation of smart public space technology (Willis & Nold, 2022).

In addition to providing a framework for the responsible use of technology in the management of smart public spaces, effective governance must also be socially inclusive and ethically responsible. Effective governance of smart public spaces should include the integration of transparent data management, protection of individual privacy rights, equitable funding, and participatory decision making processes. Embedding this framework within existing urban policy and planning practices will allow cities to create smart public spaces that are not only technologically enhanced environments but also democratically managed, inclusive, and sustainable public commons where the needs of all citizens are addressed.

Therefore, it is necessary for ethics-based design principles to be supported by institutional mechanisms and coordinated policies to address concerns related to governance, privacy, and equity in the design of smart public spaces. Thus, integrating smart public spaces into larger urban planning strategies is essential to ensure that these initiatives contribute to long term sustainability and inclusive urban development.

7. POLICY INTEGRATION AND STRATEGIC URBAN PLANNING

The development of smart public spaces has to be developed as part of a unified urban policy, plan and governance system for it to provide its maximum benefit to address the issues of pollution and congestion in urban areas. Any amount of innovation that is provided through disconnected individual interventions will never be sufficient on their own, absent of alignment to and contribution to larger scale agendas, including; climate resilience, sustainable transportation, digital equality and the creation of liveable cities. This chapter assesses how to successfully integrate the use of smart public spaces into city wide planning agendas, and offers policy recommendations to create a defined pathway for smart public spaces as part of an urban redevelopment strategy (Marasinghe et al., 2024).

Public places that are smart should be integrated into urban planning for cities with a master plan for a smart city, transportation reform policy, public health plan, and environmental action plan.

The integration will be done by considering how these public places are going to be connected with each other and to the overall urban plan to provide a clear understanding of how they fit within the long-term objectives of the city (e.g., carbon reduction, increased public transit ridership, etc.). Therefore, instead of being just individual experiments, smart public places can serve as cross-cutting facilitators in cities that have a comprehensive plan for all aspects of city-wide operations. For example, if there is a climate action plan for a city that includes targets for decreasing particulate matter from vehicles through smart air monitors placed at public plaza locations along high-traffic routes, then these air monitors can assist in providing both the diagnosis and quantification of vehicle-related pollution in real time, while also creating a mechanism for community feedback to support reduction efforts (Son et al. 2023).

One of the most critical components of a strategic plan for a city will be the implementation of data platforms and digital twins of an urban area which will allow for simulation, analysis and improvement of the numerous complexities associated with urban systems. In conjunction with data platforms, smart public spaces will be able to generate large amounts of real time data regarding how many people are moving through those spaces, the state of their environment and the experiences of users of the space. This type of real time data can then be utilized for adaptive planning purposes allowing the city to make incremental adjustments to the investment of resources they commit to infrastructure, crowd management practices and emergency response efforts. Therefore, smart public spaces not only utilize current policy frameworks, but also augment and improve upon them utilizing empirical knowledge from the employees who experience first hand the impact of those policies.

Cities need to develop legal frameworks with sufficient resources to establish smart spaces as part of their municipal policy through the use of a number of mechanisms (regulatory and financing) for smart place development, scaling up and sustainability. This includes reviewing and changing zoning regulations, city-wide plans, and building codes to require or encourage developers to build smart technology into their developments. Green purchasing agreements could give priority to vendors who provide interoperable, sustainable and open source smart infrastructure. Cities may also attract funding through public-private partnership (PPP) arrangements, and through various types of grant funding for innovation, such as funding from climate finance (green bonds, etc.), or international development organizations focused on urban resilience and clean transportation (Sanchez et al. 2025).

Besides that, there are examples of policy integration, with institutions at the local level, like the transportation department, environment department, planning department, IT department, and public works department working together for their integrated institutional planning. Smart public spaces frequently become orphaned by jurisdictions due to the separation of duties or are implemented in a haphazard manner through lack of coordination. Innovative types of governance (e.g., urban innovation office or cross-sector task forces) may provide direction for cooperative efforts and allow for the consideration of smart public spaces as an extended form of common pool resources rather than a one-off special project. Like many other cities (Vienna, Toronto), interdepartmental teams responsible for coordinating and overseeing the development and management of smart districts, integrate technological uses of public spaces into overall strategic planning (Sanchez et al., 2023).

Another important dimension of high-priority for Smart Public Spaces is the ability to replicate and scale up successful pilot programs and technologies in smart public places. Neighborhood pilots are often the first to use new technology but, once they have been piloted, it is the responsibility of local government to make the toolkit, performance metric and evaluation model available so the same pilot can be scaled throughout the entire system. Policy tools should support modules, interoperable data systems and dynamic platforms for the implementation of smart public spaces across various socio-spatial contexts (from busy downtown areas to residential parks and informal settlements).

Community engagement in the form of participatory approaches to planning, deployment and evaluation of smart public places, along with the creation of policy frameworks that will enforce these processes are important too. The input of citizens and civil society, including local business owners, is essential for prioritizing the use of public money for this initiative; identifying unintended consequences; and justifying the expenditures (Abusaada & Elshater, 2022). Moreover, in order to foster trust and transparency, such as in terms of regular updates of metrics on air quality, traffic congestion, and/or user satisfaction, etc., such data should be made available and accessible.

Governments may assist cities in both their regional and national roles as policy makers, standards developers, and capacity builders; in doing so they can foster the transformation of the understanding of smart public spaces toward the sustainable development path. National urban policies could include digital inclusion, ethical use of data and the evaluation of environmental impacts of innovations on the public space. There is also potential for knowledge transfer among cities through cross-city learning networks to provide opportunities for developing best practices and reducing the number of experiments needed to develop best practices for the public space.

In conclusion, policy integration has to be the key feature that makes smart public places transform into scalable, inclusive and effective components of large-scale urban development. In order for the strategic planning of these spaces, institutional coordination, regulatory innovations and participatory governance can lead to smart public space being part of the DNA of future cities; and as such, contributing to improved air quality, better mobility options and enhanced civic engagement. Policy frameworks provide the institutional base for smart public places, but real world examples are instructive on how conceptual frameworks are applied in practice. International case studies offer an opportunity to examine the opportunities, barriers and governance strategies for the deployment of smart public spaces in different urban settings.

8. CASE STUDIES: LESSONS FROM GLOBAL CITIES

To illustrate the development of smart public spaces; the advantages, the challenges and to provide a global comparison of the variety of ways smart public spaces have been implemented and developed throughout the world. The comparative analyses of these case studies are based on examples from Europe, Asia, North America, and Latin America. They are also reflective of the diversity of contexts within which smart public spaces have been created in an effort to make progress toward pollution control, traffic congestion relief, and civic innovation. These comparisons reflect differences in terms of citizen involvement, technological deployment, systemic governance mechanisms, and policy integration.

Barcelona, Spain: Responsive Plazas and Environmental Intelligence

Barcelona is an early example of smart urbanism and the superblock project has transformed the use of the public space from that of a transportation corridor to one of reduced commuter traffic and emissions. Public squares have been designed in the car-light zones which incorporate sensor technologies for monitoring noise levels, air quality, and pedestrian activity. This information is transmitted to the urban central platform of the city where it provides the citizens of Barcelona with real time data on pollutants in the air around them and allows the citizens to adjust various aspects of the infrastructure, such as irrigation and lighting systems, based on environmental conditions. The changes in the public space of Barcelona due to the Superblock project have produced measurable impacts in terms of air quality and attitudes toward mobility by increasing walking and cycling activities while decreasing the number of trips made by automobile. Technology and participation in the planning process have been at the heart of the success of the Barcelona experience and demonstrates how adaptable public spaces can be used to support climate actions and enhance livability (Opbroek et al. 2024).

Singapore: Smart Parks and Mobility Hubs

Smart nation initiative in Singapore is being utilized as a model for implementing intelligent public space initiatives in Singapore. The headline park in the city is Jurong Lake Garden. It features environmental monitoring devices (humidity, temperature and air quality monitoring), and interactive digital kiosks with Wi-Fi, and AR trails to encourage environmentally literate participation through education. The business district contains mobility hubs with digital displays of live transportation schedules, and shared e-scooters and a single ticket system; the mobility hubs serve to reduce reliance on personal vehicles and to solve the problem of first/last mile travel. International coordination among a wide variety of entities (both governmental and private sector) and strong regulatory frameworks that ensure data privacy and equality in terms of access to these services are key elements of the Singaporean model. The Singapore model demonstrates how national level visions and intersectoral coordination can create a robust web of operational smart public places that can be used to achieve both environmental and social goals (Carpentiere et al. 2024).

New York City, USA: Smart Streetscapes and Public Wi-Fi Infrastructure

Smart streets initiative that was run by the department of transportation, in addition to the LinkNYC program, were both initiatives of New York City; therefore, they have provided many of the smart urban environment interventions to cities. Interactive digital kiosks, air quality monitors, and pedestrian flow monitors have all been incorporated into skyscrapers such as Times Square and Union Square. All of this information is used to adjust traffic signals for better pedestrian flow and to inform emergency responders of high-traffic areas at peak times. In an effort to create a culture of community engagement, research and planning, NYC has placed emphasis on open data policies, allowing community organizations and researchers to obtain environmental and mobility data to be able to promote advocacy and planning. However, the city has also faced criticism over the inequitable nature of digital access, particularly in regards to disadvantaged neighborhoods that typically do not receive equal access to smart technology. As such, the need for equitable distribution, and ongoing public accountability in large-scale implementation, is evident (Wang, 2025).

Seoul, South Korea: Air-Purifying Bus Stops and Crowd Analytics

Smart shelters are part of the smart bus stop system. It incorporates the latest technology into the public transportation environment to reduce pollution. Smart bus stops use air purification systems, temperature control systems and UV disinfecting systems to keep passengers safe and comfortable while the pollutants are at their peak levels or there is an outbreak. Sensors track passenger flow and are combined with transit apps to monitor station usage to help minimize the overcrowding on stations. The additional data from crowd analytics provides information for the cities congestion points such as Gangnam and Myeongdong areas to aid in reducing congestion and improving the air quality in these areas. This example demonstrates how the modular smart spaces can be very effective at managing congestion and improving air quality in public spaces (Lee et al., 2020).

Bogotá, Colombia: Participatory Smart Plazas and Tactical Urbanism

The city of Bogot, Colombia has been the site for an interesting example of how low-technology driven innovation can be used to develop smart public space. Under the umbrella of the Laboratorios Urbanos program across the entire city, citizens collaborate to design and shape their own community spaces with the assistance of a mixed-modal mobile sensing kit; participatory mapping; and a temporary installation approach. Using fewer technological tools than similar projects in more affluent cities, these tactical smart place concepts have a goal to repurpose streets back into pedestrian-friendly spaces by planting trees and also to experiment with new forms of mobility nudge technology such as digital street signage and interactive polling. This may suggest a model for developing accessible, inclusive, open, and responsive to all members of society smart public spaces that rely on social innovation, local ownership, and flexible deployment models (Alvandipour, 2024).

Comparative Insights and Emerging Patterns

Numerous similarities and lessons can be extracted in these cases:

- Multifunctioning: Smartest public places should be both data nodes, mobility ports and social commons.
- Context counts: The technology application has to vary according to local environmental, social and economic context.

- materialized in governance: Good institutional coordination and open data leads to better impact and trust.
- Equity is a must: Unless inclusion is smartly incorporated, the smart spaces will merely increase prior slacks.

The transitory pilots and flexible plans can be just as efficient as permanent installations, particularly in situations that are resource-limited.

To sum up, while there are international examples of how smart public spaces can be developed and implemented differently, the way they function, their complexity, and the route to developing a smart public place differs in no way. Each example represents an innovative approach for using the public space to create cleaner, more efficient and livable urban environments through digital-environmental innovation. The experiences of various cities who have experimented with implementing smart public spaces provide insight into both the transformative nature and practical challenges related to such implementations. In light of this experience, the next chapter will explore new technologies, as well as governance models that may influence the continued evolution of smart public spaces.

9. FUTURE OUTLOOK: TOWARDS HUMAN-CENTERED SMART PUBLIC PLACES

Next generation smart public spaces will not be about simply installing digital infrastructure but instead, they will intentionally incorporate environmental sustainability, human-centered design and governance together with technological advances to meet the challenges of today's cities.

The use of new technologies for advanced urban data systems is becoming an increasingly popular trend in how cities plan and manage their urban environment. Technologies such as digital twins, AI and edge computing are being integrated into a number of urban data systems. A city's digital twin is a virtual representation of the city that can be used by urban planners and policymakers to test how various urban design interventions will perform in a simulated model before implementing them physically in the city. Using the data collected from sensors at smart public spaces in real time, a digital twin can also help predict the movement of pedestrians, where pollution will be dispersed throughout the city, and how well an infrastructure system will operate. These types of systems allow for more adaptable and evidence based decision making related to urban design and planning; thus reducing the need for reactive policy decisions and allowing cities to take proactive steps to address both environmental and mobility issues (Ahmadzai, 2025).

Another area where smart public places are becoming increasingly important is through the use of adaptive and responsive urban infrastructure. As we move toward future smart public places, they could include systems that can be adjusted based on what is happening at a particular time. In this regard, for example, some smart lighting networks can be adjusted based on the number of pedestrians using them, so that more light is provided when more people are around and less when fewer people are there. Additionally, systems that provide shade or reduce the effects of urban heat islands by providing cool air can also be used in conjunction with these smart lighting systems in dense urban environments. Smart public places can also have environmental monitoring systems that will automatically respond to changes in the environment by triggering actions such as adjusting traffic patterns or sending public health advisories to residents when pollution levels become too high. The ability of these systems to continually respond to changes in both social and environmental conditions reflects the capacity of smart public places to operate as living urban infrastructures (Moumen et al., 2024).

Technological advancements will contribute to an expansion of the experiential element of public space, as well. In this way, augmented reality, ambient computing, and location-based digital service technologies will provide new opportunities for citizen/urban environment interactions. Interactive environmental dashboards, educational installations, and immersive storytelling platforms in public spaces can educate citizens on environmental conditions, urban history, or sustainability initiatives. These technologies have the ability to increase environmental awareness and civic participation through the creation of easily accessible and understandable complex urban data for all citizens.

Although there is a potential for these technologies to enhance public spaces, ethical management of the public space through inclusive planning practices will be just as important to their long-term success. As digital technologies continue to be used and integrated into public spaces, issues related to surveillance, discrimination by algorithms, and ownership of collected information are expected to increase. For the public to have confidence in the use of digital infrastructure in public spaces, it will be necessary to protect citizens' right to privacy, provide transparency with regards to how digital systems are operated, and ensure that such digital systems are governed in a manner that is transparent and accountable (Maqousi et al., 2025). As cities continue to integrate digital technologies into their physical public spaces they will need to create regulatory frameworks that can provide guidance for algorithmic accountability, the protection of personal data, and the responsible deployment of technology in public spaces (Maqousi et al., 2025).

In addition to addressing the social equity of smart cities, there also exists a need for smart cities to address the spatial equity as well. The future development of cities must therefore take into account equitable access to digital infrastructure, especially in areas that have had an disproportionate share of the burden of pollution and other environmental impacts as well as a lack of investments in public spaces. Designing the use of technology in a manner inclusive of older adults, people with disabilities and the digitally excluded will be critical to ensuring that new technologies benefit all members of society.

Future smart public spaces will continue to evolve into testing grounds for cities to implement new technologies, new ways of citizen participation in governance and innovative sustainable structures. This is done through temporary pilots, tactical urbanism, and collaboration platforms that enable the municipality to test their concepts and receive feedback from citizens and other local stakeholders. These experiments provide a mechanism for municipal governments to learn and adapt continuously, allowing them to improve upon their smart public spaces strategy as they gain experience in the field (Park et al. 2024).

Urban planners, environmental scientists, technologists, designers, policymakers, and local residents will need to collaborate in order for the future development of intelligent public spaces to flourish. The problems that cities face regarding pollution, congestion and climate resiliency are so complex that technology is insufficient on its own. Therefore, these problems need to be solved by using an integrated approach that combines scientific knowledge about the environment with technological innovation, social inclusion and participatory governance (Bosco et al. 2024).

Smart public places are intended for long term success as a result of the application of advanced digital technology in conjunction with its ability to improve or enhance the social, environmental and civic aspects of urban living. Cities should be able to develop inclusive and sustainable urban environments which foster both democratic urban development and sustainability by developing the smart public places through the application of human centered design and through equitable access to those public spaces and through transparency and accountability in governing them.

10. CONCLUSION

Smart public spaces is an innovative strategy to help cities address major urban problems like air pollution and traffic congestion. The current chapter discusses how digital innovation can create smart public spaces with a more proactive role in city management than previously conceived. It is suggested that public spaces will become adaptive systems through integrating environmental monitoring, transportation management and citizen participation, which are all supported by sensor technology, interactive tools and data management infrastructure in the public space.

In this way, public spaces may be seen as intelligent nodes that facilitate a more sustainable and responsive urban system.

This section addresses how smart public spaces are the result of an interaction among three primary areas: social engagement, environmental intelligence, and mobility optimization. These areas interact as follows: First, environmental sensing technology and other environmental data collection systems can be used in a city's infrastructure to collect and analyze data regarding environmental factors such as air quality and other environmental data which will assist cities in developing proactive strategies for managing environmental factors. Second, when a city integrates its digital mobility systems and multimodal transportation systems into its public space environment, it has the opportunity to decrease traffic congestion while creating more sustainable mobility options through encouragement of walking, cycling and public transportation use. Finally, when cities integrate interactive technologies and/or citizen participation into their public spaces (as well as other forms of public engagement), they have the potential to increase citizens' involvement in civic activities, encourage the adoption of environmentally sustainable behaviors on a daily basis, provide citizens with greater access to environmental information, and allow them to become more involved in decision-making processes at the urban level.

The chapter clearly indicates that smart public places can be measured for success; however, it is important to recognize that there is far more than just technological advancement to smart public spaces. The creation and operation of these areas is impacted by various governmental structures, socio economic environments, ethics and many other factors. Data management (governance), privacy rights, fair and equal access to digital technology, and inclusive design are all significant elements to determine if smart public places are contributing to inclusive and sustainable urban development. If care is not taken to address the social and ethical dimensions of smart public spaces, they could potentially reinforce the same inequities already present, or introduce new forms of digital exclusion and/or surveillance.

The integration of smart public spaces in an overall urban development plan is a key to achieving maximum potential from these types of areas. Successful implementation will require multi-stakeholder involvement and coordination among urban planners, environmental managers, transportation policy makers and digital government officials. Also, it would be important to encourage collaboration with community-based organizations, private companies providing smart technologies and other relevant stakeholders. Only by coordinating efforts across all stakeholders can we create smart public spaces as part of an overall urban framework (as opposed to just using new technology).

The future of smart public spaces in cities depends on how well cities are able to integrate technology into their planning and development while also creating inclusive and human centered spaces for all residents; The emerging technologies

(AI, digital twins, adaptive infrastructure) have great potential to make cities responsive and sustainable yet they can only be successful if they support democratic participation, social inclusion, and environmental sustainability.

Smart public spaces are much more than just technological upgrades to an old urban landscape; they are also part of a greater paradigm shift in Urban planning and design of responsive (to users needs) data-informed and citizen-centered environments, where digital innovation is married to the social and ecological dimensions of urban life. The concept of rethinking public spaces as adaptable platforms for environmental management, mobility coordination and civic engagement can help cities work towards creating more sustainable, inclusive and livable urban futures.

REFERENCES

Abdelkarim, S. B., Ahmad, A. M., Ferwati, S., & Naji, K. (2023). Urban facility management improving livability through smart public spaces in smart sustainable cities. *Sustainability (Basel)*, *15*(23), 16257. DOI: 10.3390/su152316257

Abid, N., Sareen, S., & Haque, M. (2024, December). Smart cities and public space: the role of smart technologies in enhancing public spaces. In *8th IET Smart Cities Symposium (SCS 2024)* (Vol. 2024, pp. 244-249). IET.

Abusaada, H., & Elshater, A. (2022). Notes on developing research review in urban planning and urban design based on PRISMA statement. *Social Sciences (Basel, Switzerland)*, *11*(9), 391. DOI: 10.3390/socsci11090391

Ahmadzai, P. (2025). Divergent and convergent thinking processes in smart cities: A systematic review of human-centered design practices. *Cities (London, England)*, *159*, 105744. DOI: 10.1016/j.cities.2025.105744

Aldehim, G., Shahzad, T., Khan, M. A., Ghadi, Y. Y., Jiang, W., Mazhar, T., & Hamam, H. (2025). Balancing sustainability and security: A review of 5G and IoT in smart cities. *Digital Communications and Networks*, *11*(6), 1722–1737. DOI: 10.1016/j.dcan.2025.06.007

Alessandretti, L., Natera Orozco, L. G., Saberi, M., Szell, M., & Battiston, F. (2023). Multimodal urban mobility and multilayer transport networks. *Environment and Planning. B, Urban Analytics and City Science*, *50*(8), 2038–2070. DOI: 10.1177/23998083221108190

Allam, Z., & Sharifi, A. (2022). Research structure and trends of smart urban mobility. *Smart Cities*, *5*(2), 539–561. DOI: 10.3390/smartcities5020029

Almarri, K., & Boussabaine, H. (2025). Critical success factors for public–private partnerships in smart city infrastructure projects. *Construction Innovation*, *25*(2), 224–247. DOI: 10.1108/CI-04-2022-0072

Alvandipour, N. (2024). Tactical urbanism as an innovative urban governance tool: Lessons from the COVID-19 pandemic. In *Resilience vs Pandemics: Innovations in Public Places and Buildings* (pp. 69–84). Springer Nature Singapore. DOI: 10.1007/978-981-99-8672-9_5

Aurigi, A., & Odendaal, N. (2022). From "smart in the box" to "smart in the city": Rethinking the socially sustainable smart city in context. In *Sustainable Smart City Transitions* (pp. 53-68). Routledge.

Aydin, N., Seker, S., & Özkan, B. (2022). Planning location of mobility hub for sustainable urban mobility. *Sustainable Cities and Society*, *81*, 103843. DOI: 10.1016/j.scs.2022.103843

Beckers, D., & Mora, L. (2025). Overcoming the smart city governance challenge: An innovation management perspective. *Journal of Urban Technology*, *32*(2), 85–106. DOI: 10.1080/10630732.2025.2461983

Bibri, S. E., & Allam, Z. (2022). The Metaverse as a virtual form of data-driven smart cities: The ethics of the hyper-connectivity, datafication, algorithmization, and platformization of urban society. *Computational Urban Science*, *2*(1), 22. DOI: 10.1007/s43762-022-00050-1 PMID: 35915731

Bosco, G., Riccardi, V., Sciarrone, A., D'Amore, R., & Visvizi, A. (2024). *AI-driven innovation in smart city governance: achieving human-centric and sustainable outcomes. Transforming Government: People*. Process and Policy.

Carpentiere, C. D., Messeni Petruzzelli, A., & Ardito, L. (2024). Success factors in smart mobility: A new framework and implications for the EuroMed context from case study of New York, Copenhagen, Singapore, Bari and Barcelona. *EuroMed Journal of Business.*

Ceder, A. (2021). Urban mobility and public transport: Future perspectives and review. *International Journal of Urban Sciences*, *25*(4), 455–479. DOI: 10.1080/12265934.2020.1799846

Esposito, G., Terlizzi, A., Desdemoustier, J., Pichault, F., & Crutzen, N. (2025). Smart city development as public entrepreneurship: An in-depth case study of mayoral action based on actor-network theory. *International Journal of Public Administration*, *48*(3), 180–194. DOI: 10.1080/01900692.2024.2329672

Faraji, S. J., Jafari Nozar, M., & Arash, M. (2021). The analysis of smart governance scenarios of the urban culture in multicultural cities based on two concepts of "cultural intelligence" and "smart governance". *GeoJournal*, *86*(1), 357–377. DOI: 10.1007/s10708-019-10074-6

Gani, M. O., Rahman, M. S., Bag, S., & Mia, M. P. (2024). Examining behavioural intention of using smart health care technology among females: Dynamics of social influence and perceived usefulness. *Benchmarking*, *31*(2), 330–352. DOI: 10.1108/BIJ-09-2022-0585

Gretzel, U., & Koo, C. (2021). Smart tourism cities: A duality of place where technology supports the convergence of touristic and residential experiences. *Asia Pacific Journal of Tourism Research*, *26*(4), 352–364. DOI: 10.1080/10941665.2021.1897636

Hasan, M. K., Khan, M. A., Issa, G. F., Atta, A., Akram, A. S., & Hassan, M. (2022, February). Smart waste management and classification system for smart cities using deep learning. In *2022 International Conference on Business Analytics for Technology and Security (ICBATS)* (pp. 1-7). IEEE. DOI: 10.1109/ICBATS54253.2022.9759087

Hassankhani, M., Alidadi, M., Sharifi, A., & Azhdari, A. (2021). Smart city and crisis management: Lessons for the COVID-19 pandemic. *International Journal of Environmental Research and Public Health, 18*(15), 7736. DOI: 10.3390/ijerph18157736 PMID: 34360029

He, W., Li, W., & Deng, P. (2022). Legal governance in the smart cities of China: Functions, problems, and solutions. *Sustainability (Basel), 14*(15), 9738. DOI: 10.3390/su14159738

Itair, M., Shahrour, I., & Hijazi, I. (2023). The use of the smart technology for creating an inclusive urban public space. *Smart Cities, 6*(5), 2484–2498. DOI: 10.3390/smartcities6050112

Janani, R. P., Renuka, K., Aruna, A., & Lakshmi Narayanan, K. (2021). IoT in smart cities: A contemporary survey. *Global Transitions Proceedings, 2*(2), 187–193. DOI: 10.1016/j.gltp.2021.08.069

Jiang, H. (2021). Smart urban governance in the 'smart'era: Why is it urgently needed? *Cities (London, England), 111*, 103004. DOI: 10.1016/j.cities.2020.103004

Kashef, M., Visvizi, A., & Troisi, O. (2021). Smart city as a smart service system: Human-computer interaction and smart city surveillance systems. *Computers in Human Behavior, 124*, 106923. DOI: 10.1016/j.chb.2021.106923

Kasraian, D., Murdock, H. E., Imani, A. F., Yu, Y., de Nazelle, A., Stead, D., & Kahlmeier, S. (2024). Health in mobility planning: An assessment of how health is considered in Sustainable Urban Mobility Plans. *Journal of Transport & Health, 39*, 101919. DOI: 10.1016/j.jth.2024.101919

Kaur, J. (2023, November). IoT empowered smart cities for green healthcare: a sustainable pathway to transforming healthcare systems. In *2023 International Conference on Computing, Communication, and Intelligent Systems (ICCCIS)* (pp. 64-70). IEEE. DOI: 10.1109/ICCCIS60361.2023.10425484

Kolotouchkina, O., Barroso, C. L., & Sánchez, J. L. M. (2022). Smart cities, the digital divide, and people with disabilities. *Cities (London, England), 123*, 103613. DOI: 10.1016/j.cities.2022.103613

Lee, J., Kwon, G., Cheon, W., & Lim, W. (2020). A Study on the Revitalization of Forest Management by Improving the Implementation Rate of FOREST Projects. *International Journal of Human & Disaster*, *5*(2), 1–9. DOI: 10.22471/disaster.2020.5.2.01

Liu, T., Mostafa, S., Mohamed, S., & Nguyen, T. S. (2021). Emerging themes of public-private partnership application in developing smart city projects: A conceptual framework. *Built Environment Project and Asset Management*, *11*(1), 138–156. DOI: 10.1108/BEPAM-12-2019-0142

Luusua, A., Ylipulli, J., Foth, M., & Aurigi, A. (2023). Urban AI: Understanding the emerging role of artificial intelligence in smart cities. *AI & Society*, *38*(3), 1039–1044. DOI: 10.1007/s00146-022-01537-5 PMID: 36196366

Maqousi, A., Basu, K., Almomani, A., & Alkasassbeh, M. (2025). Human-Centered Design for Smart Cities: Integrating Social Aspects in Planning and Policy. In *Revolutionizing Urban Development and Governance With Emerging Technologies* (pp. 463-490). IGI Global Scientific Publishing.

Marasinghe, R., Yigitcanlar, T., Mayere, S., Washington, T., & Limb, M. (2024). Computer vision applications for urban planning: A systematic review of opportunities and constraints. *Sustainable Cities and Society*, *100*, 105047. DOI: 10.1016/j.scs.2023.105047

Mavlutova, I., Atstaja, D., Grasis, J., Kuzmina, J., Uvarova, I., & Roga, D. (2023). Urban transportation concept and sustainable urban mobility in smart cities: A review. *Energies*, *16*(8), 3585. DOI: 10.3390/en16083585

Miskolczi, M., Földes, D., Munkacsy, A., & Jaszberenyi, M. (2021). Urban mobility scenarios until the 2030s. *Sustainable Cities and Society*, *72*, 103029. DOI: 10.1016/j.scs.2021.103029

Mohapatra, H., & Rath, A. K. (2021). An IoT based efficient multi-objective real-time smart parking system. *International Journal of Sensor Networks, 37*(4), 219-232.

Moumen, N., Radoine, H., Nahiduzzaman, K. M., & Jarar Oulidi, H. (2024). Contextualizing the smart city in Africa: Balancing human-centered and techno-centric perspectives for smart urban performance. *Smart Cities*, *7*(2), 712–734. DOI: 10.3390/smartcities7020029

Nastjuk, I., Trang, S., & Papageorgiou, E. I. (2022). Smart cities and smart governance models for future cities: Current research and future directions. *Electronic Markets*, *32*(4), 1917–1924. DOI: 10.1007/s12525-022-00609-0

Nsabiyumva, S., Ngobi, D., Nyandwi, V., & Mukasa, S. (2026). Towards inclusive smart cities: Promoting digital literacy for socio-economic equity and sustainable urban futures. In *Future Smart Cities* (pp. 341–370). Elsevier. DOI: 10.1016/B978-0-443-33667-6.00009-4

Opbroek, J., Barboza, E. P., Nieuwenhuijsen, M., Dadvand, P., & Mueller, N. (2024). Urban green spaces and behavioral and cognitive development in children: A health impact assessment of the Barcelona "Eixos Verds" Plan (Green Axis Plan). *Environmental Research, 244*, 117909. DOI: 10.1016/j.envres.2023.117909 PMID: 38103780

Panori, A., Kakderi, C., Komninos, N., Fellnhofer, K., Reid, A., & Mora, L. (2021). Smart systems of innovation for smart places: Challenges in deploying digital platforms for co-creation and data-intelligence. *Land Use Policy, 111*, 104631. DOI: 10.1016/j.landusepol.2020.104631

Park, I., Kim, D., Moon, J., Kim, S., Kang, Y., & Bae, S. (2022). Searching for new technology acceptance model under social context: Analyzing the determinants of acceptance of intelligent information technology in digital transformation and implications for the requisites of digital sustainability. *Sustainability (Basel), 14*(1), 579. DOI: 10.3390/su14010579

Park, J. S., Cho, E., & Lee, S. Y. (2024, November). Towards Inclusive Smart Cities: Key Evaluation Criteria for Technology and Human-Centered Development. In *2024 International Conference on Information Science and Communications Technologies (ICISCT)* (pp. 212-219). IEEE. DOI: 10.1109/ICISCT64202.2024.10956807

Prabowo, O. M., Mulyana, E., Nugraha, I. G. B. B., & Supangkat, S. H. (2023). Cognitive city platform as digital public infrastructure for developing a smart, sustainable and resilient city in Indonesia. *IEEE Access : Practical Innovations, Open Solutions, 11*, 120157–120178. DOI: 10.1109/ACCESS.2023.3327305

Richter, M. A., Hagenmaier, M., Bandte, O., Parida, V., & Wincent, J. (2022). Smart cities, urban mobility and autonomous vehicles: How different cities needs different sustainable investment strategies. *Technological Forecasting and Social Change, 184*, 121857. DOI: 10.1016/j.techfore.2022.121857

Sanchez, T. W., Brenman, M., & Ye, X. (2025). The ethical concerns of artificial intelligence in urban planning. *Journal of the American Planning Association, 91*(2), 294–307. DOI: 10.1080/01944363.2024.2355305

Sanchez, T. W., Shumway, H., Gordner, T., & Lim, T. (2023). The prospects of artificial intelligence in urban planning. *International Journal of Urban Sciences, 27*(2), 179-194.

Son, T. H., Weedon, Z., Yigitcanlar, T., Sanchez, T., Corchado, J. M., & Mehmood, R. (2023). Algorithmic urban planning for smart and sustainable development: Systematic review of the literature. *Sustainable Cities and Society*, *94*, 104562. DOI: 10.1016/j.scs.2023.104562

Tavitiyaman, P., Qu, H., Tsang, W. S. L., & Lam, C. W. R. (2021). The influence of smart tourism applications on perceived destination image and behavioral intention: The moderating role of information search behavior. *Journal of Hospitality and Tourism Management*, *46*, 476–487. DOI: 10.1016/j.jhtm.2021.02.003

Torabi, Z. A., Shalbafian, A. A., Allam, Z., Ghaderi, Z., Murgante, B., & Khavarian-Garmsir, A. R. (2022). Enhancing memorable experiences, tourist satisfaction, and revisit intention through smart tourism technologies. *Sustainability (Basel)*, *14*(5), 2721. DOI: 10.3390/su14052721

Ushakov, D., Dudukalov, E., Kozlova, E., & Shatila, K. (2022). The Internet of Things impact on smart public transportation. *Transportation Research Procedia*, *63*, 2392–2400. DOI: 10.1016/j.trpro.2022.06.275

Vadiati, N. (2022). Alternatives to smart cities: A call for consideration of grassroots digital urbanism. *Digital Geography and Society*, *3*, 100030. DOI: 10.1016/j.diggeo.2022.100030

Varshini, B., Yogesh, H. R., Pasha, S. D., Suhail, M., Madhumitha, V., & Sasi, A. (2021). IoT-Enabled smart doors for monitoring body temperature and face mask detection. *Global Transitions Proceedings*, *2*(2), 246–254. DOI: 10.1016/j.gltp.2021.08.071

Velasquez Mendez, A., Lozoya Santos, J., & Jimenez Vargas, J. F. (2025). Strategic socio-technical innovation in urban living labs: A framework for smart city evolution. *Smart Cities*, *8*(4), 131. DOI: 10.3390/smartcities8040131

Viale, R. (2025). Behavioral city. *Frontiers in Built Environment*, *10*, 1501853. DOI: 10.3389/fbuil.2024.1501853

Vishnu, S., Ramson, S. J., Senith, S., Anagnostopoulos, T., Abu-Mahfouz, A. M., Fan, X., Srinivasan, S., & Kirubaraj, A. A. (2021). IoT-enabled solid waste management in smart cities. *Smart Cities*, *4*(3), 1004–1017. DOI: 10.3390/smartcities4030053

Wang, R. Y. (2025). From phone booths to Wi-Fi kiosks: The spatial inequality of public connectivity in New York City. *Technological Forecasting and Social Change*, *219*, 124245. DOI: 10.1016/j.techfore.2025.124245

Willis, K. S., & Nold, C. (2022). Sense and the city: An Emotion Data Framework for smart city governance. *Journal of Urban Management*, *11*(2), 142–152. DOI: 10.1016/j.jum.2022.05.009

Wirsbinna, A., Grega, L., & Juenger, M. (2023). Assessing factors influencing citizens' behavioral intention towards smart city living. *Smart Cities*, *6*(6), 3093–3111. DOI: 10.3390/smartcities6060138

Xiao, X., & Xie, C. (2021). Rational planning and urban governance based on smart cities and big data. *Environmental Technology & Innovation*, *21*, 101381. DOI: 10.1016/j.eti.2021.101381

KEY TERMS AND DEFINITIONS

Adaptive Infrastructure: Smart built environments that are adaptive to real-time information or user requests- lighting that adapts to the density of people; ventilation that automatically responds to the level of air quality.

Behavioral Nudging: A behavioral economics-based strategy, through which people are engaged by providing them with hints and feedbacking mechanism to manipulate choice of people and their behavior without compromising option.

Civic Technology: Platforms, such as digital tools which are developed to encourage people in terms of participation, increase in the transparency as well as effectiveness of civic participation and governance.

Data Governance: The structure of policies and practices defining the collection, use, sharing, and protection of data particularly in terms of the given ones such as public trust, transparency, and privacy.

Environmental Sensing: The responsive urban management uses digital sensors to monitor parameters including air quality, noise levels, temperature, humidity of a certain environment.

Internet of Things (IoT): A system of connected devices and sensors installed in physical infrastructure that detect, communicate and process data to be used to automate and make decisions.

Participatory Planning: A participatory way of shaping cities and future policymaking to include the community and stakeholders to guarantee more open and responsive decisions.

Smart City Strategy: An integrated urban development approach that leverages digital technologies to improve city services, resource management, and quality of life while addressing social and environmental challenges.

Smart Locales: Instruments installed in digitally enhanced environments to trade in a changed urban environment, mobility, and social issues through sensors, data platforms, and other interactive technologies that adjust in real time.

Sustainable Mobility: Eco-friendly transportation systems and patterns that have the least impact on the environment, frequently promoting mass transportation, walking, bicycles and low polluting vehicles.

Traffic Congestion: A state of busy transport systems caused by too many cars in the city that causes delays, more emissions, and less efficiency in the urban environments.

Urban Equity: Just and equitable access to urban resources, infrastructure, and opportunities to all individuals quite on socio-demographic lines with respect to income, race, and geography.

Urban Pollution: The concentration of toxic substances (including particulate matter, nitrogen oxides, and carbon emissions) in the air, soil or water of the densely populated territories, the generation of which is mostly associated with transportation, industry and construction.

Compilation of References

Abdelkarim, S. B., Ahmad, A. M., Ferwati, S., & Naji, K. (2023). Urban facility management improving livability through smart public spaces in smart sustainable cities. *Sustainability (Basel), 15*(23), 16257. DOI: 10.3390/su152316257

Abid, N., Sareen, S., & Haque, M. (2024, December). Smart cities and public space: the role of smart technologies in enhancing public spaces. In *8th IET Smart Cities Symposium (SCS 2024)* (Vol. 2024, pp. 244-249). IET.

Abiodun, T. P., Nwulu, N. I., & Olukanmi, P. O. (2025). Application of blockchain technology in carbon trading market: A systematic review. *IEEE Access : Practical Innovations, Open Solutions, 13*, 5446–5470. DOI: 10.1109/ACCESS.2024.3523672

Abusaada, H., & Elshater, A. (2022). Notes on developing research review in urban planning and urban design based on PRISMA statement. *Social Sciences (Basel, Switzerland), 11*(9), 391. DOI: 10.3390/socsci11090391

Ahmadian, A., Ponnambalam, K., Almansoori, A., & Elkamel, A. (2023). Optimal Management of a Virtual Power Plant Consisting of Renewable Energy Resources and Electric Vehicles Using Mixed-Integer Linear Programming and Deep Learning. *Energies, 16*(2), 1000. DOI: 10.3390/en16021000

Ahmadzai, P. (2025). Divergent and convergent thinking processes in smart cities: A systematic review of human-centered design practices. *Cities (London, England), 159*, 105744. DOI: 10.1016/j.cities.2025.105744

Akpan, E. E., Akinlade, O., Alabi, O. O., David, O. A., Afe, O. F., & Ajagbe, S. A. (2026). Optimizing Traffic Signal Control Using Machine Learning and Environmental Data. *Artificial Intelligence and Applications (Commerce, Calif.), 4*(1), 48–56. DOI: 10.47852/bonviewAIA52024199

Alam, A., & Jaffery, Z. A. (2020). Indian traffic sign detection and recognition. *International Journal of Intelligent Transportation Systems Research, 18*(1), 98–112. DOI: 10.1007/s13177-019-00178-1

Alam, T. (2024). Data privacy and security in autonomous connected vehicles in smart city environment. *Big Data and Cognitive Computing*, *8*(9), 95. DOI: 10.3390/bdcc8090095

Aldehim, G., Shahzad, T., Khan, M. A., Ghadi, Y. Y., Jiang, W., Mazhar, T., & Hamam, H. (2025). Balancing sustainability and security: A review of 5G and IoT in smart cities. *Digital Communications and Networks*, *11*(6), 1722–1737. DOI: 10.1016/j.dcan.2025.06.007

Alessandretti, L., Natera Orozco, L. G., Saberi, M., Szell, M., & Battiston, F. (2023). Multimodal urban mobility and multilayer transport networks. *Environment and Planning. B, Urban Analytics and City Science*, *50*(8), 2038–2070. DOI: 10.1177/23998083221108190

Ali, D. M. T. E., Motuzienė, V., & Džiugaitė-Tumėnienė, R. (2024). AI-Driven Innovations in Building Energy Management Systems: A Review of Potential Applications and Energy Savings. *Energies*, *17*(17), 4277. Advance online publication. DOI: 10.3390/en17174277

Ali, G. G. M. N., Sadat, M. N., Miah, M. S., Sharief, S. A., & Wang, Y. (2024). A Comprehensive Study and Analysis of the Third Generation Partnership Project's 5G New Radio for Vehicle-to-Everything Communication. *Future Internet*, *16*(1), 21. DOI: 10.3390/fi16010021

Allam, Z., & Sharifi, A. (2022). Research structure and trends of smart urban mobility. *Smart Cities*, *5*(2), 539–561. DOI: 10.3390/smartcities5020029

Almarri, K., & Boussabaine, H. (2025). Critical success factors for public–private partnerships in smart city infrastructure projects. *Construction Innovation*, *25*(2), 224–247. DOI: 10.1108/CI-04-2022-0072

Alqadhi, S., & Mallick, J. (2026). Integrating road network topology, remote sensing, and explainable machine learning to assess urban ecological resilience. *Environmental Technology & Innovation*, *41*, 104805. Advance online publication. DOI: 10.1016/j.eti.2026.104805

Al-Qudah, R., Tawil, A. A., Almuhajiri, M., Almazaydeh, L., & Suen, C. Y. (2026). Nash-regularized heterogeneous graph transformer networks for strategic task offloading in 6G edge computing. *International Journal of Data and Network Science*, *10*(1), 415–432. DOI: 10.5267/j.ijdns.2025.9.009

Alshammari, N. F., Alshahr, S., & Barakat, S. (2026). How energy management strategy shapes optimal microgrid design: A comparative analysis for EV charging stations. *Applied Energy*, *407*, 127352. Advance online publication. DOI: 10.1016/j.apenergy.2026.127352

Alshamrani, S. S., Jha, N., & Prashar, D. (2021). B5G ultrareliable low latency networks for efficient secure autonomous and smart Internet of vehicles. *Mathematical Problems in Engineering*, *2021*(1), 3697733. DOI: 10.1155/2021/3697733

Alsharbi, B. M. (2026). A Psycholinguistic Analysis of the Use of Artificial Intelligence in Foreign Language Teaching. *Journal of Multiscale Modelling*. DOI: 10.1142/S1756973726400068

Alsudani, M. (2023). The wireless communication between vehicles: exploring the potential of V2V and V2X communication for improved efficiency, safety, and sustainability: wireless communication between (V2V) and (V2I, V2X). Journal of Millimeterwave Communication. *Optimization and Modelling*, *3*(1), 9–13.

Alvandipour, N. (2024). Tactical urbanism as an innovative urban governance tool: Lessons from the COVID-19 pandemic. In *Resilience vs Pandemics: Innovations in Public Places and Buildings* (pp. 69–84). Springer Nature Singapore. DOI: 10.1007/978-981-99-8672-9_5

Ambak, K., Harun, N. E., Rosli, N., Daniel, B. D., Prasetijo, J., & Ezree, M. (2006). Driver intention to use electric cars using technology acceptance model. Age, 3(9.7), 1-4.

Annabi, M., Zeroual, A., & Messai, N. (2024). Towards zero trust security in connected vehicles: A comprehensive survey. *Computers & Security*, *145*, 104018. DOI: 10.1016/j.cose.2024.104018

Archsmith, J., Muehlegger, E., & Rapson, D. S. (2022). Future paths of electric vehicle adoption in the United States: Predictable determinants, obstacles, and opportunities. *Environmental and Energy Policy and the Economy*, *3*(1), 71–110. DOI: 10.1086/717219

Aruna, T. M., Kumar, P., Srinidhi, N. N., Divyaraj, G. N., Asha, K., Thirumalraj, A., & Naresh, E. (2023). Effective utilisation of Geospatial Data for peer-to-peer communication among autonomous vehicles using Optimized Machine learning algorithm.

Asim, M., Usman, M., Abbasi, M. S., Ahmad, S., Mujtaba, M. A., Soudagar, M. E. M., & Mohamed, A. (2022). Estimating the long-term effects of national and international sustainable transport policies on energy consumption and emissions of road transport sector of Pakistan. *Sustainability (Basel)*, *14*(9), 5732. DOI: 10.3390/su14095732

Athanasopoulou, L., Bikas, H., Papacharalampopoulos, A., Stavropoulos, P., & Chryssolouris, G. (2023). An industry 4.0 approach to electric vehicles. *International Journal of Computer Integrated Manufacturing*, *36*(2), 334–348. DOI: 10.1080/0951192X.2022.2081363

Aurigi, A., & Odendaal, N. (2022). From "smart in the box" to "smart in the city": Rethinking the socially sustainable smart city in context. In *Sustainable Smart City Transitions* (pp. 53-68). Routledge.

Aydın Yıldız, T. (2025). Sustainability Education in L2 Writing: AI-Based Multimodal Awareness and Engagement. *Sustainability (Basel)*, *17*(21), 9376. Advance online publication. DOI: 10.3390/su17219376

Aydin, N., Seker, S., & Özkan, B. (2022). Planning location of mobility hub for sustainable urban mobility. *Sustainable Cities and Society*, *81*, 103843. DOI: 10.1016/j.scs.2022.103843

Azizi, L., & Kouddane, N. (2024). The green city as a driver of sustainable development. *Journal of Umm Al-Qura University for Engineering and Architecture*, *15*(4), 384–397. DOI: 10.1007/s43995-024-00077-x

Babu, N. V., & Damle, M. (2022, November). Performance evaluation of Autonomous and Connected Electric Vehicles (ACEVs) towards buying intention in India: Forward trend in energy efficiency. In *2022 International Interdisciplinary Humanitarian Conference for Sustainability (IIHC)* (pp. 74-79). IEEE. DOI: 10.1109/IIHC55949.2022.10060349

Bagheri, H., Noor-A-Rahim, M., Liu, Z., Lee, H., Pesch, D., Moessner, K., & Xiao, P. (2021). 5G NR-V2X: Toward connected and cooperative autonomous driving. *IEEE Communications Standards Magazine*, *5*(1), 48–54. DOI: 10.1109/MCOMSTD.001.2000069

Barbarossa, C., Beckmann, S. C., De Pelsmacker, P., Moons, I., & Gwozdz, W. (2015). A self-identity based model of electric car adoption intention: A cross-cultural comparative study. *Journal of Environmental Psychology*, *42*, 149–160. DOI: 10.1016/j.jenvp.2015.04.001

Barrot, J. S., & Bui, H. P. (2026). Generative Artificial Intelligence for Automated Qualitative Feedback: A Cross-Comparison of Prompting Strategies. *RELC Journal*. Advance online publication. DOI: 10.1177/00336882251412561

Baryla, A., Karczmarczyk, A., Bus, A., & Witkowska-Dobrev, J. (2019). Surface temperature analysis of conventional roof and different use forms of the green roof. *Scientific Review Engineering and Environmental Sciences*, *28*(4), 632–640. DOI: 10.22630/PNIKS.2019.28.4.57

Bashirpour Bonab, A., Bellini, F., & Rudko, I. (2023). Theoretical and analytical assessment of smart green cities. *Journal of Cleaner Production*, *410*, 137315. Advance online publication. DOI: 10.1016/j.jclepro.2023.137315

Bawn, M., Francis, N., Alvey, E., Hassall, C., Pires-daSilva, A., Barra, P., Hough, D., Campbell, H., Hardy, M., & Canet-Perez, J. (2026). Perspectives from a workshop: Intelligent assessment in the age of artificial intelligence. *Advances in Physiology Education*, *50*(1), 73–82. DOI: 10.1152/advan.00246.2024 PMID: 41236868

Beckers, D., & Mora, L. (2025). Overcoming the smart city governance challenge: An innovation management perspective. *Journal of Urban Technology*, *32*(2), 85–106. DOI: 10.1080/10630732.2025.2461983

Begum, A. A., Abinaya, S. S., Chitrakala, G., Raghavi, M., & Savivarsha, S. (2022). A Study on Consumers' Intention and Buying Behaviour towards the Purchase of Electric Vehicles with Special Reference to Coimbatore City. Journal of Sales, Service and Marketing Research, 132-148.

Bell, G. D. (1963). Processes in the formation of adolescents' aspirations. *Social Forces*, *42*(2), 179–186. DOI: 10.2307/2575690

Bernard, T., & Seyoum Taffesse, A. (2014). Aspirations: An approach to measurement with validation using Ethiopian data. *Journal of African Economies*, *23*(2), 189–224. DOI: 10.1093/jae/ejt030

Bhandawat, A., & Jayaswall, K. (2022). Biological relevance of sound in plants. *Environmental and Experimental Botany*, *200*, 104919. DOI: 10.1016/j.envexpbot.2022.104919

Bhargava, B., Malhotra, S., Chandel, A., Rakwal, A., Kashwap, R. R., & Kumar, S. (2020). Mitigation of indoor air pollutants using Areca palm potted plants in real-life settings. *Environmental Science and Pollution Research International*, *28*(7), 8898–8906. DOI: 10.1007/s11356-020-11177-1 PMID: 33074430

Bibri, S. E., & Allam, Z. (2022). The Metaverse as a virtual form of data-driven smart cities: The ethics of the hyper-connectivity, datafication, algorithmization, and platformization of urban society. *Computational Urban Science*, *2*(1), 22. DOI: 10.1007/s43762-022-00050-1 PMID: 35915731

Bibri, S. E., Krogstie, J., & Kärrholm, M. (2020). Compact city planning and development: Emerging practices and strategies for achieving the goals of sustainability. *Developments in the Built Environment*, *4*, 100021. Advance online publication. DOI: 10.1016/j.dibe.2020.100021

Bosco, G., Riccardi, V., Sciarrone, A., D'Amore, R., & Visvizi, A. (2024). *AI-driven innovation in smart city governance: achieving human-centric and sustainable outcomes. Transforming Government: People*. Process and Policy.

Brătucu, G., Trifan, A., Dovleac, L., Chi u, I. B., Todor, R. D., & Brătucu, R. (2019). Acquisition of electric vehicles—A step towards green consumption. Empirical research among Romanian students. *Sustainability (Basel)*, *11*(23), 6639. DOI: 10.3390/su11236639

Bressane, A., Loureiro, A. I. S., & Negri, R. G. (2024). Environmental Racism in the Accessibility of Urban Green Space: A Case Study of a Metropolitan Area in an Emerging Economy. *Urban Science (Basel, Switzerland)*, *8*(4), 1–12. DOI: 10.3390/urbansci8040224

Brinkmann, D., & Bhatiasevi, V. (2023). Purchase intention for electric vehicles among young adults in Thailand. *Vision (Basel)*, *27*(1), 110–118. DOI: 10.1177/09722629211001981

Buhmann, K. M., & Criado, J. R. (2023). Consumers' preferences for electric vehicles: The role of status and reputation. *Transportation Research Part D, Transport and Environment*, *114*, 103530. DOI: 10.1016/j.trd.2022.103530

Carey, J. (2023). The other benefit of electric vehicles. *Proceedings of the National Academy of Sciences of the United States of America*, *120*(3), e2220923120. DOI: 10.1073/pnas.2220923120

Carley, S., Krause, R. M., Lane, B. W., & Graham, J. D. (2013). Intent to purchase a plug-in electric vehicle: A survey of early impressions in large US cities. *Transportation Research Part D, Transport and Environment*, *18*, 39–45. DOI: 10.1016/j.trd.2012.09.007

Carpentiere, C. D., Messeni Petruzzelli, A., & Ardito, L. (2024). Success factors in smart mobility: A new framework and implications for the EuroMed context from case study of New York, Copenhagen, Singapore, Bari and Barcelona. *EuroMed Journal of Business*.

Cavalieri, S. (2021). Semantic interoperability between IEC 61850 and oneM2M for IoT-enabled smart grids. *Sensors (Basel)*, *21*(7), 2571. Advance online publication. DOI: 10.3390/s21072571 PMID: 33917602

Ceder, A. (2021). Urban mobility and public transport: Future perspectives and review. *International Journal of Urban Sciences*, *25*(4), 455–479. DOI: 10.1080/12265934.2020.1799846

Chaudhary, I. J., & Rathore, D. (2018). Suspended particulate matter deposition and its impact on urban trees. *Atmospheric Pollution Research*, *9*(6), 1072–1082. DOI: 10.1016/j.apr.2018.04.006

Chen, R., Fan, R., Wang, D., & Yao, Q. (2023). Effects of multiple incentives on electric vehicle charging infrastructure deployment in China: An evolutionary analysis in a complex network. *Energy*, *264*, 125747. DOI: 10.1016/j.energy.2022.125747

Chéron, E., & Zins, M. (1997). Electric vehicle purchasing intentions: The concern over battery charge duration. *Transportation Research Part A, Policy and Practice*, *31*(3), 235–243. DOI: 10.1016/S0965-8564(96)00018-3

Cheshmehzangi, A., Butters, C., Xie, L., & Dawodu, A. (2021). Green infrastructures for urban sustainability: Issues, implications, and solutions for underdeveloped areas. *Urban Forestry & Urban Greening*, *59*, 127028. Advance online publication. DOI: 10.1016/j.ufug.2021.127028

Choobineh, M., Arabnya, A., Sohrabi, B., Khodaei, A., & Paaso, A. (2023). Blockchain technology in energy systems: A state-of-the-art review. *IET Blockchain*, *3*(1), 35–59. DOI: 10.1049/blc2.12020

Chu, J., Zhang, C., Yan, M., Zhang, H., & Ge, T. (2023). TRD-YOLO: A real-time, high-performance small traffic sign detection algorithm. *Sensors (Basel)*, *23*(8), 3871. DOI: 10.3390/s23083871 PMID: 37112213

Cihan Kayaçetin, N., Aslanoğlu, R., Piccardo, C., Afacan, Y., Masera, G., Li, Q., Biraghi, C. A., Pittau, F., Saelens, D., Soebarto, V., Zuo, J., Chang, R., Vrebos, H., Van Acker, K., Sebastian, R., Dikken, J., Ivan, L., Alaerts, L., Aral, D., & van Hoof, J. (2026). Ten questions concerning circularity in the built environment. *Building and Environment*, *292*, 114291. Advance online publication. DOI: 10.1016/j.buildenv.2026.114291

Cioara, T., Pop, C., Zanc, R., Anghel, I., Antal, M., & Salomie, I. (2020). Smart grid management using blockchain: Future scenarios and challenges. In *Proceedings of the RoEduNet IEEE International Conference* (2020-Decem). DOI: 10.1109/RoEduNet51892.2020.9324874

Coll-Perales, B., Lucas-Estañ, M. C., Shimizu, T., Gozalvez, J., Higuchi, T., Avedisov, S., Altintas, O., & Sepulcre, M. (2022). End-to-end V2X latency modeling and analysis in 5G networks. *IEEE Transactions on Vehicular Technology*. Advance online publication.

Cui, H., Mahfoodh, O. H. A., Dong, H., & Ulanbek, M. (2026). An assessment framework for human-AI collaborative competence in second language writing: Evidence from the Chinese EFL context. *System*, *137*, 103937. Advance online publication. DOI: 10.1016/j.system.2025.103937

Dawood, T. H., Hammad, M. J., & Hammood, M. R. (2022). Towards a New Model of Consumer Purchasing Intention of Smart Products During Crises Times; Case of Covid-19 Pandemic Outbreak: an Applied Study on Female Employees of the Faculty of Economic and Business Administration Sciences. *International Journal of Professional Business Review*, *7*(4), 25. DOI: 10.26668/businessreview/2022.v7i4.e741

de Sena Abrahão, R., Moriguchi, S. N., & Andrade, D. F. (2016). The intention of adoption of mobile payment: An analysis in the light of the Unified Theory of Acceptance and Use of Technology (UTAUT). RAI Revista de administracao e Inovacao, 13(3), 221-230.

Debrah, C., Kissi, E., Oduro-ofori, E., & Edwards, D. J. (2020). Barriers to green cities development in developing countries: evidence from Ghana development. DOI: 10.1108/SASBE-06-2020-0089

Dioha, M. O., Lukuyu, J., Virgüez, E., & Caldeira, K. (2022). Guiding the deployment of electric vehicles in the developing world. *Environmental Research Letters*, *17*(7), 071001. DOI: 10.1088/1748-9326/ac765b

Dorado, M. C., Milan, G. R., & González, A. E. (2022). Evaluation of Industrial Noise Reduction Achieved with a Green Barrier: Case Study. In *IntechOpen eBooks*. DOI: 10.5772/intechopen.108835

Dzobo, O., Malila, B., & Sithole, L. (2021). Proposed framework for blockchain technology in a decentralised energy network. *Protection and Control of Modern Power Systems*, *6*(3), 1–11. DOI: 10.1186/s41601-021-00209-8

Eguchi, M., Takizawa, K., Saeki, M., Kurata, F., Suzuki, S., Matsuyama, Y., & Sawaki, Y. (2025). Human- versus artificial intelligence-delivered roleplay tasks for assessing interactional competence: An applied conversation analytic study. *TESOL Quarterly*, *59*(S1), S183–S219. DOI: 10.1002/tesq.70028

Elkhodr, M. (2024). Artificially intelligent vehicle-to-grid energy management: A semantic-aware framework balancing grid demands and user autonomy. *Computers*, *13*(10), 249. Advance online publication. DOI: 10.3390/computers13100249

Enoma, N. (2022). A Comprehensive Review of Alternative Fuels for Automobiles: Benefits, Challenges and Future Direction. *Journal of Science and Technology Research*, *4*(4), 238–247.

Esposito, G., Terlizzi, A., Desdemoustier, J., Pichault, F., & Crutzen, N. (2025). Smart city development as public entrepreneurship: An in-depth case study of mayoral action based on actor-network theory. *International Journal of Public Administration*, *48*(3), 180–194. DOI: 10.1080/01900692.2024.2329672

Etukudoh, E. A., Adefemi, A., Ilojianya, V. I., Umoh, A. A., Ibekwe, K. I., & Zamathula, Q. S. N. (2024). A Review of sustainable transportation solutions: Innovations, challenges, and future directions. *World Journal of Advanced Research and Reviews*, *21*(1), 1440–1452. DOI: 10.30574/wjarr.2024.21.1.0173

Falai, A., Giuliacci, T. A., Misul, D., Paolieri, G., & Anselma, P. G. (2022). Modeling and on-road testing of an electric two-wheeler toward range prediction and BMS integration. *Energies*, *15*(7), 2431. DOI: 10.3390/en15072431

Faraji, S. J., Jafari Nozar, M., & Arash, M. (2021). The analysis of smart governance scenarios of the urban culture in multicultural cities based on two concepts of “cultural intelligence” and “smart governance”. *GeoJournal*, *86*(1), 357–377. DOI: 10.1007/s10708-019-10074-6

Gámez Díaz, R., Yu, Q., Ding, Y., Laamarti, F., & El Saddik, A. (2020). Digital twin coaching for physical activities: A survey. *Sensors (Basel)*, *20*(20), 1–21. DOI: 10.3390/s20205936 PMID: 33096595

Gani, M. O., Rahman, M. S., Bag, S., & Mia, M. P. (2024). Examining behavioural intention of using smart health care technology among females: Dynamics of social influence and perceived usefulness. *Benchmarking*, *31*(2), 330–352. DOI: 10.1108/BIJ-09-2022-0585

Gaoaketse, L., Ligaraba, N., & Chuchu, T. (2023). Factors influencing purchase intention of motor vehicles during the COVID-19 pandemic: An empirical study in South Africa. International Journal of Research in Business and Social Science, 12(3), 41-54.

Gao, T., Xing, K., Liu, Z., Chen, T., Yang, Z., & Li, Y. (2022). Traffic Sign Detection Algorithm based on Pyramid Multi-scale Fusion. *Journal of Traffic and Transportation Engineering*, *22*, 210–224.

Gaspar, R. M., Prasetyo, Y. T., Mariñas, K. A., Persada, S. F., & Nadlifatin, R. (2023). Exploring Consumers' Intention to Use Bikes and E-Scooters during the COVID-19 Pandemic in the Philippines: An Extended Theory of Planned Behavior Approach with a Consideration of Pro-Environmental Identity. *Sustainability (Basel)*, *15*(6), 5193. DOI: 10.3390/su15065193

Ghasemi-Marzbali, A. (2022). Fast-charging station for electric vehicles, challenges and issues: A comprehensive review. *Journal of Energy Storage*, *49*, 104136. DOI: 10.1016/j.est.2022.104136

Goh, H. H., Zong, L., Zhang, D., Liu, H., Dai, W., Lim, C. S., Kurniawan, T. A., Teo, K. T. K., & Goh, K. C. (2022). Mid-and long-term strategy based on electric vehicle charging unpredictability and ownership estimation. *International Journal of Electrical Power & Energy Systems*, *142*, 108240. DOI: 10.1016/j.ijepes.2022.108240

Gretzel, U., & Koo, C. (2021). Smart tourism cities: A duality of place where technology supports the convergence of touristic and residential experiences. *Asia Pacific Journal of Tourism Research*, *26*(4), 352–364. DOI: 10.1080/10941665.2021.1897636

Guo, J., Marsh, H. W., Morin, A. J., Parker, P. D., & Kaur, G. (2015). Directionality of the associations of high school expectancy-value, aspirations, and attainment: A longitudinal study. *American Educational Research Journal*, *52*(2), 371–402. DOI: 10.3102/0002831214565786

Guo, Y., Wan, Z., & Cheng, X. (2022). When blockchain meets smart grids: A comprehensive survey. *High-Confidence Computing*, *2*(2), 100059. Advance online publication. DOI: 10.1016/j.hcc.2022.100059

Gupta, P., Wang, R., Ard, T., Han, J., Karbowski, D., Vahidi, A., & Jia, Y. (2023, October). An x-in-the-loop (xil) testing framework for validation of connected and autonomous vehicles. In *2023 IEEE International Automated Vehicle Validation Conference (IAVVC)* (pp. 1-6). IEEE. DOI: 10.1109/IAVVC57316.2023.10328040

Gürses, A., Reddy, G., Masrur, S., Özdemir, Ö., Güvenç, İ., Sichitiu, M. L., Şahin, A., Alkhateeb, A., Mushi, M., & Dutta, R. (2025). Digital twins and testbeds for supporting AI research with autonomous vehicle networks. *IEEE Communications Magazine*, *63*(4), 56–62. DOI: 10.1109/MCOM.001.2400222

Habich-Sobiegalla, S., Kostka, G., & Anzinger, N. (2018). Electric vehicle purchase intentions of Chinese, Russian and Brazilian citizens: An international comparative study. *Journal of Cleaner Production*, *205*, 188–200. DOI: 10.1016/j.jclepro.2018.08.318

Hadjichambis, A. C., Paraskeva-Hadjichambi, D., Sinakou, E., Adamou, A., & Georgiou, Y. (2022). Green Cities for Environmental Citizenship: A Systematic Literature Review of Empirical Research from 31 Green Cities of the World. *Sustainability (Basel)*, *14*(23), 16223. Advance online publication. DOI: 10.3390/su142316223

Han, L., Wang, S., Zhao, D., & Li, J. (2017). The intention to adopt electric vehicles: Driven by functional and non-functional values. *Transportation Research Part A, Policy and Practice*, *103*, 185–197. DOI: 10.1016/j.tra.2017.05.033

Hansen, R., & Pauleit, S. (2014). From multifunctionality to multiple ecosystem services? A conceptual framework for multifunctionality in green infrastructure planning for Urban Areas. *Ambio*, *43*(4), 516–529. DOI: 10.1007/s13280-014-0510-2 PMID: 24740622

Han, Y., Lee, J., Haiping, G., Kim, K., Wanxi, P., Bhardwaj, N., Oh, J., & Brown, R. J. (2021). Plant-based remediation of air pollution: A review. *Journal of Environmental Management*, *301*, 113860. DOI: 10.1016/j.jenvman.2021.113860 PMID: 34626947

Hasan, M. K., Khan, M. A., Issa, G. F., Atta, A., Akram, A. S., & Hassan, M. (2022, February). Smart waste management and classification system for smart cities using deep learning. In *2022 International Conference on Business Analytics for Technology and Security (ICBATS)* (pp. 1-7). IEEE. DOI: 10.1109/ICBATS54253.2022.9759087

Hasan, M., Mohan, S., Shimizu, T., & Lu, H. (2020). Securing vehicle-to-everything (V2X) communication platforms. *IEEE Transactions on Intelligent Vehicles*, *5*(4), 693–713. DOI: 10.1109/TIV.2020.2987430

Hasan, S. (2021). Assessment of electric vehicle repurchase intention: A survey-based study on the Norwegian EV market. *Transportation Research Interdisciplinary Perspectives*, *11*, 100439. DOI: 10.1016/j.trip.2021.100439

Hassankhani, M., Alidadi, M., Sharifi, A., & Azhdari, A. (2021). Smart city and crisis management: Lessons for the COVID-19 pandemic. *International Journal of Environmental Research and Public Health, 18*(15), 7736. DOI: 10.3390/ijerph18157736 PMID: 34360029

Hernik, J., Sagan, A., Jarecki, W., & Grinberga-Zalite, G. (2025). Digital transformation in business process management: The role of employee engagement. *Human Technology, 21*(1), 203–221. DOI: 10.14254/1795-6889.2025.21-1.10

He, W., Li, W., & Deng, P. (2022). Legal governance in the smart cities of China: Functions, problems, and solutions. *Sustainability (Basel), 14*(15), 9738. DOI: 10.3390/su14159738

Hewitt, C. N., Ashworth, K., & MacKenzie, A. R. (2020). Using green infrastructure to improve urban air quality (GI4AQ). *Ambio, 49*(1), 62–73. DOI: 10.1007/s13280-019-01164-3 PMID: 30879268

Hiep, D. V., Tran, N. H., Tuan, N. A., Hung, T. M., Duc, N. V., & Tung, H. (2023). Assessment of Electric Two-Wheelers Development in Establishing a National E-Mobility Roadmap to Promote Sustainable Transport in Vietnam. *Sustainability (Basel), 15*(9), 7411. DOI: 10.3390/su15097411

Hoang, T. T., Pham, T. H., & Vu, T. M. H. (2022). Examining customer purchase decision towards battery electric vehicles in Vietnam market: A combination of self-interested and pro-environmental approach. *Cogent Business & Management, 9*(1), 2141671. DOI: 10.1080/23311975.2022.2141671

Honari, K., Rouhani, S., Falak, N. E., Liu, Y., Li, Y., Liang, H., Dick, S., & Miller, J. (2023). Smart contract design in distributed energy systems: A systematic review. *Energies, 16*(12), 1–28. DOI: 10.3390/en16124797

Hossain, M. S., Kumar, L., Islam, M. M., & Selvaraj, J. (2022). A comprehensive review on the integration of electric vehicles for sustainable development. *Journal of Advanced Transportation, 2022*, 1–26. DOI: 10.1155/2022/3868388

Hosseinnezhad, V., Hayes, B., O'Regan, B., & Siano, P. (2021). Practical insights to design a blockchain-based energy trading platform. *IEEE Access : Practical Innovations, Open Solutions, 9*, 154827–154844. DOI: 10.1109/ACCESS.2021.3127890

Hou, Z., & Min, S. (2026). Dialogue-based computer-assisted language learning systems for second language speaking development: A three-level meta-analysis. *ReCALL, 38*(1), 40–56. DOI: 10.1017/S0958344025100268

Huang, X., Lin, Y., Lim, M. K., Tseng, M. L., & Zhou, F. (2021). The influence of knowledge management on adoption intention of electric vehicles: A perspective on technological knowledge. *Industrial Management & Data Systems*, *121*(7), 1481–1495. DOI: 10.1108/IMDS-07-2020-0411

Ibrahim, M., Rjabtšikov, V., & Gilbert, R. (2023). Overview of digital twin platforms for EV applications. *Sensors (Basel)*, *23*(3), 1414. DOI: 10.3390/s23031414 PMID: 36772453

Imtiaz, S. (2018). The studies of a unified theory of acceptance and use of technology (utaut) in an e-commerce context. *International Journal of Information Communication Technology and Digital Convergence*, *3*(1), 42–56.

İnci Kuzu, Ç. (2026). Mathematics teachers' AI literacy, anxiety, and perceptions of AI integration in mathematics education: A mixed-methods study. *BMC Psychology*, *14*(1), 42. Advance online publication. DOI: 10.1186/s40359-025-03836-0 PMID: 41408576

Islam, M. M., & Karimoddini, A. (2022). Pedestrian detection for autonomous cars: Inference fusion of deep neural networks. *IEEE Transactions on Intelligent Transportation Systems*, *23*(12), 23358–23368. DOI: 10.1109/TITS.2022.3210186

Itair, M., Shahrour, I., & Hijazi, I. (2023). The use of the smart technology for creating an inclusive urban public space. *Smart Cities*, *6*(5), 2484–2498. DOI: 10.3390/smartcities6050112

Jaiswal, D., Kaushal, V., Kant, R., & Singh, P. K. (2021). Consumer adoption intention for electric vehicles: Insights and evidence from Indian sustainable transportation. *Technological Forecasting and Social Change*, *173*, 121089. DOI: 10.1016/j.techfore.2021.121089

Janani, R. P., Renuka, K., Aruna, A., & Lakshmi Narayanan, K. (2021). IoT in smart cities: A contemporary survey. *Global Transitions Proceedings*, *2*(2), 187–193. DOI: 10.1016/j.gltp.2021.08.069

Jiang, H. (2021). Smart urban governance in the 'smart'era: Why is it urgently needed? *Cities (London, England)*, *111*, 103004. DOI: 10.1016/j.cities.2020.103004

Jiang, S. (2016). Purchase intention for electric vehicles in China from a customer-value perspective. *Social Behavior and Personality*, *44*(4), 641–655. DOI: 10.2224/sbp.2016.44.4.641

Ji, B., Xu, J., Liu, Y., Fan, P., & Wang, M. (2024). Improved YOLOv8 for small traffic sign detection under complex environmental conditions. *Franklin Open*, *8*, 100167. DOI: 10.1016/j.fraope.2024.100167

K. S., S. S. Nath, N. T., & B. S. M. (2024). Enhancing heavy vehicle safety with intelligent driver behaviour monitoring via multi-sensor fusion and embedded systems. In *Proceedings of the 2024 International Conference on System, Computation, Automation and Networking (ICSCAN)* (pp. 1–5). IEEE. DOI: 10.1109/ICSCAN62807.2024.10894289

Karpinski, M., Kuznetsov, O., & Oliynykov, R. (2025). Security, privacy, confidentiality, and trust in the blockchain: From theory to applications. *Electronics (Basel)*, *14*(3), 581. Advance online publication. DOI: 10.3390/electronics14030581

Karyono, G., Ahmad, A., & Asmai, S. A. (2023). Image Denoising using Wavelet Cycle Spinning and Non-local Means Filter. *International Journal of Advanced Computer Science and Applications*, *14*(3). Advance online publication. DOI: 10.14569/IJACSA.2023.0140356

Kashef, M., Visvizi, A., & Troisi, O. (2021). Smart city as a smart service system: Human-computer interaction and smart city surveillance systems. *Computers in Human Behavior*, *124*, 106923. DOI: 10.1016/j.chb.2021.106923

Kasraian, D., Murdock, H. E., Imani, A. F., Yu, Y., de Nazelle, A., Stead, D., & Kahlmeier, S. (2024). Health in mobility planning: An assessment of how health is considered in Sustainable Urban Mobility Plans. *Journal of Transport & Health*, *39*, 101919. DOI: 10.1016/j.jth.2024.101919

Kaur, G., Garg, M., Gupta, S., Juneja, S., Rashid, J., Gupta, D., Shah, A., & Shaikh, A. (2023). Automatic Identification of Glomerular in Whole-Slide Images Using a Modified UNet Model. *Diagnostics (Basel)*, *13*(19), 3152. DOI: 10.3390/diagnostics13193152 PMID: 37835895

Kaur, J. (2023, November). IoT empowered smart cities for green healthcare: a sustainable pathway to transforming healthcare systems. In *2023 International Conference on Computing, Communication, and Intelligent Systems (ICCCIS)* (pp. 64-70). IEEE. DOI: 10.1109/ICCCIS60361.2023.10425484

Ke, R., Cui, Z., Chen, Y., Zhu, M., Yang, H., & Wang, Y. (2020). Edge computing for real-time near-crash detection for smart transportation applications. arXiv preprint arXiv:2008.00549

Keum, D. D., & Eggers, J. P. (2018). Setting the bar: The evaluative and allocative roles of organizational aspirations. *Organization Science*, *29*(6), 1170–1186. DOI: 10.1287/orsc.2018.1224

Khalifa, A. A., Ibrahim, A. J., Amhamed, A. I., & El-Naas, M. H. (2022). Accelerating the Transition to a Circular Economy for Net-Zero Emissions by 2050: A Systematic Review. *Sustainability (Basel), 14*(18), 1–20. DOI: 10.3390/su141811656

Kim, J., Rasouli, S., & Timmermans, H. (2014). Expanding the scope of hybrid choice models allowing for a mixture of social influences and latent attitudes: Application to intended purchase of electric cars. *Transportation Research Part A, Policy and Practice, 69*, 71–85. DOI: 10.1016/j.tra.2014.08.016

Kolotouchkina, O., Barroso, C. L., & Sánchez, J. L. M. (2022). Smart cities, the digital divide, and people with disabilities. *Cities (London, England), 123*, 103613. DOI: 10.1016/j.cities.2022.103613

Krishnan, V. V., & Koshy, B. I. (2021). Evaluating the factors influencing purchase intention of electric vehicles in households owning conventional vehicles. *Case Studies on Transport Policy, 9*(3), 1122–1129. DOI: 10.1016/j.cstp.2021.05.013

Kumari, A., Sukharamwala, U. C., Tanwar, S., Raboaca, M. S., Alqahtani, F., Tolba, A., Sharma, R., Aschilean, I., & Mihaltan, T. C. (2022). Blockchain-based peer-to-peer transactive energy management scheme for smart grid system. *Sensors (Basel), 22*(13), 1–19. DOI: 10.3390/s22134826 PMID: 35808325

Kumar, P., Sahani, J., Corada Perez, K., Ahlawat, A., Andrade, M., Athanassiadou, M., Cao, S.-J., Collins, L., Dey, S., Di Sabatino, S., Halios, C. H., Harris, F., Horton, C., Inostroza, L., Jones, L., Rodding Kjeldsen, T., McCallan, B., McNabola, A., Kumar Mishra, R., & Yao, R. (2025). Urban greening for climate resilient and sustainable cities: Grand challenges and opportunities. *Frontiers in Sustainable Cities, 7*, 1595280. Advance online publication. DOI: 10.3389/frsc.2025.1595280

Lai, I. K., Liu, Y., Sun, X., Zhang, H., & Xu, W. (2015). Factors influencing the behavioral intention towards full electric vehicles: An empirical study in Macau. *Sustainability (Basel), 7*(9), 12564–12585. DOI: 10.3390/su70912564

LaMonaca, S., & Ryan, L. (2022). The state of play in electric vehicle charging services–A review of infrastructure provision, players, and policies. *Renewable & Sustainable Energy Reviews, 154*, 111733. DOI: 10.1016/j.rser.2021.111733

Lee, D., & Hess, D. J. (2022). Public concerns and connected and automated vehicles: Safety, privacy, and data security. *Humanities & Social Sciences Communications, 9*(1), 1–13. DOI: 10.1057/s41599-022-01110-x PMID: 36187845

Lee, J., Kwon, G., Cheon, W., & Lim, W. (2020). A Study on the Revitalization of Forest Management by Improving the Implementation Rate of FOREST Projects. *International Journal of Human & Disaster, 5*(2), 1–9. DOI: 10.22471/disaster.2020.5.2.01

Licata, A. E., Bouffier, M., & Borghesani, V. (2026). A pre-registered scoping review of neuroimaging evidence concerning lexico-semantic processing in multilingual speakers. *Neuroscience and Biobehavioral Reviews*, *184*, 106591. Advance online publication. DOI: 10.1016/j.neubiorev.2026.106591 PMID: 41679413

Li, G., Luo, T., & Song, Y. (2022). Climate change mitigation efficiency of electric vehicle charging infrastructure in China: From the perspective of energy transition and circular economy. *Resources, Conservation and Recycling*, *179*, 106048. DOI: 10.1016/j.resconrec.2021.106048

Li, M., & Kang, J. (2020). Influence of leaf physical properties on Single-Leaf vibrational response to sound. *Forests*, *11*(1), 115. DOI: 10.3390/f11010115

Lin, B., & Wu, W. (2018). Why people want to buy an electric vehicle: An empirical study in first-tier cities of China. *Energy Policy*, *112*, 233–241. DOI: 10.1016/j.enpol.2017.10.026

Liu, S., Gao, C., Chen, Y., Peng, X., Kong, X., Wang, K., & Wang, M. (2023). Towards vehicle-to-everything autonomous driving: A survey on collaborative perception. *arXiv*. 2308.16714

Liu, T., Mostafa, S., Mohamed, S., & Nguyen, T. S. (2021). Emerging themes of public-private partnership application in developing smart city projects: A conceptual framework. *Built Environment Project and Asset Management*, *11*(1), 138–156. DOI: 10.1108/BEPAM-12-2019-0142

Liu, W., Agusdinata, D. B., Eakin, H., & Romero, H. (2022). Sustainable minerals extraction for electric vehicles: A pilot study of consumers' perceptions of impacts. *Resources Policy*, *75*, 102523. DOI: 10.1016/j.resourpol.2021.102523

Liu, Y., Shi, G., Li, Y., & Zhao, Z. (2022). M-YOLO: Traffic Sign Detection Algorithm Applicable to Complex Scenarios. *Symmetry*, *14*(5), 952. DOI: 10.3390/sym14050952

Liu, Z., Qi, M., Shen, C., Fang, Y., & Zhao, X. (2021). Cascade saccade machine learning network with hierarchical classes for traffic sign detection. *Sustainable Cities and Society*, *67*, 102700. DOI: 10.1016/j.scs.2020.102700

Li, X., & Zhang, W. (2010). An adaptive fault-tolerant multisensor navigation strategy for automated vehicles. *IEEE Transactions on Vehicular Technology*, *59*(6), 2815–2829. DOI: 10.1109/TVT.2010.2050014

Lu, Q., Yao, Y., Xiao, L., Zhu, X., & Yin, H. (2026). Exploring the impact of a GenAI-supported feedback practice on student feedback literacy in L2 writing. *Computer Assisted Language Learning*, 1–30. Advance online publication. DOI: 10.1080/09588221.2025.2605541

Luusua, A., Ylipulli, J., Foth, M., & Aurigi, A. (2023). Urban AI: Understanding the emerging role of artificial intelligence in smart cities. *AI & Society*, *38*(3), 1039–1044. DOI: 10.1007/s00146-022-01537-5 PMID: 36196366

Maletzky, A., Hofer, N., Thumfart, S., Bruckmüller, K., & Kasper, J. (2023). Traffic Sign Detection and Classification on the Austrian Highway Traffic Sign Data Set. *Data*, *8*(1), 16. DOI: 10.3390/data8010016

Mandal, M., Popek, R., Przybysz, A., Roy, A., Das, S., & Sarkar, A. (2023). Breathing fresh air in the city: Implementing Avenue Trees as a sustainable solution to reduce particulate pollution in urban agglomerations. *Plants*, *12*(7), 1545. DOI: 10.3390/plants12071545 PMID: 37050171

Mao, Y., Mei, Q., Jing, P., Wang, X., Xue, Y., & Zha, Y. (2023). Uncovering the behavioral determinants behind private car purchase intention during the new normal of COVID-19: An empirical investigation in China. *Mathematical Biosciences and Engineering*, *20*(4), 7316–7348. DOI: 10.3934/mbe.2023318

Maqousi, A., Basu, K., Almomani, A., & Alkasassbeh, M. (2025). Human-Centered Design for Smart Cities: Integrating Social Aspects in Planning and Policy. In *Revolutionizing Urban Development and Governance With Emerging Technologies* (pp. 463-490). IGI Global Scientific Publishing.

Marando, F., Heris, M. P., Zulian, G., Udías, A., Mentaschi, L., Chrysoulakis, N., … Maes, J. (2022). Urban heat island mitigation by green infrastructure in European Functional Urban Areas. *Sustainable Cities and Society, 77*, 103564. DOI: 10.1016/j.scs.2021.103564

Marasinghe, R., Yigitcanlar, T., Mayere, S., Washington, T., & Limb, M. (2024). Computer vision applications for urban planning: A systematic review of opportunities and constraints. *Sustainable Cities and Society*, *100*, 105047. DOI: 10.1016/j.scs.2023.105047

Martinez, F. J., Toh, C. K., Cano, J. C., Calafate, C. T., & Manzoni, P. (2011). A survey and comparative study of simulators for vehicular ad hoc networks (VANETs). *Wireless Communications and Mobile Computing*, *11*(7), 813–828. DOI: 10.1002/wcm.859

Maske, P., Chel, A., Goyal, P. K., & Kaushik, G. (2021). The sustainable perspective of electric vehicles and its future prospects. *Journal of Sustainable Materials Processing and Management*, *1*(1), 17–32. DOI: 10.30880/jsmpm.2021.01.01.003

Maurya, A., Sharma, D., Partap, M., Kumar, R., & Bhargava, B. (2023). Microbially-assisted phytoremediation toward air pollutants: Current trends and future directions. *Environmental Technology & Innovation*, *31*, 103140. DOI: 10.1016/j.eti.2023.103140

Mavlutova, I., Atstaja, D., Grasis, J., Kuzmina, J., Uvarova, I., & Roga, D. (2023). Urban transportation concept and sustainable urban mobility in smart cities: A review. *Energies*, *16*(8), 3585. DOI: 10.3390/en16083585

Meegoda, J. N., Malladi, S., & Zayas, I. C. (2022). End-of-Life Management of Electric Vehicle Lithium-Ion Batteries in the United States. *Cleanroom Technology*, *4*(4), 1162–1174. DOI: 10.3390/cleantechnol4040071

Megalingam, R. K., Thanigundala, K., Musani, S. R., Nidamanuru, H., & Gadde, L. (2023). Indian traffic sign detection and recognition using deep learning. *International Journal of Transportation Science and Technology*, *12*(3), 683–699. DOI: 10.1016/j.ijtst.2022.06.002

Metais, M. O., Jouini, O., Perez, Y., Berrada, J., & Suomalainen, E. (2022). Too much or not enough? Planning electric vehicle charging infrastructure: A review of modeling options. *Renewable & Sustainable Energy Reviews*, *153*, 111719. DOI: 10.1016/j.rser.2021.111719

Mihalakakou, G., Souliotis, M., Papadaki, M., Menounou, P., Dimopoulos, P., Kolokotsa, D., Paravantis, J. A., Tsangrassoulis, A., Panaras, G., Giannakopoulos, E., & Papaefthimiou, S. (2023). Green roofs as a nature-based solution for improving urban sustainability: Progress and perspectives. *Renewable & Sustainable Energy Reviews*, *180*, 113306. DOI: 10.1016/j.rser.2023.113306

Miskolczi, M., Földes, D., Munkacsy, A., & Jaszberenyi, M. (2021). Urban mobility scenarios until the 2030s. *Sustainable Cities and Society*, *72*, 103029. DOI: 10.1016/j.scs.2021.103029

Mocek-Płóciniak, A., Mencel, J., Zakrzewski, W., & Roszkowski, S. (2023). Phytoremediation as an Effective Remedy for Removing Trace Elements from Ecosystems. *Plants*, *12*(8), 1653. DOI: 10.3390/plants12081653 PMID: 37111876

Modrzyński, P., & Karaszewski, R. (2022). Urban energy management—A systematic literature review. *Energies*, *15*(21), 1–17. DOI: 10.3390/en15217848

Mohapatra, H., & Rath, A. K. (2021). An IoT based efficient multi-objective real-time smart parking system. *International Journal of Sensor Networks, 37*(4), 219-232.

Molinaro, A., Campolo, C., Härri, J., Esteve Rothenberg, C., & Vinel, A. (2020). 5g-v2x communications and networking for connected and autonomous vehicles. *Future Internet*, *12*(7), 116. DOI: 10.3390/fi12070116

Moon, S. J. (2021). Effect of consumer environmental propensity and innovative propensity on intention to purchase electric vehicles: Applying an extended theory of planned behavior. *International Journal of Sustainable Transportation*, *16*(11), 1032–1046. DOI: 10.1080/15568318.2021.1961950

Moons, I., & De Pelsmacker, P. (2012). Emotions as determinants of electric car usage intention. *Journal of Marketing Management*, *28*(3-4), 195–237. DOI: 10.1080/0267257X.2012.659007

Moorhouse, B. L., Wan, Y., Wu, C., Wu, M., & Ho, T. Y. (2025). Generative AI tools and empowerment in L2 academic writing. *System*, *133*, 103779. Advance online publication. DOI: 10.1016/j.system.2025.103779

Mo, T., Li, Y., Lau, K. T., Poon, C. K., Wu, Y., & Luo, Y. (2022). Trends and emerging technologies for the development of electric vehicles. *Energies*, *15*(17), 6271. DOI: 10.3390/en15176271

Moumen, N., Radoine, H., Nahiduzzaman, K. M., & Jarar Oulidi, H. (2024). Contextualizing the smart city in Africa: Balancing human-centered and techno-centric perspectives for smart urban performance. *Smart Cities*, *7*(2), 712–734. DOI: 10.3390/smartcities7020029

Moya, T. A., Van Den Dobbelsteen, A., Ottelé, M., & Bluyssen, P. M. (2018b). A review of green systems within the indoor environment. *Indoor and Built Environment*, *28*(3), 298–309. DOI: 10.1177/1420326X18783042

Mudhivarthi, B. R., Thakur, P., & Singh, G. (2023). Aspects of cyber security in autonomous and connected vehicles. *Applied Sciences (Basel, Switzerland)*, *13*(5), 3014. DOI: 10.3390/app13053014

Mustafi, N. N. (2022). An overview of hybrid electric vehicle technology. Engines and Fuels for Future Transport, 73-102.

N., R., M., B., V. N., T., Badachi, C., S., S., Balaji R., H., & Kannanugo, N. (2023). Wireless Power Transfer for High End and Low End EV Cars. In S. Angalaeswari, T. Deepa, & L. Kumar (Eds.), AI Techniques for Renewable Source Integration and Battery Charging Methods in Electric Vehicle Applications (pp. 48-66). IGI Global Scientific Publishing.

N., R., V. N., T., Badachi, C., M., B., N., M. F., S., A. K., & Kannanugo, N. (2023). Autonomous Vehicles Using OpenCV and Python With Wireless Charging. In S. Angalaeswari, T. Deepa, & L. Kumar (Eds.), AI Techniques for Renewable Source Integration and Battery Charging Methods in Electric Vehicle Applications (pp. 76-101). IGI Global Scientific Publishing.

Nagpal, M., Chakraborty, S., Gupta, M. N. R., Vigneshwari, S., & Chaudhary, P. (2025). Integrating blockchain technology for secure and decentralized network communication. In *Proceedings of the 2025 International Conference on Automation and Computation (AUTOCOM)* (pp. 512–517). IEEE. DOI: 10.1109/AUTOCOM64127.2025.10957352

Nastjuk, I., Trang, S., & Papageorgiou, E. I. (2022). Smart cities and smart governance models for future cities: Current research and future directions. *Electronic Markets*, *32*(4), 1917–1924. DOI: 10.1007/s12525-022-00609-0

Nava, M. (2017). The road ahead for electric vehicles. BBVA Research, 1-8.

Naz, I., Shah, J. H., Tahir, A., Marri, M. R., Saleem, R., & Saeed, M. E. S. (2025). Attention to detail: A conditional multi-head transformer for traffic sign recognition. *PLoS One*, *20*(11), e0335341. DOI: 10.1371/journal.pone.0335341 PMID: 41187177

Nikiforiadis, A., Stefanidou, M., & Ayfantopoulou, G. (2023). Will electric car-sharing attract citizens of touristic islands? Evidence from the island of Rhodes, Greece. *Transportation Research Procedia*, *69*, 265–272. DOI: 10.1016/j.trpro.2023.02.171

Nithya, R. (2017). Use of Tree Species in Controlling Environmental Pollution-A Review. *International Journal of Current Microbiology and Applied Sciences*, *6*(4), 893–899. DOI: 10.20546/ijcmas.2017.604.113

Nour, M., Chaves-Avila, J. P., & Sanchez-Miralles, A. (2022). Review of blockchain potential applications in the electricity sector and challenges for large scale adoption. *IEEE Access : Practical Innovations, Open Solutions*, *10*, 47384–47418. DOI: 10.1109/ACCESS.2022.3171227

Novák, V. (2012). Evapotranspiration in the Soil-Plant-Atmosphere system. In *Springer eBooks*. DOI: 10.1007/978-94-007-3840-9

Nsabiyumva, S., Ngobi, D., Nyandwi, V., & Mukasa, S. (2026). Towards inclusive smart cities: Promoting digital literacy for socio-economic equity and sustainable urban futures. In *Future Smart Cities* (pp. 341–370). Elsevier. DOI: 10.1016/B978-0-443-33667-6.00009-4

Okada, T., Tamaki, T., & Managi, S. (2019). Effect of environmental awareness on purchase intention and satisfaction pertaining to electric vehicles in Japan. *Transportation Research Part D, Transport and Environment, 67*, 503–513. DOI: 10.1016/j.trd.2019.01.012

Oksanen, E., & Kontunen-Soppela, S. (2020). Plants have different strategies to defend against air pollutants. *Current Opinion in Environmental Science & Health, 19*, 100222. DOI: 10.1016/j.coesh.2020.10.010

Opbroek, J., Barboza, E. P., Nieuwenhuijsen, M., Dadvand, P., & Mueller, N. (2024). Urban green spaces and behavioral and cognitive development in children: A health impact assessment of the Barcelona "Eixos Verds" Plan (Green Axis Plan). *Environmental Research, 244*, 117909. DOI: 10.1016/j.envres.2023.117909 PMID: 38103780

Ouaissa, M., Ouaissa, M., Houmer, M., El Hamdani, S., & Boulouard, Z. (2022). A secure vehicle to everything (v2x) communication model for intelligent transportation system. In *Computational intelligence in recent communication networks* (pp. 83–102). Springer International Publishing. DOI: 10.1007/978-3-030-77185-0_6

Ouyang, Z., Niu, J., Ren, T., Li, Y., Cui, J., & Wu, J. (2020). MBBNet: An edge IoT computing-based traffic light detection solution for autonomous bus. *Journal of Systems Architecture, 109*, 101835. DOI: 10.1016/j.sysarc.2020.101835

Ow, L. F., & Ghosh, S. (2017). Urban cities and road traffic noise: Reduction through vegetation. *Applied Acoustics, 120*, 15–20. DOI: 10.1016/j.apacoust.2017.01.007

Özkaraca, O., Bağrıaçık, O. İ., Gürüler, H., Khan, F., Hussain, J., Khan, J., & Laila, U. E. (2023). Multiple Brain Tumor Classification with Dense CNN Architecture Using Brain MRI Images. *Life (Chicago, Ill.), 13*(2), 349. DOI: 10.3390/life13020349 PMID: 36836705

Padhi, B. K., Chakravarty, S., Naik, B., Pattanayak, R. M., & Das, H. (2022). RHSOFS: Feature Selection Using the Rock Hyrax Swarm Optimization Algorithm for Credit Card Fraud Detection System. *Sensors (Basel), 22*(23), 9321. DOI: 10.3390/s22239321 PMID: 36502020

Pandey, B., & Ghosh, A. (2023). Urban ecosystem services and climate change: A dynamic interplay. *Frontiers in Sustainable Cities, 5*, 1281430. Advance online publication. DOI: 10.3389/frsc.2023.1281430

Panori, A., Kakderi, C., Komninos, N., Fellnhofer, K., Reid, A., & Mora, L. (2021). Smart systems of innovation for smart places: Challenges in deploying digital platforms for co-creation and data-intelligence. *Land Use Policy, 111*, 104631. DOI: 10.1016/j.landusepol.2020.104631

Parhamfar, M., Sadeghkhani, I., & Adeli, A. M. (2024). Towards the net zero carbon future: A review of blockchain-enabled peer-to-peer carbon trading. *Energy Science & Engineering*, *12*(3), 1242–1264. DOI: 10.1002/ese3.1697

Park, I., Kim, D., Moon, J., Kim, S., Kang, Y., & Bae, S. (2022). Searching for new technology acceptance model under social context: Analyzing the determinants of acceptance of intelligent information technology in digital transformation and implications for the requisites of digital sustainability. *Sustainability (Basel)*, *14*(1), 579. DOI: 10.3390/su14010579

Park, J. S., Cho, E., & Lee, S. Y. (2024, November). Towards Inclusive Smart Cities: Key Evaluation Criteria for Technology and Human-Centered Development. In *2024 International Conference on Information Science and Communications Technologies (ICISCT)* (pp. 212-219). IEEE. DOI: 10.1109/ICISCT64202.2024.10956807

Patel, A. R., Vyas, D. R., Markana, A., & Jayaraman, R. (2022). A Conceptual Model for Integrating Sustainable Supply Chain, Electric Vehicles, and Renewable Energy Sources. *Sustainability (Basel)*, *14*(21), 14484. DOI: 10.3390/su142114484

Perivoliotis, D., Arvanitis, I., Tzavali, A., Papakostas, V., Kappou, S., Andreakos, G., Fotiadi, A., Paravantis, J. A., Souliotis, M., & Mihalakakou, G. (2023). Sustainable Urban Environment through Green Roofs: A Literature Review with Case Studies. *Sustainability (Basel)*, *15*(22), 15976. DOI: 10.3390/su152215976

Petrea, M.-I., & Ursache, I.-M. (2023). Inside the World's most Sustainable Smart City: Lessons from Copenhagen. *International Conference on "Sustainable Development of European Smart Cities*, (October), 225–238.

Petrov, T., Pocta, P., & Kovacikova, T. (2022). Benchmarking 4G and 5G-Based Cellular-V2X for Vehicle-to-Infrastructure Communication and Urban Scenarios in Cooperative Intelligent Transportation Systems. *Applied Sciences (Basel, Switzerland)*, *12*(19), 9677. DOI: 10.3390/app12199677

Polat, A. O., Erden, B. C., Kul, S., & Nasiroglu, F. (2024). Light electric vehicle performance with digital twin technology: A comparison of motor types. *Arabian Journal for Science and Engineering*, *49*(5), 7209–7222. DOI: 10.1007/s13369-023-08668-x

Prabowo, O. M., Mulyana, E., Nugraha, I. G. B. B., & Supangkat, S. H. (2023). Cognitive city platform as digital public infrastructure for developing a smart, sustainable and resilient city in Indonesia. *IEEE Access : Practical Innovations, Open Solutions*, *11*, 120157–120178. DOI: 10.1109/ACCESS.2023.3327305

Prodonovich, S., Perry, L. B., & Taggart, A. (2014). Developing conceptual understandings of the capacity to aspire for higher education. *Issues in Educational Research, 24*(2), 174–189.

Qiu, G., Li, H., Zhang, Q., Chen, W., Liang, X., & Li, X. (2013). Effects of evapotranspiration on mitigation of urban temperature by vegetation and urban agriculture. *Journal of Integrative Agriculture, 12*(8), 1307–1315. DOI: 10.1016/S2095-3119(13)60543-2

Qiu, J., Zhang, W., Xu, S., & Zhou, H. (2025). DP-YOLO: A lightweight traffic sign detection model for small object detection. *Digital Signal Processing, 165*, 105311. DOI: 10.1016/j.dsp.2025.105311

Radić, M., Dodig, M. B., & Auer, T. (2019). Green Facades and Living Walls—A review establishing the classification of construction types and mapping the benefits. *Sustainability (Basel), 11*(17), 4579. DOI: 10.3390/su11174579

Raghu, N., Mahajan, R. A., Sivanantham, A., Bareja, L., Rayaguru, N. K., & Ganesh, R. (2024). Optimizing real-time process control through cloud-based automation and big data analysis. In *Proceedings of the 2024 15th International Conference on Computing, Communication and Networking Technologies (ICCCNT)* (pp. 1–6). IEEE. DOI: 10.1109/ICCCNT61001.2024.10725875

Raghu, N., Phadke, A., Kumar, R., & Joshi, K. (2023). Smart Traffic Light and Dynamic Navigational System for Emergency Vehicles. In Ranganathan, G., Fernando, X., & Piramuthu, S. (Eds.), *Soft Computing for Security Applications. Advances in Intelligent Systems and Computing* (Vol. 1428). Springer. DOI: 10.1007/978-981-19-3590-9_30

Ramasubramanian, P., Starry, O., Rosenstiel, T., & Gall, E. T. (2019). Pilot study on the impact of green roofs on ozone levels near building ventilation air supply. *Building and Environment, 151*, 43–53. DOI: 10.1016/j.buildenv.2019.01.023

Ravindra, K., & Mor, S. (2022). Phytoremediation potential of indoor plants in reducing air pollutants. *Frontiers in Sustainable Cities, 4*, 1039710. Advance online publication. DOI: 10.3389/frsc.2022.1039710

Raymond, C. M., Frantzeskaki, N., Kabisch, N., Berry, P., Breil, M., Nita, M. R., Geneletti, D., & Calfapietra, C. (2017). A framework for assessing and implementing the co-benefits of nature-based solutions in urban areas. *Environmental Science & Policy, 77*, 15–24. DOI: 10.1016/j.envsci.2017.07.008

Reis, A. R. N. D., Biondi, D., & De Oliveira, J. D. (2022). The role of urban green areas in noise pollution attenuation. *Dyna*, *89*(220), 210–215. DOI: 10.15446/dyna.v89n220.95822

Rey-Gozalo, G., Morillas, J. M. B., González, D. M., & Vílchez-Gómez, R. (2023). Influence of green areas on the urban sound environment. *Current Pollution Reports*, *9*(4), 746–759. DOI: 10.1007/s40726-023-00284-5

Richter, M. A., Hagenmaier, M., Bandte, O., Parida, V., & Wincent, J. (2022). Smart cities, urban mobility and autonomous vehicles: How different cities needs different sustainable investment strategies. *Technological Forecasting and Social Change*, *184*, 121857. DOI: 10.1016/j.techfore.2022.121857

Riverso, R., Altamura, C., & La Barbera, F. (2023). Consumer Intention to Buy Electric Cars: Integrating Uncertainty in the Theory of Planned Behavior. *Sustainability (Basel)*, *15*(11), 8548. DOI: 10.3390/su15118548

Rui, J., Shabrina, Z., & Gong, W. (2026). Artificial intelligence applications in urban extreme heat management: A systematic review of forecasting, monitoring, mitigation and decision support. *Environmental Impact Assessment Review*, *119*, 108363. Advance online publication. DOI: 10.1016/j.eiar.2026.108363

Rupanagudi, S. R. (2021). Optic Disk Extraction and Hard Exudate Identification in Fundus Images using Computer Vision and Machine Learning. *2021 IEEE 11th Annual Computing and Communication Workshop and Conference (CCWC)*, 655-661. DOI: 10.1109/CCWC51732.2021.9376018

Rupanagudi, S. R. (2020). A Novel Air Gesture Based Wheelchair Control and Home Automation System. In Abraham, A., Cherukuri, A., Melin, P., & Gandhi, N. (Eds.), *Intelligent Systems Design and Applications. ISDA 2018 2018. Advances in Intelligent Systems and Computing* (Vol. 941). Springer. DOI: 10.1007/978-3-030-16660-1_71

Sachan, S., Deb, S., Singh, P. P., Alam, M. S., & Shariff, S. M. (2022). A comprehensive review of standards and best practices for utility grid integration with electric vehicle charging stations. *Wiley Interdisciplinary Reviews. Energy and Environment*, *11*(3), e424. DOI: 10.1002/wene.424

Sadaf, M., Iqbal, Z., Javed, A. R., Saba, I., Krichen, M., Majeed, S., & Raza, A. (2023). Connected and automated vehicles: Infrastructure, applications, security, critical challenges, and future aspects. *Technologies*, *11*(5), 117. DOI: 10.3390/technologies11050117

Sadeghian, O., Oshnoei, A., Mohammadi-Ivatloo, B., Vahidinasab, V., & Anvari-Moghaddam, A. (2022). A comprehensive review on electric vehicles smart charging: Solutions, strategies, technologies, and challenges. *Journal of Energy Storage*, *54*, 105241. DOI: 10.1016/j.est.2022.105241

Saleem, M. U., Shakir, M., Usman, M. R., Bajwa, M. H. T., Shabbir, N., Ghafaroki, P. S., & Daniel, K. (2023). Integración del sistema de gestión de energía inteligente con Internet de las cosas y computación en la nube para una gestión eficiente del lado de la demanda en redes inteligentes. *Energies*, *16*(12).

Samak, T. V., Samak, C. V., & Krovi, V. N. (2024, July). Towards Validation of Autonomous Vehicles Across Scales using an Integrated Digital Twin Framework. In *2024 IEEE International Conference on Advanced Intelligent Mechatronics (AIM)* (pp. 1068-1075). IEEE. DOI: 10.1109/AIM55361.2024.10637205

Sanchez, T. W., Shumway, H., Gordner, T., & Lim, T. (2023). The prospects of artificial intelligence in urban planning. *International Journal of Urban Sciences*, *27*(2), 179-194.

Sanchez, T. W., Brenman, M., & Ye, X. (2025). The ethical concerns of artificial intelligence in urban planning. *Journal of the American Planning Association*, *91*(2), 294–307. DOI: 10.1080/01944363.2024.2355305

Sang, Y. N., & Bekhet, H. A. (2015). Modelling electric vehicle usage intentions: An empirical study in Malaysia. *Journal of Cleaner Production*, *92*, 75–83. DOI: 10.1016/j.jclepro.2014.12.045

Sarabdeen, J. (2024). Nexus between innovation and sustainable economic development: A bibliometrics analysis. *Journal of Infrastructure. Policy and Development*, *8*(11), 1–23. DOI: 10.24294/jipd.v8i11.8762

Sarsam, S. M. (2023). Cybersecurity challenges in autonomous vehicles: Threats, vulnerabilities, and mitigation strategies. *SHIFRA*, *2023*, 34–42. DOI: 10.70470/SHIFRA/2023/005

Schüle, R., Pollok, M., & Güleş, O. (2026). Digital justice in the smart city: Developing a framework for participatory digitalisation strategies at the local level. *Universal Access in the Information Society*, *25*(2), 42. Advance online publication. DOI: 10.1007/s10209-025-01287-3

Sekti, B. A. (2025a). AI technology management concepts and strategies. In *AI technology management and value creation* (pp. 1–32). DOI: 10.4018/979-8-3373-2497-5.ch001

Sekti, B. A. (2025a). Foundations of Artificial Intelligence Ethics. In *Navigating Social Trust in the AI Era* (pp. 23–47). DOI: 10.4018/979-8-3373-7011-8.ch002

Sekti, B. A. (2025b). IT service information security management. In *Cases on information systems service management* (pp. 61–93). DOI: 10.4018/979-8-3373-2352-7.ch003

Sekti, B. A. (2025b). Machine Learning vs. AI: Key Concepts. In *Implementing Enterprise Cybersecurity With AI* (pp. 1–27). DOI: 10.4018/979-8-3373-2252-0.ch001

Sekti, B. A., Laksono, M. N. G., Laksono, M. I. A., Widodo, A. M., Anwar, N., & Tiaraputri, Z. A. (2025). Principles of green computing in information security. In *Sustainable Information Security in the Age of AI and Green Computing* (pp. 1–16). DOI: 10.4018/979-8-3693-8034-5.ch001

Sekti, B. A. (2026). Cybersecurity Challenges in Smart City Development. In *Securing Smart Cities Through Modern Cryptography Technologies* (pp. 75–102). IGI Global Scientific Publishing. DOI: 10.4018/979-8-3373-3326-7.ch003

Shafiee Rad, H. (2025). Reinforcing L2 reading comprehension through artificial intelligence intervention: Refining engagement to foster self-regulated learning. *Smart Learning Environments*, *12*(1), 23. Advance online publication. DOI: 10.1186/s40561-025-00377-2

Shalender, K., & Sharma, N. (2021). Using the extended theory of planned behavior (TPB) to predict the adoption intention of electric vehicles in India. *Environment, Development and Sustainability*, *23*(1), 665–681. DOI: 10.1007/s10668-020-00602-7

Sharifi, A., Khavarian-Garmsir, A. R., Allam, Z., & Asadzadeh, A. (2023). Progress and prospects in planning: A bibliometric review of literature in Urban Studies and Regional and Urban Planning, 1956–2022. *Progress in Planning*, *173*, 100740. Advance online publication. DOI: 10.1016/j.progress.2023.100740

Sharma, A., Patel, M., Choudhary, A., & Kumar, G. (2023). Blockchain based security enabled smart contract for energy management. In *Proceedings of the 16th International Conference on Security of Information and Networks (SIN 2023)* (pp. 1–7). DOI: 10.1109/SIN60469.2023.10474845

Sharma, M., Sharma, B., Kumar, N., & Kumar, A. (2023). Establishing Conceptual Components for Urban Resilience: Taking Clues from Urbanization through a Planner's Lens. *Natural Hazards Review*, *24*(1), 04022040. Advance online publication. DOI: 10.1061/NHREFO.NHENG-1523

Shen, Z. J., Zhang, Y. B., Yao, Y. Q., & Liu, B. W. (2011, August). Electric vehicle: The hope of the green future. In *2011 International Conference on Management and Service Science* (pp. 1-4). IEEE. DOI: 10.1109/ICMSS.2011.5998696

Sherwood, R. A.Jr. (1989). A Conceptual Framework for the Study of Aspirations. *Research in Rural Education*, *6*(2), 61–66.

Shetty, G. S., & Raghu, N. (2025). Waterwheel Archimedes optimization and resilient consensus BiLSTM for efficient data aggregation to detect and discard malicious nodes and packets in IoT-based healthcare applications. *SN Computer Science*, *6*(4), 338. DOI: 10.1007/s42979-025-03873-x

Shishegaran, A., Shishegaran, A., Najari, M., Ghotbi, A., & Boushehri, A. N. (2020). Effect of plants on an environment with high carbon dioxide concentration. *Cleaner Engineering and Technology*, *1*, 100002. DOI: 10.1016/j.clet.2020.100002

Shoukat, M. U., Yan, L., Yan, Y., Zhang, F., Zhai, Y., Han, P., Nawaz, S. A., Raza, M. A., Akbar, M. W., & Hussain, A. (2024). Autonomous driving test system under hybrid reality: The role of digital twin technology. *Internet of Things : Engineering Cyber Physical Human Systems*, *27*, 101301. DOI: 10.1016/j.iot.2024.101301

Siano, P. (2024). Front matter: Volume 13291. *Proceedings of SPIE, 13291*, 0. DOI: 10.1117/12.3054455

Siragusa, C., Tumino, A., Mangiaracina, R., & Perego, A. (2022). Electric vehicles performing last-mile delivery in B2C e-commerce: An economic and environmental assessment. *International Journal of Sustainable Transportation*, *16*(1), 22–33. DOI: 10.1080/15568318.2020.1847367

Small, G., Jimenez, I., Salzl, M., & Shrestha, P. (2020). Urban heat island mitigation due to enhanced evapotranspiration in an urban garden in Saint Paul, Minnesota, USA. *WIT Transactions on Ecology and the Environment*, 39–45. Advance online publication. DOI: 10.2495/UA200041

Song, M. R., Chu, W., & Im, M. (2022). The effect of cultural and psychological characteristics on the purchase behavior and satisfaction of electric vehicles: A comparative study of US and China. *International Journal of Consumer Studies*, *46*(1), 345–364. DOI: 10.1111/ijcs.12684

Son, T. H., Weedon, Z., Yigitcanlar, T., Sanchez, T., Corchado, J. M., & Mehmood, R. (2023). Algorithmic urban planning for smart and sustainable development: Systematic review of the literature. *Sustainable Cities and Society*, *94*, 104562. DOI: 10.1016/j.scs.2023.104562

Sovacool, B. K., Abrahamse, W., Zhang, L., & Ren, J. (2019). Pleasure or profit? Surveying the purchasing intentions of potential electric vehicle adopters in China. *Transportation Research Part A, Policy and Practice*, *124*, 69–81. DOI: 10.1016/j.tra.2019.03.002

Štrbac, S., Kašanin-Grubin, M., Pezo, L., Stojić, N., Lončar, B., Ćurčić, L., & Pucarević, M. (2023). Green Infrastructure Designed through Nature-Based Solutions for Sustainable Urban Development. *International Journal of Environmental Research and Public Health*, *20*(2), 1102. Advance online publication. DOI: 10.3390/ijerph20021102 PMID: 36673859

Syamlal, N. C. A., George, N. A., &Sayantan, N. D. (2024). Phytoremediation: an Eco-Friendly solution for environmental contamination. *International Journal of Advanced Research in Science Communication and Technology*, 553–577. DOI: 10.48175/IJARSCT-18774

Tahir, M. N., Katz, M., & Rashid, U. (2022). Analysis of collaborative wireless vehicular technologies under realistic conditions. *Journal of Engineering*, *2022*(2), 201–209.

Taleb, T., Samdanis, K., Mada, B., Flinck, H., Dutta, S., & Sabella, D. (2017). On multi-access edge computing: A survey of the emerging 5G network edge cloud architecture and orchestration. *IEEE Communications Surveys and Tutorials*, *19*(3), 1657–1681. DOI: 10.1109/COMST.2017.2705720

Tavitiyaman, P., Qu, H., Tsang, W. S. L., & Lam, C. W. R. (2021). The influence of smart tourism applications on perceived destination image and behavioral intention: The moderating role of information search behavior. *Journal of Hospitality and Tourism Management*, *46*, 476–487. DOI: 10.1016/j.jhtm.2021.02.003

Tesar, G. (1974). New hope for the driver: An electric car. Midwest Engineer, 26(7).

Thirumalraj, A., & Rajesh, T. (2023). An Improved ARO Model for Task Offloading in Vehicular Cloud Computing in VANET.

Thoburn, J., & Natsuda, K. (2023). National Cars and Product Champions: Ways Forward for Vietnam's Automotive Industry? In *The Political Economy of Global Manufacturing, Business and Finance* (pp. 121–145). Springer International Publishing. DOI: 10.1007/978-3-031-25832-9_6

Tiwari, S., & Singh, J. G. (2022). Optimal energy management of multi-carrier networked energy hubs considering efficient integration of demand response and electrical vehicles: A cooperative energy management framework. *Journal of Energy Storage*, *51*, 104479. DOI: 10.1016/j.est.2022.104479

Torabi, Z. A., Shalbafian, A. A., Allam, Z., Ghaderi, Z., Murgante, B., & Khavarian-Garmsir, A. R. (2022). Enhancing memorable experiences, tourist satisfaction, and revisit intention through smart tourism technologies. *Sustainability (Basel), 14*(5), 2721. DOI: 10.3390/su14052721

Trebbels, M., & Trebbels, M. (2015). The concept of educational aspirations. The transition at the end of compulsory full-time education: Educational and future career aspirations of native and migrant students, 37-45.

Triki, N., Karray, M., & Ksantini, M. (2023). A real-time traffic sign recognition method using a new attention-based deep convolutional neural network for smart vehicles. *Applied Sciences (Basel, Switzerland), 13*(8), 4793. DOI: 10.3390/app13084793

Truong, T. H. (2022). Determinants of intention to purchase electric cars in Vietnam: Proposing an analysis framework from theoretical research. VNU Journal of Economics and Business, 2(1).

Unterluggauer, T., Rich, J., Andersen, P. B., & Hashemi, S. (2022). Electric vehicle charging infrastructure planning for integrated transportation and power distribution networks: A review. *ETransportation, 12*, 100163. DOI: 10.1016/j.etran.2022.100163

Ushakov, D., Dudukalov, E., Kozlova, E., & Shatila, K. (2022). The Internet of Things impact on smart public transportation. *Transportation Research Procedia, 63*, 2392–2400. DOI: 10.1016/j.trpro.2022.06.275

Utami, A. S., & Sekti, B. A. (2025). Al in Critical Sectors: Healthcare, Education, Finance, and Security - Ethical Challenges in Generative Al. In *Navigating Social Trust in the AI Era* (pp. 155–186). DOI: 10.4018/979-8-3373-7011-8.ch007

Vadiati, N. (2022). Alternatives to smart cities: A call for consideration of grass-roots digital urbanism. *Digital Geography and Society, 3*, 100030. DOI: 10.1016/j.diggeo.2022.100030

Van Renterghem, T., Botteldooren, D., & Verheyen, K. (2012). Road traffic noise shielding by vegetation belts of limited depth. *Journal of Sound and Vibration, 331*(10), 2404–2425. DOI: 10.1016/j.jsv.2012.01.006

Vanjire, S., & Naveen, R. (2024). AI on wheels: AI-powered predictive models for smart vehicles. In *Interactive media with next-gen technologies and their usability evaluation* (pp. 155–164). Chapman and Hall/CRC. DOI: 10.1201/9781032664828-11

Varshini, B., Yogesh, H. R., Pasha, S. D., Suhail, M., Madhumitha, V., & Sasi, A. (2021). IoT-Enabled smart doors for monitoring body temperature and face mask detection. *Global Transitions Proceedings*, *2*(2), 246–254. DOI: 10.1016/j.gltp.2021.08.071

Velasquez Mendez, A., Lozoya Santos, J., & Jimenez Vargas, J. F. (2025). Strategic socio-technical innovation in urban living labs: A framework for smart city evolution. *Smart Cities*, *8*(4), 131. DOI: 10.3390/smartcities8040131

Venugopal, P. (2022). Analysis of electric vehicles with an economic perspective for the future electric market. *Future Internet*, *14*(6), 172. DOI: 10.3390/fi14060172

Verma, S., Dwivedi, G., & Verma, P. (2022). Life cycle assessment of electric vehicles in comparison to combustion engine vehicles: A review. *Materials Today: Proceedings*, *49*, 217–222. DOI: 10.1016/j.matpr.2021.01.666

Verma, S., Sharma, A., Tran, B., & Alahakoon, D. (2024). A systematic review of digital twins for electric vehicles. *Journal of Traffic and Transportation Engineering*, *11*(5), 815–834. DOI: 10.1016/j.jtte.2024.04.004

Viale, R. (2025). Behavioral city. *Frontiers in Built Environment*, *10*, 1501853. DOI: 10.3389/fbuil.2024.1501853

Vishnu, S., Ramson, S. J., Senith, S., Anagnostopoulos, T., Abu-Mahfouz, A. M., Fan, X., Srinivasan, S., & Kirubaraj, A. A. (2021). IoT-enabled solid waste management in smart cities. *Smart Cities*, *4*(3), 1004–1017. DOI: 10.3390/smartcities4030053

Vourdoubas, J. (2024). Review of the benefits of green roofs. *International Journal of Current Science Research and Review*, *07*(09). Advance online publication. DOI: 10.47191/ijcsrr/V7-i9-48

Wan, D.-L., & Lin, S.-Z. (2026). Ethical challenges and governance of artificial intelligence in hepatocellular carcinoma management. *Medical Oncology (Northwood, London, England)*, *43*(2), 69. DOI: 10.1007/s12032-025-03157-7 PMID: 41452505

Wang, H., Wang, K., Cai, Y., Liu, Z., & Chen, L. (2020). Traffic Sign Recognition Based on improved Cascaded Convolutional Neural Network. *Automot. Eng.*, *42*, 1256–1262+1269.

Wang, B., Han, Y., Wang, S., Tian, D., Cai, M., Liu, M., & Wang, L. (2022). A Review of Intelligent Connected Vehicle Cooperative Driving Development. *Mathematics*, *10*(19), 3635. DOI: 10.3390/math10193635

Wang, D., Xu, P. Y., An, B. W., & Guo, Q. P. (2024). Urban green infrastructure: Bridging biodiversity conservation and sustainable urban development through adaptive management approach. *Frontiers in Ecology and Evolution*, *12*(August), 1–20. DOI: 10.3389/fevo.2024.1440477

Wang, L., Ai, Q., & Jin, H. (2026). Lightweight traffic sign detection algorithm with noise suppression and semantic enhancement. *PLoS One*, *21*(1), e0340810. DOI: 10.1371/journal.pone.0340810 PMID: 41564025

Wang, R. Y. (2025). From phone booths to Wi-Fi kiosks: The spatial inequality of public connectivity in New York City. *Technological Forecasting and Social Change*, *219*, 124245. DOI: 10.1016/j.techfore.2025.124245

Wang, R., Yin, Y., & Cao, Y. (2026). A LLM-based pedagogical framework for active, inquiry-based and adaptive learning in L2 writing. *Computers and Education: Artificial Intelligence*, *10*, 100535. Advance online publication. DOI: 10.1016/j.caeai.2025.100535

Wang, S., Fan, J., Zhao, D., Yang, S., & Fu, Y. (2016). Predicting consumers' intention to adopt hybrid electric vehicles: Using an extended version of the theory of planned behavior model. *Transportation*, *43*(1), 123–143. DOI: 10.1007/s11116-014-9567-9

Wang, Y., Su, Z., & Yan, M. (2023). Social metaverse: Challenges and solutions. *IEEE Internet of Things Magazine*, *6*(3), 144–150. DOI: 10.1109/IOTM.001.2200266

Wan, J., Ding, W., Zhu, H., Xia, M., Huang, Z., Tian, L., Zhu, Y., & Wang, H. (2021). An efficient small traffic sign detection method based on YOLOv3. *Journal of Signal Processing Systems for Signal, Image, and Video Technology*, *93*(8), 899–911. DOI: 10.1007/s11265-020-01614-2

Watling, J. R., Grant, N. M., Miller, R. E., & Robinson, S. A. (2008). Mechanisms of thermoregulation in plants. *Plant Signaling & Behavior*, *3*(8), 595–597. DOI: 10.4161/psb.3.8.6341 PMID: 19704809

Wei, H., Zhang, Q., Qian, Y., Xu, Z., & Han, J. (2023). MTSDet: Multi-scale traffic sign detection with attention and path aggregation. *Applied Intelligence*, *53*(1), 238–250. DOI: 10.1007/s10489-022-03459-7

Więckowski, J., Wątróbski, J., Kizielewicz, B., & Sałabun, W. (2023). Complex sensitivity analysis in Multi-Criteria Decision Analysis: An application to the selection of an electric car. *Journal of Cleaner Production*, *390*, 136051. DOI: 10.1016/j.jclepro.2023.136051

Willis, K. S., & Nold, C. (2022). Sense and the city: An Emotion Data Framework for smart city governance. *Journal of Urban Management, 11*(2), 142–152. DOI: 10.1016/j.jum.2022.05.009

Wirsbinna, A., Grega, L., & Juenger, M. (2023). Assessing factors influencing citizens' behavioral intention towards smart city living. *Smart Cities, 6*(6), 3093–3111. DOI: 10.3390/smartcities6060138

Wu, J., Orlandi, F., Lee, Y. H., O'Sullivan, D., & Dev, S. (2021). Organizing decentralized energy data using semantic approach. In *Proceedings of the Photonics & Electromagnetics Research Symposium (PIERS 2021)* (pp. 2213–2216). DOI: 10.1109/PIERS53385.2021.9695066

Wu, Y., Li, Z., Chen, Y., Nai, K., & Yuan, J. (2020). Real-time traffic sign detection and classification towards real traffic scene. *Multimedia Tools and Applications, 79*(25-26), 18201–18219. DOI: 10.1007/s11042-020-08722-y

Xiao, X., & Xie, C. (2021). Rational planning and urban governance based on smart cities and big data. *Environmental Technology & Innovation, 21*, 101381. DOI: 10.1016/j.eti.2021.101381

Xie, R., An, L., & Yasir, N. (2022). How Innovative Characteristics Influence Consumers' Intention to Purchase Electric Vehicle: A Moderating Role of Lifestyle. *Sustainability (Basel), 14*(8), 4467. DOI: 10.3390/su14084467

Xu, J., Huang, Y., & Ying, D. (2023). Traffic Sign Detection and Recognition Using Multi-Frame Embedding of Video-Log Images. *Remote Sensing (Basel), 15*(12), 2959. DOI: 10.3390/rs15122959

Yang, X., Shi, X., Zhang, Y., Tian, F., & Ortega-Farias, S. (2023). Response of evapotranspiration (ET) to climate factors and crop planting structures in the Shiyang River basin, northwestern China. *Remote Sensing (Basel), 15*(16), 3923. DOI: 10.3390/rs15163923

Yang, Z., Huang, H., & Lin, F. (2022). Sustainable electric vehicle batteries for a sustainable world: Perspectives on battery cathodes, environment, supply chain, manufacturing, life cycle, and policy. *Advanced Energy Materials, 12*(26), 2200383. DOI: 10.1002/aenm.202200383

Yankun, S. (2020, December). An empirical study on the influencing factors of consumers' willingness to use pure electric vehicles based on the TAM Model. In 2020 16th Dahe Fortune China Forum and Chinese High-educational Management Annual Academic Conference (DFHMC) (pp. 289-292). IEEE.

Yofianti, D., & Usman, K. (2021). Relationship of plant types to noise pollution absorption level to improve the quality of the road environment. *IOP Conference Series. Earth and Environmental Science, 926*(1), 012074. DOI: 10.1088/1755-1315/926/1/012074

Yoshida, M., Duangchinda, V., & Ruangrit, N. (2026). AI-Supported Learning in Online Discussion Forums: A Scoping Review. *Electronic Journal of e-Learning, 24*(1), 19–35. DOI: 10.34190/ejel.24.1.4409

Ysebie, W., Azaioud, H., Caers, B., & Desmet, J. (2025). RE/SOURCED pilot: Practical implementation of a DC microgrid. In *IET Conference Proceedings* (pp. 769–773). DOI: 10.1049/icp.2025.1681

Yu, Q., Nie, Y., Peng, S., Miao, Y., Zhai, C., Zhang, R., Han, J., Zhao, S., & Pecht, M. (2023). Evaluation of the safety standards system of power batteries for electric vehicles in China. *Applied Energy, 349*, 121674. DOI: 10.1016/j.apenergy.2023.121674

Zaibi, A., Ladgham, A., & Sakly, A. (2021). A lightweight model for traffic sign classification based on enhanced LeNet-5 network. *Journal of Sensors, 2021*(1), 1–13. DOI: 10.1155/2021/8870529

Zaidan, E., Truby, J., Ibrahim, I. A., & Hoppe, T. (2026). Hybrid global governance for responsible and inclusive Artificial Intelligence: Proposing a new Sustainable Development Goal 18. *Technology in Society, 85*, 103159. Advance online publication. DOI: 10.1016/j.techsoc.2025.103159

Zeng, G., Wu, Z., Xu, L., & Liang, Y. (2024). Efficient vision transformer YOLOv5 for accurate and fast traffic sign detection. *Electronics (Basel), 13*(5), 880. DOI: 10.3390/electronics13050880

Zhang, M., Xie, W., & Gao, W. (2022). Have environmental regulations promoted green technological innovation in cities? Evidence from China's green patents. *PLoS ONE, 17*(12), 1–24. DOI: 10.1371/journal.pone.0278902

Zhang, B., Liang, Z., Zhao, L., Ma, L., Zhang, S., Gao, T., & Chen, L. (2025). Optimizing Eco-Efficiency of green Infrastructure: A comparative study of woody plant species Utilizing SWMM-HYDRUS model and Analytic Hierarchy process. *Ecological Indicators, 173*, 113388. DOI: 10.1016/j.ecolind.2025.113388

Zhang, J., Wang, W., Lu, C., Wang, J., & Sangaiah, A. K. (2020). Lightweight deep network for traffic sign classification. *Annales des Télécommunications, 75*(7-8), 369–379. DOI: 10.1007/s12243-019-00731-9

Zhang, J., Xie, Z., Sun, J., Zou, X., & Wang, J. (2020). A cascaded R-CNN with multiscale attention and imbalanced samples for traffic sign detection. *IEEE Access : Practical Innovations, Open Solutions, 8*, 29742–29754. DOI: 10.1109/ACCESS.2020.2972338

Zhang, R., Zheng, K., Shi, P., Mei, Y., Li, H., & Qiu, T. (2023). Traffic Sign Detection Based on the Improved YOLOv5. *Applied Sciences (Basel, Switzerland), 13*(17), 9748. DOI: 10.3390/app13179748

Zhang, W., Fang, X., & Sun, C. (2023). The alternative path for fossil oil: Electric vehicles or hydrogen fuel cell vehicles? *Journal of Environmental Management, 341*, 118019. DOI: 10.1016/j.jenvman.2023.118019

Zhang, Y., Lin, Y., Qin, Y., Dong, M., Gao, L., & Hashemi, E. (2023). A new adaptive cruise control considering crash avoidance for intelligent vehicle. *IEEE Transactions on Industrial Electronics, 71*(1), 688–696. DOI: 10.1109/TIE.2023.3239878

Zhao, L., Wei, Z., Li, Y., Jin, J., & Li, X. (2023). SEDG-Yolov5: A Lightweight Traffic Sign Detection Model Based on Knowledge Distillation. *Electronics (Basel), 12*(2), 305. DOI: 10.3390/electronics12020305

Zhao, N., Prieur, J., Liu, Y., Kneeshaw, D., Lapointe, E. M., Paquette, A., Zinszer, K., Dupras, J., Villeneuve, P. J., Rainham, D. G., Lavigne, E., Chen, H., Van Den Bosch, M., Oiamo, T., & Smargiassi, A. (2021). Tree characteristics and environmental noise in complex urban settings – A case study from Montreal, Canada. *Environmental Research, 202*, 111887. DOI: 10.1016/j.envres.2021.111887 PMID: 34425113

Zhao, W., Li, L., & Gong, X. (2025). CPB-YOLOv8: An Enhanced Multi-Scale Traffic Sign Detector for Complex Road Environment. *Information (Basel), 16*(9), 798. DOI: 10.3390/info16090798

Zhou, G., Zhu, Z., & Luo, S. (2022). Location optimization of electric vehicle charging stations: Based on cost model and genetic algorithm. *Energy, 247*, 123437. DOI: 10.1016/j.energy.2022.123437

Zhu, Z., Pivaro, N., Gupta, S., Gupta, A., & Canova, M. (2022). Safe model-based off-policy reinforcement learning for eco-driving in connected and automated hybrid electric vehicles. *IEEE Transactions on Intelligent Vehicles, 7*(2), 387–398. DOI: 10.1109/TIV.2022.3150668

About the Contributors

Shafiqul Islam earned his PhD from the University of Dhaka, Master's and Bachelor degrees from the University of Chittagong. He was the postdoctoral fellow at London School of Economics and Political Science, London, UK. He has 39 years' experience in development sectors, teaching and research. Dr. Islam is working as an Associate Professor at International University of Business Agriculture and Technology. Prior to his current position, he worked with the United International University, State University of Bangladesh and University of Liberal Arts Bangladesh. Dr. Islam has authored and published more than 60 articles and titles in international peer-reviewed journals, as well as contributed many books and book chapters with Taylor and Francis, Apple Academic Press, Rutledge, Springer Nature, IGI Global, and Green Leaf and Nova Science Publishers.

* * *

Manish Baboo Agarwal holds M. Tech. from IIT Bombay, Ph. D. from IIT Dhanbad, has published many research papers, book chapters in Scopus Journals. Also has many patents from India and Abroad.

Seema Agarwal, M.Sc., m.Phil, has a Ph.D. from Mathematics has many National and International Publications (Scopus and SCI). Patents in National and International Platform.

S. Ida Evangeline is presently working as an Assistant Professor in the Department of Electrical and Electronics Engineering at the Government College of Engineering, Tirunelveli, Tamilnadu, India. She obtained her Bachelor's in Electrical and Electronics Engineering from Manonmaniam Sundaranar University in 2003, and Master's in Power Systems Engineering from Anna University, Chennai, Tamilnadu, India in 2005. She completed her PhD degree in 2023 at Anna University, Chennai, Tamilnadu, India. She has published six research papers in international journals. Her current research interests include optimal power flow, renewable energy, soft computing, machine learning, and deep learning.

Santosh Kumar B. did his BE in Electronics and Communication Engineering, M.Tech in VLSI and Embedded System and pursing Ph.D in Electronics and Communication Engineering. He is associated with New Horizon college of Engineering, Bengaluru since 2017. He has played a key role in implementing the innovative best practices of teaching-learning and research at NHCE since last 6 years. He is actively involved in R&D and has published good number of papers in indexed journals. He has guided UG and PG students for their project work. His research interest includes VLSI and Embedded System, Internet of Things, PCIe.

Dayananda L. N. is an Assistant Professor in the Department of Electronics and Communication Engineering (ECE) with over 11 years of experience in academia and industry. He holds a Master's degree in Microelectronics and Control Systems and a Bachelor's degree in Electrical and Electronics Engineering. His expertise includes embedded systems, electric vehicles, battery management systems, renewable energy, power electronics, and robotics. He is passionate about innovative research and effective teaching, focusing on bridging theory with practical application. Dedicated to mentoring students and lifelong learning, he actively engages in research and professional development in emerging technological domains.

Cindy Fitria Maharani is a researcher in artificial intelligence and enterprise architecture at Esa Unggul University, Jakarta, Indonesia. Her research interests include AI-driven systems, enterprise architecture frameworks, digital transformation strategies, and intelligent information systems. She has been actively involved in academic research and applied projects focusing on aligning technological innovation with organizational strategy through structured enterprise architecture design and intelligent solutions. Her work demonstrates strong analytical capabilities, strategic thinking, and technical expertise in integrating AI technologies within complex organizational environments. Cindy actively contributes to scientific publications and collaborative research initiatives aimed at advancing digital governance, enterprise systems optimization, and sustainable technological innovation.

Manu Mehrotra completed his Ph.D. in Chemistry from Jodhpur University India. He has publications in renowned SCI and Scopus journals. Dr. Mehrotra has book chapters in Scopus and Patents in National and International Platform.

Raghu N. has 15 years of experience in Academic and Research. He received the Ph.D. (2020) in Electronics Engineering from Jain University, and B.E. in

Electronics and Telecommunications Engineering from VTU University, Karnataka. His research interests were in RF Communication and Image Processing. He has published his research findings in various Scopus indexed Journals and International conferences. He is a member of various professional bodies.

Alya Nurul Qolbi is a researcher with a strong interest in artificial intelligence and emerging technologies. Her work focuses on exploring innovative digital solutions and their applications in education, data systems, and smart environments. She is passionate about advancing research that bridges technology, human interaction, and sustainable development. Alya continues to expand her academic and practical contributions in the field of intelligent systems and technological innovation.

B.Saroja is a distinguished academic and researcher in the field of Electronics and Communication Engineering. She serves as the Professor and Head of the ECE Department at Siddartha Institute of Science and Technology (SISTK). Recognized for her expertise, she is an accomplished speaker, reviewer, and academic writer. Dr. Boda is also a recognized Ph.D. supervisor under Jawaharlal Nehru Technological University (JNTU) Ananthapuram, guiding numerous research scholars in their academic pursuits. Her contributions to the academic community are marked by her commitment to excellence in teaching, research, and mentorship.

Binastya Anggara Sekti has been a lecturer at the Faculty of Computer Science, Esa Unggul University, Jakarta, since 2016. He is actively involved in the Artificial Intelligence and Information Security Study Group. He holds a Bachelor's degree in Informatics Engineering from the Bandung Institute of Technology and a Master's degree in Information Systems Management from Trisakti University, Jakarta. Prior to entering academia, he accumulated over 25 years of professional experience as an IT practitioner in various companies across Jakarta. His work focused on developing data centers for internet service providers and delivering IT solutions for the manufacturing and oil & gas sectors. His research interests include artificial intelligence, cybersecurity, and the development of IT infrastructure.

Gopikha Sundaramoorthy is an Assistant Professor in the Department of Information Technology at St. Joseph's College of Engineering, India. She holds B.E. and M.E. degrees in Computer Science and Engineering. Her research centres on artificial intelligence (AI), machine learning (ML), deep learning (DL), and natural language processing (NLP), with applications in medical image analysis—particularly automated skin cancer detection from dermoscopic images.

Arunadevi Thirumalraj did ME Computer Science Engineering in K.Ramakrishnan College of Technology, (KRCT), Tiruchirappalli and Currently working as Assistant Professor in Saranathan College of Engineering, Trichy. She is actively involved in the field of innovative teaching and Learning. She has publishing a good number of papers in indexed journals.

Muhamad Haikal Umardi is an artificial intelligence researcher at Esa Unggul University, Jakarta, Indonesia. His research interests include machine learning, deep learning, data analytics, and intelligent computing systems. He has been actively involved in academic research and applied AI projects, particularly in developing predictive models, data-driven applications, and intelligent decision-support systems. His work reflects strong analytical thinking, technical expertise, and a commitment to continuous innovation in emerging technologies. Muhamad actively contributes to collaborative research initiatives and scientific publications aimed at advancing artificial intelligence applications in education, industry, and digital transformation.

Index

S

T

U

V

www.ingramcontent.com/pod-product-compliance
Lightning Source LLC
LaVergne TN
LVHW081526300926
849161LV00006B/1313

* 9 7 9 8 2 6 0 0 0 8 8 3 6 *